Psychology for Childhood Studies

Teena Kamen

Hodder & Stoughton

A MEMBER OF THE HODDER HEADLINE GROUP

Dedication

To my son, Tom Jennings,
and my mother, Pauline White,
with love and affection

Orders: please contact Bookpoint Ltd, 78 Milton Park, Abingdon, Oxon OX14 4TD. Telephone: (44) 01235
827720, Fax: (44) 01235 400454. Lines are open from 9.00–6.00, Monday to Saturday, with a 24 hour message
answering service. Email address: orders@bookpoint.co.uk

British Library Cataloguing in Publication Data
A catalogue record for this title is available from The British Library

ISBN 0 340 780 1 5 0

First published 2000
Impression number   10 9 8 7 6 5 4 3 2 1
Year   2005 2004 2003 2002 2001 2000

Typeset by Fakenham Photosetting Ltd., Fakenham, Norfolk.
Printed in Great Britain for Hodder & Stoughton Educational, a division of Hodder Headline Plc, 338 Euston
Road, London NW1 3BH by J. W. Arrowsmith Ltd., Bristol

Contents

How to use this book

This book contains the knowledge evidence requirements for a range of topics related to young children's psychological development. The book includes practical ideas for linking knowledge evidence with performance criteria, and is suitable for students on Early Years Care and Education NVQ Level 3 and equivalent courses such as the CACHE Level 3 Diploma in Child Care and Education (DCE) and the BTEC National Diploma in Early Years.

The headings in each section are related to NVQ Level 3 for ease of reference. Read the relevant chapter(s) for the topic you are currently studying and do the exercises/activities as specified. The **key tasks** can be done in any order, as appropriate to your college and/or workplace requirements, and can contribute to your formal assessment (for example, as part of your portfolio of evidence). However, it is suggested that you read the section on observing and evaluating children's development in Chapter 1 and the information on planning activities in the appendix *before* you start planning and implementing your own activities for children. *Do* remember to follow any college/workplace guidelines you have been given.

Introduction

This book aims to provide a comprehensive look at the **psychological** aspects of child development including:

- language and communication skills;
- sensory and intellectual development;
- self-image and self-esteem.

Together with some **sociological** aspects such as socialisation and behaviour management it will be demonstrated how these two aspects work together to contribute to a **holistic** understanding of the needs of young children and how these needs may be met.

This book takes the viewpoint that *all* learning takes place within a social and cultural context. This perspective, known as *social constructivism*, is becoming established as *the* major theoretical perspective in developmental psychology, in which young children are viewed as being active participants in the structuring of their own identities.

This book is for students (and their tutors/assessors) on Early Years Care and Education courses and provides knowledge of the relevant psychological theories on child development *and* how these can be applied in early years settings. The book explains these complex issues in ways which can be easily understood, yet is sufficiently challenging to assist students in developing a sound knowledge-base to complement their practical skills.

Many thanks to the children and staff at Rood End and Withymoor primary schools where I gained much of my experience of working with young children; thanks also for their kind permission to use the photographs on pages 43, 84, and 212.

Thanks also to the students and staff at Birmingham College of Food, Tourism & Creative Studies and Sandwell College of Further & Higher Education where I developed my skills of providing learning and assessment materials for student nursery nurses; special thanks to Pam Steer and Florence Awunor.

Many thanks to Chris Helm, Tim & Sarah Crumpton and Martin Hill for technical support and computer information.

Special thanks to Helen Allan for helping to maintain my sanity while writing this book.

1

The Sequence of Language Development

• •Key Points• •

- communication is a key factor in children's development
- communication can be verbal or non-verbal
- there are several inter-related modes of language: thinking, listening, speaking, writing, reading, and non-verbal communication

- there is an identifiable sequence of children's language development
- children's communication skills depend on their chronological age *and* their language experiences

What is language ?

The word **language** is often used to describe the process of speaking and listening, but it is much more than verbal communication. Language is what makes humans different from all other animals. All animals, including humans, can communicate through the use of **signals**. For example, a cat hisses and its tail bristles when it feels threatened or a dog may bark to indicate that there is an intruder. Humans also communicate using signals such as body language and gesture; what makes us different is the use of **symbols** (e.g. words) to indicate more complex needs and feelings. While animals are only able to deal with the here and now, humans can use language to store and later recall ideas, feelings and past experiences, and to look forward to the future.

The human ability to utilise language depends on the use of **recognised systems of symbols** and a common understanding of what those symbols mean. For example:

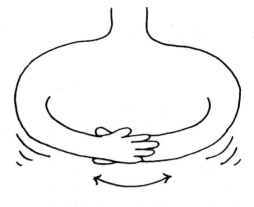

a drawing

baby
English language

sign language

bebe
French language

What is communication?

Anyone could make up their own language system, but they would not be able to communicate with others unless they shared this system or **code** with them. For example, in this country the majority of people use the language system 'English' and anyone who does not understand this code is at a disadvantage in terms of communicating effectively in an English-speaking society. Obviously there are many other systems of symbols as indicated by the many different languages and alphabet systems throughout the world.

At first, babies and young children are not able to use this complex language system; it takes time for them to learn the code of their particular home or community language. While they are learning the code they use other ways to **communicate** their needs and feelings to other people, for example, body language, gestures and facial expressions. However, these symbols can only be interpreted by others; we do not always know exactly what the child is trying to communicate to us, which can be very frustrating for both adult and child! When a baby cries it could mean:

- 'I need my nappy changed now!'
- 'I want feeding right now!'
- 'I need a nap.'

- 'I want a cuddle!'
- 'Play with me!'

Our interpretation of the baby's cry will depend on how well we know this particular baby and our understanding of this baby's needs.

Communication means:
- the passing of information, either verbally or non-verbally, to another
- the receiving of information
- the interpretation of information
- the understanding of information.

EXERCISE

Define the meaning of the terms *language* and *communication* in your own words.

Language acquisition theories

There are several differing viewpoints as to how babies and young children learn to use language and communication skills.

1 The 'nurture' theory

This **behaviourist** theory originates from the work of the philosopher John Locke (1600s) and was developed by behavioural psychologists such as **Pavlov** (1950s). This theory suggests that a baby is born with a mind like a *tabula rasa,* a 'clean slate'. This means that babies have to learn *everything,* including language, from scratch. Language has to be learned in the same way as any other skill. Children's parents and carers shape the way in which children learn language by encouraging the required sounds (and then words) while ignoring others. Children learn language by copying sounds, words and phrases around them, and through the positive reinforcement of their attempts to communicate.

2 The 'nature' theory

This **nativist** theory, put forward mainly by the linguist Noam **Chomsky** (1960s), states that babies are **born** with *some* knowledge of language. He argues that language systems are too complex to be acquired solely from being copied from and/or taught by adults. Language is **innate** and all humans have a genetic pre-disposition towards using language.

Chomsky concludes that humans have a **'language acquisition device'** (LAD) which allows them to process and to use language. To reinforce this argument, Chomsky points to how all children appear to learn language in the same way and that the early stages of language are the same for all children. For example, all children (whatever their community language) first learn to speak using **holophrases** (i.e. one word utterances to convey whole sentences) followed by **telegraphic speech** (i.e. two or three word sentences to convey meaning).

3 The 'social interaction' theory

This is part of social constructivist theory. The psychologists **Vygotsky** (1930s) and Jerome **Bruner** (1970s) suggest that young children acquire language as a means to communicate more effectively with others than can be done through non-verbal communication alone. This theory is similar to the behaviourist tradition in that children **learn** language through their interactions with others. However, this theory differs in that even very young children are seen as **active participants** in their language development. For example, research has shown that babies can *initiate and control* pre-verbal 'conversations' with their parents/carers rather than the other way round; babies make adults pay attention to them through body language, crying, babbling and end 'conversations' with adults by breaking off eye contact or simply falling asleep! The role of the adult in children's language development is to provide the **social context** in which meaningful communication can take place.

This theory also stresses the strong link between language acquisition and children's **cognitive** or intellectual development. Language arises from the need to understand the environment and from social interactions with others.

EXERCISE

What is your own view of how young children acquire language? Give a detailed account, using examples from your own experiences.

Why do we communicate?

We communicate because we need to interact with others. Humans are social animals and desire the company of others. We use language as the most effective means of communicating with other people. Communication is a **key factor** in the social interaction which is an essential part of our daily lives. This applies to babies and young children as well as to adults. Babies and young children use their communication skills (however limited these may be) to express their needs and desires in an **egocentric** way; they use language as a means of self-preservation.

Children and adults use communication to:
- interact with others
- explore the environment
- make sense of everyday experiences
- access information and understand concepts
- organise thoughts and formulate ideas
- express own feelings and understand the feelings of others.

How do we communicate?

Many people think 'language' equals 'speech', but there are many ways to communicate without talking. Humans are able to use language from birth using non-verbal communication. For example, a baby may communicate in the following ways: by crying, smiling, making eye contact or moving the body in response to sound.

Young children (and adults) use a variety of different ways to communicate. These **modes of language** are essential to being able to communicate effectively with others and to being fully involved in a wide range of social interactions. The different modes of language can be described as:

- listening   • thought   • non-verbal communication
- written language   • speech

Each mode of language involves a variety of skills which are inter-related; that is some of the skills are required in more than one mode, e.g. reading and writing both involve the processing of oral language in a written form.

Adults should provide opportunities for young children to develop the necessary skills to become competent at communicating using these different modes of language. Remember that some children may be limited in their ability to use some aspects of language due to sensory impairment or other special needs (see Chapter 2).

EXERCISE

Look at the modes of language diagram. Using the headings from the diagram, list examples of activities/experiences which would encourage each skill. Your list might look something like this:

Modes of Language	Skills	Example Activities
Thought	**Recalling images**	*Drawing/painting of event*
Speaking	**Oral language**	*Discussion or news time*
Writing	**Written language**	*Recording news*
Listening	**Processing information**	*Listening to instructions*
Reading	**Phonics**	*'Letterland' songs/stories*
Non-verbal communication	**Body language**	*Drama or role play*

Provide examples from your own experiences of working with young children.

The sequence of language development

It is more accurate to think in terms of the **sequence** of language development rather than **stages** of development. This is because:
stages = development which occurs at *fixed ages;* while
sequence = development which follows the same basic pattern *but not necessarily at fixed ages.*

We use the work of people such as Mary Sheridan as a guide to the **milestones** of *expected* development, that is the usual pattern of development or **norm**. We should use the term 'sequence' when referring to all aspects of children's development.

Language development in particular is affected by many other factors not just a child's chronological age. (See Chapter 2 for information on the factors which affect language development.)

Another important factor to remember is that physical maturity also plays a

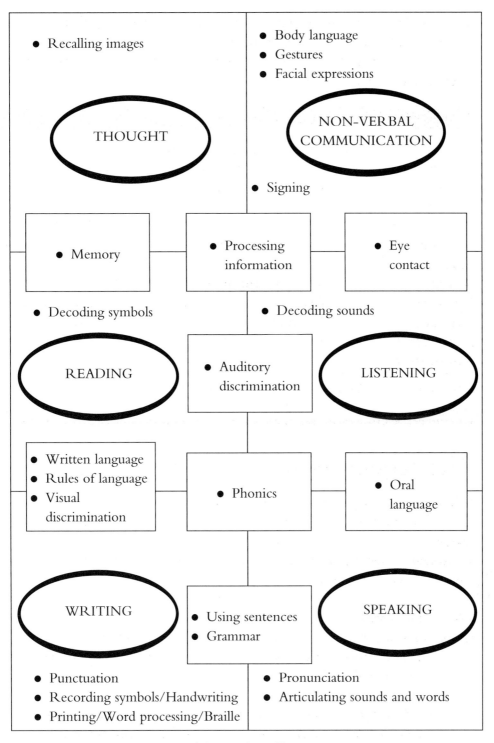

The inter-related components of the modes of language

part in children's language development. Babies need to have physical control over their vocal chords, tongue, lips and jaw muscles to be able to articulate the sounds necessary to form their first words. In addition, babies and young children have two important language ingredients:

1 a **passive** vocabulary – the language used by others which they can *understand*;
2 an **active** vocabulary – the words which they actually *use* themselves.

Babies and young children can *understand* more words than they can *speak* themselves, whatever their level of development.

The chart shown here *does* indicate specific ages, but only to provide a framework for understanding children's language development. Remember all children are individuals and develop at their own rate.

The sequence of language development

Age 0–3 months:
- recognises familiar voices; stops crying when hears them
- aware of other sounds; turns head towards sounds
- responds to smiles
- moves whole body in response to sound/to attract attention
- pauses to listen to others
- makes noises as well as crying e.g. **burbling**.

Age 3–9 months:
- responds with smiles
- recognises family names, but cannot say them
- enjoys looking at pictures and books
- even more responsive to voices and music
- participates in simple games e.g. 'peep-po'
- tries to imitate sounds e.g. during rhymes
- starts **babbling**, uses single syllable sounds e.g. 'daa', 'baa' and 'maa'
- from about 7 months uses two syllable sounds e.g. 'daada', 'baaba', 'maama'
- shouts to attract attention

Age 9–18 months:
- continues to imitate sounds
- starts **jargoning** e.g. joins up syllables so more like 'sentences'

- such as 'Maama-baaba-daa'
- learns to say first real words, usually the names of animals, every day things
- uses gestures to emphasise word meanings
- uses vocabulary of between 3 and 20 words
- participates in simple finger rhymes
- continues to enjoy books
- over-extends words, that is uses same word to identify similar objects e.g. *all* round objects are called 'ball'

Age 18 months–2 years

- uses language to gain information e.g. starts asking 'What dat?'
- repeats words said by adults
- acquires 1–3 words per month; by 2 years has vocabulary of about 200 words
- participates in action songs and nursery rhymes
- continues to enjoy books and stories
- uses **telegraphic speech** e.g. speaks in 2–3 word sentences such as 'Daddy go' or 'Milk all gone'

Age 2–3 years:

- has vocabulary of about 300 words
- uses more adult forms of speech e.g. sentences now include words like that, this, here, there, then, but, and
- can name main body parts
- uses adjectives such as big, small, tall
- uses words referring to relationships e.g. I, my, you, yours
- asks questions to gain more information
- sings songs and rhymes; continues to participate in action songs
- continues to enjoy books and stories
- can deliver simple messages

Age 3–4 years:

- has vocabulary of between 900 and 1000 words
- asks lots of questions
- uses language to ask for assistance
- talks constantly to people knows well
- gives very simple accounts of past events
- can say names of colours
- begins to vocalise ideas
- continues to enjoy books, stories, songs and rhymes

- listens to and can follow simple instructions
- can deliver verbal messages

Age 4–5 years:
- may use vocabulary of about 1500 to 2000 words
- uses more complex sentence structures
- asks even more questions using what, when, who, where, how and especially **why** !
- shows interest in more complex books and stories
- gives more detailed accounts of past events
- vocalises ideas and feelings
- can listen to and follow more detailed instructions
- can deliver more complex verbal messages
- continues to enjoy songs and rhymes
- shows interest in simple poetry

Age 5–7 years:
- has extensive vocabulary; by 7 years may use as many as 4000 words
- uses more complex sentence structures
- develops early reading skills
- develops early writing skills but possibly at slower rate than reading skills
- continues to enjoy books, stories and poetry; by age 7 can recall the story so far if book read a chapter at a time
- gives very detailed accounts of past events and can anticipate *future* events
- vocalises ideas and feelings in more depth
- listens to and follows more complex instructions
- appreciates simple jokes due to more sophisticated language knowledge
- uses developing literacy skills to communicate and to access information e.g. story and letter writing; use of dictionaries, encyclopaedia, computers, Internet, e-mail.

KEY TASK

Design a booklet which explains the sequence of language development in babies and young children. Include the following:

1 brief outline of ages and sequence of language development
2 appropriate activities and experiences to promote language development
3 the role of the adult in encouraging children's communication skills.
NVQ Level 3 links: C.11.1 C.11.2 C.11.3 C.11.4 (C.14.5)

DCE links: Units 4 and 6 (Unit 7)
BTEC links: Unit 8 (Unit 6)

The observation and assessment of children's language development

There are many reasons why it is important to observe children using language and communication skills:

- to understand the wide range of speech and language development demonstrated by babies and young children
- to know and understand the sequence of language development
- to use this knowledge to link theory with practice in your own setting
- to assess children's language development and communication skills
- to plan activities appropriate to children's individual language needs.

Thinking about observing

Adults working with young children need to be able to look and to listen attentively to how children communicate. By observing carefully you can discover the range and variety of language used by the children in your setting and improve your own skills in providing appropriate opportunities for encouraging and extending children's language development.

Regular observations are also helpful in identifying any potential problems children may have with their language and communication skills. The observing adult can identify:

- the ways in which each child communicates
- how children interact with others; their social skills
- any difficulties in communicating.

A continuous record of a child's language difficulties (for example, in a diary format) can help the adult to identify specific problems. Working with parents, colleagues and specialist advisors (if necessary) the early years worker can then plan a suitable programme to enable the child to overcome these difficulties. Observations can provide a check that children's language is progressing in the expecting ways.

Issues to think through

Portfolio building
- what to include?
- how to use your
  portfolio

Why observe?
- developing quality
  practice

Pass it on?
- whom to pass it on to?
- what to pass on?
- when to pass it on?

What to observe?
- the importance of quality
  observation
- meeting the requirements
  of the course
- recognising a suitable
  opportunity to observe

Making assessments
- background information
- aims
- areas of development
- recommendations
- personal learning
- bibliography

Where to observe
- working in a variety
  of settings

**Methods of recording
observations**
- choosing a suitable
  method
- advantages and
  disadvantages of each
  method
- record keeping

How to observe?
- planning
- preparation
- aims
- front sheet
- observing
- evaluations
- presenting work
- getting work
  assessed

FROM: *How To Make Observations and Assessments* by Jackie Harding and Liz Meldon-Smith
(Hodder and Stoughton, 2000)

Where and what should you observe?

It is important to observe in a quiet corner of the early years setting to
maximise the opportunity to hear clearly what is being said by the child.
Try to find a place in the setting which avoids too much interference or
interruptions. Make sure that the situation is realistic and not artificial; you

should be observing language activities which are part of the setting's usual routine.

For your first language observations, it might be a good idea to use picture books as an appropriate activity, because these are familiar to most young children. Making a tape recording of a conversation with a child is also a useful idea. You can then make a transcript of the tape recording (play back the tape and write down what was said). This method of observation allows you to check the child's use of language more accurately.

You can observe children's language in a variety of situations; remember we all use language in some form in *everything* we do. For example, you could observe the following situations:

- a child talking with another child or adult
- an adult talking with a small group of children
- a small group of children engaged in pretend/role play
- a child playing alone
- small or large group discussions e.g. news time
- an adult reading/telling a story to a child or group of children
- a child or group of children participating in a creative activity e.g. painting, drawing
- a child or children playing outside
- a child involved in a literacy activity e.g. writing news, story.

Basic principles

1 **Confidentiality** must be kept at all times. You *must* have permission to observe from your supervisor and/or the child's parents. Use only the child's first initial; any staff should be identified by their role (e.g. teacher or nursery nurse etc.). *Never* use surnames when referring to children or staff in an observation.

2 **Be objective** – only record what you actually see and hear, not what you think or feel.

3 **Equal opportunities**. Remember to consider children's cultural backgrounds e.g. children may be very competent at communicating in their community language, but may have more difficulty in expressing themselves in English; this does *not* mean they are behind in their language development. Also, be positive with regard to children with communication difficulties; focus on what the child *can* do in terms of language.

4 **Holistic approach**. Remember to look at the 'whole' child. Language

and communication skills do not take place in isolation; you need to look at other aspects of children's development in relation to their language development.

5 **Consider children's feelings**. Try not to make it obvious that you are observing; keep you distance where possible, but be close enough to hear the children's language.

6 **Practise**. The best way to develop your skills at observing children's language is to have a go at doing observations.

EXERCISE

Find out what the policies are in your setting with regard to:

- child observations
- language assessments
- confidentiality.

Remember to keep this information in mind when doing your own observations of children within that setting.

Assessment of children's language

Once you have recorded your observation of the child/children's language and communication skills, you need to **assess** this information in relation to:

- the aims of the observation
- what you observed about this child's language and communication skills in *this* situation
- how this compares to the expected language development for a child of this age
- any factors which may have affected the child's language ability e.g. the immediate environment, significant events, illness, child's cultural background, special needs.

Your college tutor or assessor should give you guidelines on how to present your observations.

KEY TASK

Observe a young child communicating with another child or adult. Focus on the child's language and communication skills.

In your assessment, comment on:

- any vocabulary used by the child
- the complexity of the child's sentence structure
- any non-verbal communication used (e.g. body language, gestures, facial expressions)
- the child's level of social interaction (e.g. did the child appear confident when speaking? Did they have a friendly and relaxed manner? Did they need coaxing to communicate?)

NVQ Level 3 links: C.16.1 C.16.2 C.11.1 C.11.2
DCE links: Units 1, 4 and 6
BTEC links: Units 6 and 8

The planning cycle

Following your observation and assessment of the child's language and communication skills, your recommendations can provide the basis for planning appropriate activities and experiences to encourage/extend the child's abilities in these areas.

Effective planning is based on children's individual needs, abilities and interests, hence the need for accurate child observations and assessments. These needs have to be integrated into the curriculum requirements of your particular setting.

For example, the themes and activities may be related to aspects of Key Stage One of the national curriculum or to the early learning goals for pre-school children.

When you have decided on the appropriate activities and experiences (in consultation with colleagues and/or parents as relevant to your setting) you can then implement them. Remember to evaluate the plan afterwards. Further observations will be necessary to maintain up to date information on each child's developmental needs.

KEY TASK

Plan, implement and evaluate a detailed plan for a language based activity such as:

- news time/discussion
- story time/sharing book with a baby

- game/activity book or centre with a baby
- nursery/finger rhymes
- phonics/reading activities.

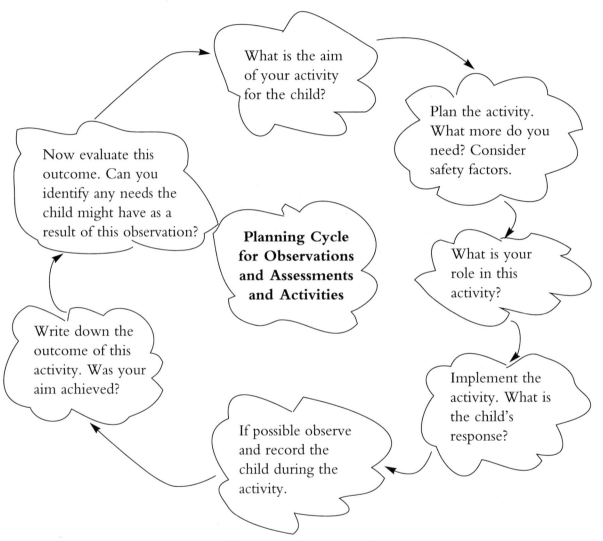

What is the aim of your activity for the child?

Plan the activity. What more do you need? Consider safety factors.

Now evaluate this outcome. Can you identify any needs the child might have as a result of this observation?

Planning Cycle for Observations and Assessments and Activities

What is your role in this activity?

Write down the outcome of this activity. Was your aim achieved?

Implement the activity. What is the child's response?

If possible observe and record the child during the activity.

From *How to Make Observations and Assessments* by Jackie Harding and Liz Meldon-Smith (Hodder and Stoughton, 2000)

Use the information gained from the observation on pages 14/15 and your recommendations for encouraging/extending that child's language and communication skills as the starting point for this activity.

Remember to review and evaluate the activity afterwards.

NVQ Level 3 links: C.11.1 C.11.2 C.11.4 C.11.5 M.7.3 (C.14.4)
(C.14.5)
DCE links: Units 2, 4 and 6 (Unit 7)
BTEC links: Units 3, 7 and 8 (Unit 6)

Further reading

Harding, J. and Meldon-Smith, L. (2000) *How to make observations and assessments.* 2nd Edition. Hodder and Stoughton.

Hobart, C. and Frankel, J. (1994) *A practical guide to child observation.* Stanley Thornes.

Matterson, E. (1989) *Play with a purpose for the under-sevens.* Penguin.

Sheridan, M. (1987) *From birth to five years.* NFER Nelson.

Steiner, B. et al (1993) *Profiling, recording and observing – a resource pack for the early years.* Routledge.

2

Factors Affecting Language Development

Factors affecting children's language acquisition and the development of their communication skills include:

- environmental factors
- social and cultural factors
- setting and group size

- group dynamics and children's temperaments
- children's social and emotional development
- language diversity
- special needs

To participate fully in all aspects of education (and society) children need to successfully develop a wide range of language and communication skills. Those working with young children need to be aware of the wide variety of language experiences that children bring to the early years care and education setting. Depending on their individual language experiences, some young children may not have reached the same level of language development as their peers or they may lack effective communication skills. Some children may even be ahead of what is usually expected for children their age.

Due to the wide range of language experiences which young children bring to the early years setting, it is important for early years workers to have a knowledge and understanding of the possible reasons for these differences.

Environmental factors and social/cultural factors

It has been suggested (for example, by Laing and Chazan in Fontana, 1984) that some children grow up within environmental and social circumstances which may restrict the children's opportunities to explore their environment and to develop language and communication skills through positive and stimulating interactions with others. For example:

- poverty • race and culture • family size • parental background/low expectations.

Poverty

Some people believe that poverty is a crucial factor affecting all aspects of children's development (Leach, 1994). No matter what level of importance parents place on language and learning, it may be very difficult to provide books and activities to stimulate children's interest in language and reading in some circumstances. For example:

- no local library
- travel costs to nearest library too high
- local parks/play areas not safe due to crime
- financial worries/unemployment make providing stimulating language opportunities more difficult.

Research indicates that poverty and related problems such as poor housing can affect children's educational success (National Commission on Education, 1993). One of the reasons for this lack of success is due to problems involving language and communication; without appropriate language and communication skills, it is impossible to access and process the information that is essential to learning.

Race and culture

We live in a multiracial and multicultural society. Many children coming into early years settings may not speak English at home. The national tests for 7 year-olds indicate that these children perform less well than children whose first language is English (National Commission on Education, 1993).

Social interaction depends on cultural patterns. How adults and children communicate with each other depends on how a culture or society views children and child development. Not so long ago, British society considered that 'children should be seen and not heard' and also that 'children should not speak until spoken to'. Children develop communication skills in line with the expectations of their culture and race. For example, English-speaking children may be used to adults who modify their speech, adults who simplify their language to help their children's comprehension; while children from many non-English speaking backgrounds may be used to more adult patterns of speech and more direct language instructions from adults in their social interactions.

Children may find communicating within the early years setting difficult at first because they find it hard to relate to staff or other children from different races and/or cultures. The lack of ethnic role models is a particular problem in educational settings where a very small number (around 2% in 1997) of teachers are black or Asian British.

However, it is dangerous to make assumptions about children's language abilities based solely on their culture or race. You should always look at each child as an *individual*.

EXERCISE

Think about your own attitudes towards race and culture. Explain how it may influence your expectations of children's language abilities and communication skills.

Family size

In the past some researchers were concerned that children in large families lacked the opportunities to interact in a meaningful way with adults, as their parents were too busy coping with so many children (Rutter in Leach, 1994). The presence of brothers and sisters was seen as a negative factor in children's development. There is little evidence to support this idea.

It has been suggested that children who are the first (or only) child in their family develop language at a faster rate and have a larger vocabulary than other children (Cunningham, 1993). This assumption should not be made as it depends on the interaction and communication the child has with his/her parent(s).

The important factor is *not* family size, but the **quality of adult and child interactions**. We will look at the importance of this aspect later on in this chapter.

Parental background and/or expectations

In the past researchers such as Bernstein suggested that 'working class' children were at a disadvantage in school because of their inability to use language in the same way as 'middle class' children. More recently it has been realised that it is the **social context of language** which is the important factor in children's language development rather than any notions related to 'class'. It depends on ***how individual families use language***: some families see language and learning as very important and pass this attitude onto their children (Foster-Cohen, 1999); some families have other priorities.

Some parents may be unaware of the ways to assist their children's language development and communication skills. Some children may have various experiences of language and literacy which are not the same as the linguistic experiences provided in early years care and education settings.

By the time most children attend an early years setting they have already developed many aspects of language and will have a wide variety of communication skills. Depending on their home experiences some children will feel at ease in talking with both adults and children, while some children will be shy and make only limited responses to others. Children who are poor communicators may come from backgrounds dissimilar to the early years workers, but this does not mean that they are incapable of communicating in meaningful ways in other contexts e.g. with other children or their own family (Meadows, 1993).

Parents who encourage their children's interest in language and literacy through: general conversation, talking about everyday/children's activities and sharing stories and books will be providing their children with a distinct advantage in terms of communication and education.

However, children who are pushed too hard by being forced to read and write before they are ready, may actually be harmed in terms of their language development as they can be put off reading, writing and other related activities. The 'early learning goals' which include social and communication skills should help parents and carers realise the importance of informal approaches to language and literacy.

The language environment

The various ideas concerning the effects of children's very early experiences on their language development may be too simplistic. While there *are* differences between children's language experiences, it is often staff attitudes towards children from differing circumstances which can create problems. Early years workers (especially in schools) may come from different backgrounds/cultures compared to the children they are working with and so *may* have low expectations of these children. This in turn can lead to low achievement by these children with regard to their language and learning (Bruce and Meggitt, 1999). We will be looking at this idea of **self-fulfilling prophecy** in Chapter 11.

In fact *later* experiences also affect children's language development, hence the importance of providing a quality, **language-rich** learning environment. For example, the early years setting could actually have a negative effect if it limits the opportunities for language.

Remember that early years workers sometimes have little or no control over the environmental/social factors *outside* the setting, but they can and should ensure maximum opportunities *within* the setting for enabling language development and encouraging communication skills by providing a stimulating, language-rich environment.

A well-planned and stimulating environment is essential to children's language development. Play and conversation are important elements in this development, because it is through these that young children learn about themselves, other people and the world around them. The relationships which children form with themselves and other children/adults is central to their language development (Ball, 1994).

E X E R C I S E

1 Draw a diagram of your work setting. Your diagram might look something like the one on page 23.
2   Look at the resources available and indicate on your diagram how you could maximise the opportunities for language and communication skills within the setting.

Setting and group size

Following the more intimate interactions which most children experience in the home, many children find the prospect of communicating within the larger early years setting extremely daunting. Even as adults it can be difficult to communicate with others in situations such as parents' evenings/open days, staff meetings, on courses at college, presentations.

Shy or less confident children may be reluctant to talk particularly in large group situations. It is important to be flexible, and to provide a variety of groupings:

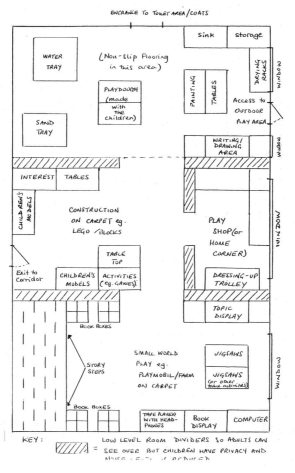

Room plan for a language-rich environment

- one-to-one
- pairs/small groups
- large groups
- whole class.

This allows for individual differences within the setting and gives every child opportunities to develop many different communication skills in a variety of meaningful ways.

Group dynamics

Each individual, whether adult or child, has different personal characteristics which affect their ability to communicate effectively and comfortably with others. From your experiences of working with young children you may have identified children's differing characteristics which influence their willingness or reluctance to communicate within a group.

For this reason, **ability groups** are not always the best way for young children to work, particularly when you want to encourage communication skills.

Ability groups are used to organise children according to academic ability, especially for literacy or numeracy, making it easier to plan activities at an appropriate level for each child's or group's ability. The difficulty with ability groups is that even very young children know if they are in the 'clever' group or the 'not-so-clever' group, no matter how the adults try to disguise the fact. This can have serious consequences for children's future development e.g. if the child *believes* they are not good at reading then they may give up trying to read. (See 'self-fulfilling prophecy' in Chapter 11.)

Friendship or temperament groups involve children with similar characteristics being encouraged to work together and/or children being free to *choose* who they work with. Friendship groups are often a better way for children to work because children feel more at ease socially and so *all* the children have the opportunity to communicate comfortably within the group, without the more articulate or confident children tending to dominate group discussions and activities. New children coming into the setting can fit in more easily too, by using the 'buddy' system where one child befriends the newcomer until they are established and can make their own choice as to which group they would like to join. This way of grouping children even works with very shy children or those who are extremely reluctant to communicate, as every child usually has at least one special friend who can be included in their group.

KEY TASK

Observe a small group of young children involved in a language activity/game.

In your evaluation comment on each child's communication skills:

- use of verbal language (e.g. vocabulary, sentence structure, babbling, imitating sounds)
- use of non-verbal language (e.g. body language, gestures, facial expressions or signing)
- level of participation in the group situation (e.g. frequency of language, need for prompts from adults/other children)

- level of social interaction (e.g. ability to take turns in listening and talking, following rules of the game)

In your recommendations include practical ideas to assist the child or children's language and communication skills in future activities.

NVQ Level 3 links: C.16.1 C.16.2 C.11.1 C.11.2 C.11.4
DCE links: Units 1, 4 and 6
BTEC links: Units 6 and 8.

Social and emotional development

Children's social and emotional development is closely linked with their language development as communication involves social interaction with at least one other person. (See information on self-talk in Chapter 6.)

Confidence, self-esteem and self-image affect the way we interact with other people, so this will necessarily affect the development of communication skills. For more information about self-esteem and self-image see Chapters 10 and 11.

KEY TASK

Plan, implement and evaluate a language activity.
(See the activity plan on page 15/16 for suggestions on possible language activities.) You could use the recommendations from the observation on page 24/25 as a starting point for planning this activity.

You should encourage the children's participation including attentive listening and communicating with others during the activity as well as supervising and maintaining the children's interest throughout the activity.

Remember to review and evaluate the activity afterwards.
NVQ Level 3 links: C.11.2 C.11.4 C.11.5 C.10.1 M.7.3 (C.14.4) (C.14.5)
DCE links: Units 2, 4 and 6 (Unit 7)
BTEC links: Units 3, 7 and 8 (Unit 6)

Language diversity

We live in a multicultural society where many languages are used to communicate. We are surrounded by different accents, dialects and other ways of communicating such as sign language. Children should have an awareness and understanding of other people's languages, while feeling proud of their own **community language** and being able to share this with others. Children in areas where only English is spoken still need an awareness of other languages to appreciate fully the multicultural society they live in.

Being **bilingual** is another factor which can affect a child's language development and communication skills. Bilingual means 'speaking two languages' which applies to many children (and adults) in the wide variety of early years care and education settings in Great Britain. 'Multilingual' is used to describe someone who uses more than two languages. However, the term 'bilingual' is widely used for all children who speak two or more languages.

There are four important factors to consider when working with children who are bilingual:

1 There are different and changing levels of competence involved in speaking several languages. For example, **emerging bilinguals** are still learning their first language while adding words to their second language and often combine words from two or more languages when they talk.
2 Different situations prompt the use of one language over another. **Fluent young bilinguals** are able to use whichever language is appropriate to a particular situation. For example, a bilingual child might have conversations with parents and siblings involving a mixture of Punjabi and English, while language used at school might be in a local dialect such as that used in the 'Black Country' in the West Midlands.
3 The range of literacy skills may be different in each language. Young children may be aware of different writing systems being used by their families and in the local community. They may be able to speak a particular language and not be able to write in that language.
4 Changing circumstances can affect children's bilingualism. For example, moving to a different area where cultural attitudes may be different so that more or less of the child's community language is used.
(Whitehead, 1996).

Children who are bilingual do not see their use of different languages as a difficulty. Early years workers need to maintain this attitude and to encourage young bilinguals to see their linguistic abilities as the *asset* it really is in our multicultural society.

Suggestions for promoting language diversity and providing for the language needs of bilingual children are in Chapter 3.

EXERCISE

1 Find out about the languages used by the children in your setting or local area.
● How many different languages are spoken by the children and adults? Which languages are spoken?
● Are there any children who are bilingual? Which languages do they use ? When do they use languages other than English?
2 Check out what resources are available locally to encourage children to development their community language and/or English. (This might include things like story time for the under-fives at the local library or lessons in Punjabi at the community centre.)
3 Design and make a leaflet using the information from your research on the above tasks.

Children with communication difficulties

All children have *individual* language needs, but some children may have *additional* or **special needs** which affect their ability to communicate effectively with others. Remember not to stereotype children with special needs; you should always look at the child *not* the disability.

Being able to structure and use language is an enormous task for every child; it takes the first seven to eight years of life to learn how to form all the different sounds correctly. Some sounds are more difficult to pronounce than others, for example: s, sh, scr, br, cr, gr and th. Most children have problems with these sounds at first, but eventually are able to pronounce them properly.

Lisping is a common problem for children learning to speak; it is caused by the child's inability to articulate a certain sound and so the child substitutes with another similar sound. Lisping usually stops without the need for adult intervention. Sometimes lisping may be a sign of a physical problem such as hearing loss, cleft palate or faulty tongue action in which case specialist advice is needed.

Some children may experience a period of **stammering**, usually around three years old. This is called **dysfluency** and is part of the normal pattern of language development: the young child cannot articulate thoughts into words quickly enough hence the stammer. About 5% of school aged children stammer, but it can be difficult to identify them, because children who stammer are often reclusive and reluctant to talk. Many children conquer this communication difficulty especially with the help of speech and language therapists and well-prepared, sympathetic early years workers; only 1% continue to stammer as adults.

Simple strategies can enable children who stammer to communicate more effectively in the early years setting:

- *Slow down your own rate of talking so children know there is plenty of time.*
- *When asking a question of a stammering child, give alternatives:*
  'Did it happen in class – or in the playground?'
- *Comment on the emotions exacerbating a stammer – 'I can see you're cross' – can be helpful. Comments on specific words or sounds often aren't.*
- *Encourage stammerers to talk about their personal interests: they are likely to feel more confident.*
- *Remain calm: with a little thought you will be able to help the stammerer.*
  (Sears in *TES*, 7 November 1997.)

Delayed and disordered language development

Some children may have difficulties with structuring language, e.g. problems with:

- **phonology** – the articulation of sounds, syllables and words (as mentioned above)
- **grammar** or **syntax** – words, phrases or sentence structure
- **semantics** – understanding language (**receptive** difficulties)
    – using language (**expressive** difficulties).

Delayed language development may be due to environmental factors such as those discussed earlier in this chapter. Children with delayed language

undemonstrative and do not like physical contact. A child with autism may have problems with:

- using verbal and/or non-verbal communication
- being aware of other people, which affects the ability to communicate effectively
- paying attention to other people (often more interested in objects) which affects listening and comprehension skills
- socialising with other children.

Children with severe autistic tendencies may not develop language at all.

Adults working with young children with autism can help in the following ways:

1 use pictorial instructions and visual cues
2 teach social skills as well as language
3 provide structured learning opportunities
4 keep to set routines
5 prepare for new situations carefully
6 use child's favourite activities as rewards
7 use music to communicate (e.g. sing instructions!)
8 work with parents and specialists to provide **consistent** care and education.

Cerebral palsy

Cerebral palsy is a condition caused by damage to the part of the brain that controls a person's movement; this damage may occur at or before birth. Cerebral palsy affects two children in every thousand and ranges from mild to severe disability. The effects on a child's language development depend on the severity of the condition. For example, the muscles necessary for speech may be affected causing communication difficulties. Speech therapy and communication aids such as specially adapted computers may be necessary. Due to their communication difficulties many people with cerebral palsy are mistakenly believed to have limited intellectual capabilities – the reverse is more often the case.

Cleft lip and/or palate

A child with a cleft lip and/or palate has structural damage to their top lip, palate or both, due to the failed development of these areas of the mouth during the early weeks in the womb. The condition is clearly diagnosed at birth. A series of operations is essential to correct this impairment; this may result in significant language delay as correct speech can not be articulated until the gaps in lips and/or palate have been successfully mended. Later speech therapy may be necessary.

Down's Syndrome

Children with Down's Syndrome have a genetic disorder which affects their physical appearance and overall development. The body's chromosomes are cell structures composed of genes; chromosomes are numbered and arranged in 23 pairs. Most children born with Down's syndrome have an extra chromosome number 21. Children with Down's Syndrome may have communication difficulties for the following reasons:

- small jaw, weak muscle tone and poorly developed nose may make articulation of sounds difficult
- language delayed compared to expected norm
- hearing loss.

Sensory impairment

Hearing loss may range from a slight impairment to profound deafness. One in four children under the age of seven experience a hearing loss of some degree at some time. The loss may affect one or both ears at different levels. There are two types of hearing impairment:

1 **Conductive** – involving the interference of the transmission of sound from the outer to the inner ear. This may be due to congestion or damage to the inner ear. The loss may be temporary or permanent; it makes sounds seem like the volume has been turned down. Hearing aids can be useful to amplify speech sounds, but unfortunately background noise is also increased. The most common form of conductive hearing loss in young children is **'glue ear'**. This temporary condition is caused by the collection of fluid behind the ear drum triggered by congestion during an ear, nose or throat infection.

Sometimes 'glue ear' can cause language delay as it interferes with a baby's or young child's hearing at an important stage of speech development. Persistent or repetitive cases of glue ear may require a minor operation to drain the fluid and to insert a **grommet** (see diagram on page 33) or small tube into the ear drum to prevent further fluid build up.

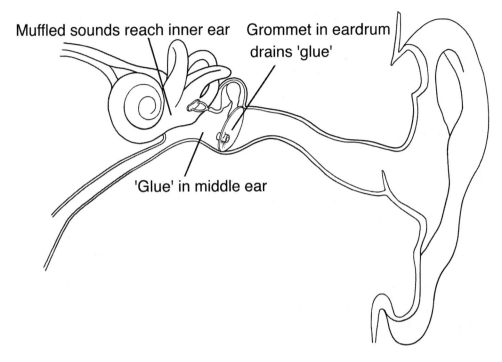

Muffled sounds reach inner ear

Grommet in eardrum drains 'glue'

'Glue' in middle ear

Ear with grommet inserted

2 **Sensori-neural** loss is a rarer condition that is more likely to result in permanent hearing impairment. The damage to the inner ear results in distorted sounds where some sounds are heard but not others. **High frequency loss** affects the child's ability to hear consonants; **low frequency loss** is a less common condition. Hearing aids are not as effective with this type of hearing impairment as the child still will not be able to hear the missing sounds. Children with sensori-neural loss therefore find it more difficult to develop speech and have a more significant language delay.

Young children with hearing impairment, especially those with conductive hearing loss, may be difficult to identify. However, even a slight hearing loss may affect a child's language development. Look out for these signs of possible hearing loss in young children:

- slow reactions
- delay in following instructions
- constantly checking what to do
- apparently day-dreaming or inattentive
- over-anxiety

- watching faces closely
- turning head to one side to listen
- asking to repeat what was said
- difficulty regulating voice
- poor language development
- spoken work more difficult to do than written work
- may have emotional or aggressive outbursts due to frustration
- problems with social interaction.

Children with hearing loss will use lip-reading and non-verbal clues such as gesture and body language to work out what is being said. Some children will wear hearing aids to improve their hearing abilities. Some early years settings may encourage the use of signing systems such as British Sign Language or Makaton and have specially trained staff to facilitate the use of sign language throughout the setting.

The following suggestions may help when working with children with hearing impairment:

- reduce background noise e.g. have carpets where possible
- ensure child is near to you
- use facial expressions and gestures
- use visual aids e.g. real objects, pictures, books, photos, etc.
- keep your mouth visible
- do not shout, speak clearly and naturally
- check child is paying attention
- develop listening skills through music and games
- include child in group activities in sensitive manner.

Visual impairment

Some children may wear glasses to correct short or long sight, but these children are not considered to be visually-impaired. A child with visual impairment has partial or total lack of vision in *both* eyes. If a child has normal vision in one eye, even if no vision in the other eye, they are *not* considered to be visually-impaired. Having one good eye is enough for most activities, although three-dimensional aspects and judging distances will be difficult.

Vision is an essential component of learning in the early years setting; visual impairment can affect language development in terms of written language and learning to read. Specialist advice and equipment may be necessary depending on the extend of the visual impairment, for example talking books and story books with Braille on plastic inserts.

The majority of children with visual impairment will have been identified before they come to the early years setting, but there may be a few children who have not, particularly in the younger age range.

Be aware of the following, a child who:

- blinks or rubs eyes a lot
- has itchy, watery or inflamed eyes
- frowns, squints or peers at work
- closes/covers one eye when looking at books
- bumps into people or furniture
- has difficulty with physical games/appears clumsy
- has difficulty forming letters and numbers
- omits words or sentences when reading
- says they cannot see the chalkboard or worksheet
- suffers from frequent headaches
- dislikes classroom/nursery lighting.

It is essential to work with parents and specialists to provide the best care and education for children with visual impairment. Make sure child wears glasses if they are supposed to. Depending on the extent of visual impairment the following strategies may help:

- ensure child is near to you
- keep the room tidy and free from obstacles
- black writing on a matt white board is better than using a chalkboard
- make worksheets clear and bold
- allow time for writing when necessary
- keep writing to a minimum—use oral methods e.g. tape recorder
- use word-processing where possible
- enlarge worksheets and books
- use other senses e.g. touch and sound to reinforce learning
- use visual aids such as magnifier
- be aware of possible mobility problems during physical activities
- provide pre-Braille and Braille activities after consulting specialist advisor.

Children with specific learning difficulties

Children with specific learning difficulties show problems in learning in one particular area of development; these children have difficulties in acquiring literacy skills and consequently other aspects of learning may be affected. The term **dyslexia** is often used when referring to children with such problems, but the phrase **specific learning difficulties** probably more accurately describes the scope of difficulties experienced by them. It is estimated that 4% of people are affected by dyslexia.

Recognising the signs of possible dyslexia in the under-fives:

- delay or difficulty in speech development
- persistent tendency to mix-up words and phrases
- persistent difficulty with tasks such as dressing
- unusual clumsiness and lack of co-ordination
- poor concentration
- family history of similar difficulties.

Note: Many young children make similar mistakes; dyslexia is only indicated where the difficulties are severe and persistent, or grouped together.

Recognising the possible signs of dyslexia in 5 to 8 year olds:

- particular difficulties in learning to read, write and spell
- persistent and continued reversing of letters and numerals (e.g. 'b' for 'd', 51 for 15)
- difficulty telling left from right
- difficulty learning the alphabet and multiplication tables
- difficulty remembering sequences e.g. days of the week/months of the year
- continued difficulty with tying shoelaces, ball-catching and other co-ordinated skills
- continued poor concentration
- frustration, possibly leading to behavioural problems
- difficulty following instructions – verbal and/or written.

Note: Not all children with dyslexia will display *all* these characteristics.

The following strategies may help when working with children with dyslexic tendencies:

- ensure child is near you or at the front of the class/group
- check unobtrusively that copy-writing, note-taking, etc. is done efficiently
- give positive feedback and encouragement, without drawing undue attention to the child
- use computers to help the child
- help the child to develop effective strategies and study skills which may differ from those used by other children.
- get specialist advice.

(Above information from The British Dyslexia Association.)

Children who will not speak

Some children can be shy, withdrawn and uncommunicative for these reasons:

- lack of confidence in group situations
- lack of social skills
- poor communication skills
- lack of experience in using English to communicate
- emotional trauma.

Check that there is no underlying cause for the children's reluctance or refusal to speak e.g. hearing loss, or stressful event such as going into hospital or a death in the family. Most children who are uncommunicative lack confidence in themselves and their ability to relate to others, so it is important to develop the children's self-esteem and improve their social skills (see Chapters 9–12 for more information). Do not try to *make* a child speak when they are reluctant to do so; it only causes further anxiety. Give the child the *opportunity* to speak in a welcoming and non-threatening environment; sometimes they may contribute, sometimes they won't. Even if the child does not say anything, make sure they can still observe and listen to what is going on in the setting.

Monitor children's language through observations (see Chapter 1); share your observations and assessments with your supervisor/assessor, that way you will be aware of any changes in a child's behaviour e.g. emotional stress can sometimes make a child become withdrawn and uncommunicative.

KEY TASK

Observe a child who has difficulty communicating. Your assessment should give particular attention to:

- the vocabulary of the child
- the complexity of his/her sentence structure
- the child's level of participation and social interaction.

Suggest possible reasons for the child's communication difficulties and make recommendations on how to encourage/develop their communication skills.
NVQ Level 3 links: C.16.1 C.16.2 C.11.1 C.11.2 C.11.4
DCE links: Units 1, 4 and 6
BTEC links: Units 6 and 8.

KEY TASK

Plan, implement and evaluate a language activity for a child with communication difficulties. Use your assessment of the child in the above observation as the starting point for planning this activity.

Remember to review and evaluate the activity.
NVQ Level 3 links: C.11.1 C.11.2 C.11. 4 C.10.1 M.7.3 (C.14.4) (C.14.5)
DCE links: Units 2, 4 and 6 (Unit 7)
BTEC links: Units 3, 7 and 8 (Unit 6)

Specialist help for children with communication difficulties

Early help is very important and effective as early assistance with communication difficulties can prevent more complex problems later on. The most important reasons for early intervention are:

1 Language and communication skills are part of intellectual development; language is an essential part of the learning process.
2 Language has vital role in the understanding of concepts.
3 The main foundations of language are constructed between the ages of 18 months and 4½ years during which time the majority of children have fully integrated language as part of the thinking and learning process. It is easier to assist with language development and communication skills

during this critical three year period then to sort out problems once children have reached school age.

4 Effective communication skills are essential to positive social interaction and emotional well-being. Communication difficulties can lead to isolation and frustration. Children who cannot communicate effectively may display emotional outbursts and/or aggressive, unwanted behaviour.

There are a number of agencies which offer specialist advice and support for children with communication difficulties, for example:

- health visitor
- speech and language therapist
- educational psychologist
- Portage worker
- nursery provision for children with special needs

- hearing impaired unit
- advisory teacher
- special language unit
- special needs assistant
- charities e.g. RNIB, RNID, AFASIC.

KEY TASK

Compile a fact file on speech and communication difficulties. Include:

- an introduction outlining the range of difficulties which may affect the language and communication skills of young children
- leaflets, booklets or information sheets on different aspects of language delay and communication difficulties
- reading list and useful addresses.

NVQ Level 3 links: C.11.1 C.11.2 C.11.4
DCE links: Unit 4
BTEC links: Units 6 and 22.

Further reading

Bruce, T. and Meggitt, C. (1999) *Child Care and Education.* 2nd Edition. Hodder & Stoughton.
Dare, A. and O'Donovan, M. (1997) *Good practice in caring for children with special needs.* Stanley Thornes.
Gulliford, R. and Upton, G. (1992) *Special educational needs.* Routledge.
Kerr, S. (1993) *Your child with special needs – a parents' handbook.* Hodder & Stoughton.

3

Developing Language and Communication Skills

- effective communication with young children
- the importance of feedback and encouragement
- the role of the adult in developing children's language and communication skills

- activities to extend/encourage speech and communication
- activities to help young children represent their experiences
- the value of young children's community languages

Effective communication with young children

The first step towards effective communication with children (and adults, too, of course) is being able to listen attentively to what they have to say. Nearly all breakdowns in communication are due to people not listening to each other.

Effective communication requires:

- **being available** – making time to listen to children.
- **being an attentive listener** – concentrating on what the children are saying.
- **using non-verbal skills** to show others we are paying attention; facing the person, leaning slightly towards them, smiling, nodding, open-handed gestures not clenched fists.
- **understanding the rules of turn-taking** in language exchanges; every person needs to have their say while the others listen.
- **being polite and courteous** – not shouting, not talking over other people, avoiding sarcasm (especially with very young children, who do not understand it and can be frightened by your strange tone of voice).
- **being relaxed, confident and articulate**.
- **using vocabulary appropriate to your listener(s)**.
- **encouraging others to talk** by asking 'open' questions
- **responding positively** to what is said.

- **being receptive** to new ideas.
- **being sympathetic** to other viewpoints (even if you totally disagree with them!).
- **providing opportunities** for meaningful communication to take place.

EXERCISE

Make a list of the opportunities for meaningful communication provided for the children within your early years setting.

Adults working with young children need to spend time listening carefully to individual children and to what children have to communicate in small or large group situations such as news time or story sessions. In order to do this effectively, early years settings should be well-staffed with a high **adult to child ratio**. When adults are not actively involved in the children's activities, perhaps because they are putting up displays or preparing materials for later activities, they should always be willing to listen to the children who will undoubtedly approach them to start up a conversation. Most communications in early years settings, especially in schools, relate to giving information or instructions e.g. setting children on to activities, discussions in preparation for tasks. However, informal 'conversations' are an important part of children's language development. Children can learn a great deal about language and the world around them from the spontaneous, unplanned communications that occur during everyday activities such as break/playtime, milk/juice time, meal times, setting up/clearing away activities.

Opportunities for conversation

Many of the following activities allow children the opportunity to talk and listen in more relaxed, informal situations. They allow children and adults to share their experiences in a more natural way through situations which may be similar to their home experiences such as meal times. Activities which can encourage conversations are:

- *natural materials*: sand, water, play dough, clay.
- *domestic activities*: milk/juice times, meal times, tidy up times, cooking and washing up, washing clothes. (Remember children's safety.)
- *books*: sharing books and stories with individual or small group.
- *special occasions*: birthdays, festivals, preparing for visits or visitors.
- *displays*: interest tables, wall displays, posters.

- *animals*: pets (in the setting or in the home), visits to farms, animal sanctuaries, safari parks.
- *toys/hobbies*: special days/times for 'show and tell' when children can talk about their special interests/favourite objects.

The language of learning

Effective communication is not just about conversations with young children. It also involves children being able to understand and use *the language of learning*. That is, the language needed:

- to understand concepts
- to participate in problem-solving
- to develop ideas and opinions.

Adults need to be able to utilise language effectively themselves in order to encourage and extend children's communication skills. A sound knowledge of children's language development plus the realistic organisation of the setting, activities and time are essential components for effective communication with children.

Organisation for effective communication

The early years setting needs to provide the space and opportunities for effective communication to take place and to enable children (and adults) to use the different modes of language. Suitable areas need to be created to facilitate the development of children's language and communication skills. For example:

- *writing tables:* enabling children to 'make their mark' using a variety of writing tools (crayons, pencils, pens, pastels, chalks) on different shapes, sizes and types of paper (e.g. plain, coloured, graph)
- *displays:* interest tables, displays of children's work and construction models, wall displays, posters to provide a stimulus for talk.
- *sand and/or water trays: science and mathematics equipment:* to encourage exploration and conversation.
- *pretend play areas:* home corner, shop, café, post office, space station to encourage language and communication skills through imaginative play.
- *book displays/story corner:* to promote children's interest in books and to develop their early literacy skills.

Children and adult talking in a reception classroom

- *computers:* to extend the children's range of language and literacy skills e.g. word processing, referencing skills.

The importance of labelling

Very young children respond to labels even before they can read them; they will ask adults what labels say. Using pictures or objects as well as written words helps children to make sense of labels and to develop their own literacy skills. Labelling introduces young children to one of the important purposes of written language: providing information or directions. Labels encourage children's independence in reading and writing. A special place for children to keep their belongings (whether on a hook, in a drawer, tray or basket) clearly labelled with each child's name, is an essential part of the effective language-rich environment. With very young children, a picture on the left-hand side of the label helps them to remember to work from left to right in reading and writing activities:

Labels on important everyday objects in the setting assist children's early literacy skills and help to extend their vocabulary within a meaningful context. Where possible use sentences rather than single words:

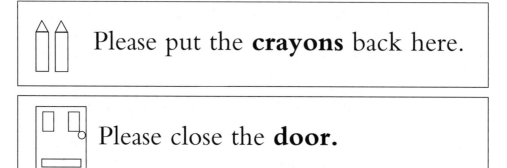

Clearly labelled areas and storage can help extend children's language as well as aiding the development of their social skills and independence:

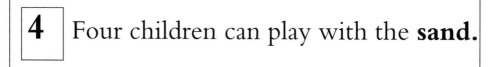

Effective communication is also promoted by encouraging children to take responsibility for everyday tasks within the setting. Young children are quite capable of making their own decisions and this helps to develop their independence and extends their communication skills even further. For example:

- be responsible for tidying up their own activities, getting equipment out (under adult supervision for safety reasons, of course)
- choose their own activities
- follow written and/or pictorial instructions for tasks/activities to be done that day
- record weather and other data.

The importance of feedback and encouragement

Praise and encouragement are essential components when working to extend and reinforce young children's language and communication skills. Young children need immediate and positive affirmations or rewards to show that their language and learning is progressing in accordance with the adult's (and child's) expectations. Adults should emphasise the **positive** aspects of children's attempts at developing their language and communication skills. Young children must be praised and/or rewarded for *effort* not just achievement. Children gain confidence and increased positive self-esteem when they receive praise and encouragement for their efforts and achievements.

There are four main methods used to praise and encourage children:

1 **Verbal** e.g. – 'Well done, Tom! This is a lovely story! Tell me what happened next..'; news time; 'circle' time.
2 **Non-verbal** e.g. – body language: leaning forward or turning towards a child to show interest in what the child is communicating; smiling; signing
3 **Symbolic** e.g. – 'smiley faces', stickers, stars or merit points.
4 **Written** e.g. – comments written (or stamped) on child's work; merit certificates

(There is detailed information on the importance of praise and rewards in Chapter 13 and on developing children's postive self-esteem in Chapter 10.)

The role of the adult in developing children's language and communication skills

Adults play a vital role in extending and encouraging the development of children's language use and communication skills. Adults provide opportunities for children to use language as a tool for exploring ideas and experiences. Opportunities for talk are especially helpful in promoting the development and use of language. Adults working with young children must be aware of and provide for appropriate experiences to enable all children to develop effective communication skills.

Adults can encourage young children's language development by:

1 **Talking** to babies and young children about anything and everything!
2 **Showing** children what you are talking about, e.g. use real objects/situations, pictures, books, and other visual or audio aids.

3 **Using straight forward sentences** with words appropriate to the children's level of understanding and development; avoid over-simplifying language; do *not* use 'baby talk' – children need adult speech to learn language.

4 **Using repetition** to introduce/reinforce new vocabulary and ideas. Do *not* make children repeat things back over and over; this is boring and frustrating.

5 **Copying** the child's sounds/words including any extensions or corrections to positively reinforce and extend the child's vocabulary, sentence structures, etc. For example: the child says: 'ball'; you could reply: 'Yes, that is Tom's red ball'. Or the child may say: 'moo!'; you could reply: 'Yes, the cow goes "moo"!' **Never** tell children off for making language errors; it will only make them reluctant to communicate in the future. Making mistakes is part of the language learning process.

6 **Being lively!** Use your tone of voice and facial expressions to convey your interest in what is being communicated.

7 **Remembering turn-taking** in language exchanges. Ask questions to stimulate children's responses and to encourage speech.

8 **Looking at the children** when talking with them. Remember to be at their level, especially when communicating with individuals or small groups of children, e.g. sit on a low chair or even on the floor; do *not* tower over them.

9 **Letting children initiate conversations** and listening to what they have to say.

10 **Sharing books, stories and rhymes** with babies and young children. (See Chapter 4.)

KEY TASK

Design and make an audio/visual aid such as a:

- puppet   - toy   - musical instrument

to extend children's language and communication skills.
Make sure the audio/visual aid is:

- safe for children (no choking hazards, sharp edges)
- sturdy and well-made
- attractive and suitable for children
- reflective of different cultural influences

- suitable for children with special language needs (e.g. children with hearing or visual impairment).

Include the following:

1 An aim and rationale explaining *why* you are making this particular audio/visual aid
2 Learning outcomes/objectives indicating *how* this aid will encourage and extend children's language and communication skills
3 How you would use the aid with children.

NVQ Level 3 links: C.11.2 C.11.4 C.11.5 C.10.1 C.10.2 (C.14.4) (C.14.5).
DCE links: Units 2, 4 and 6 (Unit 7)
BTEC links: Units 3, 7 and 8 (Unit 6).

Listening to and assessing children's language

Adults need to organise appropriate opportunities for language and to ask the right type of questions to stimulate communication. Adults can do this by providing a wide range of materials and by encouraging children to talk about their interests, what they are doing and what is happening around them, and so on. It can be difficult to be aware of your own communication skills in a busy nursery or classroom. A tape recorder is one way to obtain information on your skills. Recording your interactions with children is helpful as you can then playback recordings of various situations/activities and then assess your questions/responses to the children, your tone of voice and speed of speech.

Tape recording children's activities and discussions also enables the adult to assess the *child's* use of language and communication skills. Try it out in different situations e.g. home corner, story corner. However, be aware of the potential problems with tape recording children's activities:

- it takes time to develop the technique
- the setting may be busy and noisy
- individual children's skills may be difficult to identify.

A checklist may be an easier way to gain more precise information on children's communication skills.

Asking and answering questions

Adults need to provide **questions, prompts and cues** which encourage and extend children's language and learning. Some questions require only limited responses or answers from children. These 'closed' questions usually receive one word answers such as 'yes' or 'no' or the name of a person/object. These type of questions do not help children develop their own language and communication skills. 'Open' questions, on the other hand, are a positive way to encourage a variety of responses allowing children to give more detailed answers, descriptions and accounts of their personal experiences, feelings and ideas. For example: the question 'Did you ride your trike?' can only be answered by 'yes' or 'no'; instead it might be better to ask 'Where did you go on your trike?' and then use questions like 'What happened next?' to prompt further responses.

As well as asking questions, adults need to be able to **answer** children's questions. Encouraging children to ask questions helps them to explore their environment more fully, to look for reasons/possible answers and to reach their own conclusions as to why and how things happen. Always treat children's questions seriously. Try to answer them truthfully and accurately. If you honestly do not know the answer, then say so and suggest an alternative way for the child to obtain an answer. For example, 'I don't know where that animal comes from, let's look in the encyclopaedia to find out.' Or 'I don't know the name of that dinosaur; go and look in your dinosaur book to see if it's in there.'

EXERCISE

Listen to adults talking with young children in a variety of situations, both within and outside your setting, e.g. on buses, in shops, in the street, in the playground.

Pay particular attention to the questions asked by the adults *and* the children, and *how* they are answered.

Helping young children to understand the structure of language

As well as enabling children to use language, adults can also help children to understand the *rules of language*. Once children start to combine words to make sentences, they progress through various stages through which the structure and organisation of language becomes gradually more systematic. This systematic structuring of language is called **grammar**.

Stage 1: Children use simple two/three word phrases or sentences. Grammatical indicators are not present at this stage: no plurals e.g. 'Many car'; no possessive 's' e.g. 'Tom teddy'; no tense markers ('ed', 'ing') e.g. 'It rain'; no auxiliary verbs ('is', 'do') e.g. 'No like cake'. Children only use nouns, verbs, adjectives and adverbs such as 'now' or 'soon'.

Stage 2: Children begin to use grammatical indicators previously missing. Note the irregular use of past-tense forms, e.g. 'comed' (came), 'goed' (went) and plurals e.g. 'sheeps'. Gradually children begin to use grammar in increasingly adult forms.

Children do not learn grammar through imitation alone; children need opportunities to discover the rules of language for themselves by experimenting and being creative with words in a variety of situations.

Adults can also help children with grammar by repeating back the correct form of language when the child makes a grammatical error. Some examples are:

- **Possessive pronouns** – the child says: 'This Tom hat and that Teena hat.'; the adult replies: 'Yes, that is *your* hat and this is *my* hat.'
- **Possessive 's'** – the child says: 'Here Marly boots and teacher boots.'; the adult replies: 'Yes, these are Marly*'s* boots and those are Ms Kamen*'s* boots.'
- **Plurals** – the child says: 'We saw sheeps.'; the adult replies: 'Yes, we saw *some sheep* at the farm.'
- **Tense markers** – the child says: 'The cat goed out.'; the adult replies: 'Yes, the cat *went* outside.' Or the child says: 'Mummy come!'; the adult replies: 'Yes, your mummy is com*ing* into the nursery now.'
- **Auxiliary verbs** – the child says: 'We done play dough.': the adult replies: 'Yes, we *did* make play dough this morning.' Or the child says:

'We is walking to the park.'; The adult replies: 'Yes, we *are* walking to the park.'

- **Negatives** – the child says: 'I not eat 'nana.'; the adult replies: 'I see you *haven't* eaten your banana.'
- **Questions** – the child asks: 'More?'; the adult asks: 'Would you like some more milk?'

Finally, the adult needs to act as a **facilitator** by providing appropriate activities and experiences to enable young children to develop their language and communication skills in meaningful situations. The adult needs to:

- **provide age/level appropriate opportunities for play**
  especially activities which encourage language and communication e.g. role/pretend play, creative play.
- **provide opportunities for self-expression and self-evaluation**
  through discussion, news time, 'circle' time, painting, drawing, writing, music making, drama and dance.
- **be positive towards the child's attempts at language and communication**
  by valuing children's home experiences/cultural backgrounds; considering children's individual interests and abilities; being aware of children's special language needs.
- **give positive feedback, praise and encouragement to *all* children**
  by commenting positively on children's efforts at communicating in different ways.
- **be aware of possible developmental/psychological difficulties**
  through careful observation of children's language, learning and behaviour, e.g. children's drawings can provide information on their intellectual capabilities.

Activities to encourage/extend speech and communication

All babies and young children need activities and materials which encourage language and help to develop communication skills. These activities can be divided into five basic categories:

1 Exploration

- *toys and other interesting objects* to look at and play with such as household objects (remember safety), activity centres.
- *sounds* to listen to including voices, music, songs, rhymes, musical mobiles.
- *noise makers* such as rattles, simple musical instruments, even saucepans to bang!
- *bath toys and books*.
- *construction toys* including wooden bricks, plastic bricks like 'duplo', 'lego' and 'stickle bricks'.
- *natural materials* like water, sand, play dough, cooking ingredients.
- *creative materials* such as paint, glue.
- *outings* including visits to the park, museums, swimming.
- *animals* including visits to the farm, looking after small pets.

2 Description

- news time
- recording events, outings, visits, visitors
- a variety of books and stories including cloth books, board books, activity books, pop-up books, picture books. (See Chapter 4.)

3 Conversation

- *talking about their day, experiences, interests* in a variety of settings with other children and adults e.g. parent and toddler group, play group, nursery, school, after-school clubs.
- *talking during imaginative play activities* such as
  - playing with pretend/role play equipment including dressing-up clothes, tea set, puppets
  - playing with dolls, teddies and other cuddly toys
  - playing with small scale toys e.g. train set, dolls' house, road system
- *talking about special events* e.g. birthdays, new baby
- *talking while doing activities* (not necessarily related to the task).

4 Discussion

- *problem solving* during activities
- *follow-up* to activities e.g. after television programme or a story
- *co-operative group work*
- *games and puzzles*
- appropriate *television programmes* for their age group.

5 Instruction

- *preparation* before an activity
- *explanation* of what to do (verbal and/or written on a board)
- *instructions during an activity* to keep children on task
- *extra support* for individuals
- *introducing/extending knowledge* on a specific skill
- *step-by-step instructions*
- *worksheets*/books/cards
- *delivering verbal/written messages*, errands.

EXERCISE

Describe an example activity for each of the five categories, based on your experiences of working with young children.

Being flexible in planning activities

Careful planning of appropriate activities for babies and young children is necessary to ensure that all children have the opportunities to develop their language and communication skills within a meaningful context. Even if you are working within the national curriculum framework or towards the 'early learning goals', your planning needs to be flexible enough to allow for children's individual interests and unplanned, spontaneous opportunities for language and learning. For example, an unexpected snowfall can provide a wonderful opportunity to talk about snow and for children to share their delight and fascination for this type of weather. Or a child might bring in their collection of postcards which prompts an unplanned discussion about other children's collections; this might be developed into a 'mini-topic' on collections if the children are really interested.

Other activities may be provided within the setting which allow more spontaneous opportunities for children to express themselves without adult direction. This does not mean without adult supervision as obviously this is always necessary to maintain young children's safety. *Without adult direction* means the children are **free to choose** what and when to do particular activities. For example, drawing, painting, construction, pretend/role play and sand can often be provided as activities which children can choose (or not) to do when they feel they want/need to or after they have completed adult-directed tasks. It is important that children have this freedom of choice to help represent their experiences, feelings and ideas. Adults may still be involved in these activities, but in more subtle ways such as encouraging children to make their own decisions, talking with children while they are engaged in these types of activities.

Some early years settings take children's involvement in planning as the central basis for structuring their activities. The High/Scope philosophy encourages children to make decisions about their own choice of activities.

The 'plan-do-review' cycle of planning looks something like this:

1 **'plan'** – in a small group with an adult, children discuss which activities they would like to do that session. For example, a child might say: 'I'm going to build a sand castle first, next I will paint a picture for my mum and then play in the shop'.
2 **'do'** – the children participate in the activities of their choice. Children are encouraged to talk during this time with adults on hand to extend children's language and learning.
3 **'review'** – at the end of the session the group come together again to look back on the session's activities. For example, a child might say: 'I enjoyed making a really big sand castle with Tom. Then I painted a red dinosaur for my mum. I didn't play in the shop today 'cause Tom wanted to play with the cars instead. We made a great big traffic jam with all the cars and trucks!'

The High/Scope system encourages language and communication skills by involving children in the planning, doing and reviewing of activities. The children do participate in some adult-directed activities such as story time, PE and other larger group activities as well as work to develop specific skills such as literacy and numeracy in small groups or as individuals.

Being flexible and allowing for children's choice in planning helps children's language development by promoting:

- discussion skills
- co-operative group work (involving effective communication skills)
- opportunities for first-hand experiences and exploration
- information skills (including referencing skills, finding and using different resources).

Adults also need to be sensitive to children's individual needs and interests.

Remember to observe the children while they are involved in the activities and assess whether you need to change or extend the activities to meet the children's language needs more fully.

Television

Research shows that children benefit most when watching television with an adult and/or other children. Even programmes aimed specifically at young children lose some of their benefit in terms of children's language and learning unless shared with others. Watching television alone is a passive and non-interactive activity; children need other people to talk about programmes and to ask/answer questions in order to stimulate language and communication skills. Television should be used as an additional stimulus for discussions and ideas, not as a 'baby sitter'. Television is *not* a substitute for other forms of communication such as conversation and children's play. Television can be a useful way to introduce or reinforce information on topics/themes within the setting. Adults need to be selective in their choice of programmes for children and to avoid (as far as possible) those which portray stereotyped images as television provides powerful role models, both positive *and* negative.

Computers

Computers and other associated technology such as games consoles are now part of everyday life. They should not be used too much by children because, while they can be more interactive than television, they are no substitute for social interaction with other children and adults. However, it is as important for all children to be **computer-literate** as it is for them to develop traditional literacy and numeracy skills. Computers can make learning more attractive and interesting by providing a different, more visual way of developing and using problem-solving skills. For this reason computers can be particularly helpful for children with language and/or learning difficulties, especially as computer programs often have in-built praise or reward systems to motivate the user. Word-processing can enable children to write more easily and clearly, freed from the physical constraints of pencil control, and can encourage correct spelling through use of a spell-checker. Computers can also help referencing skills by encouraging children to access information in encyclopaedia on CD-ROM or on the Internet.

Activities to help young children represent their experiences

Children need opportunities to express their experiences, feelings and ideas through a wide range of activities and situations appropriate to their age and level of development. **Play** is an essential part of helping children to do this.

Imaginative play

This type of play, sometimes referred to as **pretend** or **role play**, is especially useful in encouraging and extending children's language and communication skills. Examples of this type of play include:

- home corner, play shop, hospital, dressing-up clothes
- dolls, puppets, teddies
- small scale toys e.g. train sets, cars
- acting out rhymes, stories, own experiences
- drama, music and movement.

Through imaginative play young children learn about themselves, other people and the world around them. Babies watch and listen to the adults and children around them, gradually young children imitate what they see others do which is often expressed through imaginative play. This includes taking on the 'role' of someone or something else; for example playing mum, dad or teacher or being a dog/cat. Eventually children go beyond copying others, they make up their own scenarios based upon their own experiences and expectations of the people and world around them.

Creative play

Creative activities in early years settings can often be dominated by too much adult-direction and by too many adult ideas. Children need opportunities to explore their own creativity, to express their experiences, feelings and ideas in their own way. Activities include:

- painting ● drawing ● model-making ● collage ● play dough and clay.

Writing

Children should be given opportunities to write about their experiences as appropriate to the age and level of development. In addition to activities

Child engaged in creative activity: finger painting

such as news and recording events, children need to be able to create their own stories and poems as a means of expressing their feelings and ideas. (See Chapter 4.)

Music

Musical activities can also provide an outlet for children's feelings and ideas. Most children have an interest in sounds from birth (unless born with a profound hearing loss) and show pleasure at hearing music. Children develop their own musical abilities by listening to and participating in musical activities from an early age. Adults need to provide opportunities for this by:

- singing songs and rhymes
- playing songs and rhymes on cassettes or compact discs
- playing musical instruments themselves (if they can!)
- encouraging children to sing
- encouraging children to make music on home-made instruments such as up-turned pots and pans, wooden spoons, shakers (remember safety!) or with commercial percussion instruments such as a xylophone, triangle, tambourine, drum.

For children to make and enjoy music, they must be able to listen first. Provide activities to encourage listening skills and auditory discrimination. For example, listening in silence 'What can you hear?' (e.g. clock ticking, wind blowing), identifying everyday sounds on a cassette or playing 'sound lotto'. Introduce children to rhythm by clapping out the beat of a rhyme, song, the syllables of a child's name or simple sentence. Let children dance to music to develop a sense of rhythm. The skills outlined above all help with children's language and communication skills; they are particularly valuable in developing children's early reading skills.

K E Y   T A S K

Observe a young child involved in an imaginative or creative play activity. Focus on the language and communication skills used by the child.
In your assessment comment on:

- the verbal and/or non-verbal communication used by the child
- the complexity of any language used
- the level of social interaction
- the role of the adult in encouraging the child's language and communication.

NVQ links: C.16.1 C.16.2 C.11.1 C.10.4
DCE links: Units 1, 4 and 6
BTEC links: Units 6, 7 and 8.

The value of young children's community languages

Early years workers must respect the languages of *all* children in the early years setting by providing an environment which promotes language diversity through:

- welcoming signs in community languages
- learning essential greetings in these languages
- photographs and pictures reflecting multicultural images
- labels with different languages/writing styles
- books, stories and songs in other languages
- multicultural play equipment e.g. ethnic dolls and dressing-up clothes.
- celebrating festivals

- preparing and sharing food from different culture.

EXERCISE

Give examples of how your setting promotes language diversity and encourages young children to use their community languages.

While promoting language diversity we need to remember that we live in a society where English is the dominant language; developing language and literacy skills in English is essential to all children if they are to become effective communicators both in and outside the setting. Most children entering the early years setting will speak English even if they have a different cultural background. However, there are some children who do start nursery or school with little or no English because they are new to this country or English is not used much at home. Early years workers can enable young children to learn English as their second language by:

- encouraging the children to use their community languages some of the time; this promotes security and social acceptance which will make learning English easier.
- inviting parents/grandparents to read or tell stories in community languages or to be involved with small groups for cooking or sewing activities.
- using action songs and rhymes to help introduce new vocabulary.
- using play opportunities to develop language skills in a meaningful context e.g. focus on words used when playing in the home corner or sand pit.
- using games to encourage language.

KEY TASK

Plan, implement and evaluate an activity which encourages/extends a baby or young child's language and communication skills. You could include the use of the audio/visual aid you made earlier.

Try to include a variety of communication techniques such as:

- active listening
- leaving time for the child to respond/talk
- careful phrasing of adult questions and responses.

Consider how you could meet the needs of children with communication difficulties with this activity. Remember equal opportunities.

NVQ Level 3 links: C.11.2 C.11.4 C.11.5 M.7.2 M.7.3 M.7.4 (C.14.4) (C.14.5)
DCE links: Units 2, 4 and 6 (Unit 7)
BTEC links: Units 3, 7 and 8 (Unit 6)

Further reading

Matterson, E. (1989) *Play with a purpose for the under-sevens*. Penguin.
Moynes, J. (1994) *The excellence of play*. The Open University Press.
Neaum, S. and Tallack, J. (1997) *Good practice in implementing the pre-school curriculum*. Stanley Thornes.
Petrie, P. (1989) *Communicating with children and adults: interpersonal skills for those working with babies and children*. Edward Arnold.
Whitehead, M. (1996) *The development of language and literacy*. Hodder & Stoughton.

Sharing Books, Stories and Rhymes

• •Key Points• •

- the importance of books to
  children's development
- choosing children's books,
  stories and rhymes
- positive images in children's
  literature
- making books for or with
  young children

Why are books important?

Books, stories and rhymes make a young child's world more attractive and interesting. They provide a lively stimulus in a variety of ways ranging from the vocal sharing of rhymes and telling stories to the visual experience of sharing well-illustrated books. By sharing books with babies and young children, we show them a positive attitude towards books and that reading is an important skill which is essential to our everyday lives. The time spent sharing books, stories and rhymes with young children is also a special time, creating a positive bond between adult and child.

Children should be introduced to books as babies. Librarians are well aware of the benefits of books for babies and young children. Many libraries have story sessions for the under-fives; some even have special story/activity sessions and homework clubs (which help children use referencing skills) for children aged 5 plus, as well as book-related activities during the school holidays.

Arrange regular library visits for your early years group. Introducing young children to the library makes them aware of this valuable local resource for all kinds of information not just books. Encourage the parents and children from your setting to use their local library; remember it's free! Attractive books for children can be expensive, but many libraries and local authorities run special loan schemes for early years settings wishing to borrow books. Paperbacks (rather than hard cover versions) covered with plastic jackets are an economical way of investing in quality children's books. Running book clubs and having book fairs also encourages children's interest in books, stories and rhymes. They can also be another useful source of free books as early years settings receive a percentage of free books depending on the number of books bought by parents, children and staff.

Sharing stories and rhymes with young children is the most positive and interesting way to encourage them to want to read for themselves.

How books, stories and rhymes help children's development

Books, stories and rhymes are ideal ways to encourage and extend children's **language and communication skills**. They do this by:

1 **encouraging listening skills and auditory discrimination** e.g. being attentive during stories, distinguishing between sounds, being aware of rhyming words, etc.
2 **providing stimulus for conversation/discussion**
3 **introducing or extending vocabulary**
4 **showing children the symbols of oral language written down**
5 **developing phonic skills** e.g. knowing letter sounds, blends.
6 **using repetition** to reinforce children's language and learning in a pleasurable, memorable way.

Books, stories and rhymes are also important in developing young children's **intellectual or cognitive skills**:

- **Observation and visual discrimination:** looking at pictures in books, observing details and differences, seeing the difference between words and pictures all help children's early reading (and writing) skills.
- **Relating sounds to symbols:** realising the printed patterns in books are speech written down and that we 'read' words; understanding they will be able to read these words too when they are older.
- **Memory:** recalling and talking about characters/events in stories. Memory is one of the key skills to learning to read.
- **Sequencing:** putting events in the correct order.
- **Predicting:** understanding 'what might happen next'; this is essential to the development of logic (an important scientific skill).
- **Imagination:** stimulating children's own ideas and creativity.
- **Curiosity:** finding out about themselves and the world around them. Books can be used for discovering new things as well as for enjoyment.

Baby, aged 5 months, looking at a nursery rhyme board book

Using reference material is an important skill, especially as children get older.

- **Concepts:** introducing and understanding concepts e.g. colour, shape, number, time.
- **Concentration:** developing attention-span by listening to progressively longer, more complex stories.

Books, stories and rhymes contribute towards young children's **social and emotional development** by providing opportunities for:

- **Enjoyment:** sharing books, stories and rhymes can be pleasurable and exciting. A sense of humour and fun are important ingredients in children's literature.
- **Reassurance:** anticipating future events/new experiences e.g. visit to dentist/hospital, the arrival of a new baby, family break-up/divorce. Dealing with positive and negative feelings in safe and positive ways.
- **Warmth and security:** sharing stories and rhymes can establish a bond

Baby enjoying a favourite nursery rhyme: 'Round and round the garden'

between adult and child in a more relaxed way then most other activities in the setting. The familiarity and repetition of rhymes and favourite stories can be particularly comforting for young children.

- **Co-operation:** sharing group story sessions involves turn-taking, listening while others talk.
- **Understanding society:** learning about the expectations concerning acceptable behaviour, the difference between 'right' and 'wrong'. Exploring the roles of men, women and children in society. Raising awareness of multicultural issues and special needs.

EXERCISE

Look at your setting's plan or timetable for a week's activities.
Highlight which activities involved books, stories or rhymes.
Describe *how* each highlighted activity encouraged and/or extended the children's language and communication skills.

Choosing children's books, stories and rhymes

Selecting *appropriate* literature for young children is essential. Children need books, stories and rhymes which reflect their individual needs and interests.

General points to consider:

1 Attractive and colourful with well-drawn, appropriate illustrations.
2 Text appropriate for age and level of development e.g. just pictures, one/two words per picture, one/two sentences per picture, several sentences and pages without pictures.
3 Safe for children and well-made in a variety of good quality materials including board, cloth, card, paper.
4 Positive images reflecting our multicultural society, the roles of men and women and people with special needs in positive ways.
5 Home-made books about familiar objects and everyday life can be just as appealing to young children as commercially produced books.
6 Photograph albums or books made using photographs of objects and people in the setting.
7 Books are a source of information not just for fun. Make sure the information provided represents the wide range of children's interests in your setting e.g. everything from animals to yo-yos! Include illustrated factual books, dictionaries, encyclopaedia, atlases.
8 Less is more! A small selection of quality books carefully chosen is better than a large collection of poor quality, unsuitable stories etc. Quality books are expensive, but can be stretched to provide variety by rotating the books at frequent intervals e.g. each group within the setting could have a selection of books which could be swapped monthly or every half-term. Remember to use any local resources as suggested earlier.

EXERCISE

1 Look at the chart showing the types of books which are suitable for children at different ages.
2 Give examples of stories for books and stories for the age group(s) you have worked with and explain why you think they were appropriate for these children.

Positive images in children's books

Positive images are important because children gain valuable information

Age	Content	Material	Examples
0–1 years	– clear, simple pictures. – single, familiar objects and animals. – bright and colourful. – large and bold pictures.	– board. – cloth. – washable/bath books. – tactile.	– 'Where's Spot?' by Eric Hill. – 'Baby in the bath'. – 'Toys' and 'Animals' by Lynn Heaton
1–2 years	– clear, slightly more complex pictures. – very simple text. – everyday objects, animals and people. – stories showing everyday routines. – bright and colourful. – rhymes and songs.	– board. – cloth. – washable/bath books. – tactile. – noisy. – lift-the-flap.	– 'Ten tired teddies' by Prue Theobalds. – 'Duck' by Anna Kiernan. – 'I don't want to go to Bed!' by J. Sykes & T. Warnes. – 'Spot's first walk' by Eric Hill.
2–3 years	– clear, more detailed pictures. – bright and colourful – stories relating to everyday life. – simple and predictable text. – stories introducing new experiences. – short stories with a happy ending. – humour and repetition. – rhymes and songs.	– board. – card/thick paper. – tactile. – noisy. – lift-the-flap. – bath books. – pop-up books.	– 'We're going on a bear hunt' by M. Rosen. – 'The baby' by J. Burlington – 'Whose mummy is this?' By Charles Reasoner. – the 'Tom and Pippo' series by Helen Oxenbury. – 'Can't you sleep little bear?' by M. Waddell & B. Firth. – 'Pudding and pie' by I . Beck & S. Williams.

Age	Content	Material	Examples
3–4 years	– bright and colourful. – more detailed illustrations. – longer stories. – humour and repetition. – stories introducing new experiences. – rhymes and songs. – pictorial factual books.	– card/thick paper. – tactile. – noisy. – lift-the-flap. – pop-up books. – story tapes.	– 'The very hungry Caterpillar' by Eric Carle. – 'Mog the forgetful cat' By Judith Kerr. – 'Little gorilla' by Ruth Bernstein. – the 'Alfie' stories by Shirley Hughes.
4–5 years	– detailed illustrations. – longer stories with more complex themes. – stories introducing new experiences. – repetition and humour. – magic. – poetry, rhymes and action songs. – pictorial reference.	– card/thick paper. – tactile. – noisy. – lift-the-flap. – pop-up books. – story tapes.	– 'Winnie the witch' by Korky Paul & V. Thomas. – 'A dark, dark tale' by Ruth Brown. – the 'Kipper' stories by Mick Inkpen. – 'Dear Zoo' by R. Campbell. – 'The bad-tempered lady-bird' by Eric Carle. – 'A balloon for grandad' by Nigel Gray.

Age	Content	Material	Examples
5–7 years	– detailed illustrations. – longer, more complex stories; anthologies of stories; different versions of traditional tales. – books with chapters. – abstract ideas e.g. magic and fantasy. – stories with strong characters. – humour. – poetry. – simple reference books.	– card/thick paper. – paper. – story tapes. – novelty books.	– 'The three little wolves and the big bad pig' by Eugene Trivizas. – the 'Happy Families' by A. and J. Ahlberg. – 'Titch' by Pat Hutchins. – 'The Twits' and other books by Roald Dahl. – 'The lighthouse keeper's lunch' by R. and D. Armitage. – 'A very first book of Poetry' compiled by John Foster.

about themselves, other people and the world around them through books and stories. In the same way that television has a powerful influence on children's perception of the world, so do books. Children believe what they see, hear or read so it is vital that books and stories:

- depict equality of opportunity in terms of gender, race, culture, special needs and age
- develop children's confidence in their own backgrounds
- promote awareness of other people's cultures
- encourage positive self-esteem and self-image.

EXERCISE

Give examples of books, stories and rhymes you have used with young children to promote positive images of the following:

1 Race/culture 2 Gender 3 Special needs/disability 4 Age.

Describe how you used each book and give examples of the children's responses.

Story telling/reading techniques

Story telling is not the same as *reading* stories from a book. Story telling involves recounting traditional tales in your own particular style or making up your own stories based on people or themes familiar to your audience. When reading from a story book you can rely on the pictures to provide the visual aids you need to maintain the children's interest and attention.

To make story telling more interesting and entertaining you can use:

- puppets
- props or objects related to the story e.g. hats to indicate different characters
- sound effects e.g. musical instruments or encouraging the children to join in with appropriate sounds such animal noises
- you own pictures, posters or photographs
- children's drawings and paintings
- children to act out key characters/situations.

Whether you read or tell a story follow these guidelines:

1 **Preparation:** you should know the story well to avoid stumbling over words or losing the thread. You should recognise where you need to change pace, pause or show excitement.
2 **Practise:** read or tell the story **aloud** to a friend or colleague or your own children (if you have any). This way you will know how long the story takes to read/tell and the outcome of the story.
3 **Organisation:** sit the children comfortably on a soft surface e.g. carpet, cushions in a semicircle. Make sure all the children in the group can see and hear you and have a clear view of the book and/or visual aids. 'Story steps' (almost like a mini-theatre) are an excellent way to set the stage for the unfolding of a story. If your setting does not have built-in story steps, you could arrange chairs, cushions to create a similar effect. (See diagram.)
4 **Introduction:** talk briefly about the story to gain the children's interest and create anticipation. Point out any links with related topics, themes or events within the setting.
5 **Eye contact:** to maintain the children's interest and involvement in the story, frequent eye contact is essential.
6 **Expression:** vary your speed and tone of voice. Keep pace with the

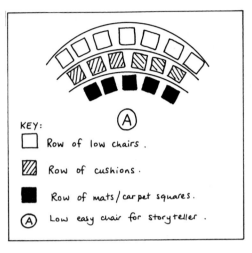

KEY:

☐ Row of low chairs.

▨ Row of cushions.

■ Row of mats/carpet squares.

Ⓐ Low easy chair for storyteller.

Story steps

story. Use facial expressions to emphasise what the characters are saying/doing. If telling a story use gestures and body language as well to bring the characters to life. You can use different 'voices' for each character, but only do this if you feel comfortable with this and if it does not spoil the flow of the story. As you become more confident, you will feel able to use different voices without losing your place or using the wrong 'voice'.

7 **Interruptions:** try to deal with these without losing the thread of the story e.g. if children want to share their own similar experiences, if possible ask them to wait until after the story. Remember to ask them what they wanted to say when you have finished the story. Keep children you know to be disruptive during story sessions close by you so that you can use a gentle touch or look to keep them under control rather that having to use verbal requests which interrupt the story.

8 **Conclusion:** usually one story at a time is enough; follow up the story with discussion, related rhymes, poems and action songs to keep your audience interested and to further develop their language and communication skills. Encourage children to look at the book and/or visual aids afterwards.

KEY TASK

Observe a story session. Focus on:
● how the adult communicates with the children ● the children's responses. In your assessment consider the benefits of the story session to the children's:
● language development ● intellectual development ● social and emotional development.

NVQ Level 3 links: C.11.1 M.7.2 C.16.1 C.16.2 (C.14.4) (C.14.5)
DCE links: Units 1, 4 and 6 (Unit 7)
BTEC links: Units 3, 6 and 8.

Count the balloons.

What is the teddy wearing ?

Tell me about your favourite teddy or toy.

Example of home-made book: drawing of teddy in card book

Making books for or with young children

Making books for children is another excellent way to develop language and communication skills as well as encouraging their interest in reading. The great advantage of home-made books is that they can be personalised to make more relevant and exciting stimuli to match children's *individual* language needs. For example, you could include pictures or photographs of the children's favourite things or interests. Nothing is guaranteed to get young children's attention more than the knowledge that you have made a book especially for them.

When making books for young children you can use a variety of materials:

- cloth book with objects designed for a baby
- pictures on thick card covered in clear sticky-backed plastic for a baby or young child
- book/file with 10–20 plastic pockets with pages of pictures and activities for an older child.

When making books for young children remember the following:

1 Ensure the book is safe for children's use, sturdy and well-made.
2 The book is attractive and stimulating.
3 Keep it simple – one picture and/or activity per page.
4 Make sure the pictures/activities are appropriate for the children's age and level of development.
5 Show awareness of equal opportunities e.g. the pictures reflect positive images of race, culture, gender, special needs.
6 Include pictures/activities which will encourage/extend the children's language and communication skills.
7 Use words that relate to the pictures/activities to maximise the opportunities for language. Use open questions. Remember the younger the children, the shorter the text. If possible, use a word processor for a more professional look. Remember to use the script preferred by your setting.

K E Y   T A S K

1 Make a book for a young child or group of young children.
   Follow the guidelines outlined above for making children's books.
2 Provide the following information to support your book:
- aim/rationale explaining *why* you made the book
- learning outcomes/objectives showing *how* the book is intended to encourage/extend children's language and communication skills
- how you would use the book with young children
- review and evaluation assessing: the effectiveness of the book; what the children learned; the children's responses to the book; any modifications for future use.

NVQ Level 3 links: C.11.2 C.11.3 C.11.4 C.11.5 M.7.3 M.7.4 (C.14.4) (C.14.5)
DCE links: Units 2, 4 and 6 (Unit 7)
BTEC links: Units 3, 7 and 8 (Unit 6).

Another exciting activity for young children is making their own books. These can be based on:

- a story which you have told rather than read to the children;
- the children's version of a favourite story or traditional tale;
- a group or class topic;
- an account of a visit or event;
- the children's daily routine;

- the children's *own* stories, poems or rhymes.

Use large sheets of thick paper (minimum size A4) and if possible cover the finished pages of the book with clear sticky-backed plastic. (If this is too expensive, make sure at least the front and back are covered to keep them clean and more durable.)

Depending on the age of the children you may need to help with the illustrations. You could draw outlines of the characters as suggested by the children which they can then complete using a variety of techniques: sponge painting; potato printing; rubbings; collage; filling in details with crayon or paint, etc. Use the children's ideas for the text too. Use a word processor to give the book the look of a printed book. Children used to working with computers should be able to do the word-processing themselves.

KEY TASK

1 Plan a story session. Read or tell a story using the guidelines in this chapter. You could use the audio/visual aid you made earlier or your home-made book to make the session more interesting.
2 Include a follow-up activity to extend the children's language development and communication skills e.g.
- discussion about the story
- rhymes and songs related to the story
- drawings or paintings about the story
- group or class book retelling the story.

NVQ Level 3 links: C.11.2 C.11.3 C.11.4 C.11.5 M.7.3 M.7.4 (C.14.4) (C.14.5)
DCE links: Units 2, 4 and 6 (Unit 7)
BTEC links: Units 3, 7 and 8 (Unit 6).

Further reading

Clay, M. (1992) *Becoming literate*. Heinemann.
Whitehead, M. (1996) *The development of language and literacy*. Hodder & Stoughton.

5

How Children Think and Learn

• •Key Points• •

- learning pathways and patterns of learning
- the importance of active learning
- the inter-related cognitive components of intellectual development

- identifying intellectual processes
- the role of play in conceptual development
- the sequence of intellectual development
- children with cognitive difficulties

Learning pathways

Every learning experience can be viewed as a journey, travelling along different pathways to reach our destination or learning goal. (Drummond, 1994).

At different points of a learning experience the learning may be:

- very easy – speeding along a clear motorway
- interesting but uncertain in parts – taking the scenic route
- very difficult and complicated – stuck in a traffic jam on Spaghetti Junction
- totally confusing – trying to find the correct exit off a big road traffic island
- completely beyond us – entered a cul-de-sac/no through road or going the wrong way down a one-way street.

Patterns of learning

Learning pathways rarely involve a straightforward journey from A to B.

The experience of learning is a never-ending cycle; learning new skills continues indefinitely. Once one skill is gained in a particular area, further skills can be learned. For example, once children have learned basic reading skills, they continue to develop their literacy skills even as adults by:

- increasing their vocabulary

- improving spelling
- decoding unfamiliar words
- reading and understanding more complex texts.

EXERCISE

Think about the learning experiences of the children in your setting.
Select two examples and draw diagrams of these children's learning
experiences.
Compare them with your own experiences of learning. Are there any
similarities or differences?
Your diagrams may look like road systems circuits or puzzles (see diagram
below).

As well as the circular nature of learning experiences, you may also have
noticed the importance of *active participation* in all learning experiences.
Watching someone else use a computer or read a book can only help so
much; to develop the relevant skills people need hands-on experience of
using the computer or handling books.

Active learning is an important part of all learning experiences. Not just
for children but for adults as well. For example, at college you may find
that learning situations take the form of workshops, group activities and
discussions rather than formal lectures.

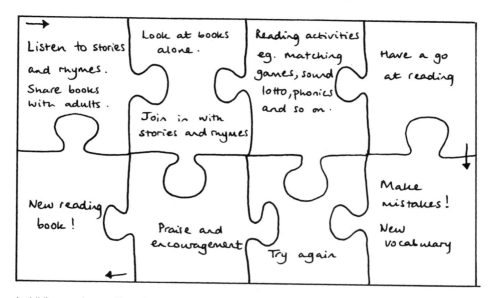

A child's experience of learning to read

For young children it is essential that they become **actively** involved in the learning process. Learning needs to be practical not theoretical. Young children need *concrete* learning experiences; that is using real objects in a meaningful context. Children (and adults) learn by *doing*. Lectures would be a waste of time for young children. Indeed, traditional lectures *are* a waste of time even for adults! This is because the average attention-span of an adult is 20 minutes! (This is why commercials are shown about every 20 minutes on television.) The average attention-span of a young child is considerably less, more like 5–10 minutes or even as little as 2–3 minutes. In all learning situations it is important to provide information in small portions with plenty of discussion and activity breaks to maintain interest and concentration.

Active learning encourages young children to be:

● Curious ● **H**andy at problem-solving ● **I**maginative ● **C**reative.

When providing learning opportunities, start from where the child is and build upon the child's experiences and interests. An awareness of children's patterns of learning and their current interests can help our knowledge and understanding of children's development.

A child's particular interest can provide a strong motivating force for learning.

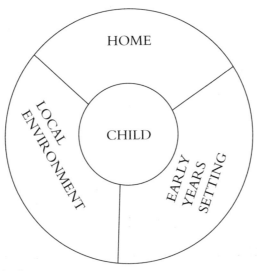

Child at centre of learning in context

EXERCISE

1 Think about the children in your setting. Focus on two children who you know reasonably well. Can you identify their current predominant interest?

2 How could you encourage and/or extend the children's learning using each child's particular interest as the starting point? Suggest practical ways to do this.

What is cognitive development?

Cognitive development involves the intellectual processes of:

- gaining
- storing
- recalling
- using

INFORMATION

These intellectual processes or cognitive components are inter-related:

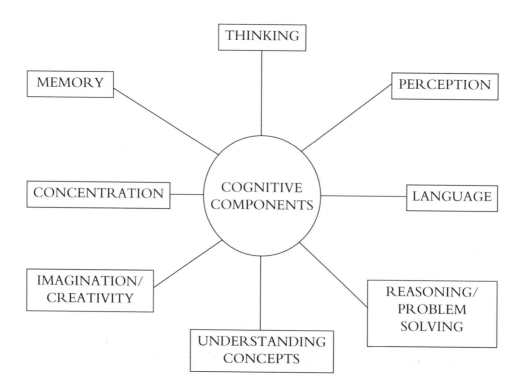

1 Thinking

Thinking can be defined as:

- *cognitive* – it occurs in the mind
- *a process* – it involves using or processing information
- *directed* – it works towards finding solutions.

We cannot see a person's thoughts because the thinking process is internal. We can *see* the process and progress of a person's thinking through their **actions** and **communications**. There are many different theories concerning thinking and its relationship to learning which are outlined in Chapter 6.

2 Perception

Perception involves the ability to identify the differences between objects or sounds. There are two types of perception:

- *auditory* – differentiating between sounds
- *visual* – differentiating between objects or the distance between objects.

Babies and young children use their senses to explore the objects and sounds in the world around them.

3 Language

Language provides the means to:

- make sense of the world around us
- process information in a more accessible form (e.g. before language, information is stored/recalled through images); language enables us to store more information and to make better connections between existing information and new information
- understand concepts
- interact with others to gain new experiences and information
- communicate more effectively with others e.g. asking questions/understanding the answers
- verbalise our thoughts
- express our opinions and ideas.

Language has such a key role to play in children's development that we have dealt with it separately in Chapter 1. Remember that **language is an integral part of children's cognitive development**.

4 Reasoning/problem-solving

Reasoning involves using intellectual processes to make personal judgements or to make connections between existing information and new information. Reasoning involves problem-solving and the ability to think logically. People use their existing knowledge and past experiences to solve problems. Children (and adults) often supplement their lack of knowledge or experience by experimenting – a process of *trial and error*. Making mistakes is part of the learning process. By using logic, people can make reasonable assumptions or predictions about what might happen in a particular situation or to a particular object. Logical thinking and problem-solving are essential to the ability to make mathematical calculations and scientific discoveries.

5 Understanding concepts

Concepts are the ways in which people make sense of and organise the information in the world around them. Concepts can be divided into two main categories: **concrete** and **abstract**.

CONCRETE CONCEPTS

Mathematical concepts include:

- sorting and counting – making comparisons, being able to discriminate between objects; matching objects, making sets.
- number – understanding and using number; number/numeral recognition and formation; number patterns; practical number operations (e.g. addition, subtraction).
- sequencing – putting things in order; knowing and understanding number sequence e.g. 1, 2, 3, 4…. and 1st, 2nd, 3rd, 4th….
- weighing and measuring – making comparisons e.g. heavy/light/long/short.
- volume and capacity – understanding that some objects hold more than others.

Scientific concepts include:

- object permanence – understanding that when an object is out of sight it still exists.
- space – relating objects to each other and the gaps between them.
- colour – distinguishing between colours; matching, naming and using colours; understanding colours in the environment e.g. *red* means stop or danger; *green* means go.

- shape – recognising different shapes and sizes is part of *classification*.
- texture – exploring the tactile qualities of objects.
- living and growing – understanding the processes of living things: humans, animals, plants.
- physical forces – understanding hot/cold, light/dark, floating/sinking; the changing properties of materials e.g. water can be steam or ice as well as liquid.

Positional relationships include:

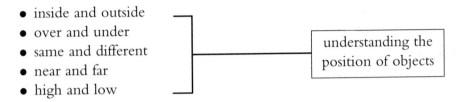

- inside and outside
- over and under
- same and different — understanding the position of objects
- near and far
- high and low

ABSTRACT CONCEPTS

Moral concepts include:

- right and wrong – understanding what is/is not acceptable behaviour.
- fairness/justice – understanding that goodness is not always rewarded, but that we still need to do what is right.
- helping others – recognising the needs and feelings of others.
- sharing – understanding the importance of turn-taking, co-operating.
- freedom – developing empathy for others and their beliefs even if we disagree with them.

TIME

Understanding the sequence of events and the passage of time. Time waits for no one, not even children! This is a difficult concept for children to understand as they think the world revolves around them. Understanding time involves knowledge and awareness of:

- today, tomorrow, yesterday
- times of the day (morning, afternoon, evening)
- days of the week, months and seasons
- *before* and *after*
- *next* – next week, next month, next year
- telling the time (e.g. 8 o'clock, half past eight; 8:00, 8:30)

Higher number operations include:

- understanding and using numbers *without* real objects e.g. mental arithmetic, doing *sums;*
- understanding and using more complex number operations such as algebra and physics.

Young children take longer to understand abstract concepts, but this depends on their individual learning experiences. For example, many children *do* understand the ideas concerning fairness and the rights of people (and animals) to live in freedom if these concepts are linked with *real* events.

6 Imagination and creativity

Imagination involves the ability to invent ideas or form images of things which are not actually there or do not exist. Creativity is the *use* of imagination in a wide variety of activities including:

- play
- art and design
- music, dance and drama
- books and stories.

Everyone is creative in their own individual ways.

7 Concentration

Concentration involves the ability to pay attention to the situation or task in hand. A person's concentration level or attention span is the length of time they are able to focus on a particular activity. Some children can concentrate for quite a long time, while some children (and adults!) find their attention starts to wander after just a few minutes. This may be due to a mismatch of activities to the individual's needs, interests and abilities which can lead to boredom and a lack of concentration.

A condition known as Attention Deficit Disorder (ADD) or Attention Deficit Hyperactive Disorder (ADHD) may also be responsible for poor concentration in certain people (see Chapter 14 for more information). Being *actively* involved helps concentration; as does doing something interesting and exciting. Concentration is a key intellectual skill, which is necessary for the development of other cognitive processes such as conceptual understanding and language.

8 Memory

The other cognitive processes would be of no use to individuals without memory. Memory involves the ability to recall or retrieve information stored in the mind. Memory skills involve:

- *recalling information* on past experiences, events, actions or feelings (e.g. a child telling you about his/her birthday party last weekend);
- *recognising information* and making connections with previous experiences (e.g. reading a story about a birthday party and discussing own experiences);
- *predicting* – using past information to anticipate future events (e.g. drawing a chart to show when each person's birthday will be).

Many cognitive processes involve all three memory skills, for example problem-solving activities in mathematics and science or the decoding and comprehension skills needed for reading.

EXERCISE

From your experiences of working with young children, provide examples of activities which you think encourage and extend children's cognitive/intellectual skills in each of the following areas:

1 Thinking	5 Understanding concepts
2 Perception	6 Imagination and creativity
3 Language	7 Concentration
4 Reasoning/problem-solving	8 Memory.

The role of play in conceptual development

Children need a combination of real and imaginary experiences to encourage language and learning. This is why **play** is an important aspect of young children's thinking and learning. Young children need to handle objects and materials to understand basic concepts. For example, in mathematics using objects for counting and addition such as buttons, cones, unifix cubes. Once children have plenty of practical mathematical experiences they can cope more easily with abstract concepts such as written sums or mental arithmetic. Through active learning, children use play opportunities to encourage and extend the problem-solving abilities which are essential to developing their intellectual processes. Suggested play opportunities include: see chart below.

CREATIVE PLAY

Activities such as painting, drawing and model-making, etc. encourage:

- understanding of concepts such as shape and colour
- development of visual discrimination and hand-eye co-ordination through pencil/brush control, using scissors
- exploration of the properties of materials e.g. textures
- problem-solving skills
- devising and using own ideas.

IMAGINATIVE PLAY

Activities such as role play, dressing-up, dolls, puppets, etc. encourage:

- language and communication skills which are essential to the thinking and learning process
- understanding of weighing and measuring through shop play
- understanding of volume/capacity and physical forces through sand and water play
- awareness of moral concepts such as sharing and helping others.

PHYSICAL PLAY

Activities like outdoor play, ball games, climbing and using apparatus encourage:

- awareness of spatial relationships
- body awareness
- understanding of positional relationships e.g. over and under
- visual perception – differentiating between objects, judging distances, ball skills
- awareness of fairness and safety.

MANIPULATIVE PLAY

Activities involving matching, grading, and fitting; jigsaws and table-top games encourage:

- hand-eye co-ordination
- awareness of spatial relationships (how things fit together and relate to each other)
- visual perception and discrimination (e.g. shape recognition)
- understanding of sequencing
- understanding of number through games which involve counting
- understanding of turn-taking, following the rules of the game.

Play opportunities are particularly useful for encouraging children to develop mathematical and scientific skills. For example:

- ***Classification*** – sorting and organising objects according to different criteria e.g. by colour, shape, size, texture.
- ***Ordination*** – Comparing numbers or sizes and putting them in the correct order e.g. first, second, third... ; big, bigger, biggest; small, smaller, smallest; big bear, medium-sized bear, small bear.
- ***Cardination*** – understanding the sequence of numbers e.g. 1, 2, 3 ...; realising that numbers remain the same whatever the objects e.g. four is four whether there are four bricks, four dolls, four buttons, four cones.
- ***Conservation*** – understanding that the quantity of objects remains the same regardless of changes in shape or appearance e.g. the conservation of number means:

$$\bigcirc \quad \bigcirc$$
$$\bigcirc \quad \bigcirc \quad \text{is the same as} \quad \bigcirc \; \bigcirc \; \bigcirc \; \bigcirc$$

Another example, this time showing how play can help children's understanding of conservation of volume:

Step 1. Children have lots of opportunities to play with water.
Step 2. Children fill various containers with water.
Step 3. Children fill big containers with water using smaller containers.

Step 4. Children pour water from one container to another of a different shape.

Step 5. When asked 'Is there the same amount of water in the second container as the first?' the children will say 'Yes!' (Without water play children under 7 would answer 'no' as they are unable to conserve.)

Play activities provide informal opportunities for children to develop ideas and to understand concepts through active learning and communication. Language is a key component in children's thinking and learning. Play is an invaluable way to provide opportunities for language and to make learning more meaningful for young children. Play enables children to learn about concepts in a safe and non-threatening environment.

EXERCISE

Give an example of a play activity which you have used to assist a young child's conceptual development. Suggest other play activities which might extend this aspect of development.

Children, aged 5 years, engaged in water play

There is more information on activities to help children's intellectual development in Chapter 8.

The sequence of children's intellectual development

We need to think in terms of a **sequence** of development rather than **stages** (see page 6) when looking at children's intellectual capabilities. This is because intellectual development is affected by other factors besides the child's chronological age, in much the same way as language development.

Factors affecting children's intellectual development include:

- lack of play opportunities
- unrewarding learning experiences
- lack of opportunities to use language and communication skills
- inappropriate learning experiences
- introduction to formal learning situations at too early an age
- physical skills e.g. fine motor control is needed for hand-eye co-ordination
- cognitive difficulties.

The chart shown here only shows specific ages to indicate the **milestones** of *expected* intellectual development to help your knowledge and understanding of children's development. Remember all children are *individuals* and develop at their own rate.

Please note that language abilities are not included in this chart although they are crucial to children's intellectual development. The sequence of language development is covered in detail in Chapter 1.

The Sequence of Intellectual Development

Age 0–3 months:
- recognises parents
- concentrates on familiar voices rather than unfamiliar ones
- aware of different smells
- explores by putting objects in mouth
- observes objects that move
- responds to bright colours and bold images

- stores and recalls information through images
- sees everything in relation to self (is egocentric).

Age 3–9 months:

- knows individuals and recognises familiar faces
- recognises certain sounds and objects
- shows interest in everything especially toys and books
- concentrates on well-defined objects and follows direction of moving object
- anticipates familiar actions and enjoys games such as 'peep-po'
- searches for hidden or dropped objects (from about 8 months)
- observes what happens at home and when out and about
- explores immediate environment once mobile
- processes information through images
- enjoys water play in the bath
- sees everything in relation to self (is still egocentric)

Age 9–18 months:

- explores immediate environment using senses, especially sight and touch; has no sense of danger
- concentrates more, due to curiosity and increased physical skills, but still has short attention-span
- follows one-step instructions and/or gestured commands
- observes other people closely and tries to imitate their actions
- uses 'trial and error' methods when playing with bricks, containers
- searches for hidden or dropped objects (aware of object permanence)
- learns that objects can be grouped together
- continues to store and recall information through images
- is still egocentric

Age 18 months–2 years:

- recognises objects from pictures and books
- points to desired objects; selects named objects
- matches basic colours; starts to match shapes
- does very simple puzzles
- follows one-step instructions
- concentrates for longer e.g. searching for hidden object, but attention-span still quite short
- shows lots of curiosity and continues exploring using senses and 'trial and error' methods

- processes information through images and increasingly through language too
- shows preferences and starts to make choices
- is still egocentric

Age 2–3 years:
- identifies facial features and main body parts
- continues to imitate other children and adults
- follows two-step instructions
- matches more colours and shapes including puzzles and other matching activities
- points to named object in pictures and books
- develops understanding of big and small
- begins to understand concept of time at basic level e.g. before/after, today/tomorrow
- enjoys imaginative play; able to use symbols in play e.g. pretend a doll is a real baby
- concentrates on intricate tasks such as creative activities or construction, but may still have short attention-span especially if not really interested in the activity
- is very pre-occupied with own activities; still egocentric
- shows some awareness of right and wrong
- processes information through language rather than images

Age 3–4 years:
- learns about basic concepts through play
- experiments with colour, shape and texture
- recalls a simple sequence of events
- follows two or three-step instructions including positional ones e.g. 'Please put your ball in the box under the table'
- continues to enjoy imaginative and creative play
- interested in more complex construction activities
- concentrates on more complex activities as attention-span increases
- plays co-operatively with other children; able to accept and share ideas in group activities
- shows some awareness of right and wrong, the needs of others
- holds strong opinions about likes and dislikes
- processes information using language

Age 4–5 years:

- is still very curious and asks lots of questions
- continues to enjoy imaginative and creative play activities
- continues to enjoy construction activities; spatial awareness increases
- knows, matches and names colours and shapes
- follows three-step instructions
- develops interest in reading for themselves
- enjoys jigsaw puzzles and games
- concentrates for longer e.g. television programmes, longer stories and can recall details
- shows awareness of right and wrong, the needs of others
- begins to see other people's points of view
- stores and recalls more complex information using language

Age 5–7 years:

- starts to learn to read
- enjoys some number work, but still needs real objects to help mathematical processes
- enjoys experimenting with materials and exploring the environment
- develops creative abilities as co-ordination improves e.g. more detailed drawings
- begins to know the difference between real and imaginary, but still enjoys imaginative play e.g. small scale toys such as cars, play people, toy farm/wild animals
- interested in more complex construction activities
- has longer attention-span; does not like to be disturbed during play activities
- follows increasingly more complex instructions
- enjoys board games and other games with rules
- develops a competitive streak
- has increased awareness of right and wrong, the needs of others
- sees other people's points of view
- seeks information from various sources e.g. encyclopaedia, computers
- processes expanding knowledge and information through language.

KEY TASK

Observe a young child involved in a play activity which encourages the child's understanding of one of the following:

- mathematical concept e.g. number, weighing/measuring, or volume/capacity

- a scientific concept e.g. colour, shape, space, texture, growth or physical forces.

In your assessment you should:
- specify which concept was the focus for the observation
- identify any other intellectual skills demonstrated by the child during the observation e.g. concentration, memory skills, imagination and creativity, problem-solving, language and communication skills
- outline the role of play in developing young children's understanding of basic concepts
- suggest further play opportunities to extend the child's understanding of the specified concept.

NVQ Level 3 links : C.10.3 C.16.1 C.16.2 (C.14.4) (C.14.5)
[C.10.1, C.10.2 and/or C.10.4 depending on other intellectual skills observed.]
DCE links: Units 1, 4 and 6 (Unit 7)
BTEC links: Units 6, 7, 8 and 12.

Children with cognitive difficulties

Some children may not develop their intellectual processes in line with the expected pattern of development for children their age for a variety of reasons:

1 sensory impairment (see Chapter 7)
2 lack of intellectual stimulation (see Chapter 8)
3 emotional and behavioural difficulties (see Chapter 14)
4 cognitive difficulties.

In this chapter we look at the cognitive difficulties which may affect children's intellectual development. Cognitive difficulties can be divided into two main areas:

- children with **specific learning difficulties** such as dyslexia (see Chapter 2)
- children with **general learning difficulties**.

The term 'slow learners' is sometimes used to describe children with below average cognitive abilities across all areas of learning; the term 'general learning difficulties' is preferable.

Children with general learning difficulties often have delayed development in other areas; they may be socially and emotionally immature and/or have problems with gross/fine motor skills.

Children with general learning difficulties need carefully structured learning opportunities where new skills are introduced step by step. Children with this type of learning difficulty may have problems processing information ; they have difficulty linking their existing knowledge and past experiences to new learning situations which makes it difficult to reach solutions or to develop ideas. Children with general learning difficulties are usually

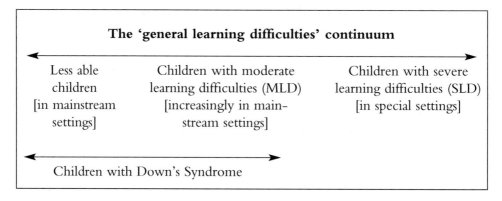

identified by the adults working with them at an early stage. Here are some common signs to look out for:

- delay in understanding new ideas/concepts
- poor concentration, shorter than usual attention-span
- inability to remember new skills without constant repetition and reinforcement
- poor listening skills
- lack of imagination and creativity
- difficulty following instructions in large group situations
- difficulty comprehending abstract ideas
- limited vocabulary; often give one-word answers
- problems with memory skills
- poor co-ordination affecting hand-eye co-ordination, pencil control, etc.
- need lots of practical support and concrete materials
- delayed reading skills, especially comprehension
- delayed understanding of maths/science concepts.

Children with general learning difficulties are often aware that their progress is behind that of their peers. This can be very damaging to their self-esteem. Some children may even feel they are incapable of learning anything at all. Adults need to convince such children that they *can* and *will* learn as long as they keep trying and do not give up.

The following strategies may help to make learning a more positive experience:

- build on what the child already knows
- let the child work at his/her own pace
- provide activities that can be completed in the time available without the child feeling under pressure
- divide the learning into small steps in a logical sequence
- present the same concept or idea in various ways to reinforce learning and understanding
- use repetition frequently; short daily sessions are more memorable than long weekly sessions
- demonstrate what to do as well as giving verbal instructions; use real examples and practical experiences/equipment wherever possible
- keep activities short; work towards increasing the child's concentration (see page 136)
- encourage active participation in discussion and group activities to extend language and communication skills.
- provide more stimuli for creative activities rather than expecting the child to develop new ideas entirely by themselves
- help the child to develop skills in accessing information e.g. use technology such as computers, Internet; also libraries, reference books; museums
- *listen* to the child; take on board their points of view.

Praise and encouragement are essential to *all* children's learning. All children, regardless of ability, are motivated by achieving success. Make sure the activities you provide are appropriate by using your observations and assessments to plan activities which are relevant to each child's abilities and interests. Praise and encouragement are especially important to raise the self-esteem of children who find learning difficult.

KEY TASK

Plan a problem-solving, mathematics or science activity for a young child or group of young children. The activity should promote the children's intellectual development through active learning. Use the information from this chapter and your assessment from the observation on page 88/89.

Review and evaluate the activity. Include information on:

- the intellectual skills demonstrated by the child or children during the activity
- the effectiveness of your planning and implementation of the activity
- how you could modify this type of activity for children with general learning difficulties.

NVQ Level 3 links: C.10.3 M.7. 2 M.7.3 M.7.4 (C.14.4) (C.14.5)
[C.10.1 C.10.2 C.10.4 depending on intellectual skills promoted by the activity]
DCE links: Units 2, 4 and 6 (Unit 7)
BTEC links: Units 3, 7, 8 and 12.

Further reading

Neaum, S. and Tallack, J. (1997) *Good practice in implementing the pre-school curriculum*. Stanley Thornes.
Willig, C. J. (1990) *Children's concepts and the primary curriculum*. Paul Chapman.
Wood, D. (1988) *How children think and learn*. Basil Blackwell.
Woolfson, R. (1989) *Understanding your child: a parents' guide to child psychology*. Faber and Faber.

6

Cognitive Development: Different Perspectives

••••••••••••••••••••••••••••Key Points••••••••••••••••••••••••••

- approaches to
  developmental psychology
- the importance of
  understanding cognitive
  development
- theories of cognitive
  development: from Froebel
  to Bruner

- the learning process: a
  social constructivist view
- nature versus nurture in
  cognitive development

Approaches to developmental psychology

Understanding cognitive development is essential for adults working with young children, because it influences:

- the quality of early years care and education provision
- the structure of the learning environment
- the provision of materials and equipment
- the communication between adults and children during learning experiences
- the adult expectations of children's development.

Research into how young children think and learn has made adults working with young children more aware of the need:

- to observe and assess children's development very carefully
- to listen to children and the way they express ideas
- to take account of children's interests and experiences when planning learning opportunities.

There are three approaches to psychology which are relevant to the study of child development:

- psycho-dynamic
- behaviourist
- cognitivist.

1 The psycho-dynamic approach

The Austrian physician, **Sigmund Freud** believed that very early childhood experiences are responsible for how people think and feel in later life. Depending on these experiences, people are either well or poorly adjusted to their everyday lives. Freud considered that most of our thinking is done on a *sub-conscious* level and is therefore beyond our control. More recently psychologists, such as **Carl Rogers**, have suggested that most of our thinking is *conscious* and that individuals *are* in control of their own lives.

2 The behaviourist approach

These psychologists focus on *behaviour* which can be observed rather than thoughts and feelings which cannot be observed. Behaviourists are concerned with how external forces can be used to control behaviour, for example, **B. F. Skinner** considered that all thinking and learning is based on responses to rewards and punishments received within our environment.

3 The cognitivist approach

These psychologists believe that human behaviour *can* be understood by studying how people think and learn. This includes the work of **Piaget**, **Vygotsky** and **Bruner**.

In this chapter we concentrate on the psychologists with a cognitive approach to development as these are the most relevant to understanding children's cognitive development. The other approaches *do* contribute to our knowledge of child development, but are of more significance to understanding children's behaviour.

Theories of cognitive development

Friedrich Wilhelm Froebel (1782–1852) was a German educator and the founder of the *kindergarten* (meaning 'children's garden') system who devised activities for young children which encouraged learning through play. He thought young women had a special rapport with young children;

prior to this, teachers were usually men or older women. Froebel trained many young women to become kindergarten teachers; some of these went to America where they established private kindergartens. The first year of compulsory schooling in America (and Canada) is still called kindergarten today. Froebel had been a student of **Heinrich Pestalozzi**, a Swiss teacher and writer. Pestalozzi established many schools for young children and also wrote books demonstrating how basic concepts could be introduced to young children. Froebel was the first educator to really see the importance of **play** in developing children's thinking and learning. He believed that play was central to children's learning and their understanding of concepts. He devised a set of specially designed play materials to encourage children's thinking and learning. Froebel pioneered the idea of *hands-on experience* which forms the basis of learning through play and active learning. He also believed that childhood was a state in its own right and not just a preparation for adulthood. It was his work that moved early education away from young children sitting in rows and learning by rote.

Maria Montessori (1869–1952) was an Italian educator and physician who became one of the best known and most influential early childhood educators. She began by working with children with special needs. She designed carefully graded self-teaching materials which stimulated children's learning through use of their senses. Montessori believed that children learn best by doing things independently without adult interference and that children concentrate better when engaged in a self-chosen activity. Adults working with young children need to be specially trained to give the appropriate support to children's independent learning. The learning environment was considered to be especially important. Montessori believed the equipment should be specifically designed for children (e.g. small, child-sized furniture, kitchen utensils, tools) and that children should have freedom to move and explore their environment.

Jean Piaget (1896–1980) was a Swiss biologist who used observations of his own children, plus a wider sample of children, to develop his theories of cognitive development. Piaget's theories of cognitive development have had a major influence on early years education during the last 40 years. Piaget believed that children went through different **stages** of cognitive development based on fixed ages. Within these stages the children's patterns of learning, or **schemas** as he called them, were very different from adult ways of problem-solving. He also believed in the importance of young children learning through action and exploration of their environment using their sensory motor skills.

General principles of Piaget's cognitive theories

1 Children are *actively* involved in structuring their own cognitive development through exploration of their environment. Children need real objects and 'concrete experiences' to discover things for themselves.
2 The adult's role is to provide children with appropriate experiences in a suitable environment to facilitate the children's instinctive ability to think and learn.
3 Cognitive development occurs in four set stages which are universal – they apply to all forms of learning and across all cultures.

Children are viewed as thinking and learning in a different way to adults. Not only do children have less experience of the world, but their understanding of it is shaped by this entirely different way of looking at their environment.

---

1 Sensori-motor (0–2 years)
- babies and very young children learn through their senses, physical activity and interaction with their immediate environment
- they understand their world in terms of actions.

2 Pre-operations (2–7 years)
- young children learn through their experiences with real objects in their immediate environment
- they use symbols (e.g. words and images) to make sense of their world.

3 Concrete operations (7–11 years)
- children continue to learn through their experiences with real objects
- they access information (using language) to make sense of their immediate and wider environment

4 Formal operations (11–adult)
- children and adults learn to make use of abstract thinking (e.g. algebra, physics, etc.)

(a) Piaget's stages of cognitive development

4 Children will only learn when they are 'ready' for different experiences as determined by their current stage of cognitive development.
5 Children's use of language demonstrates their cognitive achievements, but does not control them. Piaget did not see language and communication as central to children's cognitive development because this development begins at birth *before* children can comprehend or use words. He does see the importance of language at later stages.

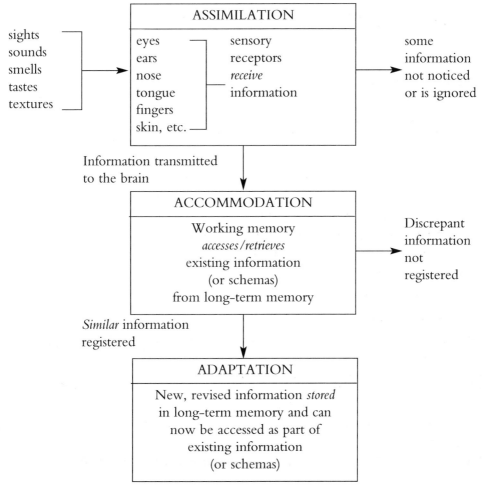

(b) Using Piaget's ideas of assimilation, accommodation and adaptation to understand how the brain processes information

6 Children are *egocentric*. They are unable to see or understand another person's viewpoint. This also means they are unable to convey information accurately or effectively to others.

7 Piaget believed that children interact with their environment to actively construct their knowledge and understanding of the world. They do this by relating new information to existing information. Piaget called this interaction:

- *assimilation*: the need for further information;
- *accommodation*: the need for organised information;
- *adaptation*: the need for revised/up-dated information.

All new information has to be built on existing information; there needs to be some connection between them. *Similar* information can be stored as it relates to existing information. *Discrepant* information cannot be stored because it is not related to existing information. (See diagram (b) above.)

8 Piaget described internal mental processes as **schemas** and the ways in which they are used when thinking as **operations**. Mental processes or schemas do not remain static; they continually develop as we acquire new information and extend our understanding of the world.

Some important criticisms of Piaget's work

There has been much disagreement concerning Piaget's theories of cognitive development in recent years, especially concerning his belief in the limitations of young children's thinking and reasoning before the age of 7 years old. Research by people such as **Margaret Donaldson** suggests Piaget underestimated young children's cognitive abilities; the use of appropriate language within a meaningful context enables 3 and 4 year olds to use logical thinking and to understand concepts such as the conservation of number, volume, weight. For example, the number conservation task involving two identical rows of objects (see diagram (c)) where young children agree that there is the same number in each row until the adult moves the objects in one of the rows so that it is longer than the other row; although the number of objects remains the same, young children will say the longer row has more objects. When this task is done using a 'naughty' teddy bear to upset the arrangement of objects, young children *can* state that the number of objects remains the same. The task has to *make sense* to the young child and the adult needs to use language which the child can understand.

" Same number in each row "

" This row has more objects "

(c) Conservation of number task

Donaldson also challenged Piaget's claim that young children under 7 years old are highly egocentric, that is they could not see things from another person's viewpoint. Piaget's evidence for this included the 'mountains' task (see diagram (d)) in which young children had to indicate what a doll would see, but instead the children would state their *own* view. Piaget described this as *egocentric illusion*. Donaldson states that evidence strongly suggests that Piaget's claim is wrong. For example, 'the policeman and little boy' task (see diagram (e)) devised by Martin Hughes, which showed that even 3 and 4 year olds could assess the policeman's viewpoint and hide the boy where the policeman would not be able to see him. This is because this task *makes sense* to young children; they can understand what they are supposed to do as even very young children can understand the motives and intentions of the policeman and the boy. The 'mountains' task is too abstract and the children do not understand what they are supposed to do (Donaldson, 1978).

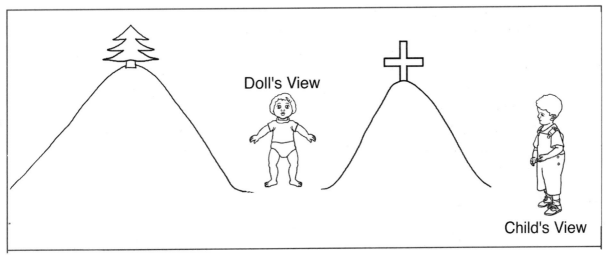

(d) Piaget's 'Mountains' task

Young children *are* capable of seeing things from another person's viewpoint, they just find it difficult; but adults find this difficult too! We are *all* egocentric in some situations and not in others.

Revisions of Piaget's work demonstrate that young children are very able thinkers as long as their learning takes place within meaningful contexts where appropriate language is used to facilitate the children's understanding. Language is seen as having a key role in young children's development; children use language to develop their understanding of the world around them.

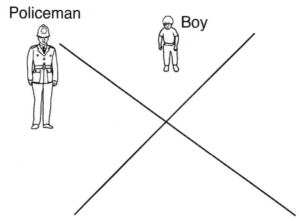

(e) 'Policeman and little boy' task

In later life, Piaget recognised the importance of social development in connection with the development of cognitive processes. Social interaction helps stimulate and formulate intelligence. Prior to this, Piaget had concluded that cognitive development progressed parallel to social development, but was not influenced by it. In his earlier work, Piaget *did* recognise the role of peers in children's cognitive development, even though he was against the idea of the adult's central role in transmitting knowledge. A child on their own might be unable to solve a problem, but working with other children could reach a solution. This also works nicely with the learning through play idea.

One of the most valuable contributions Piaget makes to our understanding of children's cognitive development is that children's thinking is an active process rather than one of passive absorption of information.

EXERCISE

Make a list of the main points of Piaget's theories of cognitive development.
Which points do *you* think accurately describe young children's thinking and learning?
Give examples from your experiences of working with young children.

Lev Semonovich Vygotsky (1896–1934) was a Russian psychologist whose book *Thought and language* was published after his death, but was quickly suppressed in Russia. This book was translated into English in 1962 and was a major influence on the work of **Bruner** and Donaldson. More recently other works of Vygotsky have been translated into English.

Like Piaget, Vygotsky was concerned with the active process of cognitive development. There were also many differences between Vygotsky's and Piaget's views of cognitive development:

Piaget's viewpoint	Vygotsky's viewpoint
Egocentric young child separate from others for a long period of development (0–7 years) but gradually becomes socialised.	Young child is a social organism who develops awareness of self through interaction with others. (Complete opposite to Piaget's idea.)
Peer interaction can be helpful. Adults provide a rich, stimulating environment; but too much adult interference can be harmful. Teaching by adults inhibits children's 'natural' development.	Social interaction with children and adults is crucial. The adult's role in teaching new skills is very important e.g. providing assisted learning situations within each child's zone of proximal development (see diagram on page 102).
Thought develops independent of language.	Language is a tool for thought.

Vygotsky argued that cognitive development was not just a matter of the maturation of intellectual processes, but of 'active adaptation' to the environment. The interaction *between* the child and other people forms the basis of the developing intellectual processes *within* the child. This social interaction enables children to develop the intellectual skills necessary for thought and logical reasoning. Language is the key to this interaction. Through language and communication children learn to think about their world and to modify their actions accordingly.

Vygotsky considered adults as having an active role in fostering children's cognitive development. So while children are active in constructing their own intellectual processes, they are not lone explorers; children need and receive knowledge through interaction with other children and adults. Vygotsky (and later Bruner) viewed the adult as supporting children's cognitive development within an appropriate framework. (See **scaffolding** on page 104.)

Adults support children's learning by assisting the children's own efforts and thus enabling children to acquire the necessary skills, knowledge and understanding. As children develop competent skills through this **assisted**

learning, the adults gradually decrease their support until the children are able to work independently. With adult assistance young children are able to complete tasks and to solve problems which they would not be able to do on their own. It is important that adults recognise when to provide support towards each child's next step of development and when this support is no longer required. Vygotsky used the idea of the **zone of proximal development** or area of next development to describe this framework of support for learning. The zone of proximal development can be represented in four stages (Tharp and Gallimore, 1991).

Children (and adults) can be in different zones for different skills or tasks. Each activity has its own zone of proximal development. For example, an adult learning to drive might progress in this way:

Step 1 – participating in driving lessons and driving test (assistance from others);

Step 2 – driving by self but need to talk through difficult manoeuvres (self-help);

Step 3 – driving confidently (auto-pilot);

Step 4 – involvement in traffic accident or different driving experiences such as motorways, driving abroad, result in need for further assistance (relapses to previous steps).

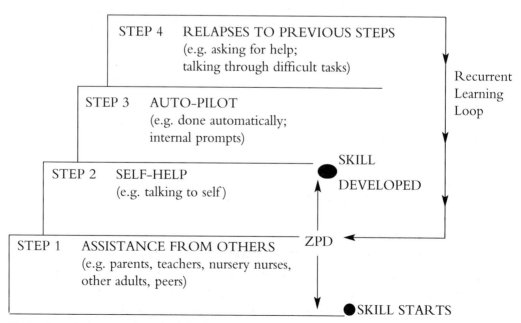

Moving through the zone of proximal development (adapted from Tharp and Gallimore, 1991; p. 50)

Another example, children learning to read may progress in this way:

Step 1 – learning phonic, decoding and comprehension skills with assistance of parents, teachers and nursery nurses (assistance from others);

Step 2 – sounding out difficult/unfamiliar words, reading aloud to self, lips moving during silent reading, etc. (self-help);

Step 3 – reading competently using internal prompts (auto-pilot);

Step 4 – new words, complicated texts, learning to read in a different language, etc. require further assistance (relapses to previous steps).

EXERCISE

Draw your own diagrams showing how the zone of proximal development could apply to:
- your own learning
- a young child's learning

An important feature of children's developing intellectual processes is the stage of *thinking aloud* which occurs between about 3 and 6 years old. Young children verbalise their thoughts and talk out loud about what they are doing. Older children and adults also use this kind of **self-talk** during complex problem-solving activities or when in difficult or stressful situations. Language also plays a key role in assisted learning. Language experiences between adults and children are essential to developing children's cognitive processes because language enables children to:

- identify thinking patterns and develop problem-solving strategies
- interpret their own experiences in relation to others
- understand how the world works e.g. scientific processes, concepts
- make judgements and decisions.

Language helps children to organise information into a structure which makes their experiences more meaningful and memorable.

Jerome S. Bruner (1915–), an American psychologist, agreed with some of Piaget's ideas but not others. Both Piaget and Bruner believed in the importance of children discovering things for themselves by exploring the environment and developing ideas in realistic situations, hence the importance of learning through play. There are three major differences involving:

1 the role of the *adult*

2 the role of *language*
3 the idea of *stages* in children's cognitive development.

The role of the adult

Bruner (like Vygotsky) emphasises the importance of the adult in supporting children's thinking and learning. Bruner uses the term **scaffolding** to describe this adult support. Picture a builder using scaffolding to support a house while it is being built. Without the scaffold the house could not be built; but once the house is finished, the scaffolding can be removed.

The adult supports the child's learning until they are ready to stand alone. Bruner also emphasises the adult's **skills** of recognising where and when this support is needed and when it should be removed. The structuring of children's learning should be flexible; the adult support or scaffold should not be rigid; it needs to change as the needs of the child change, that is as the child gains knowledge and understanding and/or acquires skills. The adult's supporting role involves:

- providing learning experiences within a meaningful context
- adapting tasks and learning experiences
- selecting appropriate materials for each child's needs and abilities
- encouraging children to make choices about what they want to do and when.

The role of language

Bruner views language as central to children's thinking and learning. Language connects a person's understanding of one situation to another. The adult has a particular role in establishing effective communication to encourage/extend children's thinking and learning. Adults use language:

- to capture children's interest and direct their attention
- to develop children's problem-solving abilities
- to assist children's understanding of concepts, etc.
- to encourage and extend children's own ideas
- to negotiate choices with children.

The idea of 'stages' in children's cognitive development

Bruner believed that any subject can be taught to any child at any age as long as it is presented in an appropriate way. Learning does not occur in

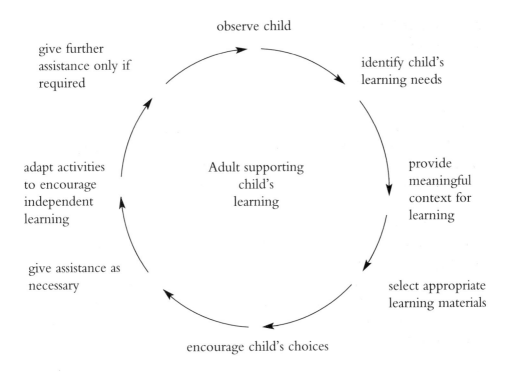

observe child

give further assistance only if required

identify child's learning needs

adapt activities to encourage independent learning

Adult supporting child's learning

provide meaningful context for learning

give assistance as necessary

select appropriate learning materials

encourage child's choices

'Scaffolding': Adult supporting child's learning

pre-determined **stages**, but is dependent on linking knowledge to children's existing knowledge in a holistic way.

Bruner's **sequence** of cognitive development is divided into three areas:

1 enactive – understanding the world through action
(relates to Piaget's sensori-motor stage)
2 iconic – manipulation of images or 'icons' in child's thinking about the world
(corresponds to Piaget's pre-operational stage)
3 symbolic – use of language and symbols to make sense of the world
(similar to Piaget's operational stage).

Bruner views language as central to cognitive development and stresses how language is used to represent experiences and how past experience/ knowledge is organised through language in ways which make information more accessible.

1 Summarise the main points of Vygotsky's and Bruner's theories concerning children's thinking and learning.
2 Think about how these ideas are related to your own experiences of working with young children.

The learning process: a social constructivist view

Children learn a great deal outside the early years setting e.g. at home, with friends.

This learning is individual, spontaneous and usually child-initiated. Within the setting (especially in schools) children's learning takes place in larger groups in more formal and planned situations which are adult-controlled. There is a danger that such learning can be less meaningful and less effective. Assisted learning occurs naturally within the home; most parents instinctively provide assistance in response to their children's needs and interests, because they know their children well. The *more* their children can do for themselves; the *less* the parents do for them.

In early years settings assisted learning can be more problematic especially if the adults do not have the necessary information regarding the children's existing level of performance before the introduction of any new experience or skill. Careful observations and assessments plus discussions with parents can provide this information. In settings where the adult to child ratio is low (notably primary schools) it can be very difficult to assess *each* child's area of next development (zone of proximal development) for *each* activity. Early years settings need to provide opportunities for conversation and interaction between adults and children in the more informal ways that make independent learning so successful within the home. These opportunities can be provided through effective organisation of the setting, for example:

- learning in small groups
- learning opportunities/activities which encourage children to work independently
- learning materials and technology (e.g. computers) which enable children to work independently.

Research shows (e.g. Donaldson) that children can be competent at one particular skill in one situation, but not in another. For example, children may be very capable of using problem-solving skills when sharing out sweets or toys among their friends in informal situations, but be unable to use these same skills in similar tasks within formal settings, such as completing mathematical activties in nursery or school. Children may also demonstrate highly imaginative skills and an extensive vocabulary when engaged in pretend/role play with siblings at home or with friends in the playground, but appear to lack imagination and communication skills within the classroom.

It is not the skill or task which poses the problem, but the **context**. It is the context of the learning experience which either encourages or inhibits children's cognitive abilities.

The other factor is the *skill of the adult in offering appropriate assistance* to encourage and extend the children's learning within that context. The adult's role is more than just one of providing appropriate resources within a stimulating environment and leaving the child to soak up knowledge like a sponge; the *adult and child work together* to build a network of knowledge and understanding. Learning is an *interactive* process in which the stimulus for learning can come from either the adult or the child; instruction from the adult springs from the child's need for more information (Rowland, 1987).

Young children have less experiences to draw on, so in order to make sense of the world they need assistance from more knowledgeable others. Adults and children are partners in the learning process, but it is an uneven relationship because adults know more than children *and* have the responsibility of sharing their knowledge with children in appropriate ways. Children know things about themselves and their world which the adults in the early years setting do *not* know. The effectiveness of assisted learning depends on the adults understanding of what children already know and building on the children's existing knowledge and experiences.

The social constructivist perspective on cognitive development emphasises the importance of the social context and social interactions with regard to the learning process. Cognitive development should not be viewed as a separate developmental process. In particular, social aspects and cultural influences are integral components of adult expectations concerning children's cognitive abilities.

In western society we have a high regard for abstract intellectual skills such as mathematics and science, but little regard for emotional skills e.g. social sciences, humanities. Cognitive development is part of the social process whereby adults help children to increase the scope of their intellectual abilities within a wide variety of social situations or contexts – in the home, the setting and the wider environment.

KEY TASK

Plan an activity which involves children learning within the social context of the wider environment e.g. outing or educational visit.

State the ages of the children and the aims/objectives of the outing (e.g. what are the learning goals for the children?) and include information on the following:

- choice of appropriate destination and length of outing
- preliminary visit by adult
- parental permission for children going on outing
- requests for adult helpers
- transport and other resources
- children's safety and first aid
- plan of activities during the outing and ideas for follow-up activities
- additional support for children with special needs (if required).

Child, aged 3 years, feeding the goats on nursery outing

Discuss your plan with your supervisor and, if possible, implement your outing.

Review and evaluate the outing afterwards considering the benefits to the children's thinking and learning.

NVQ Level 3 links: M.7.1 M.7.2 M.7.3 M.7.4 C.11.4 (C.14.4) (C.14.5)
DCE links: Units 2, 4 and 6 (Unit 7)
BTEC links: Units 3, 6, 7, and 8.

The social constructivist view of the learning process takes into account more recent research concerning how children think and learn within the context of home, setting and the wider environment. Social constructivism integrates children's cognitive and social development within a useful framework. It moves away from the idea that the development of children's cognitive abilities occurs in stages at particular ages and that adults simply provide the means for this natural process. Rather adults assist children's cognitive development as part of the **social process** of childhood. Age is not the critical factor in cognitive development; assisted learning can and does occur at *any age*. An emphasis on 'lifelong learning' recognises that as adults we continue to learn as we develop new skills and ideas throughout our adult lives. The **key factor** is the learner's *existing* knowledge and/or experience in connection with the *current* problem or learning situation.

EXERCISE

List the key features of the social constructivist view of children's cognitive development. Think about how these relate to your experiences of children's learning.

The nature versus nurture debate in cognitive development

Is children's cognitive development derived from their genetic inheritance (nature) or the result of their upbringing and experiences (nurture)?

This is one of the major questions concerning children's cognitive or intellectual development. If a person's intellectual abilities are dependent on heredity (nature) than it is possible to believe that people are born with a predetermined level of intelligence which remains the same all their lives;

they can only be as intelligent as those abilities permit. However, if a person's intellectual abilities arise as the result of their environment (nurture) it is then possible to believe that people are as intelligent as their learning experiences allow.

Research indicates that the development of children's cognitive abilities depends on both nature and nurture; babies and young children have a predisposition towards learning which is activated by environmental triggers such as social interaction, language and learning opportunities. Research with twins, separated and raised in different environments, shows that genetics is a key factor because the twins had similar IQ scores despite their different life experiences. Environment is also important. Research on children from ethnic minority groups shows that where there is racial discrimination the children did less well educationally; when their families moved to areas where there was little or no discrimination these children's IQ scores were the same as non-minority children. Intelligence is not determined by just one factor, similar to the way children's linguistic capabilities are affected by other factors (see Chapter 2).

We look at factors which may affect children's cognitive development in Chapter 8. A note of caution! It is easier for some parents, educators and politicians to say that intelligence is a matter of genetics because it avoids taking personal responsibility for children's failure to learn. As adults working with young children, we must ensure that we provide the appropriate and stimulating learning environments where children's intellectual processes can flourish.

EXERCISE

Having read the information on children's cognitive development in this chapter, what is your own opinion regarding the nature versus nurture debate?

Further reading

Britton, J. (1992) *Language and learning*. Penguin.
Bruce, T. and Meggitt, C. (1999) *Child care and education*. 2nd Edition. Hodder & Stoughton.
Donaldson, M. (1978) *Children's minds*. Fontana.
Wood, D. (1988) *How children think and learn*. Basil Blackwell.

7

Developing Children's Sensory Experiences

•••••••••••••••••••••••••••Key Points••••••••••••••••••••••••••••

- how babies and young children use their senses to understand the natural and physical world
- the sequence of sensory and perceptual development
- how to encourage young children to explore their environment
- the importance of play in promoting sensory experiences
- the development of children's drawings
- children with sensory impairment

Using the five senses to understand the natural and physical world

Babies and young children use their senses:

- to explore their environment;
- to investigate and participate in new experiences;
- to develop new skills and abilities;
- to discover how things work in the world around them.

Research shows that babies are born with a wide range of sensory skills and perceptual abilities which enable them to explore their environment in a variety of ways.

Hearing

Ears receive sounds and transmit them as signals to the brain which makes sense of these sounds. Research has shown that babies respond to sounds before they are born. Newborn babies can hear very well (unless they are born with a hearing impairment); they prefer the sound of human voices and respond to their mother's voice.

Sight

Eyes provide people with images, but the process of seeing involves the brain's ability to interpret these images. Each eye forms a slightly different image of what the individual sees, these two images combine to provide the person with binocular vision. Thus the person can see things with depth and is able to judge the distance of objects; that is, they have depth perception. Initially, babies are unable to make both eyes work together and so have no sense of distance. Visual perception together with improved physical co-ordination enables the hands and eyes to work together (i.e. hand-eye co-ordination) with increasing competence throughout the child's early years.

Touch

Babies are born with a grasping reflex, for example automatically gripping another person's finger. Newborn babies can reach for objects placed in front of them, but their hands may be closed before they can actually touch the object. Young babies respond to even delicate touches such as a puff of air. Different parts of the body are more sensitive than others; the mouth and hands (especially the fingers) are particularly sensitive to touch. Babies discover new experiences through touch, for example, by handling objects and putting everything in their mouths. As they get older, children

Child, aged 2 years, exploring outdoor wider environment using touch

continue to use their tactile abilities to explore their environment and to discover the properties of different materials such as rough/smooth, hard/soft, sharp/curved, and so on. The sense of touch also enables children to learn about temperature (e.g. hot/cold) and sensation (e.g. pain, pleasure, pressure).

Taste

As food dissolves in the mouth, a chemical reaction activates the taste buds which transmit messages to the brain as to whether the food (or liquid) is sweet, sour, bitter or salty.

Young babies respond to tastes in a way similar to adults; that is, they smile when tasting sweet things and frown when experiencing bitter and sour tastes. Newborn babies prefer sweet tastes like breast milk. Gradually they are able to discriminate between a range of tastes and flavours. Tasting and smelling work together; what many people think of as tasting is really smelling.

Smell

As a person breathes in, their nose senses the smells around them through tiny particles released by anything which has an odour. Nerve cells then transmit this information to the brain. A sense of smell is present in newborn babies; they can recognise the smell of their own mother. Babies smile when smelling fruit and frown when smelling strong odours such as fish. As children get older they can discriminate between a wide range of smells.

E X E R C I S E

Think about how young children explore their environment using their senses.
Give examples of the sensory experiences provided for the children in your setting.

The sequence of sensory and perceptual development

Babies' responses initially consist of automatic reflexes such as grasping and sucking; within a few months, they are able to explore objects in more purposeful ways. Babies and young children use different strategies for exploring their environment as they mature, gain more experience and develop their physical skills. The more opportunities they have to explore, the more they will develop their sensory skills and perceptual abilities. As their senses develop, babies and young children begin to make sense of the world around them as they perceive and process information in their environment.

To begin with babies focus on human faces and brightly coloured objects. Later they are able to perceive more detailed information and begin to make sense of that information. For example, being able to reach for and grasp a desired object; telling the difference between two bricks, etc. As well as developing their **visual perception**, babies gradually develop their **auditory perception** from merely reacting to noise to being able to concentrate on and make sense of specific sounds e.g. listening to an adult's voice without being distracted by other sounds during a story or rhyme. The young child's visual and auditory experiences are supplemented by tactile exploration of their environment. Intellectual development is closely linked with young children's physical development. For example, increasing mobility (from rolling to crawling to walking) enables further exploration of the environment. Developing hand-eye co-ordination and manipulative skills enable young children to participate in a wide range of creative and construction activities, jigsaws and games. These activities assist children's powers of observation and perception.

The chart below outlines the general sequence of young children's sensory and perceptual development. Remember that the ages referred to in the chart are only guidelines to *expected* development. Some children will acquire these sensory skills and perceptual abilities earlier than indicated, some children later than shown here.

The Ages of Discovery: The Sequence of Sensory and Perceptual Development

Age 0–3 months:
- in first month, babies' responses are reflexes e.g. sucking, grasping
- learns to modify reflex responses
- alert to voices when awake
- blinks when surprised or alarmed
- can focus 18 to 23 centimetres
- can distinguish between light and dark

- responds to bright light and bold colours (not pastels)
- from about 2 months, can discriminate between shades and colours
- can focus further and images become clearer as eye muscles become trained
- recognises faces of well-known adults and responds with smiles and arm movements
- looks around purposefully and responds to visual stimulation by smiling and/or reaching out towards objects e.g. mobiles, activity centres, board books, plastic mirrors, etc.
- repeats basic actions e.g. thumb/fist sucking, wiggling fingers
- reacts to prolonged noises such as washing machines or vacuum cleaners.

Age 3–9 months
- can focus more accurately; taking in more visual detail
- follows the progress of moving objects
- enjoys bright, bold patterns; starts to notice different patterns
- from about 5 months begins to perceive differences between objects e.g. size, shapes, colours
- can discriminate between different facial expressions
- quietens or smiles in response to parent's/carer's voice; turns head towards voice
- developing curiosity encourages adjusting own position to look at objects
- still puts things in mouth, but fingers used increasingly to explore objects
- responds to visual stimuli by touching activity centre, hitting mobile, etc
- reaches out and grasps objects e.g. shakes rattle to make a noise
- rolls towards desired object; once can crawl will do this to reach object
- enjoys putting things in containers and taking them out again
- from about 8 months, begins to understand object permanence e.g. if drops a toy will look in appropriate direction for it
- by about 9 months, listens attentively to everyday sounds and reacts to quiet sounds out of sight.

Age 9–18 months
- can focus like an adult, but still learning how to interpret visual information
- can follow objects moving quickly with eyes and see them clearly
- will physically follow a moving object if mobile and reach for it; if not yet mobile will point to an object out of reach
- experiments with toys and everyday objects to see what will happen; still puts things in mouth, but uses fingers more to explore objects and what can be done with them
- enjoys stacking, posting and/or pulling toys

- enjoys finger rhymes and clapping games such as pat-a-cake
- as becomes more mobile, physically explores environment – watch out!
- responds to own name and other familiar words such as 'no' and 'bye-bye'
- from about 12 months, scribbles with crayons; enjoys sensation of finger painting.

Age 18 months–2 years

- may be able to concentrate on short stories with clear pictures
- enjoys pop-up/novelty books with flaps (needs supervision)
- continues to develop visual perception and hand-eye co-ordination through activities which involve sorting and matching e.g. simple in-set jigsaws, 3-4 piece jigsaws, building towers, sorting bricks, etc.
- continues to scribble with crayons and enjoys tactile/visual qualities of paint
- able to use symbols in play activities e.g. doll represents a real baby
- increased mobility/co-ordination allows further exploration of their environment
- visual memory increases – can remember where favourite things are kept (and has physical ability to go and get them!)

Age 2–3 years

- desire to explore continues
- enjoys 'hide and seek' games e.g. hiding toys to find
- continues to develop visual perception and hand-eye co-ordination through doing more complex jigsaws, sorting/matching activities, modelling, construction
- more confident with crayons; using paintbrush as well as finger/sponge painting
- enjoys looking at books with clear illustrations
- can identify different letters of the alphabet and match some letters when asked
- increasingly uses language to discover what is going on e.g. asking questions and listening to conversations of others, listening to stories.

Age 3–4 years

- visual perception continues to improve as physical co-ordination develops through creative play, construction activities, threading, jigsaws etc.
- pencil control improving; learns use scissors and other simple tools
- developing colour and shape recognition

- continues to enjoy books with clear, meaningful illustrations related to their own interests
- developing observational skills through exploration of environment e.g. looking through simple binoculars, etc.
- curiosity increases along with 'who, what, why, when, how' questions
- auditory perception develops through activities such as listening to stories, joining in with songs/rhymes and other simple musical activities.

Age 4–5 years
- continues to develop observational skills through detailed examination of their environment e.g. using binoculars, magnifying glasses, telescopes
- visual perception/discrimination and hand–eye co-ordination improve through activities such as painting, drawing, writing, lotto, dominoes, jigsaws
- continues to develop visual memory through activities such as 'matching pairs'
- awareness of signs in local environment e.g. street names, shop signs, road signs
- developing auditory perception through listening activities e.g. sound lotto, 'what's that sound?' games, musical activities
- improved physical skills lead to interest in climbing and swinging activities
- discovering more about their world through language, television, books.

Age 5–7 years
- continues detailed exploration of the environment
- may be interested in maps and plans e.g. layout of classroom, school, local streets, atlases (including making own maps and plans)
- discovers more about own abilities through physical activities such as running, jumping, climbing, throwing and catching; increasingly competitive
- continues to use language to discover more about their environment and how things work, but also interested in why *people* do things as well as objects
- shows particular interest in sources of information e.g. television, computers, books, encyclopaedia, museums.
- as hand–eye co-ordination and manipulative skills develop further, writing, drawing and painting skills also improve
- auditory perception/discrimination improves through listening to stories, participating in singing and other musical activities.

The young explorer: 12 ways to encourage children to explore their environment

Babies and young children have a natural desire to explore their immediate environment. Below are some ideas on how to encourage and extend their discovery skills.

1 **Provide opportunities and materials to increase curiosity** e.g. mobiles, posters, pictures, toys, games and books.

2 **Encourage them to be observant by pointing out details in the environment** e.g. colours, shapes, smells, textures; interesting objects such as birds, vehicles; talking about weather conditions; take them on outings; gardening; keeping pets.

3 **Provide opportunities and materials for exploratory play** e.g. sand/water play; construction activities; modelling with 'junk' materials, playdough, clay.

4 **Participate in children's play to extend their learning** by asking questions, providing answers and demonstrating possible ways to use equipment.

5 **Demonstrate how things work or fit together** when the child is not sure what to do. For example, a child can become very frustrated when struggling to do a jigsaw, but make sure your help is wanted (and necessary); use verbal prompts where possible to encourage children to solve the problem themselves.

6 **Provide repetition** by encouraging children to play with toys and games more than once; each time they play, they will discover different things about these activities.

7 **Provide gradually more challenging activities** but do not push children to hard by providing activities which are obviously too complex; instead of extending children's abilities this will only put them off due to the frustration at not being able to complete the task.

8 **Remember safety**. It is important to allow children the freedom to explore their environment and to experiment with the properties of different materials. Make sure that these materials are suitable for young children. Objects which can pose a choking hazard or glass objects which could be broken causing cuts **must** be kept well out of young children's reach.

9 **Encourage auditory perception** through activities such as: singing rhymes and songs; clapping games; awareness of animal noises/environmental sounds; taped songs, rhymes, music, everyday

sounds and stories; sharing books and stories; sound lotto; identifying musical instruments; speaking and listening activities.

10 **Encourage visual perception** through activities involving exploration of the environment including outings to the park, farm; looking at books, pictures, displays, photographs; using magnification to highlight details e.g. magnifying glass, binoculars, telescope; matching games, jigsaws, lotto; using mirrors; activities requiring letter and/or number recognition including simple board games.

11 **Encourage tactile exploration** through activities which involve exploratory play – handling sand, water, clay, dough, wood; using manufactured materials e.g. plastic construction kits (Duplo, Lego, Stickle bricks); making collages using different textures; 'feely' box or bag.

12 **Encourage use of taste and smell senses** through cooking activities; finding out about different tastes: sweet, sour, bitter, salty; and different smells: sweet and savoury, flowers, fruit and vegetables.

KEY TASK

Observe a child or group of children engaged in an activity which encourages sensory exploration.

In your assessment focus on:

- which senses were used by the child
- the child's responses, including any language used
- the child's concentration level
- the physical skills demonstrated by the child e.g. hand-eye co-ordination, manual dexterity, mobility.

Suggest how the adult could extend the child's use of sensory skills and/or perceptual abilities.

NVQ Level 3 links: C.16.1 C.16.2 C.10.2
DCE links: Units 1, 4 and 6
BTEC links: Units 6, 7, 8 and 12.

The importance of play

Exploratory play encourages and extends young children's discovery skills. Play is an important way to motivate children and to assist their thinking

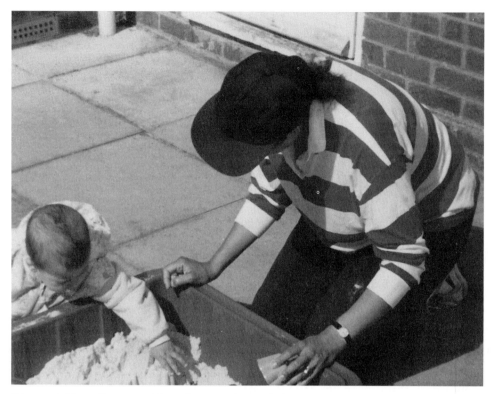

Baby, aged 12 months, engaged in exploratory play: sand pit

and learning in a wide variety of settings. It is not just the youngest children who benefit from play experiences; 7 year olds (and older children) can learn from play situations which give them 'hands-on' experience. Exploratory play encourages children to use their senses to discover the properties of different materials in pleasurable and meaningful ways. For example, playing with sand encourages children to consider textures and the functions of sand – getting the right consistency of sand to build sand castles, too wet or too dry and the sand will not stick together.

Play allows children to explore their environment in non-threatening ways which are less damaging to their self-esteem than more formal learning situations which involve right and wrong answers. Play enables direct learning through hands-on experiences often involving trial and error methods. We *all* experiment with new objects or situations. Adults will 'play' with new equipment such as a television, video recorder or hi-fi system e.g. pushing buttons to see what they will do, even before we have read the instructions. Adults and older children have more experiences and knowledge to draw on to make sense of new situations and can usually *read* to gain additional information. Young children have less experiences to refer to, so require more exploration and experimentation to make sense of the materials in the world around them.

EXERCISE

1 Think about what you do when you have a new machine/gadget or when you visit a new place e.g. checking out holiday accommodation.
2 Give examples of exploratory play from your own experiences of working with young children.

Research shows that play activities are effective in developing children's thinking and learning by providing opportunities for:

- well-motivated learning
- challenging and interesting learning experiences
- children to take responsibility for their own learning and to gain independence
- co-operative work between children
- developing problem-solving skills and improving concentration
- encouraging imagination and creativity.

Children learn through play. The term 'play' is often used to refer to activities which are considered to be unimportant and frivolous by many people (notably some teachers, parents and especially politicians!) It is up to early years workers to stress the importance of play to those who are sceptical about its benefits.

To children of *all* ages play involves:

- investigation – *What can this do? How does it work?*
- frustration – *I can't get it to work!*
- concentration – *trying hard to work it out.*
- satisfaction – *it works! Now what else can it do?*

Play is not an extra – something to be done to keep children quiet and occupied while adults are busy or as a reward for when other (more important) tasks have been done.

Play is an essential part of the learning process, especially for young children.

Play enables children to:

- learn about and understand the physical world
- develop individual skills and personal resources
- communicate and co-operate with others
- develop empathy for others
- make sense of the world in relation to themselves
- do their own learning, in their own time and in their own way.

The role of the adult in promoting learning through play is to:

1 Providing challenging and interesting play opportunities appropriate to children's needs, interests and abilities.
2 Provide varied resources and encourage children to use them.
3 Participate in children's play where appropriate to stimulate language and extend learning.
4 Intervene only when appropriate; adult participation can sometimes stifle children's language or creativity.
5 Encourage social interaction during play; some children may need coaxing to join in, others may need guidance on taking turns, sharing.
6 Link play activities to real life situations (e.g. shop play links with real shopping trips).
7 Encourage children's own imagination and creative ideas.
8 Be clear about their plans for play e.g. what are the learning goals for the children?

(See Appendix for information on planning activities for children.)

Children's drawings

Children's drawings are often used as indicators of children's intellectual abilities. For example, intelligence tests such as Florence Goodenough's 'draw-a-man' test (1926) and the up-dated test of drawing a man, woman and self by Dale Harris (1963) which have been used to measure children's intelligence according to the presence of set criteria e.g. head, mouth, fingers, etc. The more detailed the drawings, the more intelligent the child. The difficulty with this is that children's drawing abilities depend on a number of factors:

- physical ability e.g. manipulative skills in holding and using a pencil or crayon
- opportunities for mark-making
- interest in drawing activity
- concentration level

- visual input from books, television, displays, posters
- the teaching of drawing skills
- the drawings of other children
- adult reactions to children's artistic attempts.

None of these factors are related to **IQ**. Children can demonstrate obvious intelligence in other ways (e.g. reading ability and comprehension skills) but fail to complete the drawing of a recognisable person with the expected detail for a child of their particular age. The validity of such tests has been challenged and their use has declined. Research also shows that some children with cognitive and language difficulties (e.g. children with autistic tendencies) have exceptional drawing abilities perhaps because this is their only means of self-expression.

Children's drawings (and paintings) are also used as a way to assess young children's emotional development. For example, preoccupation with the use of black may be seen as a warning sign of emotional trauma, but could equally be a reflection of the child's interest in exploring dark colours and nothing more sinister.

Similarly, anatomically correct drawings of people do not necessarily indicate that a child is being sexually abused; they may have seen people in quite natural situations (e.g. bath time, getting dressed) or had inappropriate access to sexually explicit material (e.g. magazines, television programmes, videos).

We need instead to look at *what children mean to express* through their drawings rather than use adult interpretations of them. This is easier once children have language to express their ideas verbally as well as pictorially, but is more difficult with babies, toddlers and children with communication difficulties.

Another factor to consider is that western society does not place much importance on the *teaching* of drawing. Especially for young children, the emphasis is on allowing children to develop their drawing and painting skills in their own way. Children do not see many adults drawing and painting unless they receive a Rudolf Steiner education where a specific artistic technique is taught from 5 years old and upwards. The national curriculum *has* promoted the idea of introducing young children to the work of famous artists such as Van Gogh and Monet, and encouraging children to try out different techniques. The results have been surprising, children have produced paintings with detail far exceeding the children's usual artistic output.

You may have noticed that if an adult draws or paints alongside the children in your setting and talks about what they are all doing, the detail in the children's drawings/paintings increases quite markedly. The *process* of drawing and the *context* in which the drawing activity takes place are as important as the drawing itself, the end *product*.

Drawing is often seen as children's first attempts at writing. While the same skills (e.g. hand-eye co-ordination and pencil control) are required for both, drawing and writing are actually two distinct activities. Writing is speech written down; drawing is an individual's pictorial representation of their world. Both activities *do* involve the use of **symbols**. The simplistic and stylised nature of young children's drawings shows more about their *use of drawing* rather than their cognitive abilities or drawing skills. Young children use their drawings to convey meaning in the same way as they later on will use words e.g. the drawing is a pictorial symbol for 'bird' in the same way as the written word *bird*. From the age of seven years visual realism becomes more important as children's understanding of the function of drawings changes. Through drawing and painting children express themselves, their understanding of the world around them and their relationship to it. Limitations for this expression are imposed by the medium used (e.g. crayons, paints) and the ability to translate 3-D objects into 2-D images. (Even adults have problems with perspective in drawing and plans/maps rely on symbolic representation rather than realism.)

How children's drawings develop

Drawing and painting are important to children's development because they help:

- the expression of feelings, fears and fantasies
- hand-eye co-ordination and pencil control
- represent the people and world around them
- the recall of memorable events e.g. birthdays, holidays, falling off the swings.

Age 12–18 months
- cannot lift crayon off paper, moves it up and down in random marks
- has no control of stroke direction
- experiments with sensation of feeling paint rather than creating pictures.

Age 18 months–2 years
- cannot lift crayon off paper, draws round and round in circular movements

- very limited control of stroke direction
- explores sensation of paint textures rather than creating pictures
- imitates adults' and other children's efforts.

Age 2–3 years
- can lift a crayon off paper and continue in different place, makes lines, circles, dots
- begins to control stroke direction
- begins to draw shapes representing objects and people
- does not know what drawing beforehand, but will say what they have drawn afterwards once they can see a resemblance between the marks they have made and an object/person
- experiments with textures and colours.

Age 3–4 years
- can start and finish lines, draw dashes and dots
- does planned drawings but objects may not always be recognisable
- draws recognisable people e.g. 'tadpole' person with circular body-head, arms and legs (which may or may not be joined to body), basic facial features, possibly hair, fingers may be present (but may be too few/too many), possibly has feet.

Age 4–5 years
- drawings are right way up
- more like adult representations, but still child-like e.g. sun always shining with rays coming out
- drawings of people more detailed e.g. 'tadpole' person includes more obvious body shape, solid arms and legs, hair on head, more detailed facial features including eyebrows, five fingers on each arm, etc.

Age 5–6 years
- people have more detailed bodies e.g. neck, two-part bodies, ears, fingers, eyelashes, etc.
- people with details of clothes e.g. skirt styles, etc.
- scenes have ground and sky
- more adult representations but still child-stylised e.g. 'classic' house with roof, chimney, 4 windows and central door.

Age 6–7 years
- more adult representations e.g. clearly recognisable people and scenes
- gradually more and more detailed pictures

- very detailed people e.g. facial features include chins, freckles etc., details on clothes
- background details increasingly important e.g. flowers, vehicles, fences, trees, birds, etc.
- houses become more elaborate, reflecting reality e.g. child who lives in a flat will draw a block of flats, where before drew 'classic' house as above.
- some children may be reluctant to draw or become frustrated at inability to accurately represent what they see; they become self-critical and want to get details just right.

How to encourage children's drawing

1 Provide lots of paper and crayons, pencils. Chunky crayons and thick stemmed pencils are best for young children.
2 Encourage children to hold the pencil or crayon as best they can. They will control these better with a grip about 2 centimetres from the point.
3 Keep drawing sessions short. Be guided by the child's interest and concentration. A child's first attempt is usually their best – so do not ask them to do a picture over and over to get a better copy.
4 Let the children in your setting see *you* drawing and painting.
5 Draw outlines for children to fill in details e.g. adding facial features to a circle. (Do not do this all the time; children need freedom to draw what they like, how they like, when they like.)
6 Encourage observation skills by getting children to copy patterns and shapes. As children get older, encourage them to represent 3-D objects in 2-D and pay attention to detail e.g. self-portraits, drawing pictures of their own models, still-life (flowers, fruit, toys).
7 Provide variety in drawing and painting activities by offering different materials, tools and techniques
 e.g. – chalks, pastels, charcoal, felt-tips
   – sponges, different sized brushes, rollers
   – different sized paper, shaped paper, different textures
8 Provide plenty of interesting experiences (e.g. outings) to provide stimuli for drawing and painting.

KEY TASK

Observe a young child drawing or painting a picture of a person.
In your assessment comment on the child's:

- imaginative/creative skills
- concentration level

- use of colour
- manipulative skills (e.g. pencil or brush control).

You might also consider the emotional value of the activity.
Compare to the usual pattern of development of drawing/painting for a child of this age. (See chart on pages 124–126.)
NVQ Level 3 links: C.16.1 C.16.2 C.10.1 C.10.2 C.10.4 C.11.4
DCE links: Units 1, 4 and 6
BTEC links: Units 6, 7, 8 and 12.

Children with sensory impairment

The identification of children with sensory impairment and strategies for helping them to communicate more effectively have already been outlined in Chapter 2. Adults in early years settings need to enable children with sensory impairment to take part in a wide range of sensory and exploratory experiences by:

- providing a stimulating language-rich learning environment which is visually attractive, tactile and interactive
- maximising the use of space in the setting to allow freedom of movement for *all* children (including those who are visually impaired)
- ensuring accessibility of materials and equipment
- providing opportunities for all children to explore different materials and activities
- encouraging children to use their senses (whichever ones they can use) to their fullest extent
- providing sufficient time for children to explore their environment and materials; some children may need extra time to complete tasks
- encouraging independence e.g. use computers, word processing, tape recorders
- praising *all* children's *efforts* as well as achievements.

Two additional visual problems need to be considered.

CHILDREN WITH MONOCULAR VISION

Children with normal vision in one eye are not considered to be visually impaired, because one eye enables them to see quite well for most activities. Children with monocular vision will be affected in terms of 3-D perception and judging distances. Remember children with a squint may be relying on the vision of the one 'good' eye.

CHILDREN WHO ARE 'COLOUR BLIND'

Some children may have difficulty differentiating between certain colours, usually red and green. Again this is not a visual impairment, but may cause occasional difficulties in the setting e.g. when doing activities involving colour recognition, colour mixing, etc. There is also a safety implication e.g. red for danger/stop may be confused with green for go.

KEY TASK

Plan a sensory experience for young children. A suitable activity might be:

- providing a visual stimulus for a baby such as a mobile or activity toy/centre
- devising a musical activity or sound game to encourage auditory perception
- designing a tactile activity such as a 'feely' box or bag
- implementing a cooking or tasting session (remember safety, food allergies and dietary restrictions)
- organising an outing where the focus is on exploring the environment using the senses e.g. visit to local park, nature centre/trail; going on a 'bug hunt'.

You could use your suggestions from the observation on page 119 as a starting point.

Include suggestions for promoting the sensory development of a child with a hearing or visual impairment.

Review and evaluate the activity afterwards.

NVQ Level 3 links: C.10.2 M.7.1 M.7.2 M.7.3 (C.14. 3) (C.14.4)
DCE links: Units 2, 4 and 6 (Unit 7)
BTEC links: Units 3, 6, 7, 8 and 12.

Further reading

Cox, M. (1995) *Children's drawings*. Penguin.
Dare, A. and O'Donovan, M. (1997) *Good practice in caring for children with special needs*. Stanley Thornes.
Hobart, C. and Frankel, J. (1994) *A practical guide to activities for young children*. Stanley Thornes.
Matterson, E. (1989) *Play with a purpose for the under-sevens*. Penguin.

8

Meeting Children's Intellectual Needs

- identifying young children's intellectual needs
- the possible effects of inadequate intellectual stimulation
- the needs of more able children
- developing children's memory skills and attention-span
- developing children's imagination and creativity
- developing children's mathematical and scientific skills
- developing children's early literacy skills

What are children's intellectual needs?

To develop as healthy, considerate and intelligent human beings, babies and young children require intellectual stimulation as well as physical care and emotional security. Babies and young children are constantly thinking and learning; gathering new information and formulating new ideas about themselves, other people and the world around them.

The intellectual needs of babies and young children include:

- **freedom to explore their environment** and to investigate new information/ideas through interaction with other children and adults.
- **freedom to think and learn** through a wide variety of experiences and to discover things for themselves.
- **freedom to make their own mistakes** in a safe and secure environment, without feeling inadequate; 'trial and error' are important to the learning process.
- **appropriate support from adults (and other children)** to encourage and extend their learning.
- **developing autonomy** through increased responsibility and opportunities to perform tasks independently.
- **access to information and an appropriate learning framework** in which to make sense of new information and ideas.

The possible effects of inadequate intellectual stimulation include:

1 **Low self-esteem**. The lack of opportunities to explore, experiment and create within a stimulating, language-rich environment, can result in children having no sense of purpose or achievement. A person's emotional well-being is based on positive interactions with others *and* the world around them.

2 **Inability to concentrate** and poor attention-span due to lack of opportunities to discover things for themselves. Poor concentration leads to poor listening skills and difficulty in following instructions. Play opportunities are a good way to motivate children's learning; children are more likely to concentrate on self-chosen activities they enjoy. If they have not had play opportunities they will find it especially difficult to concentrate in more formal learning situations.

3 **Boredom**. Lack of concentration can lead to boredom. If children have not had discovery opportunities they will often lack interest in others and the world around them. This can lead to disruptive and/or attention-seeking behaviour. (See Chapter 14.)

4 **Reluctance to participate** and a tendency to withdraw from activities (especially those involving problem-solving skills) for fear of 'failing'. Children who have lacked play opportunities have missed out on learning in safe, non-threatening situations.

5 **Over-dependency on adult support**. Some children may be reluctant to do things for themselves if they have not had opportunities to engage in play and independent learning activities. Dependency on adults can also be linked to children's fear of 'failing'.

6 **Learning difficulties**. The inability to concentrate, to work independently or to use investigative skills may make it very difficult for some children to participate fully in early learning situations. This may lead to subsequent difficulties in curriculum areas such as English, mathematics, science, technology, etc. Some children are inaccurately thought to have learning difficulties, when they are really suffering from a severe lack of intellectual stimulation. Children with little or no intellectual stimulation cannot develop their own thinking skills or formulate new ideas.

It is vital that **all** children have access to a stimulating environment which enables learning to take place in exciting and challenging ways. Intellectual stimulation through play and other learning opportunities allows children to develop their cognitive abilities and fulfil their potential as individuals.

Some children may have intellectual abilities which are well above the expected norm for their age group. More able or 'gifted' children may have:

1 Reached developmental milestones *much* earlier than the norm.
2 More energy than is usual for their age.
3 A never-ending curiosity.
4 Sharp powers of observation.
5 Advanced thinking and reasoning skills.
6 A preference for interaction with older children and adults.

More able children need additional challenges and innovative ideas to stretch their cognitive capabilities. They need access to advanced resources with plenty of opportunities for independent, original and creative thought/action. Remember the children's social and emotional needs as well as their intellectual needs; if they are made to feel different or extraordinary they may find it difficult to mix with other children in the setting.

Developing children's memory skills

A person's mind is like a computer which stores information using a system of files to link different pieces of information together. Relating new information to existing information through this system makes it easier to access and use information. Information is stored in the short-term (or working) memory for about 10–20 seconds; from there the information is either forgotten or is passed on to the long-term memory where it is linked to existing stored information and 'filed' for future reference. (Look back at the diagram on how the brain processes information on page 97.) Information is more likely to be stored and therefore remembered if:

- **it is repeated many times**
- **it is linked effectively to existing information** (e.g. through personal experiences).

Young children have a limited number of experiences so their 'filing' system is quite basic. Gradually children create new files and have more complex filing systems to store the ever-increasing amount of information they receive through:

- their own experiences
- interaction with others
- a developing knowledge and understanding of their environment.

For example, if a young child has a cat at home, they may store all information about animals in the file labelled 'cat'. All animals will be called 'cat' by the child until s/he has enough information about other animals to create new files; eventually the child will have a complex network of files relating to information on animals.

There is no limit to the amount of information that can be stored in the long-term memory. The difficulty lies in accessing this stored information.

EXERCISE

1 What is your earliest memory?   2 How old were you?

Babies and memory

Your earliest memory was probably of some significant personal event when you were about 3 years old. Most people are unable to recall events or experiences before the age of three. From birth to about 3 years old our memories are stored using our senses (sight, sound, smell and touch) rather than language. For example, babies can remember the sound of their mother's voice and her smell, mealtimes and sleep routines. Once we develop language, we use words rather than our senses to recall information and lose the ability to remember our earlier sensory memories. It is as if these earlier memories were stored using a card-index file and once we have installed our 'computerised' filing system we no longer require the old card files or cannot find them.

As young children's language develops they are able to remember a great deal of information. For example, 2 and 3 year-olds can recall interesting experiences such as visits to the nature centre or farm. As children get older the process of remembering relies more and more on being able to use language to organise and retrieve information effectively.

Adults and children recall films, stories, songs and rhymes because they usually have a theme running through them and a continuity which makes them more meaningful and therefore more memorable. Positive thinking is also an important part of remembering. If you think you *can* remember you are more likely to recall information.

Children may have poor memory skills because they are:

● not paying attention or listening carefully in the first place

- anxious about remembering; being nervous and feeling under pressure can have a negative effect on memory skills
- upset by unpleasant associations with previous similar experiences and so subconsciously do not want to remember the new information
- not aware that the information is important and needs to be remembered
- unable to connect the information to existing knowledge or experiences
- not able to understand or process the information because it is too difficult or inappropriate.

10 ways to help young children develop memory skills

1 Encourage children to use their senses to remember new experiences, especially sight, sound *and* touch.
2 Make sure the children are *looking* and *listening* attentively when telling them something new.
3 Encourage children to repeat instructions or new information to check their understanding.
4 Explain how new information is connected to the children's existing experiences and knowledge (e.g. by linking activities with a common theme).
5 Use *action* to reinforce new ideas. Remember active learning.
6 Give new information in small pieces so children can learn bit by bit.
7 Do not pressurise children into recalling information. They will remember more if they feel relaxed.
8 Encourage children to feel confident about their memory skills.
9 Demonstrate your own memory skills and show them that remembering is not too difficult.
10 Provide lots of opportunities for children to practise and revise information. Use a variety of ways to reinforce learning e.g. games, play activities, etc.

Activities to develop memory skills

Involving young children in games and activities which require observation and recall helps improve their memory skills. (Note: children can usually remember as many objects as their age minus one e.g. a 5 year old will remember about 4 things in a game.)

THE GUESSING GAME

Arrange a few objects on a tray or table. Encourage the child to look at the objects and name them; use other senses too e.g. touch the objects, listen to them (have some that make a sound). Cover the tray/table. Ask the child to recall as many objects as they can. Give clues e.g. 'There was something red, something shiny . . .' etc.

THE OBSERVATION GAME

Arrange a display of interesting objects such as musical instruments, toys, etc. Ask the child to choose an object and examine it carefully. Put the object out of sight and ask the child to describe it in detail. Give prompts e.g. 'What did it *look* like? How did it *feel*? Did it make a *sound* or have a certain *smell*?' etc.

MATCHING PAIRS

Using matching cards (such as those for snap games) lay them face down. Each child turns over 2 cards at a time, trying to find a matching pair.

SONGS AND RHYMES

Singing songs and rhymes is easier than remembering prose because the rhythms, rhymes and melodies help recall. Young children love the repetition of favourite songs and rhymes. Knowing they can remember songs and rhymes gives children confidence in their memory skills.

KEY TASK

Design a game to help develop young children's memory skills. Implement the game.

Review and evaluate the game afterwards including information on:

- the benefits of the game to the children's development
- the children's responses including language.

NVQ Level 3 links: C.10.1 M.7.1 M.7.2 M.7.3
DCE links: Units 2, 4 and 6
BTEC links: Units 3, 6, 7, 8 and 12.

Developing children's attention-span and concentration
Being able to concentrate is an important part of the learning process.

Children with short attention-spans find it more difficult to take in new information; they may also need extra time to complete activities. Young children need to be able to focus on one activity at a time without being distracted by other things. This is an essential skill for learning, particularly within schools. Concentrating enables children to get the most out of learning opportunities.

Activities within the early years setting may require different kinds of concentration:

- **passive concentration** – e.g. listening to instructions, listening to stories, watching television, assemblies.
- **active concentration** – e.g. creative activities, construction, sand/water play, imaginative play, problem-solving activities including mathematics and science, reading/writing activities.

Some children have no difficulty paying attention to activities requiring **passive** concentration for quite long periods, for example watching a favourite video or television programme or listening to a story tape. Other children may not be able to pay attention to such activities for long but are totally engrossed in activities requiring **active** concentration such as constructing a model or completing a complex jigsaw.

All children have times when they find it more difficult to concentrate because:

- they are simply not interested in the activity
- the activity is inappropriate e.g. too difficult or too easy
- they are distracted by inner thoughts (day dreaming!)
- they are distracted by outside influences e.g. other children talking to them or around them; noises such as traffic or other groups/classes; weather conditions (*windy* days often make children more boisterous and inattentive, *snow* may make them too excited to concentrate, *rain* may make them restless if they are cooped up indoors all day).
- they are too tired or unwell
- they are emotionally distressed
- they have Attention Deficit Hyperactivity Disorder (see Chapter 14).

12 ways to improve children's concentration

1 **Minimise distractions** by providing a suitable learning environment where children can concentrate without being continually distracted or interrupted. For example, provide a quiet area for activities which require more concentration; quiet times when noisy activities are not permitted; carpets and screens to minimise noise levels.

2 **Be sensitive to children's individual needs and concentration levels**. Be flexible. Provide enough time for activities to be completed without children feeling under pressure. Too much time and children can become bored and disruptive.

3 **Keep activities short** to begin with, then gradually increase the time as the children's concentration improves. Divide complex activities into smaller tasks to make it easier for children to concentrate.

4 **Check the children understand the instructions** by asking them to repeat back instructions. Repeat instructions yourself as necessary.

5 **Use children's names** when asking them a question or giving an instruction. This attracts their attention and can help to maintain concentration.

6 **Use eye contact**. Make sure the children are looking at you when you talk to them. This encourages better understanding and minimises distractions.

7 **Use positive feedback and praise to encourage concentration**. Provide small incentives or rewards for achieving targets e.g. smiley faces for completing tasks.

8 **Use memory games** to encourage and extend children's concentration levels.

9 **Encourage observational and investigative skills** by asking children to look for specific items e.g. 'treasure' hunt, bug hunt, colour search, Easter egg hunt.

10 **Identifying sounds**; encourage children to listen out for a specific sound e.g. bell ringing, car passing, person walking in corridor. They will need to concentrate and screen for that sound. Identify everyday sounds on a tape or musical instruments behind a screen.

11 **Reading or telling stories** is an enjoyable way to encourage children's listening skills. Choosing stories of particular interest to the children will encourage their concentration. Increase the length/complexity of the story as the children's attention-span increases.

12 **Singing songs and rhymes** also improves concentration. For example, following a number sequence in songs like *Five brown teddies, Ten green bottles, When I was One . . ., Five little speckled frogs*.

Developing children's imagination and creativity

Imagination involves the individuals ability to invent ideas or to form images. Young children express their imagination through imitative play to begin with and then gradually through imaginary play. Imagination is important to the development of children's thinking and learning. As young children explore their environment and find out what objects and materials can do, they use their imagination to increase their understanding of the world and their role within it. For example, through pretend or imaginative play children can become other people by dressing-up and behaving like them.

Imaginative play assists the development of children's imagination through activities such as dressing-up, doll play, shop play, hospital play, small scale toys.

Creativity is the **use** of the imagination in a wide variety of activities including play, art and design, music, dance, drama, stories and poetry. Young children express their creativity mostly through creative activities such as painting, drawing, model making, etc. Creativity involves a process rather than an end product; it cannot be measured by the end result of an activity, but is based upon *how* the child worked and *why*. Creativity involves:

- exploring and experimenting with a wide range of materials
- thinking and learning about the properties of materials e.g. colour, shape, size, texture, etc.
- developing physical skills to manipulate materials
- developing problem-solving techniques
- a life-long process of developing our individual understanding of the world and our personal contribution to it.

EXERCISE

1 Give an example of an activity which encourages a group of children to express themselves freely in an imaginative and creative way.
2 Suggest ways to develop the children's imagination and creativity.

Creative activities are essential to developing children's imagination and creativity:

- **Painting** with brushes, sponges, string; finger painting, bubble painting, 'butterfly' or 'blob' painting; printing (e.g. with potatoes, cotton reels) and pattern-making (e.g. with rollers, stamps).
- **Drawing** using a variety of tools (e.g. crayons, pencils) and paper which children can use when they feel the need to express themselves through this medium.
- **Model-making** using commercial kits (like Duplo, Lego, Stickle bricks) or clean and safe 'junk' materials to create their own designs.
- **Collage** using glue and interesting materials to create pictures involving different textures, colours and shapes; this gives children an enjoyable sensory experience too.
- **Play dough** and other materials such as clay can be used creatively; they are tactile too.
- **Cooking** can be a creative activity; it is an experience similar to working with play dough or clay except that the end product is (usually) edible. Remember to include 'no cook' activities such as icing biscuits, making sandwiches or peppermint creams where the children can create their own designs.

KEY TASK

Observe a group of young children during a creative activity.
In your assessment focus on the children's intellectual skills especially:

- imaginative and creative skills
- problem-solving skills
- concentration levels
- use of language.

Suggest ways to extend the children's creative skills including appropriate resources.

NVQ Level 3 links: C.16.1 C.16.2 C.10.4 C.11.2
DCE links: Units 1, 4 and 6
BTEC links: Units 6, 7, 8 and 12.

Making music

Young children enjoy the experience of making music using a wide range of musical instruments. Music provides an interesting and exciting way for children to be creative e.g. making their own combinations of different sounds plus simple rhythmic patterns and tunes. Use percussion instruments with young children as it is easy for them to make rhythmic and melodic sounds without the experience and expertise required for more complex instruments such as recorders, guitars, pianos, etc. Provide a portable box or trolley with a range of percussion instruments including: drums, tambourines, castanets, wood blocks, shakers, bell sticks, Indian bells, triangles, xylophones and chime bars. To begin with provide young children with opportunities to play along with favourite songs. Encourage the children to decide which instruments might be suitable for particular songs e.g. triangles and bells for *Twinkle, twinkle little star*. Also provide opportunities for children to experiment freely with the musical instruments.

Gradually, encourage children to create their own music by getting them to copy clapping patterns, making clapping patterns using their own names, etc. Use pictures, stories or rhymes as a stimulus for children to make their own musical creations on their own, with a partner or as a group. Encourage them to represent their music using symbols and/or words, for example:

Creative writing

Children can also demonstrate their imagination and creativity through their writing for example, stories and poems. (See also Chapters 3 and 9.)

KEY TASK

Plan and implement a creative activity with a young child or group of young children.
Review and evaluate the activity afterwards.

NVQ Level 3 links: C.10.4 C.10.1 M.7.2 M.7.3 M.7.4 C.11.2
DCE links: Units 2, 4 and 6
BTEC links: Units 3, 6, 7, 8 and 12.

Helping children to develop understanding in mathematics and science

Mathematics and science rely on the ability to understand abstract ideas. For young children this means developing a sound knowledge and understanding of concrete concepts first such as number, weighing/measuring, volume/capacity, shape, colour, space, textures, growth and physical forces. Experiences with real objects enable young children to develop problem-solving skills and to acquire understanding of these concepts. Some concepts require the understanding of other concepts beforehand e.g. understanding *number* and *counting* comes before *addition*; understanding *addition* comes before *multiplication*, etc. Adults working with young children need to ensure that they provide activities at the appropriate level for the children's conceptual development (see Chapter 5). There should be a balance between encouraging the children to develop their own problem-solving skills through play with minimal adult intervention and complying with the objectives of the national curriculum (e.g. numeracy hour) or the early learning goals for mathematics and knowledge/understanding of the world.

Suggestions for developing children's mathematical skills

1　**Sorting and counting involving stories, rhymes and songs** like 'Goldilocks and the three bears; matching games e.g. lotto, snap; play activities such as dressing-up (e.g. pairs of socks, gloves, mittens) and organising sets of plates, cutlery, boxes, toys in the home corner or play shop; using toy vehicles for counting and matching activities.

2 **Understanding and using number** through playing games like dominoes, 'snakes and ladders' and other simple board games; looking for shapes/sizes and making comparisons, price tags and quantities in shop play and real shopping trips; number songs and rhymes like 'One, two, three, four, five, Once I caught a fish alive . . .'.

3 **Sequencing** through activities involving comparing and ordering e.g. in-set jigsaws, doll/toy sizes; putting events in order e.g. stories, pattern of the day/week.

4 **Weighing and measuring** activities such as shop play (using balance scales to compare toys and other items); real shopping (helping to weigh fruit and vegetables); sand play (heavy and light); cooking activities (weighing ingredients to show importance of standard measures).

Encourage children to develop understanding of length by comparing everyday objects/toys and using mathematical language such as tall/taller/tallest, short/shorter/shortest, long/longer/longest, same height, same length. Encourage them to record information. Use non-standard measures e.g. hand-spans to measure everyday objects; gradually introduce standard measures e.g. metre, centimetres.

5 **Volume and capacity**. Using sand and water play including filling various containers to encourage understanding of full, empty, half-full, half-empty, nearly full, nearly empty, more/less than, the same amount. Use coloured water to make activities more interesting. Gradually introduce idea of standard measures e.g. litre of juice, pint of milk.

Suggestions for developing children's scientific skills

Young children need lots of opportunities to develop these scientific skills:

● observe   ● investigate   ● predict   ● hypothesise   ● record.

1 *Shape and space*. Observing shape and patterns in the setting and wider environment. Exploring shapes during model-making, collage and other creative activities. Exploring space and shapes during outdoor/physical play, PE and movement sessions by looking at body shapes and how they move with and without apparatus.

2 *Colour*. Creative activities including collage, colour-mixing, making rainbows. Colour tables or weeks with books, stories and songs linked

to colours. Playing 'Traffic lights' in PE or movement sessions – red for stop/stand still, green for go/move, yellow for make a shape. Talk about colours in the environment e.g. blue lights for emergency vehicles; plants.

3 *Texture*. Provide tactile experiences such as sand/water play, collage, touch table, 'feely' bag/box, play dough, clay, and cooking sessions.

4 *Living and growing*. Sing songs and rhymes about ourselves and the human body e.g. 'I've got a body, a very busy body...', 'Head and shoulders...'. Do topics on babies. Study animals and plants by: visiting nature/garden centres, parks and farms; keeping pets; growing seeds like beans, mustard and cress; having a nature table. Remember health and safety.

5 *Physical forces*. Use toys to explore ideas about *energy* e.g. pulling, pushing, pull-back, wind-up, battery, remote-controlled and electrical toys. Explore ideas about the *weather* by: observing and talking about different weather conditions; keeping a weather chart; making a windmill; making paper snowflakes; sharing weather stories and rhymes e.g. discussing *temperature* differences like hot and cold, suitable clothing for different weather conditions; changing states of materials e.g. frozen water is ice, water vapour is steam. Experiment with different objects to see which will *float* or *sink*. Use questions to encourage predictions: will all heavy objects sink? Will all light objects float? What happens if change object's shape? (e.g. plasticine in a ball sinks, when reshaped as a bowl or boat it floats).

KEY TASK

Plan and implement an activity for a group of young children which involves developing their mathematical or scientific skills such as:

- matching/counting
- number recognition or number operations
- cookery
- sand or water play
- using patterns
- investigating the environment or weather conditions.

Encourage the children to explore using their senses and to use mathematical/scientific language as appropriate. Review and evaluate the activity afterwards.

NVQ Level 3 links: C.10.2 C.10.3 C.11.2 C.11.4 C.11.5 M.7.2 M.7.3 M.7.4
DCE links: Units 2, 4 and 6
BTEC links: Units 3, 6, 7, 8 and 12.

Helping to develop young children's literacy skills

An important aspect of children's cognitive development is developing literacy skills; learning to read and write. Without literacy skills individuals are very restricted in their ability to:

- function effectively in the school (or work) setting
- access information and new ideas
- communicate their own ideas to others
- participate fully and safely in society.

Education depends on individuals being able to read and write. Nearly all jobs and careers require at least basic literacy (and numeracy) skills.
Our society also requires people to use literacy skills in everyday life:

- reading signs: street names, shop names, traffic and warnings
- reading newspapers, magazines, instructions, recipes, food ingredients, etc.
- dealing with correspondence: reading and replying to letters; household bills; bank statements; benefits; wage slips, etc.
- using computers
- writing shopping lists, memos, notes.

Activities which help develop young children's early literacy skills

1. **Talking:** children who are effective communicators often transfer these skills to reading
2. **Listening games** like 'guess the sound', sound lotto and using everyday objects or musical instruments to encourage auditory discrimination.
3. **Sharing books**, *stories and rhymes* (see Chapter 4)
4. **Matching games** like snap, matching pairs, jigsaws to encourage visual discrimination.
5. **Memory games** like 'I went shopping . . .'
6. **Looking at other printed materials** e.g. newspapers, magazines, comics, signs, packaging

7 **Fun with letters**: 'I spy . . .' using letter sounds; going on a 'letter hunt' (looking around the setting for things beginning with a particular letter); hang up an 'alphabet washing line'; sing alphabet songs and rhymes.

8 **Television**: use programmes like 'Sesame Street' and 'Words and Pictures' to encourage and extend children's literacy skills.

Alphabet washing line

'Reading readiness'

There is no set age at which children are magically ready to read although most children learn to read between the ages of 4½ and 6 years old. The age at which a child learns to read depends on a number of factors:

- physical maturity and co-ordination
- social and emotional development
- language experiences especially access to books
- interest in stories and rhymes
- attention-span and memory skills
- opportunities for play.

Reading readiness checklist

1 Can the child see and hear properly?
2 Are the child's co-ordination skills developing within the expected norm?
3 Can the child understand and follow simple verbal instructions?
4 Can the child co-operate with an adult and concentrate on an activity for short periods?

5 Does the child enjoy looking at books plus joining in with rhymes and stories?

6 Does the child show interest in the details of pictures?

7 Can the child retell parts of a story in the right order?

8 Can the child tell a story using pictures?

9 Can the child remember letter sounds and recognise them at the beginning of words?

10 Does the child show pleasure or excitement when able to read words in the setting? If the answer is 'yes' to most of these questions, the child is probably ready to read; if the answer is 'no' to any of the questions, the child may need additional support or experiences in those areas before they are ready to read.

Reading methods

Whole word or 'look and say'

Children are taught to recognise a small set of key words (usually related to a reading scheme) by means of individual words printed on flashcards. Children recognise the different words by shape and other visual differences. Once the children have developed a satisfactory sight vocabulary, they go onto the actual reading scheme. The whole word method is useful for learning difficult words which do not follow the usual rules of English language. The drawback is that this method does not help children to work out new words for themselves.

Phonics

With this approach children learn the sounds that letters usually make. This method helps children establish a much larger reading vocabulary fairly quickly as they can 'sound out' new words for themselves. The disadvantage is that there are many irregular words in the English language, e.g. bough, rough, through.

However, children do better with this method than any other approach.

Apprenticeship approach

This method, also known as the 'story' or 'real books' approach, does not formally teach children to read. Instead the child sits with an adult and listens to the adult read; the child starts reading along with the adult until the child can read some or all of the book alone. This method does not help children with the process of decoding symbols. There has been much criticism of this method, but it has proved effective in this country and New Zealand as part of the 'Reading Recovery' programme for older less able readers.

Most adults helping young children to develop reading skills use a combination of the 'look and say' method to introduce early sight vocabulary and then move onto the more intensive phonics approach to establish the children's reading vocabulary. It is important to be flexible to meet the individual language needs of young children. Adults in the early years setting should work with parents to develop children's reading skills.

EXERCISE

1 Investigate the approaches to developing young children's reading skills. Think about:
   - how you learned to read
   - how your own children (if any) learned or are learning to read
   - approaches to reading used in the early years setting where you are/have worked.
2 Consider the similarities and differences between these approaches in developing young children's reading skills.

Learning to write

Most of the activities used to develop children's early reading skills will also help children's early writing skills. In addition, young children need plenty of opportunities to develop the *co-ordination* skills necessary for writing:

- hand–eye co-ordination
- fine manipulative skills for pencil control
- being able to sit still with the correct posture for writing.

Some children may have special needs which require writing using alternative means e.g. Braille, word processor, voice-activated computer.

It is usual to teach writing skills alongside reading. This helps the children to make the connection between written letters and the sounds they make when read. Young children experience written language through books and stories (see Chapter 4) and learn that writing is made up of symbols or patterns organised on paper in a particular way. In English this means 26 letters in the alphabet written from left to right horizontally.

Young children also learn through watching adults and other children at home and in the setting that writing can be used for:

- recording past events and experiences e.g. news, outings, visitors, special events
- exchanging information e.g. notes, memos, letters, postcards
- functional writing e.g. shopping lists, recipes, menus, recording experiments or data
- sharing stories and ideas e.g. story writing, poetry.

Developing writing skills is much more difficult then reading because of:

- the considerable physical and cognitive demands e.g. co-ordinating movements to write
- the need for legible writing e.g. letters of consistent size and shape; gaps between words
- the need for punctuation and sentence structure
- correct spelling requirements
- the need for writing of the required length which makes sense.

EXERCISE

1 How did you learn to write?
2 Which activities for developing children's writing skills have you observed in early years settings?

Provide lots of opportunities for young children to develop the co-ordination skills needed for writing. Include activities such as:

- drawing/painting   • colouring in   • tracing
- threading beads   • cutting and sticking   • sewing (remember safety).

Learning to write takes lots of practise so provide plenty of opportunities for young children to form letters in a variety of ways;
- in the air   • in sand   • using paints
- with crayons, pencils, felt-tips   • using plasticine, clay or playdough.

KEY TASK

Observe a young child engaged in a writing activity.
In your assessment comment on:

- the child's manipulative skills
- the child's concentration
- the creativity of the finished piece of writing.

Suggest ways to encourage and extend the child's writing skills.

NVQ Level 3 links: C.10.1 C.10.4 C.11.2 C.16.1 C.16.2
DCE links: Units 1, 4 and 6
BTEC links: Units 6, 7, 8 and 12.

Let children use their preferred hand when writing. Some children swap around for sometime until they establish which hand they feel most comfortable writing with. Give children lots of praise for their attempts at writing and put their efforts on display. Do not worry that it does not look neat in the early stages, it is having a go at writing that is important.

Encourage independent spelling techniques e.g. word banks, key words on permanent display, topic words on the board/on paper at children's tables, personal word books and dictionaries. Release young children from their physical limitations of writing by allowing them to dictate their ideas while an adult acts as scribe, using a tape recorder or word processor.

Further reading

Clay, M. (1992) *Becoming literate*. Heinemann.
Einon, D. (1986) *Creative play*. Penguin.
Morris, J. and Mort, J. (1991) *Bright ideas for the early years: learning through play*. Scholastic.
Neaum, S. and Tallack, J. (1997) *Good practice in implementing the pre-school curriculum*. Stanley Thornes.
Whitehead, M. (1996) *The development of language and literacy*. Hodder & Stoughton.
Willig, C. J. (1990) *Children's concepts and the primary curriculum*. Paul Chapman.

9

Socialisation: Relating to Others

· ·Key Points· ·

- understanding the importance of children's social and emotional development
- nature versus nurture in personality development
- factors affecting social and emotional development
- the sequence of social and emotional development

- observing and assessing children's social and emotional development
- the importance of play
- helping children to respect and care for others
- helping children deal with conflict situations

Social and emotional development can be defined as the development of **personality** and **temperament**. This involves how each person:

- develops as a unique individual
- *thinks* other people see them and feelings
- relates to others
- sees and feels about themselves
- expresses their individual needs, desires
- interacts with their environment.

Adults working with young children need to understand the process of children's personality development in order to provide appropriate assistance and guidance.

Nature versus nurture in personality development

Research indicates that genetics plays its part in this development; babies only a few weeks old already have distinct personalities. Children inherit their particular temperaments which are then influenced by the environment they are raised in. Researchers agree that personality is derived from a combination of inheritance (nature) and environment (nurture).

Genetic inheritance

In the same way as babies inherit their physical characteristics, they also inherit genetic information which contributes towards their **personality** development. Studies of very young babies show that they already have distinct temperaments or personality types e.g.

- 40% were easy-going   • 10% were 'difficult'
- 15% were 'slow to warm up'   • 35% did not fit any category!
(Fontana, 1984.)

Note: *Labelling* personalities is not really a good idea, as every child is a unique individual.

Environmental factors

1 *Attachments*: having at least one secure and personal relationship e.g. with parent/carer enables children to form other relationships.
2 *Parental care*: consistent, loving care from parent/carer who is sensitive to the child's particular needs enables children to feel secure and to develop self-worth. Physical care is not enough; children need love and attention from their parent and/or carer.
3 *Role models*: observing the behaviour of parents and other significant adults (carers, teachers). **Aggressive** arguments, shouting or **assertive** discussions and compromise or **passive**, silent 'doormat' responses will affect children's own behaviour, how they deal with their own feelings and how they relate to others.
4 *Social context*: positive interactions with other people in various settings will lead to positive ways of relating to others and appropriate social skills. Children's social and emotional development may be affected by social factors such as:
   - family occupation and income
   - type of accommodation family can afford to buy or rent
   - the area where they live
   - parental expectations
   - society's expectations.
5 *Culture and gender:* cultural expectations and child-rearing practices vary. Different cultures within society may have differing cultural expectations relating to what is considered to be appropriate behaviour including the expected roles for men and women. For example, research shows that parents treat boys and girls differently, often subconsciously i.e. girls get more cuddles.
6 *Family size and birth order:* children in large families may find it more difficult to get their parents' attention and this may affect their social adjustment especially in group settings. Some research studies indicate

that the position of children in the family may also affect their personality. First-born (or only) children are more likely to be conscientious, co-operative, sensitive and academically ambitious. Second-born children are more likely to be out-going, aggressive, and competitive. The youngest child in a family tends to be the most sociable, spontaneous, passive and lacking in maturity. Any differences in personality are probably due to the way in which adults treat the children rather than birth order. First time parents are more likely to be anxious and over-protective of their first born; parents may be more relaxed with the second child who may feel they are in the older child's 'shadow'; the youngest child may be 'babied' by the rest of the family.

7 *Other factors:* children's social and emotional development may also be affected by:
  - special needs and/or difficulties at birth (e.g. premature baby, forceps or caesarian delivery) which are often stated as being the cause for a baby being 'difficult'. Again this is more likely to be the result of the adult's treatment of the child (e.g. over-anxiety due to low-birth weight of a premature baby or concern over the child's special needs) which then affects the child's behaviour.
  - family circumstances such as separation/divorce, one-parent families, step-families.
  - death, abandonment or other permanent separation from parent or main caregiver
  - adoption, foster care or other temporary/permanent residential care.

These factors do not necessarily have negative effects on children's social and emotional development; there are usually additional factors (such as financial hardship, poor quality substitute care) which can lead to poor social adjustment and/or emotional difficulties.

The effects of the environment are *interactive* because children also influence their environment by the way they respond to the experiences provided by their family and others within any social context. For example, adults who provide inconsistent or inappropriate care due to anxiety or uncertainty about care-giving may unwittingly encourage difficult behaviour in their children which then leads to the adult spending less time interacting with the child resulting in the child having poor communication skills and poor attachment which may mean difficulties in forming other relationships. Some babies do not cry much, have consistent feeding and sleeping patterns; while others do not. An 'easy' baby responds well to parent/caregiver and encourages confidence; while a 'difficult' baby can undermine the parent/carer's confidence especially if its their first child. There is a spiralling interaction between child and adult.

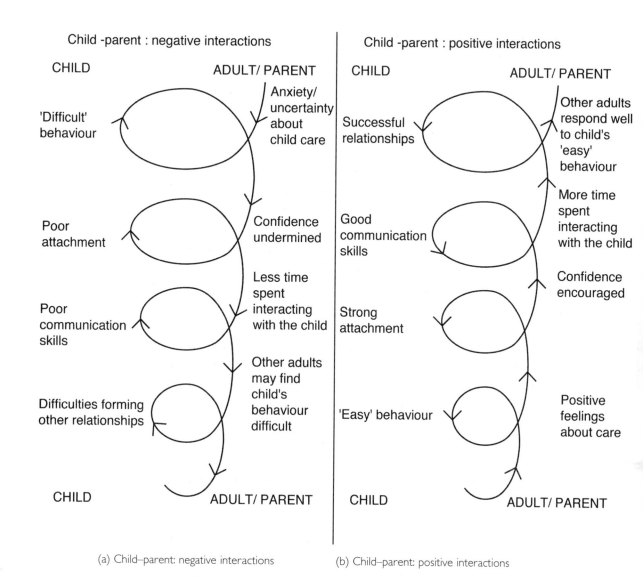

(a) Child–parent: negative interactions   (b) Child–parent: positive interactions

All children need:

- affection   • security   • acceptance   • encouragement
- patience   • a stimulating environment.

A child who has been deprived of these in the first 5 to 6 years of life may remain deprived throughout childhood (and even adulthood) because they may find it difficult to relate to other people. However, children are amazingly resilient and subsequent, sustained relationships with caring adults in a supportive environment can help children overcome early parental separation, rejection or neglect.

Socialisation involves the development of:
- behaviour patterns
- self-control
- independence (including self-help skills such as feeding, toileting, dressing, washing, etc.)
- awareness of self in relation to others
- relationships
- understanding the needs and rights of others
- moral concepts (e.g. understanding the difference between right and wrong; making decisions based on individual morality).

Socialisation determines how children relate socially and emotionally to others. Children need to learn how to deal appropriately with a whole range of emotions including anger and frustration within a supportive environment. (See pages 176–178.)

An essential aspect of socialisation is getting young children to behave in socially acceptable ways without damaging their self-esteem; that is, rejecting the unacceptable behaviour *not* the child. Socialisation begins from birth as babies interact with the people around them and respond to their environment. Babies develop an awareness of others in relation to themselves e.g. people who fulfil their needs for:

- food and drink ● warmth and shelter ● sleep ● physical comfort
- entertainment!

Babies develop strong attachments to the people seen most often and who satisfy the above needs. One attachment is usually stronger than the others and is usually to the baby's mother, but the attachment can be to another family member or anyone outside the immediate family who spends a significant amount of time with the young child such as a grandparent or nanny.

The security of these early attachments is essential to babies and young children because they provide:

- a firm foundation for emotional well-being
- confidence to explore the environment and to relate to others.
(There is more detailed information on attachment theory in Chapter 12.)

These early attachments enable children to feel secure about their relationships and to develop trust in others. Security and trust are important

elements in the young child's ability to separate from parents and others; to develop their own independence and ideas. Young children want to do things for themselves (e.g. getting dressed, making things) and become frustrated if they cannot.

Many conflicts arise between young children and other people as children increase their independence and expand the boundaries of their world. Adults should avoid:

- *inhibiting* the child's need for independence as this can lead to either
  - emotional dependence, excessive shyness and an over-cautious nature;
  or
  - emotional detachment, anti-social behaviour and a rebellious nature.
- *unrestricted* independence for the child who may be exposed to danger and physical harm (e.g. from fire, boiling water, traffic) and/or a child who becomes selfish and unable to recognise the needs and rights of others.

Adults caring for young children need to strike a balance between these two extremes. Adults also need to provide a balance between allowing for the *individual* child's need for independence and providing supervision with appropriate guidelines for socially acceptable behaviour which takes into consideration the needs of *everyone* in the setting. Encouraging appropriate behaviour from children does not mean adults being aggressive or using bullying tactics. Firm discipline should include warmth and affection to show the children they are cared for and accepted for who they are regardless of any inappropriate behaviour demonstrated by the child.

By about four years old, most young children will have achieved the ability to:

- be fairly independent
- be realistically self-controlled
- understand the needs and rights of others (to some extent)
- participate in group activities
- make friends with other children
- meet the challenge of new experiences without too much anxiety.

These abilities enable young children to adjust to starting school which can be a daunting experience. Schools involve society's attempts at socialisation; as well as educating children by providing opportunities to gain knowledge and understanding in a wide range of subjects, schools influence children's

attitudes and actions by providing a framework for socially acceptable behaviour with rules that have to be followed by all. (See Chapter 13 on behaviour.)

Socialisation occurs through:

- observation ⎤
- identification ⎥
- imitation ⎥—— of the behaviour of other people
- assimilation ⎦

Children model their attitudes and actions on the behaviour of others. They imitate the actions and speech of those they are closest to e.g. acting out being 'mum', 'dad' or 'teacher'; copying the actions and mannerisms of adults around the home or setting. All adults caring for young children need to be aware of the significant impact they make to children's social and emotional development by providing *positive role models*.

Language is important to socialisation as it enables children to:
- understand verbal explanations of *what* is and is not acceptable behaviour
- understand verbal explanations of *why* certain behaviour is not acceptable
- express their own needs and feelings more clearly
- avoid conflicts when handled by sensitive adults
- reach compromises more easily
- have a positive outlet for feelings through discussion, imaginative play.

The sequence of social and emotional development

The progression of social and emotional development is similar to cognitive and language development in that there is a recognised **sequence** of development which occurs in and around particular ages depending on the children's interaction with others and their environment. For ease of reference and to assist your understanding of young children's social and emotional development the following sequence of development has been related to specific ages. Remember that children are unique individuals who develop in their own way and at their own pace depending on their individual life experiences. Note that social and emotional development have been listed *separately* to assist your observations, assessments and understanding of these two complex aspects of psychological development; but you will notice that there are *overlaps* between the two aspects.

The Sequence of Social and Emotional Development

Age 0–3 months

Social:

- cries to communicate needs to others
- stops crying to listen to others
- responds to smiles from others
- responds positively to others e.g. family members and even friendly strangers unless very upset (when only main caregiver will do!)
- considers others only in relation to satisfying own needs for food, drink, warmth, sleep, comfort and reassurance.

Emotional:

- becomes very attached to parent/carer (usually the mother)
- experiences extreme emotions e.g. very scared, very happy, or very angry; these moods change in an instant
- requires the security and reassurance of familiar routines
- may be upset by unfamiliar methods of handling and care.

Age 3–9 months

Social:

- responds positively to others, especially to familiar people such as family members; by 9 months is very wary of strangers
- communicates with others by making noises and participating in 'conversation-like' exchanges
- responds to own name
- begins to see self as separate from others

Emotional:

- has strong attachment to parent/carer (usually the mother)
- develops other attachments to people sees regularly
- by 6 or 7 months shows clear preferences for familiar adults as can differentiate between individuals
- demonstrates strong emotions through body language, gestures and facial expressions
- dislikes anger in others and becomes distressed by it

- has clear likes and dislikes e.g. will push away food, drink or toys does not want.

Age 9–18 months

Social:
- responds to simple instructions (if wants to!)
- communicates using (limited) range of recognisable words
- shows egocentric behaviour e.g. expects to be considered first; all toys belong to them
- is unintentionally aggressive to other children.

Emotional:
- likes to get own way; gets very angry when adult says 'No!'
- has emotional outbursts ('temper tantrums') when does not get own way or is otherwise frustrated e.g. unable to do activity because of physical limitations
- shows fear in new situations e.g. attending parent/toddler group, visiting somewhere new such as the farm, nature centre
- relies on parent/carer for reassurance and support in new situations
- is upset by the distress of other children (even if they caused it)
- seeks reassurance and contact with familiar adults throughout waking hours.

Age 18 months–2 years

Social:
- responds positively to others e.g. plays alongside other children and enjoys games with known adults
- communicates more effectively with others
- responds to simple instructions
- wants to help adults and enjoys imitating their activities
- may be interested in older children and their activities; imitates these activities
- may unintentionally disrupt the play of others e.g. takes toys away to play with by self
- becomes very independent e.g. wants to do things by self
- still demonstrates egocentric behaviour; wants their own way and says 'No!' a lot.

Emotional:
- begins to disengage from secure attachment e.g. wants to do things by self 'Me do it!'

- still emotionally dependent on familiar adult(s) but this leads to conflict as need for independence grows
- has mood swings e.g. clingy one moment, then fiercely independent the next
- becomes very frustrated when unable/not allowed to do a particular activity which leads to frequent but short-lived emotional outbursts ('temper tantrums')
- explores environment; even new situations are less frightening as long as parent/carer is present.

Age 2–3 years
Social:
- continues to enjoy the company of others
- wants to please and seeks approval from adults
- is still very egocentric and very protective of own possessions; unable to share with other children although may give toy to another child if *adult* requests it, but this is to please the adult and is not really sharing
- may find group experiences difficult due to this egocentric behaviour
- uses language more effectively to communicate with others.

Emotional:
- may still rely on parent/carer for reassurance in new situations or when with strangers
- still experiences emotional outbursts as independence grows and frustration at own limitations continues e.g. aggressive towards toys that cannot get to work
- begins to understand the feelings of others but own feelings are still the most important
- has very limited understanding of other people's pain e.g. if hits another child
- feels curious about their environment but has no sense of danger e.g. that they or other people can be hurt by their actions.

Age 3–4 years
Social:
- enjoys the company of others; learns to play *with* other children, not just alongside them
- uses language to communicate more and more effectively with others
- develops self-help skills e.g. dressing self, going to the toilet as becomes more competent and confident in own abilities

- still wants to please and seeks approval from adults
- observes closely how others behave and imitates them
- still fairly egocentric; may get angry with other children if disrupt play activities or snatch play items required for own play; expects adults to take *their* side in any dispute.
- gradually is able to share group possessions at nursery or playgroup.

Emotional:
- less reliant on parent/carer for reassurance in new situations so able to stay at nursery or playgroup without them
- may be jealous of adult attention given to others e.g. to younger sibling or other children in group situations
- argues with other children but is quick to forgive and forget
- has limited awareness of the feelings and needs of others
- may be quite caring towards others who are distressed
- begins to use language to express feelings and wishes
- still has emotional outbursts especially when tired, stressed or frustrated.

Age 4–5 years

Social:
- continues to enjoy the company of other children; may have special friend(s)
- uses language even more effectively to communicate, share ideas, engage in more complex play activities
- appears confident and competent in own abilities
- co-operates with others, takes turns and begins to follow rules in games
- still seeks adult approval; will even blame others for own mistakes to escape disapproval
- continues to observe how others behave and will imitate them; has a particular role model
- may copy unwanted behaviour e.g. swearing, biting, kicking to gain adult attention.

Emotional:
- becomes more aware of the feelings and needs of others
- tries to comfort others who are upset, hurt or unwell
- may occasionally be aggressive as still learning to deal with negative emotions
- uses language to express feelings and wishes
- uses imaginative play to express worries and fears over past/future experiences e.g. hospital visits, family disputes/upheaval

- has occasional emotional outbursts when tired, stressed or frustrated
- argues with other children but may take longer to forgive and forget
- confidence in self can be shaken by 'failure'
- may have an 'imaginary friend'.

Age 5–7 years

Social:

- continues to enjoy the company of other children; wants to belong to a group; may have a special friend
- uses language to communicate very effectively, but may use in negative ways e.g. name-calling or telling tales as well as positively to share ideas and participate in complex play activities often based on television characters or computer games.
- is able to play on own; appreciates own space away from others on occasion
- becomes less concerned with adult approval and more concerned with peer approval
- is able to participate in games with rules and other co-operative activities.

Emotional:

- becomes less egocentric as understands feelings, needs and rights of others
- still wants things that belong solely to them e.g. very possessive of own toys, puts own name on everything they possess!
- becomes more aware of own achievements in relation to others but this can lead to a sense of failure if feels does not measure up; hates to lose
- may be very competitive; rivalry may lead to aggressive behaviour
- argues with other children but may take even longer to forgive and forget
- has increased awareness of the wider environment e.g. the weather, plants, animals, people in other countries.

Observing and assessing children's social and emotional development

Observing these aspects of development can be difficult because it is easy to become **subjective** that is, recording our *interpretation* of what we see and hear. Interpretations may be included in the *assessment* of observations, but need to be based on accurate and **objective** information. Being objective means only recording what you actually *see* and *hear*. Observing social development requires recording the interactions between children and other people which can sometimes be influenced by our own interpretations of the events and interactions observed.

One way to ensure objectivity is to use a **chart** to record the social skills and interactions observed e.g. tick chart, pie chart or bar graph. (See diagrams on page 161/162.) This allows you to record information more accurately. Observing emotional development is even more problematic as we cannot *see* feelings. We can see the **expression** of feelings or the **reactions** to people and situations which indicate the individual's emotional responses. For example, *crying* can indicate a variety of emotional responses such as joy, relief, physical hurt or distress. Looking at the **social context** and the particular event or situation being observed should make it clearer as to which emotional response is indicated.

Examples of observation charts:

Tick chart : Group observation of children at snack/meal time

SELF-HELP SKILLS	CHILDREN'S NAMES			
	Shafik	*Sukhvinder*	*Ruth*	*Tom*
goes to the toilet				
washes hands				
dries hands				
chooses own snack/meal				
uses fingers				
uses spoon				
uses fork				
uses knife				
holds cup with 2 hands				
holds cup with 1 hand				

KEY: ✓ = competent at skill.
\ = attempts skill/needs adult direction.
✗ = no attempt/requires adult assistance.

Pie chart: Time sample observation of child's play activities

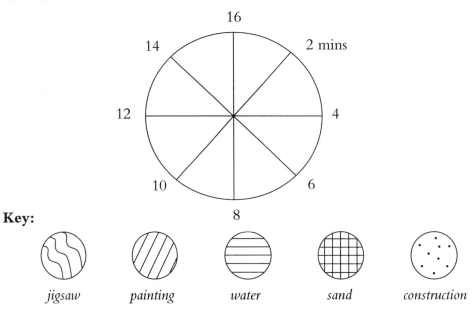

Key:

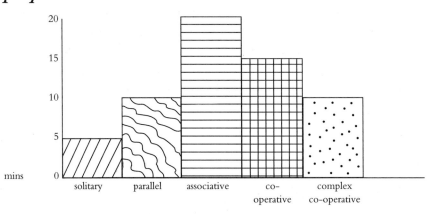

| jigsaw | painting | water | sand | construction |

Bar graph: Time sample observation of child's social play

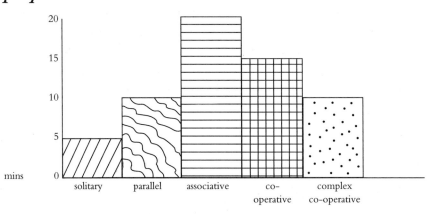

Key:

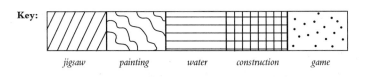

| jigsaw | painting | water | construction | game |

Social play

Play is an essential aspect of children's social and emotional development as it enables them to:

- learn and develop new social skills
- practice and improve existing social skills
- experiment with new social situations e.g. anticipate what they *might* do in new situations
- prepare for new experiences
- act out past experiences
- express emotions in positive ways.

How children interact with other children in play situations also gives adults valuable insights on children's social and emotional development. Observing children at play is a useful way of assessing children's:

- level of social interaction   • social skills   • emotional responses.

Children go through a recognised sequence of social play. Younger children tend to engage in more solitary or parallel play activities because they are more egocentric; while older children are capable of more co-operative play activities as they can take turns, share play equipment and follow rules more easily. There will be times when quite young children can be engaged happily in play activities with some interaction with other children (associative play) such as dressing-up, home corner, doing jigsaws, simple construction, painting. There will be occasions when older children become engrossed in solitary or parallel play activities with no interaction with other children, e.g. doing detailed drawings and paintings, building intricate constructions that require complete concentration to the exclusion of everyone else.

The sequence of social play

- SOLITARY PLAY: playing alone.
- PARALLEL PLAY: playing alongside other children without interaction.
- ASSOCIATIVE PLAY: playing alongside other children with limited interaction.
- CO-OPERATIVE PLAY: playing together.
- COMPLEX CO-OPERATIVE PLAY: playing together including following agreed rules.

The sequence of social play

The level of social interaction during play depends on:

- individual children
- the play activity itself
- children's previous experiences of play
- the social context.

K E Y   T A S.K

Observe the social interaction of a young child during play activities over 20-30 minutes. Indicate the social play for each activity. You could record your observation using a chart like the one shown on page 162.

NVQ Level 3 links: C.16.1 C.16.2 C.5.2 C.5.3 C.11.2 (C.14.4)
DCE links: Units 1, 4 and 6 (Unit 7)
BTEC links: Units 6, 7, 8 and 12.

Helping children to respect and care for others

Babies and very young children are naturally egocentric; they believe the world revolves around them and their wishes which makes them selfish and possessive. As children develop they begin to think and care about others as well as themselves.

This egocentric behaviour results in the need for:

- adult attention
- the *most* attention
- the *best* toys, clothes.

We have all experienced jealousy in our relationships with others e.g. with siblings, friends, neighbours, colleagues, employers. Unchecked jealousy can become a very destructive and hurtful emotion which prevents children (and adults) from developing respect and care for others. Jealousy starts at the same time as babies begin to realise they are separate from their main caregiver (usually their mother). At about 6 months old they realise they do not have their main caregiver's complete and undivided attention. The child sees the adult sharing their attention with:

- siblings, other family members or friends
- other children and adults in the early years setting.

Children will show their jealousy by:

- crying
- being clingy
- displaying attention-seeking behaviour e.g. shouting or biting
- regressing to previous levels of development.

By the age of 2 or 3 years children can share adult's attention more easily and handle their jealousy better. Young children can be extremely jealous of their own brothers and sisters as well as children outside the family. You may care for children from the same family especially if you work as a nanny, childminder or with children who are close in age and attend the same early years setting. It is important that you help children to cope with any feelings of jealousy they may have towards other children whether related to them or not.

1 *Never make comparisons between children (especially siblings)* e.g. 'You're not as quiet as your brother' or 'Why can't you behave more like the children in green group?'
2 *Encourage children to focus on their own abilities.* Emphasise co-operation and sharing rather than competition. Comparisons should be related to improving their own individual skills. Class star chart are too competitive, individual books are better.
3 *Show understanding for children's jealousy.* Children feel better when adults acknowledge their feelings. Do not make children feel guilty about being jealous.
4 *Treat children with respect and fairness.* Take children's individual needs into account; children require different amounts of adult attention at different times. Equal opportunities does not mean treating everyone exactly the same as this would mean ignoring individual needs; it means treating individuals fairly and providing the same *chances*.
5 *Reassure the children that they are accepted for who they are regardless of what they do.* Try to spend a few minutes with each child in the setting. Giving regular individual attention helps to reduce jealousy and increase children's emotional security.

Linked to young children's egocentricity is the ability to interact positively with other children. Very young children are often unable to co-operate with other children in group activities. Even school age children can find it difficult to share with others. Disputes are frequent among young children. Often these disputes are short-lived; early friendships are easily broken but just as quickly mended. Learning to deal with these disputes is an important part of children's social and emotional development. Very

young children will use physical force to maintain ownership of a toy, but by 3–4 years they begin to use language to resolve disputes e.g. 'That's mine!' By 5–6 years children continue to use language to resolve disputes and co-operate with others e.g. 'After Luke's go, it's my turn.' Older children will use language to negotiate and compromise when there are disagreements e.g. 'Let me borrow your aeroplane and you can use my train.'

We live in a highly competitive society where the media – television, magazines, newspapers – focuses our attention on being the best. Most sports and games have only one *winner* which means all the other participants are *losers*.

Competitive sports and games can be beneficial to children's social and emotional development as long as they emphasise:
- co-operation • working as a team • mutual respect
- agreeing on rules and following them • participation and the pleasure of taking part are more important than winning • doing our personal best.

Competitive play in early years settings can prepare children for the competitiveness of real life.

Young children also need opportunities to participate in co-operative activities which encourage:
- self-confidence and positive self-esteem
- relating positively to others
- working together and helping others
- making joint decisions
- full participation (no one is left out or eliminated)
- a sense of belonging.

10 Golden Rules for respecting and caring for others

1 Welcome and celebrate our differences; we are all important, valued and unique individuals.
2 Listen and be attentive to what others have to communicate.
3 Regard and value the needs and rights of others.
4 Recognise and respect the culture and beliefs of other people (whether we share them or not)
5 Be considerate and courteous towards others.

6 Help and care for each other as much as we are able.

7 Co-operate and work together to reach the best solutions.

8 Sharing and taking turns; remember compromise equals wise.

9 Praise and encourage others to raise their self-esteem.

10 Inspire respect in others through our own kindness, fairness and honesty.

KEY TASK

Plan and implement an activity which encourages young children to relate positively towards others. Evaluate the activity afterwards.

NVQ Level 3 links: M.7.2 M.7.3 M.7.4 C.5.1
DCE links: Units 2 and 4
BTEC links: Units 3, 6, 7 and 8.

Helping young children to deal with conflict situations

All young children will experience situations where they feel that life is not fair. They will have disagreements and disputes with other children. Initially children rely on adults to help resolve these disputes, but gradually they learn how to deal with these for themselves. Children need to learn how to use language to reach agreements so that as far as possible their needs and other people's can be met fairly. Children need to learn that resolving conflicts does not mean getting your own way all the time (being aggressive) or allowing others to get their own way all the time (being submissive/passive). There is a better way which allows everyone to reach a satisfactory compromise: being **assertive**.

Ways to resolve conflicts:

- Fight/Bully   = Aggressive   → 'I win so you lose'.

- Submit/Retreat   = Submissive/Passive → 'I lose because you win'.

- Discuss/Negotiate   = Assertive   → 'I win and you win'.

Point out to children that shouting or physical violence never resolves conflicts, they usually make matters worse and only demonstrate who is the

loudest or strongest or has more power. Conflicts need to be discussed in a calm manner so that a mutually agreed compromise can be reached.

EXERCISE

1 Describe how *you* have dealt with a conflict situation.
2 Look at the conflict situations listed below. Suggest how these could be resolved to achieve a 'win/win' result.

With young children you can use books, stories and short videos which depict other children in conflict situations such as:

- sharing or borrowing toys
- deciding on rules for a game or choosing a game
- choosing partners or teams fairly
- knocking over models or spoiling work *accidentally*
- disrupting other children's activities *deliberately*.

Discuss with the children afterwards:

- what caused the conflict or disagreement? • how were they resolved?
- what were the best solutions? • how would they have resolved it?

Even very young children can do this with appropriate situations and guidance from sensitive adults. Using puppets and play people can also help. Where children are used to doing role play or drama, adults can get them to act out how to resolve conflicts in peaceful ways.

Further reading

Harding, J. and Meldon-Smith, L. (2000) *How to make observations and assessments.* 2nd Edition. Hodder & Stoughton
Hobart, C. and Frankel, J. (1994) *A practical guide to child observation.* Stanley Thornes.
Matterson, E. (1989) *Play with a purpose for the under-sevens.* Penguin.
Masheder, M. (1989) *Let's play together.* Green Print.
Sheridan, M. (1987) *From birth to five years.* NFER Nelson.

10

Developing Self-reliance and Self-esteem

· ·Key Points· · · · · · · · · · · · · · · · · · · ·

- what is self-reliance?
- encouraging children's self-reliance
- what is self-esteem?
- factors affecting self-esteem
- promoting positive self-esteem
- how maturation and the development of cognitive and communication skills affect self-reliance and self-esteem

- the expression of feelings
- helping children cope with fears and phobias
- strategies for dealing with emotional outbursts

What is self-reliance?

Self-reliance involves:

- dependence on own capabilities and personal resources   • the ability to think and act for oneself   • not being dependent or relying entirely on others   • autonomy i.e. independence   • competence in looking after self   • trust in own judgement and actions   • confidence in own abilities and actions.

Children gain self-reliance by:

- developing self-help skills   • making choices and decisions   • taking responsibility for their own actions.

Children need the freedom to develop their independence in ways appropriate to their overall development. Some children may need more encouragement than others to become increasingly more independent and less reliant on other people. Most children start wanting to do things for themselves from about 18 months to 2 years onwards. Adults should encourage children's self-reliance by:

1 Providing *freedom* for children to become more independent.
2 Being *patient* and providing *time* for children to do things for themselves e.g. letting young children dress themselves takes longer, but is an essential self-help skill; with practice they will get faster so do not rush them.
3 *Praising* and *encouraging* children's efforts at becoming more independent.
4 Being *aware of children's individual needs* for independence; every child is different and requires encouragement relevant to their particular level of development. Do not insist children be self-reliant in a particular area until they are ready.
5 Being *sensitive to children's changing needs* for independence. Remember a child who is tired, distressed or unwell may require more adult assistance than usual.
6 Offering limited *choices* to make children feel more in control e.g. let them choose which bowl, cup, jumper. As children develop, increase the scope of choices.
7 Providing *opportunities for play* which encourage self-reliance e.g. dressing-up helps children learn to dress independently in a fun way.

KEY TASK

Observe a young child demonstrating their self-help skills such as:

- feeding self • going to the toilet • washing hands • getting dressed/undressed (e.g. for PE) • tidying up.

Assess the child's ability to perform the skill independently. Outline the adult's role in developing the child's self-reliance in this area.

NVQ Level 3 links: C.16.1 C.16.2 C.2.1 C.2.2 C.5.3 (C.14.1)
DCE links: Units 1, 3 and 4 (Unit 7)
BTEC links: Units 6, 7, 8 and 12.

What is self-esteem?

Self-esteem involves:
- feelings and thoughts about oneself (positive or negative) • respect or regard for self (or lack of it) • consideration of self • self-worth (i.e. value of self) • self-image (i.e. perception of self).

How we feel about ourselves depends on a number of factors:

- *who* we are with at the time
- current and past *relationships*
- the social context e.g. *where* we are
- past *experiences* (especially in early childhood).

A person's self-esteem is changeable; sometimes we feel more positive about ourselves than other times. Even if we have had past experiences which resulted in negative or poor self-esteem, we can overcome this and learn to feel more positive about ourselves.

We cannot *see* self-esteem, but we can assess children's (and adults') levels of self-esteem by their emotional responses, attitudes and actions.
People with positive or high self-esteem are usually:

- calm and relaxed
- energetic, enthusiastic and well-motivated
- open and expressive
- positive and optimistic
- self-reliant and self-confident
- assertive
- reflective e.g. aware of own strengths and weaknesses
- sociable, co-operative, friendly and trusting.

People with negative or low self-esteem tend to be:

- anxious and tense
- lacking in enthusiasm, poorly motivated and easily frustrated
- secretive and/or pretentious
- negative and pessimistic
- over-dependent, lacking in confidence and constantly seeking the approval of others; *or* over-confident, arrogant and attention seeking
- aggressive *or* passive
- self-destructive *or* abusive towards others
- resentful and distrustful of others.

Reasons for low self-esteem

Babies and very young children feel positive about themselves and what they do/do not want. As their self-reliance develops, children become more aware of their own capabilities in comparison with others and this begins to affect the way they feel about themselves.

All children begin with the *potential* for *high* self-esteem, but their interactions with others contribute to whether positive self-esteem is encouraged or diminished. Experiences in early childhood have the most significant affect on children's self-esteem; sometimes these affects may not become apparent until adolescence or adulthood when serious psychological and social problems may result due to very low self-esteem. Children (and adults) are very resilient and can learn to have greater self-esteem even if their earlier experiences were detrimental to their esteem.

Factors which lead to low self-esteem include being:

- deprived of basic needs or having these needs inadequately met. (This includes social and emotional needs as well as physical care and intellectual stimulation.)
- denied their expression of feelings or having these feelings ignored.
- put-down, ridiculed or humiliated
- coerced into participating in inappropriate activities
- made to feel that their ideas and opinions are unimportant
- denied appropriate information or explanations
- labelled (*all* labels deny a person's individuality as human personalities are too complex and diverse to be describe by a single word or phrase)
- over-protected (we all learn more through our own efforts and making our own mistakes)
- excessively disciplined (especially if labelled as *being* 'bad' or 'naughty')
- under-disciplined; lack of rules and discipline can lead to inappropriate behaviour
- exposed to inconsistent behaviour
- physically abused or threatened with violence
- sexually abused.

(Lindenfield, 1995.)

15 ways for adults to promote positive self-esteem

1 Listening calmly and attentively to children.
2 Taking time before replying to what children have to say; using prompts to encourage children to continue talking or to answer questions.
3 Encouraging children to talk about and express their feelings including anger and jealousy; reassuring children that having strong feelings is acceptable.
4 Taking an interest in children's drawings, paintings, stories and other activities.

5 Praising and encouraging children's *attempts* at activities not just the end result.

6 Showing an interest and appreciation of children's personal qualities such as kindness or humour not just their academic abilities.

7 Using language which is appropriate to the children's level of understanding without being condescending or using 'baby talk'.

8 Communicating with children *literally* at their level e.g. squatting down or sitting down so that children are not intimidated.

9 Providing a child-centred, language-rich and stimulating learning environment.

10 Responding to children's *individual* needs.

11 Providing a clear framework for behaviour and using rewards rather than punishments.

12 Encouraging children to value their individuality.

13 Encouraging children to be self-reliant by helping them to develop self-help skills and to make choices.

14 Asking children for their ideas and opinions and listening to these with respect and interest.

15 Being a positive adult role model; increasing their own self-esteem will help adults inspire feelings of self-worth in children.

How maturation and the development of cognitive and communication skills affect children's self-reliance and self-esteem

Physical maturity is important to children's self-reliance because physical skills are necessary to children's ability to do things for themselves.

Physical skills	Self-help skills
Manipulative skills and hand-eye co-ordination to hold spoon (later fork, knife), to get food to mouth; to hold cup, etc.	feeding self
Bladder and bowel control. Manipulative skills and co-ordination to pull down/up pants, wipe bottom using toilet paper.	going to the toilet

Physical skills	Self-help skills
Manipulative skills and co-ordination to put plug in/pull out, turn taps on/off, handle soap; apply face cloth.	washing hands and face
Manipulative skills to hold brush; co-ordination to clean teeth.	brushing teeth
Manipulative skills and co-ordination to take off clothes/ put them on; undo/do up buttons, zips and laces.	getting dressed/undressed
Manipulative skills and co-ordination to put toys and equipment in appropriate places.	tidying up

Encouraging children's self-reliance and developing positive self-esteem gives children the confidence to explore their environment and interact with others. This exploration stimulates physical development: gross motor skills, manipulation and co-ordination.

Cognitive development is also linked with children's self-reliance and self-esteem. Curiosity and exploration help develop children's independence. Social and cognitive development are inter-related. All learning and development takes place within a social context. Adults who provide appropriate assistance in the early years setting encourage children's learning and acquisition of social skills. Adults need to know when to reduce the level of their assistance so that children can become increasingly more independent. (See Chapter 6.)

Memory skills are also important to social and emotional development because children remember past experiences and interactions with others. Remembering past experiences helps children to:

- learn from past mistakes and so avoid repeating them
- recall skills (e.g. how to do up laces)
- recall past events and share them with others
- develop a sense of time.

Young children have a limited *understanding of time* which means they find it difficult to wait for things – they want it *now*!

Language and communication skills are essential to social development. Young children's developing ability to communicate with others assists their self-reliance. Listening to and communicating positively with young children increases their self-esteem and boosts their self-confidence in themselves and their abilities. Children who are not listened to properly or have limited/negative communication with adults may grow up to feel that what they have to say is not valued or that as a person they are not important or interesting. Children who are never listened to by their parents or carers may become withdrawn or demonstrate behavioural difficulties such as aggression or frequent emotional outbursts.

The expression of feelings

An essential aspect of children's social and emotional development is helping children to recognise and deal with their own feelings and those of other people.

Feelings can be defined as:
- an *awareness* of pleasure or pain
- physical and/or psychological *impressions*
- the *experience of emotions* such as anger, joy, fear or sorrow.

There is an enormous range of emotions that are experienced by humans as feelings. We all experience a variety of **personal emotions** which are related to our individual perceptions of and responses to ourselves and our life experiences. We also experience **interpersonal** emotions which affect the way we relate to other people and how they respond to us.

In British society we are encouraged to keep our feelings to ourselves. Males are discouraged from showing sensitive emotions; females are discouraged from demonstrating aggressive emotions. Babies and very young children naturally demonstrate clearly how they feel by crying, shouting, rejecting objects. They will openly show affection and other emotions such as jealousy or anger. Young children do not understand that others can be physically or *emotionally* hurt by what they say or do. Gradually, children become conditioned to accept that the feelings and needs of others *do* matter. We need to ensure that children do not forget their own feelings and emotional needs by becoming too concerned with the feelings of others or trying to please others. This can be a particular problem for females in a male dominated society. Children need to know that it is natural to feel a wide range of emotions and that it is acceptable to express strong feelings such as love and anger openly as long as they do so in positive and appropriate ways.

Adults should encourage children to:
- identify and name their own feelings • express these feelings in positive ways • recognise feelings in other people • deal with emotional responses from others in appropriate ways • deal with conflict situations.

Adults can help young children to do these by using:
- **books, stories and poems** about feelings and common events experienced by other children to help them recognise and deal with these in their own lives
- **creative activities** to provide positive outlets for feelings e.g. pummelling clay to express anger; painting/drawing pictures or writing stories and poems which reflect their feelings about particular events/experiences
- **physical and/or outdoor play** involving vigorous physical activity which allows a positive outlet for anger or frustration
- **imaginative play** activities to act out feelings e.g. jealousy over new baby; worries over past experiences; fears about future events such as visit to dentist, hospital.

Imaginative play enables young children to:
- *release emotional tension/frustration or expression of feelings* such as anger or jealousy in positive ways e.g. jealousy over a new baby can be expressed by shouting at a teddy or doll
- *practise and rehearse real-life situations* e.g. domestic play, playing/imitating 'mum' or 'dad'; later imitates other role models such as carers, teachers, characters from television, books; shop play including post office, hairdressers, café where can explore other roles.
- *look and feel things from another person's viewpoint* e.g. pretending to be someone else helps children to understand what it is like to be that person and encourages empathy and consideration for others
- *share ideas and co-operate with other children* e.g. play with small-scale toys (such as dolls' houses or farm animals) and vehicle play where children can act out previous experiences or situations while sharing ideas and equipment with other children; this can also help them establish early friendships

- *develop communication skills to interact more effectively with others*; puppets are a useful way of providing children with a 'voice' and may encourage shy/withdrawn children to express themselves more easily
- *overcome fears and worries about new experiences or people* e.g. pretending to visit the dentist, clinic, optician or hospital; changing the home corner into a health centre or hospital can provide for this type of play
- *feel important and powerful* e.g. pretending to be television super-heroes, characters from games consoles, kings and queens, parents, carers and teachers allows children to experiment with being powerful and in control
- *feel more secure by being able to temporarily regress to earlier development* e.g. pretending to be a baby while other children act as parents.

EXERCISE

Describe how you would set up a pretend or imaginative play area based on the following themes:

1 home corner   2 shopping   3 health centre or hospital   4 post office
5 café

Draw diagrams of the play areas and list the resources required. Remember equal opportunities.

Helping children to cope with fears and phobias

All children feel frightened or worried sometimes.

A **fear** is: – an emotion caused by a real or imagined danger;
           – a feeling of anxiety caused by the anticipation of danger.
A **phobia** is: – an irrational fear
           – a fear or hatred of a specific object(s) resulting in avoiding behaviour.

While phobias are extremely rare among young children, fears are a common aspect of their social and emotional development. Childhood fears can be very upsetting for the children experiencing them and the adults helping the children to cope with these fears. Learning how to overcome fears helps to build self-confidence. Most childhood fears are due to children's:

- *reactions* from previous frightening experiences
- *expectations* concerning the unknown or new experiences
- *observations* of other people's responses to situations/experiences.

Being aware of your own fears and how you deal with them, will help your understanding of young children's fears and helping them to cope. Most children copy the reactions of other children or adults when responding to potentially frightening situations/experiences. Recognising your own fears may stop you passing them onto the children in your setting.

Common childhood fears include being frightened of loud noises, water, animals, insects and the dark.

Ten tips for helping children to cope with their fears

1 Recognise and acknowledge the child's fear.
2 Listen to children when they express their fears.
3 Do not pass on your own fears. Hiding your own fears is not the answer; instead acknowledge your own fears but show children positive ways of coping with them.
4 Do not rationalise irrational fears.
5 Remain calm and act confidently.
6 Reassure and comfort the child when they are frightened.
7 Let children have comforters such as cuddly toy or transition object (see Chapter 12).
8 Let children keep their distance from whatever frightens them; encourage them to get closer at their own pace.
9 Never force a child to do something or face their fear before they are ready.
10 Prepare children for potentially frightening experiences in advance.

Remember most childhood fears pass as quickly as they come; these fears disappear of their own accord without any need for special help. Very rarely a fear becomes so severe that it dominates the child's life. A child's fear may be developing into a phobia if it:

- causes major disruption to the child's life
- necessitates rituals e.g. checking under the bed several times
- restricts behaviour so that child avoids situations in case fear is present

- widens to include more fears e.g. not just dogs but all animals
- distorts perceptions of reality.

Children with phobias need specialist help. Suggest their parents discuss this with their GP who will refer the child to a child psychologist.

KEY TASK

Devise a routine for dealing with a young child who is emotionally upset:

- helping a child to deal with strong feelings such as anger or jealousy.
- helping a child to cope with a childhood fear.

NVQ Level 3 links: C.5.4 (M.8.1) (C.14.2) (C.14.4)
DCE links: Units 2, 3 and 4 (Unit 7)
BTEC links: Units 3, 6, 7 and 8.

Strategies for dealing with children's emotional outbursts

Sometimes young children are overwhelmed by their emotions and will act inappropriately or regress to previous patterns of behaviour. Before children are able to use language to express their feelings, they are more prone to demonstrate their emotional responses in physical ways e.g. biting, scratching, kicking, shouting, screaming, throwing things, throwing themselves on the floor, etc. These emotional outbursts or 'temper tantrums' can be very frightening to the child and other children present. Adults too can find children's emotional outbursts difficult to deal with. It is essential that adults:

- remain calm; speak quietly but confidently, shouting will only make things worse
- ignore the emotional outburst as much as possible while maintaining the children's safety
- avoid direct confrontations
- give the child time and space to calm down
- reassure the child afterwards but do not reward them
- when the child has calmed down talk about what upset them in a quiet manner

- suggest to the child what they could do instead if they feel this way again.

The best way to deal with emotional outbursts is to minimise the likelihood of them happening in the first place:

- Avoid setting up situations where emotional outbursts are likely to happen e.g. making unrealistic demands or doing complex activities when a child is tired.
- Give advance warning e.g. prepare child for new experiences; give 5 minute warning that activity is coming to an end and that you want them to do something else.
- Provide reasonable choices and alternatives to give child a sense of responsibility and control e.g. choice of activity to do next; choice of materials.
- Make potential problem situations more fun and interesting to engage child's attention and co-operation e.g. use toys to make bath time or journeys more exciting.
- Encourage children to express their feelings in more positive ways.

EXERCISE

1 Outline your setting's policy for dealing with children's emotional outbursts.
2 Describe how *you* have dealt with a young child's emotional outburst.

Further reading

Goleman, D. (1996) *Emotional intelligence*. Bloomsbury.
Houghton, D. and McColgan, M. (1995) *Working with children*. Collins Educational.
Lindenfield, G. (1995) *Self esteem*. Thorsons.
Woolfson, R. (1989) *Understanding your child: a parents' guide to child psychology*. Faber and Faber.

11

Developing a Positive Self-image and Identity

•••••••••••••••••••••••••••Key Points•••••••••••••••••••••••

- what are self-image and identity?
- the development of self-image and identity
- factors influencing self-image and identity
- reasons for poor self-image
- self-fulfilling prophecy
- encouraging children to feel positive about themselves and their identity
- children with special needs
- awareness of gender, racial and cultural stereotypes
- promoting equal opportunities and avoiding stereotypes
- activities and experiences which help children to explore their self-image and identity in positive ways.

What are self-image and identity?

The development of self-image and identity are strongly linked to self-esteem. Self-image and identity can be defined as:

- the individual's view of their own personality and abilities
- the individual's *perception* of how other people view them and their abilities.

This involves recognising:

- ourselves as *separate* individuals
- we are *unique* individuals with characteristics and abilities that make us separate and different from others
- the factors which influence how we *identify with* other people e.g. gender, culture, race, nationality, religion, language, social status/occupation, disability/special needs, early experiences and relationships.

Adults working with young children need to be aware of their *own* self-image/identity and the importance of having positive self-esteem. Adults may need to deal with issues regarding their own self-image/identity and to raise their own level of self-esteem before they can help develop children's positive self-image/identity.

Think about your own self-image and identity.

1 How do you view your own personality and abilities? Write down 5 positive things about yourself.
2 Consider the factors influencing self-image and identity. Make a list related to your own identity (e.g. male or female, full or part-time student, British, etc.) How do you think these factors influence your identity and the way you *think* other people see you? (e.g. some people may consider a female studying child care is appropriate for a woman, but a male studying child care may be regarded differently).

The development of self-image and identity

Children develop their self-image/identity through interactions with others starting with family members and gradually including carers, teachers, friends, school mates. Through positive interactions, children learn to value themselves and their abilities *if* they receive approval, respect and empathy.

Reasons for poor self-image and identity

Early childhood experiences and relationships may have positive or negative influences on children's self-image/identity.

Children with positive self-image and high self-esteem:
- tend to come from homes where they are regarded as significant and interesting people
- have their views invited and listened to
- have parents/carers with high, but reasonable and consistent expectations
- receive firm discipline based on rewards and sanctions not physical punishment.

Children with negative or poor self-image and low self-esteem:
- tend to come from homes where no one takes any real interest in them

- have parents/carers with limited, negative or unreasonable expectations
- are given little consistent guidance and/or care
- receive too little discipline or overly strict discipline or a confusing mixture of the two.

In early years settings, especially schools, young children become very aware that certain levels of performance are expected by adults and begin to compare their own achievements with that of other children. If children regularly feel that their achievements do not compare favourably with those of other children, then they begin to experience a sense of failure and inferiority. Children may react to this feeling by:

- passively accepting that they are a failure and being reluctant to attempt new activities; *or*
- rebelling against and rejecting all activities that remind them of failure.

Children may respond to their perceived lack of achievement/success by demonstrating attention-seeking behaviour such as: tears, sulks, emotional outbursts, or aggressive behaviour.

Research suggests that children have high, medium or low self-esteem (Fontana, 1984). Self-esteem is an important indicator of children's self-image and identity.

Children with high self-esteem:

- have a positive self-image • are active, confident and expressive
  • are willing to participate in a wide range of activities
  • communicate effectively with others • can accept criticisms more easily • can accurately assess their own abilities • have good exam and/or career prospects.

Children with medium self-esteem:
- have reasonable positive self-image • have many of the same qualities as children with high self-esteem • tend to be more anxious to gain adult approval • desire peer approval and are therefore easily lead by others.

Children with low self-esteem:
- have poor or negative self-image • tend to feel isolated • may be

shy and/or withdrawn   ● may feel anxious and self-conscious   ● can be reluctant to participate in activities or conversations   ● are very sensitive to criticism   ● tend to under-estimate their own abilities.

Research shows that intelligence or physical attractiveness are *not* factors in children's self-esteem; very intelligent or attractive children may still have poor self-esteem and self-image. **The main reason for poor self-image and low self-esteem is the treatment which children receive from their parents** (Fontana, 1984).

However, it is not just parents who influence children's self-image and self-esteem. **All adults who work with young children influence children's self-image and identity through their attitudes, words and actions; this includes teachers, and nursery nurses.** Adults can encourage children to have a positive view of themselves and their abilities by:

● praising and encouraging children's efforts as well as achievements
● demonstrating that children are valued and important by listening to children's ideas/views
● taking an active interest in children's activities.

Other factors such as gender, race, culture, nationality, disability/special needs may also have positive or negative influences on an individual's self-image and identity. See chart below.

Influences	Positive	Negative
Gender	Positive role models showing that gender does not matter in terms of jobs, etc. Feeling secure and confident as a strong woman; sensitive, caring man. Both men and women should be assertive.	Poor role models e.g. passive women; aggressive men. Stereotyped images in the media. Experience of sexual discrimination e.g. not allowed to do things because of gender; restricted choices in play.
Race	Positive role models e.g. Black, Asian, etc. Race should not matter in terms of jobs, etc.	Experiences of prejudice due to skin colour; racial discrimination. Stereotypes; restricted choices.

Influences	Positive	Negative
Culture	Clear cultural identity. Pride in cultural heritage. Celebration of festivals. Pride in dress and other symbols of culture. Acceptance from others.	Experiences of prejudice due to culture. Stereotyped images in the media. Restricted choices. Ridicule over dress and food.
Language	Pride in home language(s), dialect, or accent. Being encouraged to communicate with others. Being spoken to in positive ways.	Experiences of ridicule due to different language, dialect or accent. Limited or restricted communication with others.
Nationality	In Britain, a clear sense of identity usually includes being *British* regardless of race and culture. Pride in nationality without feeling superior. Welcoming people of other nationalities.	Feeling isolated from society if not part of white British majority. Restricted choices/discrimination e.g. immigration laws. Excessive pride in nationality, no acceptance of others who are 'inferior'.
Social status	Having high expectations for life – e.g. education, relationships, jobs – regardless of family background. Equal opportunities in terms of education, occupations, etc.	Having low expectations for life e.g. education, relationships, jobs if considered to be 'working class' or from 'disadvantaged' backgrounds. Limited/restricted choices in terms of education, occupations, etc.
Disability/ Special Needs	Recognition as an individual not a condition e.g. child with autism not autistic child. Positive role models;	Stereotyped images in the media. Being labelled rather than seen as an individual. Restricted or limited choices. Being

Influences	Positive	Negative
	recognising everyone's potential; having high expectations. Being encouraged to get the 'able' world to adapt to their needs not the other way round.	viewed as 'handicapped'. Being seen as disabled and having to adapt to fit into the 'able' world.
Religion	Belief in own faith (or not) and freedom to worship. Knowledge and tolerance of other people's religions even if do not share or accept their beliefs. Respect for all places of worship.	Ignorance or intolerance of other people's beliefs leading to discrimination or persecution. Disrespect for places of worship (including vandalism of such places).

Beware of self-fulfilling prophecies!

Children's perceptions of themselves and their abilities are influenced by other people's expectations. If children are aware of these expectations, they often behave in ways which fulfil these expectations. The expectations become true *only* because they were made in the first place. This is called **self-fulfilling prophecy** which means:

- an inaccurate or inappropriate expectation which influences a person's behaviour so that the expectation becomes fact.

The cycle of expectation:

1 Adult forms inaccurate expectation of child's behaviour.
2 Adult's behaviour changes towards the child.
3 The child notices change in adult's behaviour.
4 Child believes in adult's expectation.
5 Child responds according to adult's expectation.
6 Child's behaviour deteriorates.
7 Adult's expectation confirmed.
8 Adult forms further inaccurate expectations of child's behaviour.

Research suggests that children from disadvantaged backgrounds or from ethnic minorities (especially Black children) are more likely to have emotional and behavioural difficulties and/or be excluded from school. Having such backgrounds is *not* the cause of their difficulties; there are other more important factors:

- the way society views children from disadvantaged or ethnic minorities
- adults' expectations for such children e.g. carers, teachers, social workers.

Adult expectations influence not only children's self-image and self-esteem, but children's *potential* achievements. Higher expectations of children make it more likely that the children *will* succeed.

Adults working with young children have to make frequent judgements about children's achievements in comparison with other children. Adults must be *aware* of this social context, where the emphasis is on competition and 'good' academic results and *beware* of its affects on the expectations for children. Assessment, both formal and informal, creates labels for children which can affect adult expectations; such labelling may affect children adversely for years to come.

A **social constuctivist** approach to children's development and learning views children as being active participants in the structuring of their own identities. A social constructivist perspective could help avoid negative adult expectations of children and their abilities (i.e. self-fulfilling prophecies) in the following ways:

1 By creating awareness of the effects of adult expectations e.g. adults need to be aware of bias within the early years setting (and society as a whole) and to avoid stereotypical assumptions.
2 By working within the cultural and social context of the setting e.g. *use* the children's backgrounds positively; know that limitations exist, but *use* them to advantage even with the constraints of the national curriculum.
3 By actively promoting equal opportunities (see page 193).
4 By using the children's own perceptions of themselves e.g. acknowledging their personal views of their individual capabilities; using friendship/temperament groups instead of ability groups (see page 24); giving children more choice over their activities and involving them in decisions.

EXERCISE

List ways in which you think your setting promotes positive self-image/identity.

10 ways to encourage young children to feel positive about themselves:

1   Treat every child as an individual. Each child has unique abilities and needs. Help them to maximise their individual potential.
2   Be positive by using praise and encouragement to help children focus on what they are good at. Point out all the things which make each child special.
3   Encourage children to measure their achievements by comparing them to *own* efforts.
4   Have high but realistic expectations of *all* children. Remember *nothing succeeds like success* so provide appropriate activities which are challenging but allow children the opportunities to succeed.
5   Take an interest in children's efforts as well as achievements. Remember the way children participate in activities is as important as the end results e.g. sharing resources, helping others, contributing ideas.
6   Encourage children to engage in a variety of activities in the setting/local environment.
7   Give children opportunities to make decisions and choices. Letting children participate in decision-making, even in a small way, helps them to feel positive and important; it also teaches them how to make appropriate judgements and sensible decisions later on.
8   Challenge stereotypical assumptions about children with special needs or from ethnic minorities. Focus on the child as an individual *not* on their special need, disability or ethnic background.
9   Promote equality of opportunity by providing positive images of children and adults through books, stories, songs.
10 Be consistent about rules and discipline within the setting. Children need consistency and a clearly structured framework for behaviour so that they know what is expected of them. Remember to label the behaviour not the child as this is less damaging to their self-image e.g. 'That was an unkind thing to say' rather than 'You are unkind'. (There is more on behaviour in Chapter 13.)

Some children may experience difficulties in developing a positive self-image and identity. For example:

- children with special needs
- children who are/have been abused
- children who are HIV positive
- children from ethnic minorities.

These children may be experiencing prejudice and/or discrimination on a regular basis which affects their ability to maintain a positive self-image or identity. By praising *all* children and encouraging them to feel good about themselves and their achievements, adults can help *all* children to establish and maintain a positive self-image/identity.

Children with special needs

All children have individual needs, but some children have special or additional needs which mean that they may require:

- special equipment or resources
- modified surroundings e.g. wheelchair access, ramps
- a special or modified curriculum.

Twenty per cent of children within early years setting have some kind of special need:

- physical disability
- learning difficulty
- emotional or behavioural problem.

Early years settings often play a crucial role in the identification and assessment of young children with special needs. It is now established policy to integrate children with special needs within mainstream settings wherever possible. This integration means that children with special needs may not feel so isolated from other children because:

- they are part of the mainstream education system and have access to the same educational opportunities
- they are able to have their needs identified, assessed and provided for as soon as possible to avoid/decrease potential difficulties (but beware early labelling)
- it discourages stereotypical views of people with disabilities or learning difficulties
- it encourages other children to view children with special needs in positive ways.

Gender stereotypes

Even very young children are aware of gender identity. Research shows that by 2½ years, children *think* girls prefer to play with dolls and engage in domestic activities with mum while boys prefer to play with cars or construction toys and helping dad! By 5 years gender identity is clearly established, children *think*:

- girls are more easily hurt • boys are stronger than girls • girls are more polite • boys fight more • girls are more open about showing their feelings • boys are more capable.

It is disturbing that such young children have developed these stereotyped views on gender.

The origins of these perceived differences between the behaviour/temperament of boys and girls can be difficult to work out, because social conditioning begins from birth especially with regard to the expectations for female and male behaviour. These expectations are reinforced throughout childhood by parents, siblings, other family members, as well as by other adults and children in the following ways:

- clothes • toys given • comments on behaviour • expectations in play and learning.

Stereotyped gender expectations are also reinforced through:

- advertising • television programmes • magazines/comic • books

Despite the general acceptance of equal opportunities as an important aspect of modern, western society, gender differences of behaviour and social/emotional expectations are still very apparent:

- most carers and teachers of young children are *women*
- the top jobs in education and most other occupations are done by men
- the majority of women are still responsible for child care in the home (whether they work outside the home or not)
- most men do significantly less around the home than women.

Gender stereotyping is especially damaging to the self-image and identity of girls because it can lessen their confidence and lower their self-esteem. Boys too can be limited by gender stereotypes by being forced to behave in tough or less caring ways in order to conform and be accepted by others.

Adults should:

1 Be aware of social and cultural expectations for boys and girls e.g. gender stereotypes in the media, literature and everyday life.
2 Give children the opportunities to play with a wide variety of toys and games.
3 Provide role play opportunities including dressing-up clothes which allow children to explore different roles.
4 Encourage children to participate in everyday activities around the setting; do not let just the girls tidy up or give out the milk/juice.
5 Avoid books and games which demonstrate gender stereotypes.
6 Use stories, films and television programmes which promote positive images.
7 Ensure that neither boys nor girls think they are superior to the other sex.
8 Expect the same standards of behaviour from both boys and girls.

Racial and cultural stereotypes

Even very young children are aware of racial differences and racial prejudices. Young children are influenced by images, ideas and attributes which create prejudice and lead to discrimination or disadvantage. Research shows that by 3 years old children can differentiate between skin colours and allocate different values to them e.g. light skin colour is positively valued, while dark skin colour is less respected. Research also shows that by the age of 5 years, many white children believe black people are inferior; while many black children believe that they are viewed with less respect than white people. Children are not born with these attitudes; they *learn* them. Adults in early years settings have an essential part to play in promoting children's positive attitudes towards themselves, other people and cultures. Being proud of one's own identity is not the same as thinking you are superior to others.

Adults working with young children must not have stereotyped views about children's potential or have low expectations of children from particular ethnic or cultural groups. Many ethnic minority families have a strong commitment to education and their children's academic progress.

Different child-rearing practices are evident in different cultures, but differences are also apparent in different families within the same culture.

Adults need to:

- recognise and eliminate racial discrimination
- maximise children's motivation and potential by encouraging them to feel a positive sense of identity within the setting in an environment which reflects themselves and their cultures in positive ways.

Promoting equal opportunities and avoiding stereotypes

It is important to select and provide resources which:

- promote positive images and non-stereotypical views of people
- provide positive role models for children within the setting.

Children need positive role models which counteract the stereotyped images in our society as demonstrated through the media especially television. Children need to see examples of:

- Black/Asian people and women from all ethnic groups in prominent roles in society e.g. politicians, doctors, lawyers, business people, teachers.
- Black/Asian people's past contributions to politics, medicine, science, education, etc. Look at important historical figures like Martin Luther King, Mahatma Gandhi, Mary Seabrook.
- people with disabilities participating fully in society.

Activities and experiences which help children to explore their self-image and identity in positive ways

1 Books and stories about real-life situations with children and adults the children within the setting can identify with.
2 Posters, pictures, photographs, displays, jigsaws, puzzles, toys and other learning materials which reflect positive images of race, culture, gender and disability.
3 Activities which encourage children to look at their physical appearance in a positive light e.g. games looking in mirrors; self-portraits (ensuring paints provided for all skin tones); drawing round each other to create life-size portraits.
4 Activities which encourage children to focus on their skills and abilities

Self-potraits by reception children

in positive ways e.g. 'I can . . .' tree with leaves showing positive
statements about what each child *can* do.

5 Activities which encourage children to express their likes and dislikes,
plus confidence in their own name and who they are e.g. circle games
such as *The name game* where each child takes it in turn to say 'My
name is . . . and I like to . . . because . . .' or *Circle jump* where each child
takes a turn at jumping into the circle, making an action which they feel
expresses them and saying 'Hello, I'm . . .'; then the rest of the children
copy the action and reply 'Hello . . . [repeating the child's name]'.

6 Sharing experiences about themselves and their families through topics
like *All about me* and by inviting family members such as
parents/grandparents to come into the setting to talk about themselves
and their backgrounds.

7 Providing opportunities for imaginative/role play which encourages
children to explore different roles in positive ways e.g. dressing-up
clothes, cooking utensils, dolls, puppets, which reflect different cultures.

8 Visiting local shops, businesses and community groups that reflect the
cultural diversity of the setting and the local community.

9 Inviting visitors into the setting to talk positively about their roles and
lives e.g.

- (female) police officer or fire fighter
- (male) nurse

- people with disabilities
- people from ethnic minorities

(**Note**: Avoid tokenism; include these visitors as part of on-going topics or themes within the setting.)

10 Celebrating cultural diversity by celebrating the major festivals of the faiths in the local community; comparing similarities and differences between religions e.g. the festivals of light include Diwali (Hindu), Channuka (Jewish), Christmas (Christian); sharing food such as different types of bread (naan, chapati, soda); looking at clothes and why different cultures dress differently (e.g. tradition, religion, climate).

11 Valuing language diversity by displaying welcome signs and other information in community languages. Language and culture are central to children's self-image and identity. (See Chapter 2 for more information.)

K E Y   T A S K

1 Compile a resource pack which promotes equal opportunities and helps young children to explore their self-image and identity in positive ways. Include information and resources from the local community as well as materials you have made yourself. You might include the following:

- posters and wall charts
- photographs and pictures
- booklets and leaflets
- suggested activities
- copies of worksheets, work cards, etc.
- book list of relevant children's books and stories
- list of useful organisations and addresses.

2 Plan, implement and evaluate at least one activity suggested in your resource pack.

NVQ Level 3 links: C.5.5 C.5.2 C.5.3
DCE links: Unit 4
BTEC links: Unit 6, 7, 8 and 12.

Further reading

Masheder, M. (1989) *Let's play together.* Green Print.

Massey, I. (1991) *More than skin deep: developing anti-racist multicultural education in schools.* Hodder & Stoughton.

Sirjai-Blatchford, I. (1994) *The early years: laying the foundations for racial equality.* Trentham Books.

Yeo, A. and Lovell, T. (1998) *Sociology for childhood studies.* Hodder & Stoughton.

12

Transitions: Adjusting to New Settings and Situations

·······················Key Points·····················

- attachment theory
- the effects of separation
- early years care and education
- preparation for new settings and situations
- transition objects
- activities and strategies for settling into new settings
- exchanging information with parents

Attachment theory and the effects of separation

John Bowlby's theory was that to ensure a child's mental health the child required a continuous relationship with *one* mother or mother-substitute. If not the child would be psychological damaged by the deprivation experienced. Bowlby believed there was a parallel between the animal instinct for *imprinting* and the human need for *attachment* between mother and child. This belief was a firm foundation of Bowlby's theory of **maternal deprivation**. An important concept in Bowlby's theory of maternal deprivation is **attachment theory** which suggests that the mother-baby attachment is unique and unlike any other relationship the child may have with another person. This instinctive attachment which a child has to one mother-figure is described as **monotropism**.

Bowlby's theories have been strongly criticised as children are able to form many attachments/distinct relationships with other family members and day care staff. The term maternal deprivation has been described as unsatisfactory. Michael Rutter disagrees with the term maternal deprivation as stated by Bowlby because children can experience deprivation in other ways not just through separation from their mothers; children can also experience maternal deprivation within the family setting even if the mother is actually present (Rutter, 1972).

Instead Michael Rutter prefers these definitions of deprivation:

1 **Privation** – the child has no opportunity to form secure attachments/relationships.
2 **Disruption** – the child experiences broken attachments/relationships due to death or other separation.
3 **Distortion** – the child experiences distorted family relationships due to marital discord, inconsistent treatment or any form of abuse.

According to Bowlby separation from their mothers causes intense distress in young children particularly in the critical period between the ages of 7 months and 3 years. This distress sets up a chain of events: distress → protest → despair → emotional detachment.

Following reunion with their mothers detachment may still continue leading to contradictory feelings towards their mothers alternating between being clingy and hostile. Bowlby believed that continued and persistent periods of this sort of separation caused permanent psychological damage. Although young children do experience distress when first separating from their mother when starting nursery or school, it is short-lived and has no lasting affect on children's psychological development. Long-term effects *have* been found in children in residential care; teachers' reports indicate behavioural problems in such children with effects including:

- extreme need for adult attention
- difficulties in making friendships with peers (Tizard, 1991).

These effects can also be apparent in young children who have been mothered at home where they are used to one-to-one with their mother and so sometimes find it difficult to be a part of a group e.g. in nursery or school. Research shows that children who have attended nursery/playgroup or been cared for by a relative/childminder before they start school are often:

- more independent
- better able to interact with their peers
- more willing to share and co-operate with other children
- more sociable towards unfamiliar people
- less timid or shy.

However, there was no difference in the percentage of behavioural difficulties between children cared for by their mothers and children who have attended day care prior to nursery or school.

Bowlby's theory suggests that any family no matter how 'bad' provides children with the care they need so that they do not experience maternal deprivation; children in 'good' residential care do less well than children in 'bad' homes. Rutter suggests that children in 'bad' families are suffering distortion; the children are still experiencing deprivation even though they remain in the family setting. Children can experience violence, cruelty or neglect at the hands of their mothers (and fathers); many children can and do receive better care away from their biological parents in foster homes, small residential homes or with adoptive parents.

The strange situation

This is a common psychological test to see if children have a secure/insecure attachment with their mothers. The child is put in a strange room with mother, the mother goes away, then a stranger comes in, the stranger leaves, finally the mother returns. The children's reactions to these events are used to determine the child's emotional security. However, in this strange situation test children of working mothers are not distressed about being in a strange place or by their mothers leaving or by being comforted by the stranger because they have experienced these events before e.g. being left at nursery or with a childminder, etc. This does not mean that these children have insecure attachments to their mothers. The children's reactions are because they are more independent (Tizard, 1991.)

The social and cultural context

The theory of maternal deprivation is related to social, cultural and even political ideas. Bowlby's theory of maternal deprivation was established in the 1950s following post-World War 2 anxieties concerning the care of children in residential nurseries; it was also politically motivated by the fact that when men returned from the war they wanted the jobs back that had been done by women during the war. Many women had enjoyed being part of the work force and were reluctant to give up their freedom and status. Women were made to feel guilty about going out to work; the theory of maternal deprivation effectively black-mailed women into staying at home for the sake of their children's psychological well-being.

In Britain today, women are still viewed as children's primary caregivers. Women who work, especially if their children are under five years old, are seen by many as not being maternal (Stoppard, 1990). Many people still feel that women with children should stay at home and not go out to work.

This is reflected in the lack of adequate, affordable child care facilities for working mothers in many areas. In the short-term, it can be cheaper for the government to encourage mothers (in two-parent families) to stay at home looking after their own children than to provide government funded child care for the under-fives, especially in times of high unemployment. Single parents (mostly mothers) on the other hand are encouraged to work and offered financial help towards child care costs.

Different cultures have different attitudes towards child-rearing and the role of women as primary care-givers. For example, the *kibbutz* model in Israel where everyone shares work/chores equally including child care. In Scandinavian countries a high proportion of young children are in child care facilities provided through government funding and both parents have access to paid parental leave to enable them to spend more time with their children.

Children do not have to be cared for solely by their mothers; there is strong cross-cultural evidence that a child can make strong and secure attachments with five or more 'caretakers' (Woodhead, 1991).

Bowlby himself recognised that the *amount* of time children spend with their mothers is not the crucial factor; it is the *quality* of the time spent together, not the *quantity*. *Quality* is also the key factor in children's other attachments. There is no evidence that quality day care has a detrimental affect on young children and it is unlikely that young children will suffer psychological damage because their mothers work (Tizard, 1991). This has important implications for the relevance of maternal deprivation theory to early years care and education.

Transitions in early years care and education

A transition involves the transfer of a child from one care setting to another:

- from home to nursery, playgroup or school
- from home to childminder
- from nursery or playgroup to school
- from one year group to another e.g. reception to Year 1; Year 1 to Year 2
- from Key Stage 1 (infants) to Key stage 2 (juniors).

Sometimes a transition involves only a change in carer e.g. a nanny working in the child's own home.

Transitions involve change, separation and loss; so young children need:

- help to prepare for such transitions
- help to accept transitions and settle into new settings
- reassurance from adults to maintain their feelings of stability, security and trust
- adult assistance to adjust to different social rules and social expectations
- help in adapting to group situations.

Young children may experience transitions in a variety of settings for a variety of reasons. There are four main types:

1 **Early years settings** where children under eight receive care and education provided by qualified staff on a full or part time basis day time only. These include: day nurseries; pre-school playgroups; nursery schools and classes; Key Stage 1 in primary schools (Infants); before and after school clubs/holiday schemes.
2 **Other child care arrangements** where children receive care/education on a full or part time basis in a family setting which is provided by adults who may or may not have child care qualifications and/or experience. These include: relatives; childminders; nannies; mothers' help; au pairs.
3 **Residential care** where children are cared for day and night on a temporary or permanent basis. These include: foster homes; children's homes; boarding schools; hostels (e.g. for holidays or respite care).
4 **Hospitals** where children receive care, education and medical attention day and night usually on a temporary basis. These include: children's wards/hospitals; hospices for children; respite care for children with severe disabilities.

KEY TASK

Observe a young child in a situation which may be stressful e.g.

- child's first day/week at nursery or school
- child who finds it difficult when parent leaves the setting
- child meeting a visitor or unfamiliar adult in the setting.

In your assessment include the following:

- the child's level of social interaction (e.g. communication)
- the child's behaviour (e.g. was the child co-operative, disruptive?)
- the child's emotional responses
- suggest ways to make this type of situation less stressful for the child.

NVQ Level 3 links: C.16. 1 C.16.2 C.5.1 C.5.2 C.5.4 (C.14.2) (C.14.4)
DCE links: Units 1, 3 and 4 (Unit 7)
BTEC links: Units 6, 7, 8 and 12.

Preparing children for new settings and situations

Children's responses to transitions often depends on the way they are prepared for the new setting or situation. The need for preparation was not recognised in the past; children started school or went into hospital and were left to cope with the situation with little or no preparation beforehand and parental involvement was positively discouraged.

EXERCISE

Can you remember your first day at school? What was it like?
Describe how you were prepared for this new situation.

Many children experience anxiety and stress when they first attend a new setting due to:

- separation from their parent or previous care-giver.
- encountering an unfamiliar group of children who may have established friendships.
- the length of time spent in the setting e.g. 8.00am to 6.00pm in a day nursery or 9.00am to 3.30pm in school.
- differences in culture and language of the setting to child's previous experiences.
- unfamiliar routines and rules.
- worry about doing the wrong thing.
- activities such as PE, playtime, lunch time or even story time which may be unfamiliar.
- the unfamiliar physical environment which may seem overwhelming and scary.

- difficulties in following more structured activities and adult directions.
- concentrating on activities for longer than previously used to.

To alleviate some of this anxiety and stress, preparation is now seen as an essential part of successful transitions in most settings including nurseries, schools, childminders, foster care and hospitals. Most settings have established procedures for preparing children for such transitions.

Prepare babies and very young children (0–2 years) for transitions

- talk to the parents and children about what is going to happen
- obtain detailed information from the parents so that the children's individual needs can be identified, this includes the baby's existing daily routine, eating and sleeping patterns; likes/dislikes regarding food, toys; as well as emergency contact numbers, medical history e.g. allergies, asthma, eczema.
- provide information pack/brochure about the setting for the parents
- arrange introductory visits for the children and their parents
- plan appropriate activities for the first few days/weeks which provide reassurance to both children and parents
- organise a key worker system so that the children can establish a one-to-one relationship with a specific person in the setting especially in the settling-in period.

Prepare older children (2–7 years) for transitions

- talk to the children and explain what is going to happen
- listen to the children and reassure them that it will be fine
- read relevant books, stories and poems about transitions e.g. starting playgroup, nursery, school; going into hospital.
- watch appropriate videos/television programmes which demonstrate the positive features of the new setting or situation
- provide opportunities for imaginative play to let children express their feelings and fears about the transition
- organise introductory visits for the children and their parents/carers so that the children can become familiar with the setting and the adults who will be caring for them
- provide information appropriate to both children and adults e.g. information pack/brochure plus activity pack for the child
- obtain relevant information about the children e.g. correct name and address, contact details, medical information, dietary requirements

- plan appropriate activities for an induction programme (the children's first day/week in the new setting).

Describe the procedures in your setting for preparing children new to the setting.

How well do you think these procedures meet children's social and emotional needs?

Think about possible improvements.

Transition objects

A transition object is a comfort object which a young child uses to provide reassurance and security when separated from a parent (usually the mother). The child feels connected to them by holding, cuddling, stroking or sucking the object. Transition objects are usually something soft like a small blanket, muslin cloth (nappy), or cuddly toy such as a teddy bear.

Transition objects provide a link between the child and the absent parent/caregiver which enables the child to feel more secure in new situations without the parent. Reliance on a comfort object does not mean

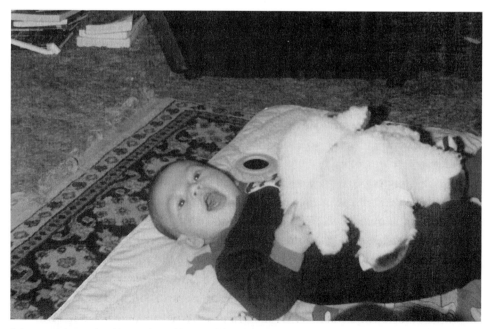

Baby, aged 1 month with comfort object: cuddly toy

a child is insecure or too dependent on the parent. It may actually enable the child to become more independent and secure as they have the object to reassure them in the parent's absence. A child *without* a comfort object may not have this reassurance or feeling of security.

Some children have their comfort object with them at all times; some just at bed time, during naps or to relax with when they need a break; others only when entering new situations such as visiting GP, clinic or hospital, starting nursery, playgroup.

A strong attachment to a comfort object usually begins in a child's first year and often increases between the ages of 1 and 2 years. By the time a child is 3 or 4 years old the need for their comfort object usually lessens. Many children are less attached to their comfort object by the time they start school. A child may continue to need their comfort object for the occasional snuggle when they are very tired or distressed until they are teenagers. There is no set age for giving up a comfort object.

Bottles should not be used as comfort objects because:

- they are unhygienic e.g. bacteria in milk kept around too long
- prolonged contact with teeth can lead to dental decay
- can contribute to problems with bite.

Dummies can be acceptable as comfort objects if well-kept (they are no less hygienic than thumb sucking) but discourage prolonged use as this can restrict the child's communication.

Comfort habits include thumb sucking and twiddling/sucking hair. These can be difficult to stop as the comfort 'object' is with the child forever!

One of the first priorities of all early years settings is to meet the individual needs of children; if children feel more emotionally secure, reassured and relaxed due to the presence of their comfort objects then these should be accommodated.

Attitudes towards transition/comfort objects or habits vary between settings and individuals within the setting. Consider these points:

1 Allow very young children to have free access to their comfort objects at all times as this can assist their sense of security especially during transitional periods.

2 With older children keep comfort objects out of sight e.g. in child's personal drawer/bag where they can get it if they really need it.

3 Separation from a comfort object (e.g. in order to participate in messy activities or meal times) must be done gently; it is the most precious thing the child has.

4 Comfort objects are usually irreplaceable so check with parents that a replacement or substitute is available if the worst happens.

5 Let the children decide when they no longer need their comfort objects.

6 With older children (and as their confidence in being in the setting increases) set time limits as to when they can have their comfort object e.g. they can bring it to the setting but it remains in their drawer the whole time unless the child becomes ill, distressed or has an accident.

7 Reception children may be allowed their comfort objects during their first days/weeks in school to help them settle in.

8 School age children should be encouraged to leave their comfort objects at home.

9 Some children may need access to their comfort objects while experiencing exceptional distress on separating from parents or where other factors make this necessary e.g. emotional or behavioural difficulties.

10 Anything which makes transitions (e.g. comfort objects) easier for young children should be regarded in a positive way.

Activities and strategies for settling into new settings

The first days (or even weeks) that children spend in a new setting/situation require a sensitive approach from adults to enable young children to cope with separation from their parents and to adjust to new routines and/or people.

Remember the following points:

1 Follow a clear, structured daily routine to provide stability and security for the children.

2 Ensure children's transition objects are easily accessible to them.

3 Provide play opportunities for children to express their feelings and concerns over separating from parents, starting in new setting.

4 Identify children's individual needs.

5 Provide activities and experiences appropriate to these needs.

6 Show an active interest in the children's activities.

7 Work with the children to establish clear boundaries and rules.

Welcome
to
Little Acorns

'mighty oaks from little acorns grow'

Welcome to Little Acorns
Day Nursery

This booklet provides information for parents and children interested in Little Acorns Day Nursery.

It includes information on:
- the nursery's aims and objectives
- how the nursery is organised
- the nursery's policies
- early learning

8 Reassure the children about their parents eventual return.

9 Provide reminders of the children's parents e.g. talk about them, display photographs.

10 Encourage parental involvement as far as is practical and appropriate to the setting/situation.

11 Prepare parents for possible *temporary* effects of separation e.g. children may demonstrate their feelings of anxiety by being clingy, hostile, aggressive or by regressing to previous developmental level.

12 Settling in can often be more stressful for the parents than the children; encouraging them to be relaxed, calm and confident will help their children who can sense their parents' anxiety.

Exchanging information with parents

Sharing information is an essential part of working with young children and their parents. Parents often know more about their children and their needs so it is important to listen to what parents have to say.

Adults working with young children need essential information *from* parents including:

1 *Routine information* e.g. child's name, date of birth, gender, home address and telephone number; medical history/conditions such as allergies; home/community language; cultural or religious practices which may have implications for the care of the child such as special diets; names and addresses of adults with parental responsibilities for the child; who will collect the child from the setting; any siblings already in the setting; the child's particular likes and dislikes.
2 *Emergency information* e.g. contact numbers for parents, GP.
3 *Other information* e.g. factors in child's life which may affect the child's behaviour within the setting including family difficulties and crises such as divorce, bereavement.

Always remember **confidentiality** with regard to information provided by parents.

Adults working with young children will also need to *give* parents information on:

- the aims and objectives of the setting
- age range of children
- ratio of adults to children
- staff qualifications
- session structures including session times and holidays
- outdoor facilities
- admission procedures
- settling in procedures
- record keeping and assessment
- outline of approaches to learning e.g. early learning goals or national curriculum
- children with special needs including the administration of medicines within the setting e.g. the use of inhalers by children with asthma
- miscellaneous e.g. procedures regarding discipline, food, drink, meal times in the setting; rules regarding uniform, dress code, jewellery.

This information is usually given to parents in the setting's brochure, prospectus or information pack. Information can also be given to parents via letters, notice boards, newsletters, open or parents' evenings.

K E Y   T A S K

Compile/devise a brochure, prospectus or information pack for an early years care and education setting. Include the following:

- information about the setting e.g. aims and objectives, ratio of adults to children, age range of children, staff qualifications, session structures, opening times, holiday dates, outdoor facilities
- information about admission policy, introductory visits, induction programme and settling in procedures including sample timetable of first week's activities
- activities and pictures demonstrating the setting's approaches to learning
- information on record keeping and assessment
- statement on equal opportunities including special needs
- policies regarding medicines, discipline, meal times, jewellery, dress code, etc.
- an activity pack for children to prepare them for starting at the setting
- examples of new child/pupil form, consent forms, etc.

NVQ Level 3 links: C.5.1 C.5.6 M.7.1
DCE links: Units 2, 4 and 11
BTEC links: Units 3, 6, 7 and 8.

Further reading

Bartholomew, L. and Bruce, T. (1993) *Getting to know you: a guide to record-keeping in early childhood education and care.* Hodder & Stoughton.
Geraghty, P. (1994) *Caring for children.* Bailliere Tindall.
Mort, L. and Morris, J. (1989) *Bright ideas for early years: getting started.* Scholastic.

13

Promoting Positive Behaviour

- what is positive behaviour?
- parental expectations and their influence on children's behaviour
- other influences on children's behaviour
- the benefits of positive behaviour
- the behaviour of babies and toddlers
- ways to encourage children's positive behaviour
- negotiating and setting achievable goals and boundaries
- involving children in goal and boundary setting
- the importance of praise and encouragement
- the principles of positive reinforcement
- the effective use of rewards and sanctions
- preventing or reducing disruptive behaviour

Behaviour can be defined as:

- a person's actions and reactions
- a person's treatment of others.

Behaviour involves a person's *learning to conform* to:

- parental expectations for behaviour
- group setting expectations for behaviour
- society's expectations for behaviour.

Those who are not prepared (or are unable) to conform have to accept the consequences e.g. sanctions or punishments for unacceptable behaviour.

Learning about behaviour (as with all learning) always takes place within a social context. Certain behaviour may be acceptable in one context but not in another e.g. families may make allowances for their child's behaviour, but different rules may apply in a group setting. In group settings, adults must consider the needs of *all* the children and have rules to reflect this. What is acceptable in one situation may not be acceptable in another, even within the same setting e.g. loud, boisterous behaviour *is* acceptable in the playground but *not* in the classroom. Conforming brings limitations to children's behaviour e.g. in school, participating in all national curriculum areas even those they do not like. In some early years settings, such as day nurseries or pre-school playgroups, there may be more freedom to choose activities but there will still be times when children have to comply with adult demands (e.g. snack/mealtimes, story times) or follow rules concerning sharing toys or equipment.

E X E R C I S E

What are your own expectations regarding what is acceptable behaviour

- for yourself?
- for the children in your setting?
- for the individual in society?

What is positive behaviour?

What is considered to be positive behaviour depends on:

- the individual
- the setting   and their expectations of what is acceptable behaviour.
- society

Tolerance is often the key factor as to what is considered to be acceptable or desirable behaviour. Each person has different levels of tolerance for different kinds of behaviour depending on:

- how that person feels at the time
- the expected behaviour in relation to age/level of development
- the social context.

Examples of:

Positive Behaviour	Negative Behaviour
sharing resources and adult's attention	not sharing; attention-seeking; jealousy
taking turns	taking things; stealing
playing co-operatively	fighting or arguing; disrupting activities
helping/comforting others	hurting others
being friendly	being aggressive/abusive inc. bullying

Positive Behaviour	Negative Behaviour
remaining on task	easily frustrated or distracted
concentrating on activities	not concentrating on activities
complying with adult requests	refusing reasonable requests; defiant
contributing creative ideas	overriding/ridiculing other people's ideas
expressing self effectively	emotional outbursts; whining; nagging
being aware of danger	no sense of danger; too compulsive
being polite	rude, cheeky; interrupting others
being responsible for own actions	blaming others, lying
being independent	being easily led; too dependent on others
being flexible	resisting change; overly upset by change
being an active participant	over-active or passive

Children playing co-operatively: circle game.

List positive and negative behaviours which you consider to be appropriate to the age/level of development of the children in your setting. State the activity and the social context for each behaviour.

Parental expectations of behaviour

Many parents may have idealised or unrealistic expectations concerning their children's behaviour because:

1 Many child care books and the media promote unrealistic age-related expectations; many children do not 'measure up' to what the experts say.
2 Parents compare their children to other children (of relatives, friends, neighbours), not realising that all children are individuals and develop at their own rate.
3 Parents have expectations for behaviour based on perceptions of their own childhood and *their* parents' attitudes to behaviour.
4 Smaller families (often with few or no relatives nearby) mean many parents lack first-hand experience of caring for young children *before* they have their own children and may feel less confident about their parenting skills.

Parents have social/cultural expectations relating to their children's behaviour based on:

- cultural or religious beliefs
- individual variations in child-rearing practices
- adherence to traditional child-rearing practices.

Traditionally children did not dare challenge parental authority for fear of physical punishment. Today some parents still feel that if they were brought up this way, then this is what they expect from their children. In the twenty-first century, society recognises the rights of the child and has the expectation that all parents should be more caring and responsive to their children's needs by using positive methods such as praise, encouragement, negotiation and rewards to achieve socially acceptable behaviour. The UN Convention on the Rights of the Child states that 'children have the right to be protected from all forms of physical and mental violence and deliberate humiliation'. Where parental expectations concerning punishment conflict with those of the setting, staff should point out to parents the setting's **legal** requirements under the Children Act 1989, that is *no* physical punishment. (See page 224.)

Children are influenced by their parents' expectations for behaviour. Children learn:

- what is or is not acceptable behaviour   • which rules can be bent or broken   • which boundaries can be crossed.

Through their parents, children learn about the rules for acceptable behaviour which apply in:

- their family   • the local community   • the wider environment/society.

Children will challenge parents by saying 'no!' or 'I don't want to' etc. Children will also try to change the rules or negotiate new ones. Parents (and other family members) also act as role models for children's behaviour. Children will imitate both positive and negative aspects of their parents' behaviour.

Children may observe parental behaviour which is:

- *assertive*; sensitive to their own *and* other people's needs
- *passive*; too sensitive to other people's needs so *ignores own needs*
- *aggressive*; obsessed with own needs so *ignores other people's needs*.

Children learn what their parents consider to be acceptable behaviour and will bring these expectations to the early years setting.

Other influences on children's behaviour

We live in a very competitive society as demonstrated in sport, business and politics. Early years settings, especially schools, actively encourage competition through sports and team points. Children may also be aware of being assessed and may start comparing their achievements with others. Most children want to be part of a group and are willing to co-operate with others, but they can also be very competitive on behalf of themselves and their group or team. This type of competition may be seen as 'team spirit' or demonstrating loyalty to the group. **Competition** can be used to promote positive behaviour, for example:

- winning merit points for self and team;
- sharing common interests and activities within the setting e.g. clubs, sports or hobbies.
- belonging to clubs in the local community.

Peer pressure may have a negative influence on children's behaviour; children may be:

- persuaded by others to participate in dangerous activities including 'dares'
- pressured into socially unacceptable behaviour such as lying, stealing or bullying
- excluded from or threatened by the group unless they conform which puts pressure on children to behave like the rest of the group
- encouraged to behave in ways they never would as an individual e.g. 'mob rule'.

Adults can use peer pressure to encourage positive behaviour by highlighting the positive benefits of certain behaviour for the group. The **media** (television, magazines, comics) and computer games can be positive or negative influences on children's behaviour. It depends what children see and how they are affected by it.

Children exposed to violent images may see aggressive behaviour as an acceptable way to deal with others. Children who observe more assertive behaviour (with its emphasis on negotiation and compromise) are likely to demonstrate similar positive behaviour. Television programmes, characters and personalities provide powerful role models for children. Consider the effectiveness of advertising!

The benefits of positive behaviour

Promoting positive behaviour can bring many benefits to children, adults and early years settings. These benefits include:

- creating a positive framework with realistic expectations for children's behaviour
- providing consistent care for children with clear rules and boundaries
- the security and stability of a welcoming and structured environment
- positive motivation through praise, encouragement and rewards

- positive social interaction between children and adults
- encouraging children's self-reliance, self-confidence and positive self-esteem
- encouraging adult confidence in caring for children
- a positive atmosphere which makes caring for children more interesting and enjoyable
- opportunities for more effective thinking and learning leading to improved educational achievement/test results

There are also potential benefits for society such as:

- more positive social interactions including friendships, clubs, etc.
- re-development of community spirit and belief in citizenship
- positive attitudes towards others e.g. equal opportunities, racial harmony, etc.
- research shows that young children who have positive early years experiences are more likely to maintain an interest in education leading to further training/qualifications and are less likely to go on to experience 'juvenile delinquency' and adult unemployment (Ball, 1994).

Negotiating and setting achievable goals and boundaries

Setting goals and boundaries involves teaching children to:

- respect other people
- respect the possessions of others
- develop self-control.

Setting goals and boundaries involves adults:

- seeing things from a child's point of view
- respecting children's ideas and needs
- realising children will test boundaries from time to time
- having realistic expectations for children's behaviour
- recognising the limitations of young children's level of understanding and memory skills.

Goals are the *expectations* for behaviour; usually starting with '**Do** ...'
Boundaries are the *limitations* to behaviour, often starting with '**Don't** ...'
The key factor in negotiating and setting achievable goals and boundaries is having :

- Realistic expectations
- Reasonable limitations

Adults need to set goals and boundaries which take into account:

1 the age/level of development of the children
2 the children's individual needs and abilities in all areas of development
3 the social context e.g. the setting, activity, group size, etc.

Babies and behaviour

Babies have limited cognitive and communication abilities so negotiating goals and boundaries is not possible because they cannot understand what is required or be reasoned with. Adults can show what is required by being positive role models for behaviour. Babies are not deliberately 'naughty' so sanctions or punishments for unwanted behaviour are *not* appropriate. Babies may display 'difficult' behaviour such as persistent crying, being irritable or unco-operative because these are the only ways they have to communicate things like hunger, tiredness, illness, anxiety or frustration.

Behaviour guidelines for babies:

1 Be calm; do not get annoyed with babies' behaviour.
2 Praise and reward desired behaviour; ignore unwanted behaviour.
3 Give babies appropriate care and adult assistance.
4 Make potentially difficult situations more fun e.g. using games and rhymes during routines such as meal times, nappy changing, dressing, etc.
5 Be positive! Try not to say 'Don't . . .' or 'No' too often.
6 Use diversionary tactics e.g. removing the baby from the situation or removing the object from the baby's reach.
7 Do not force or pressurise babies into behaving in certain ways; aggressive adult behaviour such as shouting only frightens babies and does not change their behaviour.
8 **Never** use physical punishment (e.g. smacking, shaking, etc.) as this can cause serious or even fatal injuries to a baby. In any case such punishment does not work; babies have no understanding of what they are being 'punished' for.

As babies develop they become more independent and will demonstrate this through challenging behaviour because they still lack the communication skills to express their needs effectively and are often frustrated by their lack of physical skills to do what they want e.g.

- challenges or refuses adult's choices of food, clothing and activities;
- asserts own likes and dislikes;
- starts to have frequent emotional outbursts or 'temper tantrums'.

Toddlers and behaviour

Adults need to have realistic expectations for very young children and accept that certain types of behaviour are characteristic of the under-threes. For example, children in this age group may be:

- attention-seeking; they dislike being ignored so will interrupt adults
- very sensitive to changes; upset if separated from parent or carer
- very active; keen to explore environment
- unaware of potential dangers
- unable to respect the possessions of others
- stubborn and insist on having their own way
- easily frustrated and prone to emotional outbursts
- unpredictable and contrary with changeable behaviour.

Behaviour guidelines for toddlers

The guidelines for babies also apply to toddlers, but in addition this age group need a positive framework for behaviour. Young children learn to behave in socially acceptable ways through positive interaction with adults who provide:

- opportunities for channelling their frustration through play
- diversions to distract the child
- clear and consistent guidelines about what is and is not acceptable behaviour.

10 ways to encourage positive behaviour in young children

1 *Keep rules to a minimum.* Too many rules make it difficult for children to remember and follow them. Children will often accept and keep to a few rules if they have some freedom. Children also need to learn self-control and make their own decisions regarding behaviour.

2 *Be realistic about children's behaviour.* Accept that children will be inquisitive, noisy and messy at times! Organise a child-orientated environment and implement activities in appropriate areas e.g. quiet activities in areas where children can concentrate without too many distractions.

3 *Be flexible.* Children often behave inappropriately when their needs or wishes conflict with adult expectations. Altering the setting's routines to fit in with children's individual needs may provide fewer opportunities for such conflicts. While clear structures and routines are essential, there should be room for flexibility e.g.

- when children are not responding well to an activity, be prepared to adapt or abandon the activity
- do less demanding activities when children are tired.

4 *Be prepared to compromise*; negotiate goals and boundaries with children. Children should develop independence and have some control over their lives. Their wishes should be considered and their ideas respected. Give children some freedom:

- to explore (within safety limits)
- to select and carry out activities
- to choose and/or make snacks and meals
- to choose clothes and/or dress themselves.

Some activities and routines *have* to be done, but it may be possible to negotiate with children as to *when* these tasks are done or give an *incentive* for completion e.g. when they have finished tidying up the children can choose a story or a rhyme.

5 *Be positive.* Once goals have been negotiated and set, encourage the children to keep them through rewards or other positive incentives. Reward positive behaviour using verbal praise, stickers or merit points. Keep smiling! A sense of humour goes a long way.

6 *Ignore certain behaviour.* Ignore unwanted behaviour especially attention-seeking or behaviour that is not dangerous or life-threatening e.g. a toy left in the corner of a room will not hurt anyone, but left in the corridor or on the stairs could be a trip hazard.

7 *Use diversionary tactics.* Sometimes it is not possible or appropriate to ignore unwanted behaviour e.g. if the child is in danger. With younger children it may be more effective to distract the child (e.g. by playing a game) or to divert their attention to another activity (e.g. giving them another more suitable toy, while quietly taking the other one away). Diversionary tactics can often avoid the confrontations which can lead to emotional outbursts. Recognise and try to avoid the

possible triggers to unwanted behaviour e.g. doing demanding tasks when a child is tired.

8 *Be consistent.* Once rules, goals and boundaries have been negotiated and set, stick to them. Children need to know where they stand; they feel very insecure if rules and boundaries keep changing for no apparent reason. Children need to understand that 'no' always means 'no' especially where safety is concerned.

9 *Give clear instructions and explanations.* Explain why certain rules are necessary e.g. for safety. Gradually young children will understand the need for rules and this will help them to develop their own self-control.

10 *Keep calm.* Be calm, quiet, firm and in control; shouting only makes matters worse. If you feel you are losing control, count to 5 and then proceed calmly. You may need to use strategies like **time out** to give the child a chance to calm down, but keep it short – ignore or remove for only a few seconds until the child is a little calmer.

Children may not recognise the rules of the setting or share the same views as to what is acceptable behaviour. Remember children from different social or cultural backgrounds may have different expectations regarding behaviour. Where children are given clear guidelines for behaviour at home, they are much more likely to understand and keep to rules, goals and boundaries in the setting.

Involving children in goal and boundary setting

Children are more likely to keep to goals and boundaries if they have some say about them. Children need to be active participants, not only in following rules, but in establishing them. Having a feeling of ownership makes rules more real and gives children a sense of control.

GOAL AND BOUNDARY SETTING

1 *What* is the goal or boundary?
Focus on the behaviour would like to change. Encourage children to talk about, draw a picture or write down what *they* would like to change. Remember to be positive.

2 *Why* is the goal necessary?
To improve behaviour, to provide happier atmosphere, to encourage co-operation or for safety reasons.

4 *Who* does the goal or boundary apply to?
Does it apply to everyone in the setting, just the group/class, or one particular individual?

4 *Where* does the goal or boundary apply?
Does it apply everywhere in the setting, in a particular room/class, indoors or outdoors?

5 *When* will the children start working towards the goal? *When* will the boundary apply? Will it apply at all times in the setting or only at certain times?

6 *How* will the goal or boundary be implemented? *How* will the children be encouraged to keep to the goal or boundary? Include positive incentives such as smiley faces, stickers or merit points.

7 What happens when the *goal* is *achieved*?
Ask the children what *they* would like. Rewards might include a badge, certificate, assembly praise or a special treat.

8 *Set new goal.* Start with the next goal or boundary which needs changing.

EXERCISE

1 Think about goals and boundaries which might be appropriate to the children in your setting.

2 If possible, encourage the children in your setting to draw up a list of rules which promote positive behaviour.

The importance of praise and encouragement

Praise and encouragement promote positive behaviour in children by encouraging:

- emotional well-being and high self-esteem • strong motivation for behaving in positive ways • positive attitudes to behaviour and learning • effective communication and social interaction

The principles of positive reinforcement include:

1 Positive expectations lead to positive behaviour.
2 Rules, goals and boundaries are framed in positive and realistic terms.
3 Positive feedback leads to positive behaviour.
4 Effort is as important as achieving goals or desired behaviour.
5 Rewards encourage or reinforce appropriate behaviour; sanctions are kept to a minimum.

Positive feedback for positive behaviour can make an enormous difference to the atmosphere of the setting, to children's concentration levels and learning abilities.

Praise is most effective when it:

- provides positive feedback about a specific behaviour or achievement e.g. 'Well done, Tom, you've played with Alex really nicely today by working together to make a super rocket!' rather than just 'Well done, Tom!'
- is sincere and given with maximum attention
- recognises effort not just achievement, especially with difficult tasks or goals
- encourages children to focus on their *own* individual behaviour or achievement
- shows the adult's positive expectations for the child's behaviour and learning.

Rewards can provide positive incentives for positive behaviour. Children can be motivated by rewards such as:
- choice of favourite activity • smiley faces, stars or stamps • stickers or badges • merit points and certificates • mention in praise assembly • mention in Head teacher's praise book.

Rewards are most effective when they are:
- immediate and clearly linked to the child's behaviour, effort or achievement so that the child connects the reward with the behaviour
- meaningful and appropriate to the child's age/level of development e.g. smiley faces and stickers are more real to young children than points
- related to an *individual's* behaviour, effort or achievement rather than a group; every child needs the chance to obtain rewards for some positive aspect of their own behaviour
- recognised and consistently applied by *all* the adults in the setting e.g. some adults hand out rewards like confetti (making them meaningless), while others strictly ration them (making rewards virtually unobtainable); either way children will not be motivated.

The difficulty with some reward systems is that children who find it easier to behave appropriately may do very well, but children with emotional or behavioural difficulties may not do so. Reward systems which display stars or points for the whole group can be particularly damaging to children's self-esteem and often they do not indicate what the reward was for. An individual chart or book for each child can be better as the child is clearly competing against their own past efforts or improving their own behaviour.

Examples of rewards for positive behaviour.

For example, each child could have a small exercise book with a page a week for stickers, smiley faces or merit points which are clearly linked to the child's behaviour and/or learning. The adult can negotiate with each child the targets they are expected to achieve that particular week. If they achieve this target the child receives an appropriate reward such as a certificate or choosing a favourite activity. This makes it easier for children to see their individual efforts and achievements and can help to set future goals for behaviour and learning. (See example on page 224.)

While the emphasis should be on promoting positive behaviour through praise, encouragement and rewards, there may be times when these do not work. Some early years settings may feel it necessary to impose **sanctions** for children whose behaviour goes beyond acceptable boundaries or who break the rules.

example cover

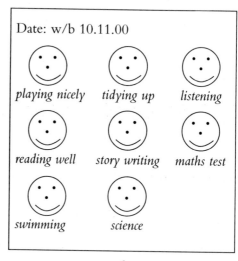

example page

Sanctions are most effective when they are:

- balanced against appropriate rewards
- reasonable and appropriate to the child's action so that major sanctions do not apply to minor lapses in acceptable behaviour
- applied to the children responsible and not the whole group
- aimed at discouraging unwanted/unacceptable behaviour without damaging children's self-esteem
- used as a last resort; every effort should be made to be positive and to encourage acceptable behaviour through *positive* rather than negative reinforcement.

Physical or corporal punishment is illegal in maintained schools and is not permissible in all other early years settings:

Corporal punishment (smacking, slapping or shaking) is illegal in maintained schools and should not be used by any other parties within the scope of this guidance. It is permissible to take necessary physical action to prevent personal injury either to the child, other children or an adult or serious damage to property.
(The Children Act 1989 Guidance and regulations: Volume 2 Family Support, day care and educational provision for young children, Section 6.22.)

Dealing with unacceptable behaviour using physical punishment is also inappropriate as it teaches children that violence is an acceptable means of getting your own way. Smacking and shouting do not work; adults end up smacking harder and shouting louder to get the desired behaviour. Children do not learn anything by being smacked; they are just hurt and humiliated.

EXERCISE

Outline your setting's policy on rewards and sanctions relating to children's behaviour.

Preventing and reducing disruptive behaviour

Adults can promote positive behaviour and thus prevent or reduce disruptive behaviour by:

- learning and using children's names
- using effective communication skills and encouraging these in children
- identifying children's needs and interests to provide appropriate learning opportunities
- organising a stimulating environment to encourage learning opportunities
- having well prepared learning materials
- encouraging children to take appropriate responsibilities e.g. tidying up
- encouraging parental involvement.

KEY TASK

1 Negotiate and set some achievable goals and/or boundaries with a young child or group of young children as part of a framework of positive behaviour.
2 Outline how you would implement this framework. Remember to emphasise the positive aspects of behaviour.
3 Devise a system of rewards for encouraging the children to demonstrate the targeted positive behaviour. If appropriate, include possible sanctions for unwanted/unacceptable behaviour.

NVQ Level 3 links: C.7.1 C.7.2 C.5.3 C.5.5
DCE links: Unit 4
BTEC links: Units 6, 8 and 12.

Further reading

Leach, P. (1994) *Children first*. Penguin.

Lindenfield, G. (1994) *Confident Children*. Thorsons.

Lyus, V. (1998) *Management in the early years*. Hodder & Stoughton.

Yeo, A. and Lovell, T. (1998) *Sociology for childhood studies*. Hodder & Stoughton.

14

Responding to Unwanted Behaviour

················Key Points······················

- key indicators of withdrawn and aggressive behaviour
- contributing factors to unwanted behaviour
- observing and monitoring children's behaviour
- children with Attention Deficit Hyperactivity Disorder (ADHD)
- approaches to persistent unwanted behaviour
- the principles of behaviour modification
- sharing concerns with parents, colleagues and other professionals
- dealing with bullying

The key indicators of unwanted behaviour

The adult response to a child's behaviour is as important as the behaviour itself. Different people have different attitudes to what is or is not acceptable behaviour. The social context also affects adult attitudes towards children's behaviour (see Chapter 13). Certain types of behaviour should be considered unacceptable by all adults; these include behaviour which causes:

- physical harm to others • self-harm • emotional/psychological harm to others • destruction to property.

Children whose unwanted behaviour is demonstrated through aggressive or disruptive behaviour are usually the children to attract the most adult attention as they are easily identified and hard to ignore.

Key indicators of aggressive behaviour include being:
- very noisy e.g. shouting
- disruptive during group activities e.g. games, story time
- physically over-active
- verbally abusive e.g. swearing, name-calling, taunting
- physically abusive e.g. biting, kicking, scratching
- destructive e.g. towards property, other children's work or possessions

- attention-seeking
- immature
- disobedient, defiant or unco-operative
- easily distracted
- prone to emotional outbursts or 'tantrums'.

Children who demonstrate unwanted behaviour in a withdrawn manner may be overlooked especially by inexperienced adults or in very busy settings.

Key indicators of withdrawn behaviour include being:
- very quiet
- very passive or under-active
- over sensitive to criticism
- over-anxious or obsessive
- engaged in self-damaging activities e.g. head-banging, pulling out hair or picking at skin
- solitary and isolated
- shy/timid
- inattentive e.g. 'day dreaming'
- disoriented e.g. aimless wandering or looking confused
- absorbed in excessive/repetitive use of comfort habits e.g. rocking, thumb-sucking or masturbation.

Children may have some or all of the indicators characteristic of either group of behaviours or a mixture from both groups depending on:
- the individual child
- the social context e.g. *where* they are and *who* they are with
- how they feel that particular day/moment.

Key indicators common to both groups of behaviour include having:
- limited attention-span and concentration levels
- restricted range of communication skills
- hostile, uncaring or indifferent attitude towards others
- negative self-image and low self-esteem
- behaviour and/or learning patterns which are inconsistent with expected development.

Labelling children's behaviour is not usually helpful, but it may help when observing children's behaviour to recognise the key indicators of unwanted behaviour.

Contributing factors to unwanted behaviour

It is also important to be aware of the factors which can affect children's behaviour.

Contributing factors include environmental, social or emotional factors such as:
- family bereavement or prolonged illness
- divorce or separation
- family violence
- emotional damage through physical, verbal or sexual abuse
- insecure early relationships
- depression
- changes e.g. moving house, school
- sibling jealousy/rivalry
- inappropriate role models outside the setting
- lack of parental care and control
- financial problems, poverty or homelessness
- negative early years experiences in previous settings.

Adults in the early years setting may have little or no control over these contributing factors but they *do* have control over **additional factors** such as:

- their response to children's unwanted behaviour
- inadequate preparation for and introduction to the setting/transition to other settings
- the demands of the setting e.g. unfamiliar routines, strict regimes.
- insensitivity or inflexibility towards individual needs
- stressful, boring or frustrating activities and experiences
- inappropriate learning opportunities
- unrealistic adult expectations or limitations
- inappropriate role models *within* the setting
- poor adult to child ratio; very large group size
- over-emphasis on competition and not enough on co-operation
- unwarranted disapproval from adults/other children in the setting
- children being bullied.

Children are more likely to demonstrate unwanted behaviour if they are:

- under-stimulated
- bored or frustrated
- uncertain of what is required e.g. rules are unclear or unrealistic
- with adults who have low/negative expectations about children's behaviour and learning.

Children are more likely to behave in positive ways if they are:

- in a welcoming and stimulating environment
- engaged in interesting and challenging activities which are appropriate to their age and level of development
- given clear and realistic guidelines on behaviour with adults who have high/positive expectations for children's behaviour and learning.

No single factor causes a child's unwanted behaviour; there is usually a combination of factors. By identifying the contributing factors which make such behaviour more likely, adults in the early years setting can often avoid the additional factors which result in unwanted behaviour. By responding positively to children, adults can encourage positive self-image/high self-esteem and stop a negative self-image being reinforced because of unwanted behaviour.

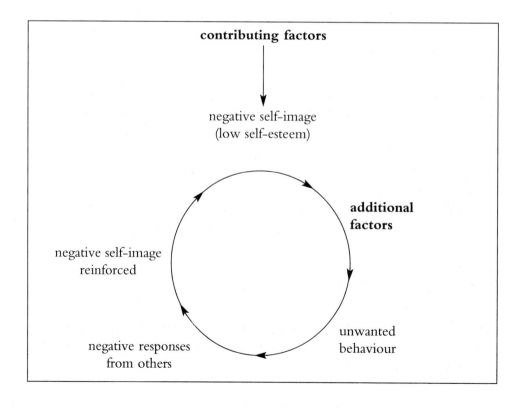

Rare factors causing unwanted behaviour include:

- *psychosis* – a serious psychological disorder characterised by mental confusion, hallucination and delusions; in young children symptoms include: regression, speech loss and extreme hyperactivity
- *autism* – a rare and complex condition usually present from birth (although identification may not be made until 3 years +) ; autistic tendencies include speech loss or unusual speech patterns, isolation and withdrawal, intense dislike of environmental changes (see Chapter 2)
- *Attention Deficit Hyperactivity Disorder* (ADHD) – a biological condition affecting children's behaviour and concentration (see pages 233–235).

The effects of preservatives and additives in food and drink on children's behaviour

Food and drink which contain preservatives or additives (such as blue, orange or red colorants) may affect some children's behaviour; the child's behaviour improves when particular colourings or additives are excluded from the child's diet. Concerns over a child's diet should be discussed with their parents who may be advised to see their GP or paediatrician. Preservatives and additives do *not* cause hyperactivity, but they may worsen the behaviour of children with existing behavioural difficulties or conditions such as ADHD. Research suggests that only 10% of children with ADHD are affected by preservatives or additives.

Observing and monitoring children's behaviour

It is essential to observe and assess children within the early years setting to evaluate each child's needs and to monitor their behaviour. As children develop, their needs and behaviour patterns change. Regular observations can help identify *pronounced* changes in a child's usual behaviour patterns.

Through accurate observation and assessment adults can:

- *identify* the child's main areas of difficulty.
- *respond* to the child's behaviour in appropriate ways.
- *devise* strategies to encourage the child to demonstrate more positive behaviour.
- *seek* professional advice for the child with more persistent behavioural difficulties.

When observing and monitoring children's behaviour remember it is not possible or helpful to record everything children say and do at all times. It is therefore necessary to decide:

1 *who* is to be observed?
2 *why* do they need to be observed?
3 *what* activities and which aspects of behaviour to focus on?
4 *when* and how often to observe?
5 *where* to do the observations?
6 *how* to observe e.g. which observation method(s) to use?

Time sampling is a useful method of observing a child's behaviour at regular intervals. It can provide a clearer picture of behaviour changes throughout the session/day and help to identify when certain behaviour occurs during which activities.

Event sampling involves recording specific events or behaviour as they happen. A record is made of the number of times the target behaviour occurs, when it occurs and how long it lasts.

Trail or movement observations can also be used to monitor behaviour. On a plan of the setting, lines are drawn indicating the movements of the child over a period of time with brief notes about the length of time spent in each area, the child's behaviour and any social interaction.

Other useful methods for observing behaviour include checklists, target child/coded observations and diaries. (See Chapter 1 for more information on observations.)

KEY TASK

Observe a young child who demonstrates unwanted behaviour during a group activity such as:

- story time
- singing session
- play activity or game
- PE or movement lesson.

In your assessment include information on:
- the child's behaviour during the activity
- the child's communication skills
- how the adult responds
- how the other children respond to the child's behaviour.

Suggest ways to monitor the child's future behaviour.

Suggest ways to encourage the child to behave more appropriately (see Chapter 13).

NVQ Level 3 links: C.7.1 C.7.2 C.16.1 C.16.2 C.5.1 C.5.2 C.5.3
DCE links: Units 1 and 4
BTEC links: Units 6, 7, 8 and 12.

Attention Deficit Hyperactivity Disorder (ADHD)

About 3% of children have ADHD and it is possible that about 10% of children have a milder form of the disorder. Boys are more likely to be affected than girls. ADHD is rarely diagnosed before the age of 6 years because many young children demonstrate the behaviours characteristic of this disorder as part of the usual sequence of development. From about 6 years old it is easier to assess whether the child's behaviour is *significantly* different from the expected norm. Most children with ADHD are formally identified between 5 and 9 years old.

Children with ADHD are usually:
- *inattentive* with a short attention-span; unable to concentrate on tasks, easily distracted; they forget instructions due to poor short-term memory; they may seem distant or be prone to 'day dreaming'.
- *over-active* with high levels of activity and movement; restless and fiddle with objects.
- *extremely impulsive* which may lead to accidents as they have no sense of danger; they often speak and act without thinking.

Children with ADHD may also be:
- *discontent*; they are rarely satisfied with themselves or others; they generate lots of tension by interrogating, nagging or pestering others.
- *lacking in social skills* as they do not know how to behave with others; very bossy and domineering; unable to make or keep friends; they may demonstrate inappropriate behaviour or misread social cues e.g. treating complete strangers as close friends.
- *lacking in co-ordination skills* and may have poor pencil control resulting in untidy written work; they may be accident prone.

- *disorganised* and unable to structure their own time; unable to motivate themselves unless directed on a one-to-one basis; they may be very untidy.
- *changeable and unpredictable* with severe, unexplained mood swings; short-tempered with frequent emotional or extremely aggressive outbursts.

Some children with ADHD may also have specific learning difficulties such as dyslexia. Most children with ADHD have problems with handwriting but this could be due to poor hand-eye co-ordination and short attention-span.

ADHD is a hereditary, biological condition caused by a slight difference in brain function which can be seen clearly on a brain scan. The medication Ritalin (a stimulant which enhances brain function) has been very effective in about 80% of children with ADHD. Such medication helps focus the child's attention, keeps them on task and allows the child to think before they act. Once the child's concentration and behaviour improves the dose can be decreased. With or without medication, it is important to have a consistent system for managing the child's behaviour within the setting and at home.

Within the setting adults need to provide:
- a quiet group/class with one or two adults who are firm but fair and can provide consistent care and education throughout the year
- calmness and a clear routine
- seating near a known adult away from distracting children
- step-by-step instructions
- constant feedback, praise and encouragement.

At home parents or caregivers need to:
- be patient and ignore minor irritations
- be calm and provide a clear routine
- provide special times with the child without distractions e.g. cosy story times, playing quiet games
- use step-by-step methods for modifying the child's behaviour
- give small, frequent and constant rewards.

Even with medication and/or behaviour management, ADHD currently cannot be cured.

Adults working with children with ADHD should be aiming to:

1 Encourage the children's enthusiasm for learning.
2 Improve the children's self-esteem.
3 Maintain harmony and peace (as far as possible) within the setting.

EXERCISE

Describe how you have responded to a child with challenging or unwanted behaviour.

Approaches to responding to persistent unwanted behaviour

1 *Approaches not solutions*. There are no easy answers or quick solutions to dealing with challenging or unwanted behaviour. Adults may need to use a variety of approaches.
2 *Past experiences*. Children learn about behaviour through their early relationships and experiences. The effects these have depends on the individual's personality (see Chapter 9). No one's behaviour is static; they can acquire new behaviour patterns and discard behaviour which is ineffective or inappropriate.
3 *Adult influences on children's behaviour*. Parents and carers have major influences on children's behaviour. Adult responses to children's behaviour can make things better or worse. Adults may need to modify their own behaviour and responses.
4 *Patience and perseverance*. Changing children's behaviour takes time, so do not expect too much all at once. Take things one step at a time. Remember that behaviour may get worse before it gets better because some children will resist attempts to change their behaviour (particularly if they have behaved this way for some time) and will demonstrate even more challenging behaviour especially if minor irritations are being ignored.
5 *Temporary phases*. Some unwanted or difficult behaviour is part of the usual sequence of young children's development e.g. emotional outbursts or 'temper tantrums' in the under-threes. Provide a positive framework for the child's behaviour appropriate to their age and level of development.
6 *Establish clear rules, boundaries and routines*. Children need to understand the rules and the consequences if they do not follow the rules. Children need clear boundaries as to what is or is not acceptable

behaviour, including frequent reminders about what these are. Try to include the children in deciding some rules, goals and boundaries.

7 *Consistency from adults*. Adults need to be consistent when responding to children with persistent unwanted behaviour or the children become confused. Adults need to discuss and agree on responses to the child's behaviour. Adults within the setting need to work with the child's parents so the child sees that both are working together to provide a consistent framework for behaviour.

8 *Diversionary tactics*. Adults can sometimes divert the child from an emotional or aggressive outburst or self-damaging behaviour. This does not always work but often does. Be aware of possible triggers to unwanted behaviour and intervene or divert the child's attention *before* difficulties begin.

9 *Giving children choices*. Children can also be diverted by being offered alternative choices or being involved in decision making.

10 *Encouraging positive social interaction*. Help children to develop their social skills so they can join in activities with other children. Start off with one to one, then small groups and then larger groups. Play tutoring can help e.g. adult involvement to develop and extend social play.

11 *Alternative ways to gain attention*. Most children want adult attention; it is the way they behave to gain attention that may need changing. Instead of being disruptive, children need to be encouraged to use more acceptable ways to get adult attention by asking or showing the adult that they have something to share.

12 *Helping children to express their feelings*. Adults need to encourage children to express strong feelings such as anger, frustration or fear in positive ways e.g. through play and communication. (See Chapter 10.)

13 *Looking at the environment*. Identifying and, where possible, changing aspects of the environment and routines within the setting which may be contributing towards the child's unwanted behaviour.

14 *Label the behaviour not the child*. Make sure any response to unwanted behaviour allows the child to still feel valued without any loss of self-esteem e.g. 'I like you, Tom, but I don't like it when you . . .'

15 *Be positive*. Emphasise the positive and encourage children to be positive too. Phrase rules in positive ways e.g. 'do' rather than 'don't'. Think about which unwanted behaviour must be stopped and which can simply be ignored so that children are not being told 'No' or 'Don't do . . .' all the time.

16 *Punishments do not work*. Punishments may satisfy the people giving them, but they are of little value in changing children's behaviour. Children may become devious or blame others in order to avoid being

punished. Quiet reprimands are more effective than a public 'telling off' which only causes humiliation in front of other children and increases the child's resentment towards the adult. Rewarding positive behaviour is more effective than punishing unacceptable behaviour.

17 *Praise, encouragement and rewards*. Set realistic and achievable goals and use children's interests to motivate them. Use regular positive feedback to encourage children to behave in acceptable ways and raise their self-esteem. Praise children's *efforts* as well as achievements. Find out which kinds of rewards matter to the child and use them.

18 *Avoid confrontation if at all possible*. Use eye contact and the child's name to gain/hold their attention. Keep calm, sound confident and in control. If the child is too wound up to listen, give them a chance to calm down e.g. '**time out**' (see page 220).

19 *Give individual attention and support*. This encourages children to share their worries or concerns with a trusted adult. 'Time in' involves giving children special individual attention to reinforce positive behaviour and decreases the need for them to gain adult attention through unwanted behaviour. It involves children talking one to one (or in a small group of children) with an adult about their day including reviewing positive aspects of the day.

20 *Behaviour modification*. Using positive reinforcement to encourage acceptable behaviour; ignoring all but harmful unwanted behaviour. Work on one aspect of behaviour at a time and reward the child for any progress no matter how small.

See Chapter 13 for more information on promoting positive behaviour.

EXERCISE

List appropriate strategies for responding to at least one of the following persistent unwanted behaviour:

- 1–2 year old having an emotional outburst or 'temper tantrum'
- 3–4 year old who appears anxious and withdrawn
- 5–6 year old deliberately disrupting an activity
- 6–7 year old teasing, taunting or other verbal abuse directed at other children.

Behaviour modification

The background to behaviour modification

Ivan Petrovich Pavlov (1849–1936) was a Russian biologist who studied animal behaviour. His experiments involved teaching dogs to salivate in response to the sound of a bell. Before giving the dogs their food, Pavlov rang a bell. Eventually the dogs began to salivate when the bell rang even when there was no food. The dogs had learned to respond to the bell sound with their salivating reflex. This type of learned response or behaviour is called a *conditioned reflex*. Pavlov extended his ideas concerning conditioning to human psychology; he believed that human behaviour consists of many conditioned reflexes which are triggered by external influences.

B. F. Skinner (1904–1990) was an American psychologist who discovered that the behaviour of rats could be controlled by food rewards. This idea of *operant conditioning* can be applied to any situation where the required behaviour is reinforced with a reward. Skinner believed that positive reinforcement (rewards) and negative reinforcement (punishments or sanctions) both contribute towards an individual's motivation for learning and behaviour.

The basic principles of behaviour modification:

- **P**raise and reward acceptable behaviour
- **R**educe the opportunities for unwanted behaviour
- **A**void confrontations
- **I**gnore minor unwanted behaviour
- **S**tructure appropriate sanctions
- **E**stablish clear rules, boundaries and routines.

Using behaviour modification techniques

1 Focus on the child's behaviour.
2 Target which aspect of unwanted behaviour needs to be changed first.
3 Observe and monitor the specific behaviour e.g. how often the behaviour occurs, when, where and in what situations.
4 Outline the usual response to this behaviour and the result.
5 Observe and record which activities/rewards the child responds to positively.
6 Discuss possible strategies and decide on appropriate responses to the behaviour e.g.

      – adapt routines

      – change sanctions

      – rewards for appropriate behaviour.

      Discussions should include the child, their parents as well as colleagues.

7 Implement the proposed strategies. Remember to be positive.

8 Continue to observe, monitor and record the child's behaviour using simple, straightforward recording systems which can also involve the child and their parents.

9 Use regular positive feedback, praise and rewards to encourage the child.

10 Assess the effectiveness of the strategies. If they *are* working, continue to use them; if they are not, adapt them or try new ones. It may also be necessary to consult more senior colleagues or other professionals. Once the agreed behaviour target has been reached, focus on the next aspect of unwanted behaviour that needs changing.

KEY TASK

Think about the basic principles of behaviour modification.

Look back at the observation on page 232/233 and focus on one aspect of that child's behaviour.

Outline a step-by-step approach to encourage the child to behave in more acceptable ways. Remember to include appropriate rewards (and sanctions).

NVQ Level 3 links: C.7.3

DCE links: Unit 4

BTEC links: Units 6 and 12.

Sharing concerns about children's behaviour with their parents

It is easier to discuss concerns about a child's behaviour with their parents if sharing information with parents and parental involvement are established practices within the setting.

- *Be welcoming* and create an environment which provides opportunities to talk with parents. If face to face contact is difficult use a home-setting diary to share information.
- *Be clear* about which aspects of the child's behaviour are causing difficulties within the setting. Ask the parents about any similar difficulties in the child's behaviour at home and how they respond to it.

- *Be sensitive* when talking with children's parents; be willing to share positive information about the child's behaviour not just the negative.
- *Be tactful* when asking the parents if they think their child may be worried or upset about anything.
- *Be attentive* and listen carefully to the parents' views and any particular concerns *they* may have concerning their child's behaviour. Show parents that their involvement in their child's care and education is respected and valued.

Sharing concerns with colleagues and other professionals

Serious concerns about a child's persistent unwanted behaviour should be discussed with colleagues and possibly with other professionals. Remember confidentiality. However, all early years workers have a legal duty to report serious concerns about a child's welfare e.g. possible child abuse; each setting should have guidelines about this.

Adults may need specialist advice, guidance or support to provide the best possible approaches to responding to some children's behavioural and/or emotional difficulties.

Colleagues **may include**:
- the child's key worker or class teacher
- nursery supervisor or manager
- early years co-ordinator
- special educational needs co-ordinator
- head teacher.

Each setting should have a clear structure for reporting concerns about children's behaviour to colleagues and appropriate ways to deal with these concerns. Be aware of your own role and responsibilities within this structure.

Other professionals **may include**:
- health visitor • paediatrician • clinical psychologist • educational psychologist • social worker • education welfare officer • play therapist • music therapist.

Compile an information pack about responding to unwanted behaviour. Include the following:

- a list of key indicators of unwanted behaviour e.g. regression, withdrawal, attention-seeking, aggressive or self-damaging behaviour
- contributing factors to unwanted behaviour
- strategies for dealing with unwanted behaviour
- the setting's policy regarding behaviour and discipline
- sources of specialist advice and support.

NVQ Level 3 links: C.7.3
DCE links: Unit 4
BTEC links: Units 6 and 12.

Bullying

Bullying occurs in early years settings not just in secondary schools. Recent studies suggest that 85% of 5–11 year olds have experienced bullying in some form e.g. name calling, being hit or kicked. Bullying is such a serious problem that schools must now have an anti-bullying policy which clearly sets out the ways in which they try to prevent bullying and deal with bullying behaviour.

Dealing with bullying behaviour

1 Have clear strategies for dealing with bullying behaviour.
2 Have clear sanctions for such behaviour.
3 Provide help for the bully so they can recognise that this behaviour is unacceptable e.g. discussion, mediation, peer counselling.
4 Work with parents to establish community awareness of bullying.
5 Make sure all children know that bullying will *not* be tolerated.
6 Exclude children who demonstrate persistent bullying behaviour especially if they use physical violence towards other children.

Recognising when a child is being bullied

- a child who usually enjoys nursery/school suddenly does not want to go

- a child has unexplained cuts and bruises
- a child's possessions have unexplained damage or are persistently 'lost'
- a child's academic performance declines for no apparent reason
- a child becomes withdrawn or depressed but will not say what is the matter.

Example of anti-bullying poster

Helping children who have been bullied

1 Encourage the child to talk.
2 Listen to the child's problems.
3 Believe the child if they say they are being bullied.
4 Reassure the child that it is not their fault; no one deserves to be bullied.
5 Discuss the matter with the child's parents.
6 Take appropriate action, following the setting's policy on anti-bullying.

EXERCISE

1 Outline your setting's policy regarding bullying behaviour; if there is no policy, work with colleagues to devise one.
2 Devise an activity to encourage children to speak up about bullying e.g. story/discussion, role play/drama or poster making.

Further reading

Bartholomew, L. and Bruce, T. (1993) *Getting to know you: a guide to record-keeping in early childhood education and care.* Hodder & Stoughton.

Green, C. and Chee, K. (1995) *Understanding ADD.* Vermilion.

Harding, J. and Meldon-Smith, L. (2000) *How to make observations and assessments.* 2nd Edition. Hodder & Stoughton.

Train, A. (1996) *ADHD: How to deal with very difficult children.* Souvenir Press.

Appendix

Planning, implementing and evaluating learning activities and experiences

Activity plans should be appropriate to the ages, individual needs and interests of the chilren in your particular early years setting. Discuss each plan with your supervisor/assessor and negotiate when it would be appropriate for you to implement each activity.

Your college tutor or assessor should give you guidelines on how to present your activity plans. Otherwise you might find this suggested format useful:

- **Title:** brief description of the activity
- **Date:** the date of the activity
- **Plan duration:** how long will the activity last?
- **Aim and rationale:** the main purpose of the activity including how it will encourage the child's or children's learning and development. The rationale should outline why you have selected this particular activity (e.g. identified particular child's need through observation; links to topics/themes within the setting). How does the activity link with any early learning goals or national curriculum subjects relevant to the setting?
- **Staff and setting:** the role (do not use names) and number of staff involved in the activity plus the type of setting.
- **Details of children:** activity plans involving an individual child or small group should specify first name, age in years and months plus any relevant special needs; activity plans involving larger groups should specify the age range and ability levels.
- **Objectives/learning outcomes for the children:** these should indicate what the children should gain from participating in the activity in each developmental area:
  Social   Physical   Intellectual   Communication   Emotional
- **Preparation:** what do you need to prepare in advance? (e.g. selecting or making appropriate materials; checking availability of equipment). Think about the instructions and/or questions for the children; will these be spoken and/or written down e.g. on a worksheet, workcard or on the board? Will *you* need prompt cards to remind you of key instructions or questions?
- **Resources:** what materials and equipment will you need? Where will you get them from? Are there any special requirements? Remember

equal opportunities. How will you set out the necessary resources? (e.g. set out on the table ready or children getting materials and equipment out for themselves).

- **Organisation:** whereabouts in the setting will you implement the activity? How will you organise the activity? How will you give out any instructions the children need? Will you work with children one at a time or as a group? Are there any particular safety requirements? How will you organise any tidying up after the activity? Will the children be encouraged to help tidy up?
- **Implementation:** describe what happened when you implemented the activity with the child or children. Include any alterations to your original plan e.g. changes in resources, modifications to the activity.
- **Equal opportunities:** indicate any multicultural aspects to the activity and any additional considerations for children with special needs.
- **Review and evaluation:** review and evaluate the following:
  – the aims and objectives/learning outcomes
  – the effectiveness of your preparation, organisation and implementation
  – what you learn about children's learning/development
  – what you learned about curriculum planning
  – possible modifications for future similar activities.
- **References and/or bibliography:** the review and evaluation may include references appropriate to children's learning/development. Include a bibliography of any books used as references or for ideas when planning the activity.

Bibliography

ATL Special Educational Needs Working Group (April 1994) 'Achievement for all'. London: ATL Association of Teachers and Lecturers.

Ball, C. (1994) *Start Right: The importance of early learning.* London: RSA.

Bartholomew, L. and **Bruce,** T. (1993) *Getting to know you: a guide to record-keeping in early childhood education and care.* London: Hodder & Stoughton.

British Dyslexia Association (October 1997) 'Dyslexia: an introduction for parents and teachers and others with an interest in dyslexia'. London: BDA.

Bruce, T. and **Meggitt,** C. (1999) *Child care and education.* 2nd edition. London: Hodder & Stoughton.

Commission for Racial Equality (December 1989) ' From cradle to school: a practical guide to race equality and childcare'. London: CRE.

Cox, M. (1995) *Children's drawings.* London: Penguin.

Cunningham, B. (1993) *Child development.* London: Harpercollins.

Davenport, C. (1994) *An introduction to child development.* London: Collins Educational.

Davie, R. (1984) 'Social development and social behaviour' (see **Fontana,** D.)

Donaldson, M. (1978) *Children's minds.* London: Fontana.

Drummond, M. et al. (1994) *Making assessment work.* NFER Nelson.

Department of Health (1991) *The Children Act 1989: Guidance and regulations, Volume 2: Family support, day care and educational provision and young children.* London: HMSO.

Einon, D. (1986) *Creative play.* London: Penguin.

Fontana, D. (1984) 'Personality and personal development' in D. Fontana (ed.) *The education of the young child.* Oxford: Blackwell.

Foster-Cohen, S. (1999) *Introduction to child language development.* Harlow: Longman.

Goleman, D. (1996) *Emotional intelligence.* London: Bloomsbury.

Green, C. (1990) *Toddler taming: a parents' guide to the first four years.* London: Vermilion.

Green, C. and **Chee,** K. (1995) *Understanding ADD.* London: Vermilion.

Harding, J. and **Melton-Smith,** L. (2000) *How to make observations and assessments.* 2nd edition. London: Hodder & Stoughton.

Houghton, D. and **McColgan,** M. (1995) *Working with children.* London: Collins Educational.

Hutchcroft, D. (1981) *Making language work.* London: McGraw-Hill.

Laing, A. and **Chazan**, M. (1984) 'Young children with special educational needs' (see **Fontana**, D.).

Laishley, J. (1987) *Working with young children*. London: Edward Arnold.

Leach, P. (1994) *Children first*. London: Penguin.

Lee, V. and **Das Gupta**, P. (eds.) (1995) *Children's cognitive and language development*. Oxford: Blackwell.

Lindenfield, G. (1995) *Self esteem*. London: Thorsons.

Light, P., **Sheldon**, S. and **Woodhead**, M. (eds.) (1991) *Learning to think*. London: Routledge.

Masheder, M. (1989) *Let's play together*. London: Green Print.

Matterson, E. (1989) *Play with a purpose for the under-sevens*. London: Penguin.

Meadows, S. (1993) *Child as thinker: the development of cognition in childhood*. London: Routledge.

Mort, L. and **Morris**, J. (1989) *Bright ideas for early years: getting started*. London: Scholastic.

Moyle, D. (1976) *The teaching of reading*. London: Ward Lock Educational.

Modgil, C. and **Modgil**, S. (1984) 'The development of thinking and reasoning' (see **Fontana**, D.).

Mulvaney, A. (1995) *Talking with kids*. Sydney: Simon & Schuster.

National Commission on Education (1993) *Learning to succeed*. London: Heinemann.

Neaum, S. and **Tallack**, J. (1997) *Good practice in implementing the pre-school curriculum*. London: Stanley Thornes.

Petrie, P. (1989) *Communicating with children and adults*. London: Edward Arnold.

Rogoff, B., **Gauvain**, M. and **Ellis**, S. (1991) 'Development viewed in its cultural context' (see **Light**, P.).

Rogers, C. (1991) 'Early admission: early labelling' (see **Woodhead**, M.).

Rowland, S. (1987) 'Child in control: Towards an interpretive model of teaching and learning' in A. Pollard (ed.) *Children and their primary schools*. London: Falmer Press.

Rutter, M. (1991) *Maternal deprivation reassessed*. London: Penguin.

Sameroff, A. (1991) 'The social context of development' in M. Woodhead, R. Carr and P. Light (eds.) *Becoming a person*. London: Routledge.

Sears, N. 'Stammerers offered the time to talk', *The Times Educational Supplement* (7.11.97)

Stoppard, M. (1990) *The new baby care book*. London: Dorling Kindersley.

Taylor, J. (1973) *Reading and writing in the first school*. London: George Allen and Unwin.

Tharp, R. and **Gallimore**, R. (1991) 'A theory of teaching as assisted performance' (see **Light**, P.).

Tizard, B. (1991) 'Working mothers and the care of young children' (see **Woodhead**, M.).

Tough, J. (1976) *Listening to children talking*. London: Ward Lock Educational.

Tough, J. (1984) 'How young children develop and use language' (see **Fontana**, D.).

Train, A. (1996) *ADHD: How to deal with very difficult children*. London: Souvenir Press.

Whitehead, M. (1996) *The development of language and literacy*. London: Hodder & Stoughton.

Wood, D. (1991) 'Aspects of teaching and learning' (see **Light**, P.).

Wood, D. (1988) *How children think and learn*. Oxford: Blackwell.

Woodhead, M. (1991) 'Psychology and the cultural construction of children's needs' in M. Woodhead, P. Light and R. Carr (eds.) *Growing up in a changing society*. London: Routledge.

Woolfson, R. (1991) *Children with special needs: a guide for parents and carers*. London: Faber & Faber.

Woolfson, R. (1989) *Understanding your child: a parents' guide to child psychology*. London: Faber & Faber.

Yardley, A. (1984) 'Understanding and encouraging children's play' (see **Fontana**, D.).

Index

HIS STOLEN INNOCENT'S VOW

MARCELLA BELL

WAYS TO RUIN A ROYAL REPUTATION

DANI COLLINS

MILLS & BOON

First Published in Great Britain 2021
by Mills & Boon, an imprint of HarperCollins*Publishers*
1 London Bridge Street, London, SE1 9GF

His Stolen Innocent's Vow © 2021 Marcella Bell

Ways to Ruin a Royal Reputation © 2021 Harlequin Books S.A.

Special thanks and acknowledgement are given to Dani Collins
for her contribution to the Signed, Sealed...Seduced miniseries.

ISBN: 978-0-263-28240-5

MIX
Paper from
responsible sources
FSC™ C007454

Printed and bound in Spain
by CPI, Barcelona

HIS STOLEN INNOCENT'S VOW

MARCELLA BELL

To Kaleen, my real-life Hel.

CHAPTER ONE

HELENE COSIMA D'TIERRZA, inheritor of the great d'Tierrza fortune and titles—including the duchy—and seventh in line for the throne of Cyrano, stood unsteadily before the marble statue that dominated her family's private courtyard.

Her silver-blond bangs feathered across her brow, swaying in time with her body's slight motion, while her normally sharp sapphire-blue eyes glared with unfocused intensity at the carved figure's face. Her dress was a long column of azure. Strapless and simple, it emphasized the elegant length of her figure rather than the unexpected muscle tone of her arms and chest. The dress flared gently at its base to provide what she supposed was a generous allowance for walking...if one minced.

Disgust curled her lips, the effect all the more striking for the fullness of her wide mouth.

Today might be the one day of the year she conceded to wearing a dress, but she never minced.

It was also the one day of the year when she drank.

Both the dress and the drink contributed to the uncharacteristic wobble in her stance.

With her arms crossed in front of her chest and a

half-empty flute of champagne loosely clasped in one hand, angled at a slight tilt, she was also uncharacteristically alone. She had no one to guard and no staff lingered in the shadows. They were occupied with the guests gathered in the large seascape courtyard who mingled and drank, all in the dubious name of her father's legacy.

The king and queen, two of her most constant companions, were in attendance, as was her fellow queen's guard, Jenna Moustafa, who was on solo duty with backup from the king's guard while Hel played dress-up.

The crease between her eyebrows deepened. She should be out there with her friends, alert and ready to back up Moustafa should the need arise. It would certainly be a better use of her time than standing in front of her father's likeness, once again engaged in the silent battle of wills that hadn't so much as ended with the end of his life, as become unwinnable. Not that she ever had a chance when he'd been alive. No one stood a chance against Dominic d'Tierrza.

Hel wouldn't be the one to throw in the towel, though. Her father didn't deserve the satisfaction.

Not even in death.

Instead, she sneered at the statue. "You've really outdone yourself this year, Papa. Already raised two million and we haven't even had dinner yet."

He said nothing in response.

He wouldn't have, had he been alive, either. Speaking about money was gauche and two million a paltry sum. He would have raised four by this point in the afternoon had he been around to run things. His permanently raised eyebrow said as much.

Not up to the standard of the d'Tierrza name.

Though just a memory, the oft-repeated words remained an acid refrain.

Her father had been old-fashioned, autocratic and hateful. She'd only learned the last in her teens. He cared about the family line and that alone.

A daughter was a bargaining chip to be played to the family's best advantage, nothing more. A wife past childbearing years, even less.

He had encouraged Helene, named after the beautiful cause of the Trojan War, to be lovely and amenable, a prize all men would covet.

So she had become loud and opinionated and learned to fight.

She'd also gone out into the world and gotten involved, gotten dirty, done everything she could to prove that Helene d'Tierrza was the furthest thing from the marriage material her father wanted her to be as was possible.

It hadn't been enough.

Nothing, not even truly diverging from her "correct" path to become a royal guard, had truly been enough to get back at him, to balance the scales. Not when he'd been alive and certainly not now that he was dead.

Not when he still cast such a long shadow over her life. Over her mother's.

She couldn't even believe they were doing an event in his name. There was nothing honorable about her father's legacy—it was only criminal.

She could literally recite a list of crimes.

But she never did, merely carried it around with her—a small penance for the ills he wrought on the world, and the only one she'd been allowed. On the point that the d'Tierrzas were important to national security, it seemed the world agreed with her father.

She and her mother kept their dirty laundry hidden in the dark and everyone benefitted. And maybe if she dedicated every living and breathing moment to serving justice, it might make up for the lie…if not the actual sins of her father.

Besides, the money they raised went to charities across the entire island nation.

That wouldn't have mattered to her father, though. Only the d'Tierrza name mattered to him. Nothing else. No other name, not even that of the royal family, could be allowed to outshine it.

God help you if you had the misfortune to be born with that name.

The charities mattered to her, though. People mattered to her. She was related to him in name only, and if she'd at first cultivated heart and honor just to spite him, in the end, those qualities had been too pure to pollute and had instead molded her. Including the voice that told her all of this was wrong.

Hel broke her stare, unfolded her arms and lazily downed the remainder of her champagne. Effervescent and smooth, it bubbled gently down her throat while she contemplated the perfect crystal stem twirling between her fingers. Then, without turning her gaze back to the statue, she stopped twirling the glass and flicked her wrist, the action decisive and controlled.

The glass sailed toward her father's likeness, spinning end over end in a perfect circle, before it crashed into the marble statue, shattering on impact. Bright clear pieces of crystal caught the light as they fell, filling the space with her own personal rainbow, all to the sound of tiny brittle stars cracking on the ground.

Suddenly, she heard a throat clear and the scuffing of feet on the paving stones behind her. In an instant, she snapped into full alertness, her wobble and dead father abandoned.

Behind her, the stranger quickened. She moved faster, feinting to the right and dropping into a crouch, before a large hand came around to catch her around the mouth. Her dress seam split as she executed the move, but she ignored it, spinning around to shoot her heeled foot out at the shin of her would-be abductor.

The person anticipated the move, though, jumping out of both her reach and sight. She tried to leap upright but lost precious time, slowed down as she was by her torn evening gown. Their arms, large and strong, came around hers, holding her tight in an iron grip.

This was exactly why she refused to wear dresses. She wouldn't have been caught if she'd had pants on.

She slammed her head back toward her attacker's face, but once again the stranger anticipated her move and shifted their head to the side in time to avoid her. Arms tightened around her. She lifted her feet, surprising them with her entire body weight. There was a grunt behind her, but the person held on, the powerful grip loosening only a fraction.

The fraction was all she needed.

She twisted down and out of the hold, dropping to the ground at the same time as she swept his feet out from under him. She could see that he was a man now. He landed well, but the move managed to give her enough time to put space between them and take a reasonable, if narrow, fighting stance.

He leaped from the ground effortlessly and advanced toward her, and for an instant, she was frozen.

He was stunning.

Well over six feet tall, his skin shone a rich, dark brown. His suit was impeccably tailored but not of Cyranese cut or style. Instead, it nodded toward their Sidran neighbors to the south with a long jacket and short collar.

In all her life, she had never been stopped short by another soul, and yet this man had paralyzed her. It wasn't his clothing, though it fit him flawlessly, highlighting his perfect proportions. The bulk of the people who inhabited her world had been wearing bespoke couture since they could first toddle. It wasn't his height. Her father had been a tall man and her cousin, the current king and her lifelong best friend, was a towering man.

The man was older than she was, his trim beard lightly salt and peppered, though his skin was as smooth as marble. His eyebrows were thick and black, and low over his eyes.

Those eyes. Something about them grabbed at her and pulled, urging her to move closer, as if she was his prey, helplessly ensnared.

He smiled, the expression filling his deep brown eyes with an arrogant gleam. The smile drew her eyes to his mouth, which was full. Her lips parted, dry suddenly, and she licked them.

"It seems I might have underestimated the difficulty I'd face in convincing you today…" he mused in Cyranese, his low whisper a skin-tingling bass that caressed her ears.

She shivered, breath hitching, as her body kick-started systems she'd been certain were defective after years of being dormant.

And then his words sank in.

He knew the effect he was having on her. And he thought he could use it against her.

Heat flooded Hel's face, a combination of irritation at his arrogance and embarrassment at her stupefaction—because that's the only thing it could be called, as stupid as it was—but this time she didn't let her reaction to him slow her down.

In one smooth motion, she reached down, took off a heel and hurled it at his face, quickly repeating the motion with the other shoe before bolting toward the courtyard's exit.

He avoided the first shoe, but not the second, giving her precious seconds of advantage.

They weren't enough.

Beating her to the archway, he blocked the way and she halted, not willing to get within arm's reach again. Without taking her eyes off him, she grabbed the ripped seam of her dress and ripped it farther.

His cocky grin returned. "Eager, are we?"

She flipped him a rude gesture and he threw his head back and laughed. The sound hummed through her bones before coming to a heated rest at her core, though she resisted the urge to press her legs together.

"Who are you?" she asked.

"Not who you expected to meet here?" he asked with mock surprise, the laughter in his voice setting off inner fires she didn't know could burn.

The heat from her core made its way up her neck to merge with the bright blush spots on her cheeks until her normally cool, pale skin burned a bright red across her entire body.

"This is a private courtyard."

He nodded. "I know."

"What are you here for?"

He tilted his head in a chiding fashion that somehow reminded her of her mother, as if he knew she could do better. "To speak with you. Isn't it rather obvious?"

"Normally, people who wish to speak with me approach from the front," she observed.

He shrugged, the movement fluttering his jacket. "It wouldn't be the first time I've come at things from a different angle."

She laughed, unable to help herself in the face of his blasé attitude. "What did you want to talk about?"

A wicked spark came to his eyes as he took in her partially exposed body, beginning at her bare feet and traveling slowly up, lingering at her breasts, before his gaze locked on hers.

She felt the look like a caress, making her breathing go short and heavy.

"Many things—reunions, new unions…" he said, the words trailing off slow like honey.

"We've never met." She spoke casually as she shifted her weight to the balls of her feet.

Something like pain flashed across his eyes, but was gone by the time his words came out, his voice entirely nonchalant as he said, "The two of us? No. But we've known each other our whole lives."

His words were intriguing, a siren mystery tempting her to ponder his meaning instead of thinking through her next move, but she wasn't going to bite. She couldn't afford the time it would take. She'd only requested one day off, no matter how fascinating the stranger who dangled the lure.

With shocking speed, she pivoted on her heel and erupted into a sprint, wincing as she dashed barefoot through the shards of broken champagne glass along the way.

And it was her own fault. Her father always said her rashness would come home to roost.

Her would-be kidnapper was on her tail alarmingly quickly, but she had the advantages of a head start and greater familiarity with the terrain.

Running right at the statue, she leaped, her feet planting squarely on her father's nose with an ominous crack as she used it to spring onto the tiled rooftop surrounding the courtyard. She landed hard, sliding slightly as she dislodged the tiles, sending some falling to crack on the marbled floor below.

Once she caught her balance, she scrambled toward the top bar of the roofs—the only place where running was actually feasible.

A loud thud behind her and a quick glance over her shoulder confirmed that her pursuer had not yet given up. That was fine. She hadn't, either.

She ran across the roof, her bare feet finding easy purchase on the familiar old wood. She followed the same route she and her cousin had taken as young daredevils looking for a bit of fun and a chance to terrify their tutors.

With any luck, the old trick would work on the man behind her, because his long strides were rapidly closing the space between them.

In the distance, she could hear the tasteful music and muffled chatter of the party. There was still time to veer right and head in that direction. Moustafa and the king's guard wouldn't hesitate to provide backup. However, there was a chance that the man was actually coming after her in an effort to get near to the king and queen. In which case, protecting them meant keeping him away. Besides, she could just imagine the horror on her mother's face when her daughter literally dropped into the middle of her party wearing nothing but a tattered evening gown.

But then again, maybe her mother wouldn't mind. The party would certainly be talked about long afterward.

She had promised her mother that she would settle down, though, and—her profession notwithstanding—for the most part, she had.

After her father's death, the need to tarnish the family name had lost its sense of urgency.

Her mother, her companion in the trenches, understood her motivation for upsetting the family wheelhouse and cared little for what gossip surrounded her daughter. Their relationship was close and open and far too strong to be shaken by rumor. But her behavior could still impact the way her mother was treated in society, whom she was allowed to see, what services she could solicit. Hel knew her mother would say it saved her from frequenting with fools, but hearing that her mother had been denied an appointment at her salon after Helene joined the royal guard had triggered the protective response that years of living with her father had developed in her. She wouldn't do anything that might limit her mother's hard-earned freedom.

So rather than seek backup, Hel stayed her course, nearly to the spot that she and her cousin had named The Leap of Death.

They'd discovered it when they were eleven, once again illicitly exploring the ducal palace's roof.

"If you jump from here you would land in the deep pool," Zayn had said with a frown on his face, the one young Helene recognized as his figuring face. She'd looked, gauged the necessary arch, then given him a wide grin. He'd shaken his head. She'd taken a running start and jumped.

He'd been right. Thankfully.

After that, The Leap of Death had become the preferred method of testing the mettle of each and every educator and mentor assigned to bring them to heel. With the exception of one, none had realized the jump was safe until their charges returned hours later.

Hel was banking on the phenomenon that watching her leap to her death at sea would have the same demoralizing effect on the man chasing her as it had on so many of her would-be educators.

Meanwhile, she could swim into the natural caves, then take the path back up to the palace and figure out who in the hell the guy was. And she could do it with pants on.

She made the final turn on the roof, a sharp left that angled her toward the sunrise balconies—it was the turn that would lead her to the leap.

The man remained close on her heels.

Abruptly, she sprang off the beam, her body arching into a perfect dive, her blood singing a thrilling song she hadn't heard in too long.

Blood rushed in her ears as she angled toward the water, her body lighting to the experience like a long-lost friend.

Laughter bubbled out of her underwater.

She needed to do this more often.

She'd entered the water as slick as a seal, her momentum taking her another thirty yards before she surfaced.

Breathing heavily, she looked up at the corner of the roof she had jumped from, taken, as always, by how small and far away it looked. Her pursuer was nowhere to be seen. A wide grin spread across her face. The Leap of Death had come through once again.

She set a leisurely pace swimming back toward the caves, entering their shadowed depths quietly, her feet appreciating the cool and cleansing sting of the salt water after running through the broken glass.

And then she heard the sound of something large landing in the water.

Spinning around, she treaded water as she squinted in the direction of the sound. For a moment, all she saw was gently waving sea.

Then he surfaced.

She turned back to the cave, swimming furiously now, but he cut through the water behind her like some kind of sinister merman.

As she pushed deeper into the cave, a large shape took form, and she stopped in her swim. Once again treading water, her gasp was magnified and echoed by the curvature of the cave's walls.

There was a ship anchored in the cave.

Masculine laughter broke out behind her, swirling around her, surrounding her in the high-ceilinged space.

Mere feet separated them in the water. She considered her next move. There was no way she could outswim him. She sensed it without a doubt, not needing to test the hypothesis.

There was something about him, his aura somehow half sea creature. Or maybe it was the fact that he seemed completely at one with the water, despite the fact that he swam in soaking-wet formal wear.

Of course, even against impossible odds, it never hurt to try.

Darting away from him, she put all her energy into speed and zoomed with a mad burst through the water.

And it worked. Shooting yards ahead of him, she felt the exhilaration of defeating a worthy opponent. It was certainly a better way to spend her father's birthday than pretending to love and honor him.

At that moment, the strength of her surge circled back to bite her. Swimming with enough speed to retain her lead required her full power, all of her energy driving ahead…straight into a tangle of net.

Caught in thoughts and swimming through churning waters, she'd missed it, floating in the water ahead of her.

Her momentum sent her into the net in a tangle of limbs before the heavy waterlogged ropes, now knotted around, began to drag her below the surface. She struggled, but only tangled herself further.

He was on her in seconds, securing her around the waist with the iron band of his arm. He was treading water while untangling the ropes from her limbs with the other arm.

The water was his ally, accepting him as one of its own while he worked smoothly, as if they weren't bobbing in a cove.

Smoothly, until the palace alarm sounded above them. Her absence had been noted.

Cursing under his breath, he made quick work of the last of the grasping ropes before pulling them with fast strokes toward the ship.

"None of this is going according to my plan." He sounded like a weary grandfather.

She ignored him, aiming for a casual tone, though it was strained. "At least this answers how you got in."

The whole experience was turning out to be enough to throw her off balance. It wasn't every day a handsome stranger snuck his ship into her harbor and beat her at sparring. She was usually the one who won.

"I assume that's your ship?" she asked, as if the answer was of no importance.

He laughed, the sound once again echoing in the chamber of the cave, but said nothing.

They were nearly to the hanging rope ladder that would carry them onto the ship. She was exhausted, with welts beginning to form on her skin from her bout with the fishing net, and she blamed it on the dress.

If she hadn't been wearing a dress, they wouldn't have even made it to the harbor. She would have easily subdued the mesmerizing man in the family courtyard, learned what he wanted and ended the day nestled snugly in her childhood bed. It was becoming clearer and clearer to her that he had never intended to kidnap her, and that, as he carried them up the ladder with a slight huff to his breath and a new, more serious intensity now that the alarm had sounded, it might have actually made things more inconvenient for him.

Pondering all of this meant she didn't fight as he scaled the rope ladder with one arm and climbed aboard, his other arm holding her all the while.

Men and women of assorted shapes and sizes milled about on the deck, but no one seemed to bat an eye as he carried Hel aboard. A few even paused in what they were doing to wave and nod in greeting.

He acknowledged them with the briefest nod en route to wherever they were going.

The cabin he took her into was like walking into a Moroccan library—bright, airy and warm, with blindingly white walls lined with sleek bookshelves made from a honey-colored wood and large-sized porticos and skylights that drenched the room with sunbeams. It was utterly masculine, with its streamlined, low-profile decor, with soft, low-profile furniture, and each and every surface bare and clean enough to eat from. Each bookshelf was quite full and had a small lip. The lip, she presumed, was to keep the books where they were meant to be in the event of turbulent seas. The immense collection, she presumed, was for show, though the tradition was to pretend otherwise. In her lifetime, Hel had observed that men of action were rarely readers. Readers spent their evenings at home, not out at sea.

Yet, looking closer, she noticed signs of wear and tear—and not light—marking each volume: cracked spines, slightly bent covers, warped lines.

His books had not just been read. They'd been loved soft.

Despite the utter maleness of the room, no one would have called the space sterile or aggressive. Instead, it was warm and natural. Rich, vibrant-hued upholstery—goldenrod-yellow suede leather for the accent chair and deep burgundy silk for the matching sofa—and the woven wool throw pillows made the room homey. At their feet was a handwoven rug in a black-and-white Berber style on gleaming hardwood whose honey tones matched the bookshelves. Centered on the rug was a large, single-slab driftwood table, three inches thick and gleaming in the room's natural lighting, unabash-edly gorgeous in all its Technicolor wood-grain glory.

So unless she was mistaken and this was *not* the wealthiest vessel she'd ever stumbled upon, the absolute lap of luxury, boasting subtle features here and there that even an aristocrat like herself might have trouble getting her hands on, this man was not hurting for cash.

Beneath the room's warmth, however, were signs she was dealing with a professional.

Surveillance cameras whispered in the corners of the room and there were items cleverly designed to look like pieces of the room that she was certain were weap-ons—a bookend, the unique detachable legs of a globe stand and an evil eye that hung on a long slender cord that she would have called a garret, if it hadn't been at-tached to one of the few pieces of decor in the cabin. There was a safe camouflaged among the books. It was one of the best jobs Hel had ever seen.

The man had money, a ship and he was paranoid. Putting the three things together, she could come to just one conclusion.

He was a pirate.

Hel had been kidnapped by pirates.

But why would a pirate kidnap her? Tierrza, her es-tate, was a port, but she didn't have any problems with pirates. They'd never truly had pirates, just smugglers, and her ancestors had dealt with them long ago.

But modern pirates still plagued the Mediterranean.

Just not usually Cyrano.

Hel quirked her lips, the private joke sliding across her mind that it was a sign her cousin, King Zayn, was succeeding in putting their island nation on the map. The fact that she was once again the one making jokes, even if just privately and in her mind, felt like a sign she'd only momentarily lost her groove—a brief blip in what was otherwise a perfect record.

Well, no one would really ever call her record perfect, but she was a damn good guard.

"Are you done with your tour? Forgive me if not, it just seemed like you had moved on." His voice was dry, filled with a joke just for him, leaving Hel with the strangest sense of being left out…and caring about it.

Hel's eyes narrowed, but she was determined to meet him head-on, even if she was barely clothed. "It's all right, some nice stuff in here, but it's just one room." She paused and looked around again, exaggerating the whole thing, then added with a disappointed frown, "And it's kind of small."

He let out a bark of laughter and she started, the sound entrancing her momentarily, a real-life version of the Pied Piper's flute. "Size doesn't matter, it's the motion of the ocean." His eyes laughed as he delivered the line with no shame, his open palm gesturing at the open sea around them through the porticos.

Hel forced herself to look away, following the path of his hand to stare hard at the water and grumbled, "That's not the ocean."

She didn't know what was wrong with her, but it was certainly not helping her regain her accustomed advantage. It was hard to maintain discomfiting nonchalance, the strategy that seemed to most put her opponents off balance, when her breath kept catching every time her eyes snagged on this man's form, carrying her away with reactions and…staring, rather than cool observation.

Thinking while she could, while the strange distraction of him was out of sight, she reviewed what else she knew. Based on the level of luxury of the cabin, the obvious wealth it required to create such a space, let alone what might lie behind the two doors in the room, indicated this was the cabin's quarters. She could be wrong, of course, but she doubted it. She didn't know many people with the kind of wealth that could outfit a passenger or crew cabin so well. Very few were *that* rich, and she knew most of them.

Pirates were a rare thing in this day and age—in the Mediterranean or elsewhere, for that matter.

Incredibly wealthy pirates even less so.

In fact, there was only one who fit the bill that she knew of, and it was, fortunately to the present context, her job to know things, but he wasn't a pirate. He was a privateer, and his name wasn't whispered with fear, but called out for in desperation.

Hel's stomach fluttered and it dawned on her that this is what people meant when they said they had butterflies, but she turned back to face him. Caught all over again by his arresting beauty, it took her a moment to speak, but when she did, despite the strength and steadiness of her voice, the strange absurdity of her words was enough to almost turn them into a question. Because in no scenario in all of the world did it make sense for a man famous through the entire Mediterranean for fighting human trafficking to be kidnapping her, she thought, as she said, "You're the Sea Wolf."

CHAPTER TWO

EYEING HIS CAPTIVE, with her long, deadly limbs, her mop of silver-blond hair, her flashing gemstone eyes and skin that gave off a faint radiance—as if moonglow emanated from her very core, or she was a pearl come to life—Drake Andros, retired admiral, occasional investor, eternal sailor, licensed privateer and Sidran duke, held back a laugh.

"Caught me," he said with a smile instead.

That she'd put the pieces of his high-seas identity together was as irrelevant as it was charming, but he hadn't expected it of her. Not that he had been operating under the impression that she was stupid. Certainly not. A stupid woman didn't graduate at the top of her class from a military academy and rise through the ranks of the royal guard while successfully managing multiple complex estates. He was simply surprised that she'd maintained such an incredible level of coolheaded composure through the process of being accidentally kidnapped and literally dragged out to sea.

A phenomenal bout, superb high dive and hundred-meter swim, all wrapped it up with her being carried off, and she still had the wherewithal to come to an accurate conclusion with very little input—it was impressive. He could recognize that being impressed was sexist—he wouldn't be of a man in her position—but his inner demons were as irrelevant to the situation as was her lovely mind.

That he was the Sea Wolf was business. What sat between them was entirely personal.

Thirty years ago her father had tried to murder his family.

Today he'd achieved his vengeance.

But his plan hinged on her cooperation.

"So why did the Sea Wolf capture the Cyranese captain of the queen's guard?" she asked, adorably nonchalant about the whole thing.

"The Sea Wolf," he said, "doesn't have anything to do with you. Drake Andros, son of Ibrahim and Amira Andros, rightful heir to the Andros Duchy of Cyrano, however, has a few things he'd like to discuss."

She froze, her face losing its pretty glow, replaced by a more deathly pallor.

Her reaction was…interesting. He had expected to have to feed her a few more tidbits before she began to realize the more sinister nature to their connection. Perhaps she wasn't unaware of what her father had done to him?

If that was true, it would change things. His gut tightened. He worked hard to account for contingencies, but by their nature, not every one could be anticipated. The tightness tilted toward a slow burn as his mind played out the ways his plan would be impacted if she wasn't as innocent as he'd assumed. Her original involvement would have been impossible—she'd been a small child—but had she a part in keeping the event covered up?

After all the years, all the loss…could he let it crumble if touching her was unconscionable? He hadn't had a problem touching her to this point. If she was guilty in the whole thing, as well, what did that say about the trust he could place in his own instincts where she was concerned?

As seconds passed, her reaction only seemed to deepen, actual horror dawning on her face just before she began to shake her head.

The suspicion that had started sick and slick and warm in his gut turned hot and dangerous as it unfurled.

She might not have been involved in the original plot, but her reaction suggested she wasn't innocent of it.

Emotion made him impatient, edgy. Life had consistently proved to him that the only thing he could rely on was himself, but what if even that wasn't true? What if he'd misread such a critical piece in her presumed innocence? If he'd been wrong he'd wasted years on a plot with a critical flaw. He'd done what his mother had warned him of and drilled so deep into the dark that he'd lost the light of clarity.

"Ibrahim Andros, your father's dearest friend and oldest childhood playmate, and his companion well into adulthood. They were two peas in one pod—right up until Ibrahim, his wife, Amira, their son, Drake, and their daughter, Nya, all of them at once, were killed when their boat tragically capsized at sea."

Doubt turned his voice harsh and made his words run fast. His gaze was ultra penetrating as he watched her for hints or clues of guilt as he spoke, but if she already knew, then he wanted to be sure she felt at least something in his reveal—that she was moved, somehow, as she came to understand just exactly who he was, and what her family had made him.

"In the wake of the tragedy, your father became steward, and for all intents and purposes, inheritor of the slightly smaller duchy to the east, with its incredible maritime prospects, named as such, to the surprise of no one, by his very best friend."

"My father arranged the accident…" Her words were a breathless combination of horror, rage and knowing, all braided together.

But the knowing was a new knowing, and with taking it on, it seemed, she took on an invisible anchor of responsibility, her shoulders visibly sinking, though she had been barely old enough for school when it had all occurred.

Out of the storm of his emotions, he made the wild swing from suspicion to—to what exactly, he couldn't say, but something filled him with the urge to reach out to her, to place a hand on her shoulder and say something conciliatory, to remind her that she had been too young to have been meaningfully involved in the ancient plot.

He resisted the urge. Comforting her because her father was a monster was not on the current agenda. Wrenching his plan back on track and toward fruition was.

Though off to a less-than-smooth start, and thirty years delayed, justice would finally be served. His relief was shaky at best, the bumps and hurdles thus far only proving what he'd known since he was a disillusioned child: a person could only rely on themselves. That his plan hinged on her, a stranger and the daughter of his enemy, was a weakness, but one that could be adjusted to.

She was crucial to it all, the only one who could help him find the closure that he'd chased his whole life—closure that his mother had insisted had to come from within, not knowing that he didn't have anything inside but a gaping hunger for the wrongs committed against them to be righted—and already his plans had taken a significant detour because of it.

He had intended to approach her privately, smoothly lay his cards on the table based on his suspicion that she was of a mind with him, charm her into thinking she might be interested in destroying her father's legacy and leave the harbor with her none the wiser. He'd contemplated how to approach her for months, with the loft of their titles, the respective careers they were well known for in the world and the friendliness of their nations all on the line. Discretion, charm and mystery had been the key components of his planned approach.

Instead, they'd fought and set off a national alarm, and he'd unintentionally abducted her. And now he had to convince her to go along with his plan.

It was incredibly trying to work with others. He was cut from the cloth to lead or go alone—teamwork was inefficient.

But he could find no other way. Her father had been meticulous in his lineage obsession, ensuring that only another one of his blood, another d'Tierrza, could undo his work.

And so Drake had studied his would-be partner, reading every tabloid article about her and tracking down every whisper of her name from the moment his plans had settled into their final shape. He'd held his mother's hand as she struggled with her last breaths—

cancer the foe that finally took her down after murder plots and poverty had tried their best and failed.

Before that moment, he had simply turned his entire life into a catalog of triumph and success, his metaphorical rude gesture to spite the man who'd tried to stamp out him and his family. But when he'd learned that that man had died, peacefully in his sleep, the death of the innocent and the just, while his mother had struggled to draw in air, it didn't matter that he'd made sure she'd had the best care money could provide and the all the comfort human beings had been able to invent. Drake had been consumed with impotent rage. That a good and strong woman would go, her passing a thing of pain, while her tormentor had gone easy ate at him, driving him from sleep, from home, from ease, from even the satisfaction of having earned everything back that had been taken from him and then some.

It wasn't enough. The only thing that could possibly be enough was to take everything that man held dear.

When the shocking announcement was made that the old duke had passed up his wife to name his daughter his successor, Drake realized he'd been given his opportunity.

Whether or not the father could see it, the daughter hated his guts.

Marrying her would be Drake's means to not just regaining his own ancestral home, but to taking Tierrza's, as well. He would exact his revenge in the only way that a man like Dominic d'Tierrza would have understood: by taking everything he had.

Helene might be the daughter of his greatest enemy, but she was also the key to his revenge. He was going to marry her. He was going to marry her and get her pregnant, and his sons—and his name—were going to rule not just Andros, but Tierrza, as well, the famous jewel of Cyrano.

And he had strong reason and evidence to believe that she would be amenable to the idea…if he hadn't irritated her too much by kidnapping and towering over her.

He didn't expect, however, her to place a hand over her heart as she said, "You have my most sincere apologies. If this world were a just one, my father would reap the punishment his actions deserved, but it is not, and this is just one more of the many evils he died without accounting for. I cannot undo what he did, but I offer you my deepest apologies." She concluded her speech with a deep bow.

He frowned.

This was not the solidarity he had been looking for.

He needed a rebellious daughter, not a battle-weary soldier.

Though, he supposed, her response was a sort of confirmation of his suspicion that bad blood existed between father and daughter.

From age eleven to sixteen, she had used every public appearance and every form of acting out possible to present a clear picture, at least to Drake, of exactly what she thought of the man.

She had exhausted the typical means of wealthy children by the age of thirteen—wrecking cars, being caught on film smoking, dating older men. It had seemed her actions were more than adolescent rebellions. But then she'd turned to more mature methods.

At thirteen, she became famous for being the youngest accepted applicant for Cyrano's International Young

People's Volunteer Corps, a humanitarian organization comprised of Cyranese citizens aged eighteen to twenty-six, sparking a sea of rumors of corruption and buying access that were no doubt true, but didn't prevent her from spending two years in Kazakhstan, mastering the Russian language and establishing an orphanage…into which she funneled an inordinate amount of d'Tierrza cash. The amount itself was the next scandal, far exceeding the highest recorded charitable donations in the nation of Cyrano prior to it. For a while, the joke was that daddy's little girl had a great big heart and no sense of the value of money. Again, it was clear to Drake, though, that she'd been entirely aware of her actions, and they were intentional.

She was hitting her father strategically.

Looking at her now, though, he realized it went deeper than that.

She wasn't merely a spoiled girl pushing back against her powerful father.

She was engaged in an honor war.

Helene d'Tierrza hated her father, and she had always taken pains to strike where she could to do the most damage—his pocketbook and his reputation.

The age of sixteen had brought an end to her obviously rebellious days, and by the end the year, marked a lull in her scandalous behavior. That birthday, Dominic d'Tierrza had announced her engagement to a Cyranese lord, the son of a known crony of her father's.

Three months later, the engagement was over under murky circumstances. The young man left the country. Then, just before she turned seventeen, Helene shocked the world with her greatest scandal yet: enrolling in the Cyranese military academy. She kept a low profile for the remainder of her time in the academy, where she graduated six years later at the top of her class with top honors, as well as a master's degree in military sciences, making the society pages only for her academy honors.

She shocked Cyrano once more, however, upon graduation. Rather than return to her place in society, she enlisted in and was accepted as a member of the royal guard. That the female heir to the wealthiest aristocratic family in the country would postpone marriage in favor of active military duty was outrageous.

But by twenty-two it was clear that the Rebel Heiress, as she'd been dubbed by the tabloids, had settled into who she was. She'd been assigned to guard the then prince, Zayn, her cousin through her mother's family, and when his father was assassinated eleven years later, she found herself the guard of a king. Six months after that, upon the death of her father, she nonetheless became the Duchess d'Tierrza, the first female to hold the title in the history of the line. In fact, because there had never been a female head of the family, it had become a colloquial joke to refer to her as the duke.

This was all public knowledge. What Drake had pieced together from his own research, however, was that even after her father died, she continued to attack his legacy.

Rather than growing the d'Tierrza coffers, she managed her estates to perfection, bringing in greater incomes than they ever had under her father's watch, and donated all but what was required to manage each to charities around the nation. On the surface, it appeared she was increasing her family's income, but if one looked closely—as Drake had—she was incrementally shrinking the d'Tierrza estate and fortune, funneling wealth back into the community, little by little, through the charitable foundation she and her mother had created in her father's name.

And if he'd been left with any doubt before he approached her, she'd ended it by throwing a custom champagne flute at his likeness.

As Drake had suspected, her father's death didn't seem to have eased any of his daughter's animosity toward him, and for that, Drake was grateful, as his vengeance hinged on it.

"I'm sorry." She met his eyes—hers as blue as the deepest ocean—commander to commander, and he knew that her words weren't empty. He appreciated them, he truly did. But he needed a lot more than an apology from her.

But she wasn't done yet.

Wrapping her arms around her chest, a gesture that returned his attention to the fact that while she wasn't naked, she was also not what anyone would reliably describe as fully clothed, she said, "My father was a real bastard."

The reminder of her state of undress brought with it an unwelcome tightening in his groin, even as discussing her father left a sour taste in his mouth, so he was sharper than he intended to be when he said, "Take one of my shirts," then nodded toward the door closest to her, which led to his bedroom.

Without commenting on his sudden change of subject, she walked in the direction he indicated and returned with a shirt from his wardrobe.

She had selected quickly, choosing a navy blue button-up. She turned her back to him before she put it on. The back of her blue dress revealed bare shoulders and what remained of it after their chase hugged the long line of her spine before ending at midthigh, where jagged edges revealed the supple skin of her lower derriere as she put her arms in the sleeves... Then his shirt dropped down to cover it all up and for a split second he hated the garment.

When she turned around, however, he decided he loved it once more—would perhaps even call it his favorite shirt.

The dark blue fabric, which should have made her look washed out, only served to deepen the flashing blue of her eyes and make her white-blond hair shine like silver.

She was truly a stunning creature, what he imagined a Valkyrie might look like, crossbred with a literal star.

Her eyebrows were deep golden blond, highlighting the elegant bone structure of her face. Her lips were sinful—bright coral, lush and carnal. They were a stark contrast to the rest of her untouchable cool beauty. And her nose was long and straight—aristocratic to the bone.

And all of that, coupled with her obvious hatred of her father, meant that when it came to this particular path to revenge, he might even enjoy the journey. Even if it did involve marrying and making love to the daughter of his greatest enemy.

"As you were saying...your father was a real bastard, which brings us to what I was hoping to speak with you about."

She nodded with a half smile, sitting on the arm of his chair as she did so, and his skin heated, his entire system thrilling as he circled ever closer to the achievement of his goals.

"I have a proposal for you, a way for you to 'right

the wrongs,' as you say. What I'm asking for is no small commitment, I recognize that, but the wrong your father committed against my family is no small thing, either. What I am asking for requires a two-or possibly three-year sacrifice from you and a great deal of physical discomfort, but afterward, you will be free to go your own, returning entirely to your life as it is now."

Crossing her arms in from her chest, she lifted an eyebrow. "A great deal of physical discomfort, eh? You're not selling this well."

Drake laughed, the sound starting as a low rumble in his gut and rising out of his reach and deep until his eyes watered. Wiping them at the corners, he shook his head. "Oh, it's nothing that women don't go through all over the world every day—I just want you to be the mother of my children."

CHAPTER THREE

HEL'S MOUTH DROPPED OPEN.

It made her look like a fish. Roz, her childhood etiquette tutor and lifelong ally, had drilled this into her. She knew it like she knew her name, and yet there she was.

The man before her certainly kept her on her toes, that was for sure. He threw her off balance with an ease that no one but her father had ever been able to achieve.

He was gorgeous and tragic and dangerous and everything the angry daughter of a wealthy man could ask for when it came to flipping her father and family legacy the bird—everything she might have conjured up for herself, late at night in her room as a young girl, as yet powerless to stand up to her autocratic parent.

But she wasn't that girl anymore, and while this thrilling man and his thrilling and indecent proposal were a temptation the likes of which her thrill-seeking heart might have leaped at earlier in her life, she had grown into the kind of woman that realized her responsibilities were more important than her desires. And if she was tempted in a way a part of her was ashamed of, she could at least find comfort in the truth of that fact, because she certainly wasn't finding it in the words she had to say.

"I can't," she said, though her mouth fought the words the whole time.

He smiled, and the smile was as entrancing as her first look at him had been. She had never had this reaction to another human. Yes, she had been wild and reckless in her youth, but it had all been for show. She hadn't been attracted to anyone she'd made sure to be photographed with, just like she'd never actually gone out with any of them. Though the scandal had suited her narrative, the reality had been the obvious truth: she had been too young for that kind of thing.

Later, in the Volunteer Corps and later in the military academy, she had been too busy for it. And then she had been a royal guard and her job made it too risky. Then her father had died and her vow had put an end to even thinking about it. Until this shockingly magnetic man had dropped into her world out of the sky and brought desire to the forefront after it was far too late to do anything about it.

For the first time since she'd made it, she regretted her vow. Not the actual making of it—that she stood by—and not because she wanted to take it back, but because she'd had no idea what she'd been giving up when she had. Promises made in ignorance required keeping no less than those made in full knowledge, but if she'd known men like him existed in the world…

His voice was its own lure, warm like an embrace, confident in its assuredness that it could change her mind. "Of course you can't. It isn't done. You don't know me. What would people think…? But ignore that, ignore them. Think instead of what your father would think. Think about how angr—"

As much as she loved to imagine her father angry, she held up her hand to stop him where he was. "I can't," she repeated, her voice low and earnest. "I can't, because when I went to him as he lay dying, I looked him in his eye and swore to him that the d'Tierrza line would end with me, that there would be no d'Tierrza children to inherit the lands or title and that I would see to it that the family name was wiped from the face of the earth so that everything he had ever worked for, or cared about, was lost to history, the legacy he cared so much about nothing but dust. I swore to him that I would never marry and never have children, that not a trace of his legacy would be left on this planet."

For a moment, there was a pause, as if the room itself had sucked in a hiss of irritation. The muscles in his neck tensed, then flexed, though he remained otherwise motionless. He blinked as if in slow motion, the movement a sigh, carrying something much deeper than frustration, though no sound came out. Hel's chest squeezed as she merely observed him. She felt like she'd let him down in some monumental way though they'd only just become reacquainted. She struggled to understand why the sensation was so familiar until she recognized the experience of being in the presence of her father.

Then he opened his eyes again, and instead of the cold green disdain her heart expected, they still burned that fascinating warm brown—a heat that was a steady home fire, as comforting as the imaginary family she'd dreamed up as a child—and all of the taut disappointment in the air was gone.

Her vow was a hiccup in his plans. That he had a

low tolerance for hiccups was becoming clear. How she knew any of this when he had revealed so little in his reaction, and her mind only now offered up hazy memories of him as a young man, she didn't know.

She offered a shrug and an airy laugh in consolation, mildly embarrassed about the whole thing though she was simultaneously unsure as to exactly why. "Otherwise, you know, I'd be all in. Despite the whole abduction…" Her cheeks were hot, likely bright pink, but it couldn't be helped so she made the joke, anyway, despite the risk that it might bring his eyes to her face, that it might mean their eyes locked again and he stole her breath again.

Of course, that is what happened. And then there was that smile again, the one that said he knew all about the strange mesmerizing power he had over her, and it pleased him.

Whether he was the kind of man who used his power for good or evil had yet to be determined.

Either way, beneath that infuriating smile, deep in his endless brown eyes, was the sharp attunement of a predator locked on its target. "Give me a week." His face may not have changed, but his voice gave him away, a trace of hoarseness, as if his sails had been slashed and the wind slipped through them, threaded it, a strange hint of something Hel might have described as desperation…if it had come from anyone other than him.

"What?" she asked.

"Give me a week to change your mind."

Hel's sympathy dried up like a desert pool. She shook her head. "No, thank you. I'm pretty set on this. And while I appreciate the seriousness, as well as the lack of intention, you did kidnap me…"

He laughed, and the sound of it eased some of the tightness in her chest. She brought a hand to the spot in the center of her breastbone, where the sensation seemed to coalesce, and rubbed as he continued, his eyes sharp on her every movement. "Give me seven days to bring you around to my plan. We want the same thing, in the end. Let me convince you."

Hel snorted. They didn't exactly want the same thing. He wanted revenge. She wanted eradication. But she didn't say that. Instead, she asked, "And if you can't? What do I get?"

His eyes lit, voice picking up a charge as he said with a shrug, "I bring you back home, forgiven—no harm, no foul. You did your part to right the wrong."

She sucked in a little breath, the only outward sign of the allure of that promise. But, clearing her mind, she shook her head and said, "My job prevents things being that simple."

He chuckled. "It's not just your job."

Hel smiled. "Agreed. My absence is likely already rather visible."

He nodded sagely and she almost laughed.

"Now, and I know this is rather unconventional, " he began, "but, seeing as how you are already 'kidnapped,' my suggestion would be to keep things simple and just remain so."

Now Hel did laugh. A lot.

Shaking her head, she wiped at the tears that escaped from the corners of her eyes. When she had collected herself, she said, "So you're suggesting I take this as an enforced holiday, if you will?"

He gave a single, firm, grave nod in response and another chuckle bubbled out of her.

"And on this enforced vacation, you're going to try and seduce me out of the deathbed vow I made to my father?" She lifted an eyebrow with the question.

He smiled, his grin quick and wicked. "If you want me to. I just said I'd change your mind, though."

Hel's blush was an immediate inferno—hot enough that she glanced surreptitiously at her arm just to make sure she hadn't caught fire.

"You're not," he said, reading her mind.

"What?" she asked, irritation threading the question.

"On fire," he said, chuckling. "You looked worried."

"What are you talking about?" she snapped, knowing exactly what he was talking about.

"Well, you're as red as a ripe tomato and even look a little sweaty, so I only thought…"

Her mouth dropped open again. "I'm not sweaty," she said.

He inclined his head and raised his palms. "My mistake. Glistening."

There was no match for his audacity, Hel realized. No attack she could be assured he wouldn't deflect smoothly…except one.

"Yes." The word danced out of her mouth, relaxed and self-assured, while her stomach spiraled and her palms went clammy. She had the sense of things picking up speed, right before they spun out of control—the moment before the crash she knew so well from her days of high-performance racing, but it was too late to take her foot off the gas now.

Once again, his entire body stilled, his cocky smile gone for a frozen moment as he stared her dead in the eye, gaze searching and intense. Uncertainty, raw emotion and...vulnerability all poured out of the deep, soul-revealing orbs of his eyes, and in the face of it, she was nearly lost, though to what she didn't know.

She had thrown him off balance for once. It had taken offering herself up on a platter in order to do so, but she had been successful. But as things shifted within her, she realized he wasn't the only one.

"You're sure?" His eyes left no room for anything but absolute and irrefutable commitment.

Hel swallowed. Was she? Jenna and the king's guard could handle her absence, but could she handle the man before her? There had never been a shadow of a doubt before, but there had also never been a challenge before. In fact, she'd yet to meet a challenge she wasn't a match for.

The reminder shored her when her heart was less certain.

"Yes," she answered.

Triumph lit his eyes, his grin returning, his canines catching the light streaming in through the skylights, to shine bright white and sharp. He licked his lips and she was helpless to do anything but watch, fascinated, rapt, absolutely trapped.

He pushed away from the desk he was leaning against and closed the space between them until she was forced to tilt up her head to maintain their eye contact.

Instinctively she knew not to break it, knew it would trigger a chase that she wasn't sure she was fast enough to outrun.

In truth, she wasn't sure it hadn't already begun.

He brought his hands to her jaw and ran his fingers along its stubborn line, tiny jolts of electricity shooting through her skin in the wake of their contact. She sucked in a breath and his smile reached his eyes, though it could never have been called warm.

No. Warmth was pacts and partnership. The light that lit his eyes was triumph—cold, bright and biting.

He angled her face up, tilting it toward his even farther for greater access. His eyebrows had drawn together while his eyes stormed, both pleasure and anticipation weaving together with his win.

"Seven days. No more, no less—unless, of course, it doesn't take that long." And then he kissed her.

If she hadn't already been lost at sea, she would have sworn the earth roiled beneath her when their lips met.

Like magnets with opposite poles, they locked on contact, neither of them in control of the attractive force that held them. He plundered, of course—what else would he have done? He was a pirate.

She surprised herself, though, when she opened to the onslaught, rather than pushing him away immediately and with grand retribution—what she would have done with any other man.

Sensing the surrender in her softening, he took more. More surprise came as she welcomed his dominance, pouring her own fierce nature into it, just this one time completely unafraid of overwhelming someone else.

With his free hand he undid the top buttons and slipped his shirt over her shoulders—all without breaking the kiss.

Hel, drowning as she was in the sensations of his generous lips pressed against hers, didn't care what else he did as long as he held his line, his tongue marauding, her system reveling in this rare moment of being overpowered.

Pressing closer, he drew her body against the long length of his hard body, heedless of his sea-soaked clothing, which did nothing to cool the heat building in her veins.

As he drew her nearer, his thigh pressed against the crease of her thighs, wedging an opening between them, his wet clothes a sensual abrasion against her sensitive bare skin.

The echo of a sharp inhalation bounced around the room when he made contact with the molten core of her, and it took her mind a moment to process the fact that the sound came from her. Rational mind struggling to come back to itself, back to its home in the driver's seat of her consciousness, she tried to remember the terms of their deal and her vow and her very name, but couldn't seem to hold thought in the face of each sensory revelation.

He tasted like salted caramel on a shortbread cookie, the sweet savory combination of the one thing her mother knew how to cook that she looked forward to every holiday season. A flavor she couldn't get enough of.

He smelled like salt water and leather and rope, and something she had never encountered before but her mind told her was his skin, a scent she'd find nowhere else but here.

He completely encompassed her, hard and hot, pressing against her like a molten iron bar, reshaping her into something new.

Waves of electricity rode through the remaking of her until she couldn't be sure that she hadn't become merely a conduit—a vessel created to contain all his energy and power.

He growled and the sound rippled across her skin, leaving a trail of shivers before burrowing deep in her core.

Eyes closed, her remaining inputs heightened, overloading her system with information.

His fingertips were rough, his skin was smooth and soft. His lips were full and he was in absolute control of their kiss, not so much guiding her into new territory as grabbing her hand to take her running into the unknown, fast, heady and daring. And though the destination was forbidden, it was hard to remember that, when his invitation had been delivered in exactly her language.

Though her balance was excellent she was filled suddenly with a sense of vertigo, falling, the only constant thing his kiss as she went.

From far away, she heard the sound of laughter, growing closer as her breath turned shallow and quick. Her breasts were sensitive beacons on her chest, alert in a way she hadn't known they had the capacity to be, straining for contact she wasn't supposed to want.

Reading her mind again, his hand came to her breast, the thin fabric of his shirt serving only to enhance the erotic sensation of the searing heat of his hand cupping her swollen flesh. She gasped, and in her mind, the laughing grew louder until she could recognize whose it was.

Like an ice bucket from the underworld, her father's ghostly cackles bounced around her head, reminding her that he would always win in the end, even from beyond the grave.

Gasping, though no pleasure lingered, Hel brought the flexed side of her palm down against Drake's aorta before gut checking him with a one-inch punch to the solar plexus. Remarkably, he remained upright, taking a step back with a grunt, sucking in a breath, eyes squeezing shut, before he cracked open an eye to look at her.

She remained bent over, hands on her knees, breathing hard.

Looking up, she caught his open eye.

For a moment they simply stared at each other, Hel's bangs falling in front of her face, which she knew was a mask of exasperation. She had never been good at hiding her feelings. No amount of practice in front of the mirror could remedy her of the failing.

Then he cracked a one-eyed smile, white teeth flashing, and reached out a hand to her. "Deal?"

Hel stared at the hand offered. It was massive, rope-scarred, marked with faded tattoos, and she couldn't help herself. Rising to meet his hand with one of hers, the woman who'd grown out of the girl known for making risky wagers with the devil, the woman who had learned to put responsibility above desire, said, "Deal."

God help her.

CHAPTER FOUR

TRIUMPH WAS TOO small a description for the rush of sensation in his veins. Joy, relief, rage, pride—all of them coalesced into a throbbing new emotion that threatened to overwhelm him. It wasn't closure—that would take bringing his father back, saving his mother from the hard life and exposure that had taken her early from him. But it was close. Close enough that he was tempted to let out a little of the tidal wave.

But he also didn't respond to threats, not even his own emotional ones, and so none of it escaped.

Once again, he had grasped victory from the jaws of certain defeat. And all he'd had to do to do it was catch a high-voltage current wrapped in moonglow. His plan had hinged on her, that had always been true, but he realized he'd underestimated the power that gave her all the way up to her declaration. The fact that she had a choice had been in his mind the whole time. That she might refuse had never truly crossed it.

He had come this far through relentless self-assuredness, and emerged as the natural leader in every group effort he'd been a part of. He had been irritated by the element of uncertainty she introduced into his endeavor, and yet he'd underestimated it all the same.

Her eyes had steel in them as she'd spoken. She'd been serious. He'd been prepared to break down defenses that were social—they were weak at best. He was an excellent catch and had her disdain for her father on his side. Despite the absurdity of it, he'd never imagined her walls would be of such a deep and personal nature. Nor so irrevocable.

In her gorgeous blue eyes, bright and inviting as the Caribbean Sea, he'd seen her resolution, as binding as his own promise to himself and his mother's memory. She would not be moved. And in that liquid firmament, his grand plans began to drown. He would return to Calla a failure, just as he'd arrived decades before. The admiral and captain, everything he'd done going down with the ship because in the end, he was just like his father—brought down by the d'Tierrzas.

His offer had been a desperate call to the wind—her simple *yes* the light of a lighthouse flickering to life on the shore. It had been a risky and near thing, but he'd escaped the gale force just before it tore apart his soul.

So if he'd nearly lost control, nearly let the tide of emotions break free of the dam of his control, it could be understood.

And by the way she'd responded to his kiss, her vow would be forgotten before they even arrived in Calla.

Even accounting for the sucker punch.

He grinned, allowing the expression as his mind raced ahead, plotting and planning his campaign, even as his stomach continued to roll.

The woman had an arm.

But she was naive and as clear as glass when it came to what lovers did.

She was completely ignorant of the rarity of the thing

that had sparked between them. It was a feeling even he, as experienced as any respectable sailor, had never had before. And he could use that.

With the heat of their kiss still electric on his tongue and the elation of his success throbbing in his system, he gestured for her to sit, every inch the magnanimous host.

"Would you like anything?" he asked. "The galley is well-stocked. My chef can make virtually anything."

She must have been feeling the beginning of hunger by now. A body that strong needed regular fuel. And even without the experience of sparring with her, the fact of her strength was impossible to miss when it was muscle tone that gave her body dimension, and, he observed, its hints of curves.

Had she not been the captain of the royal queen's guard of Cyrano, he imagined she might have had the same willowy slenderness that her mother and aunt had been famous for in their heyday. It had been rare for his mother to speak of the past, but when she did, her best friend, Seraphina d'Tierrza, famous beauty, featured heavily.

Like her mother, Helene was tall and long. Unlike her mother, she had filled out, and incredible strength hummed under the pretty packaging like a high-performance racer.

She lifted an eyebrow. "Anything?"

His grin grew even wider. She doubted him.

He loved it when people doubted him. Their ignorance was his advantage.

"Dragon fruit," she declared.

Throwing his head back, he laughed, the sound rich and warm and booming. The laugh was his father's, famous among those who had known him, and just another feature on the long list of traits Drake had inherited from him. Everything but his open heart, it seemed.

"Easy. Try again."

"Star fruit."

He snorted, nodding without bothering to answer.

"Pickled herring."

He tsked, crossing his arms in front of his chest and shaking his head. "I am ashamed at you, Helene. We might be high-class, but we're still sailors. Of course, we have pickled herring."

Chuckling, she challenged, "Durian."

He stopped laughing, gave her a stern frown and pointed a finger at her. "That's cheating."

She nodded, smiling, gemstone eyes sparkling like freshly cut and cleaned diamonds.

"No durian. Too smelly. Despite our spacious and luxurious accommodations, it is still a confined space."

This time she tsked at him. "And you said anything…" At ease, exactly as he'd intended, her voice was all smiles when she said, "A glass of water would be wonderful, please."

That she was comfortable enough to ask him for something was more significant than he thought she realized, but music to his ears. "Certainly." He smiled. "I don't even need to call for that."

He walked to a set of bookshelves and pressed a small button, then a shelf of books slid to the side, a quiet swoosh the only sound as the secret shelf-door revealed a crisp minibar. Filling a chilled crystal glass, he asked, "Bubbles?"

She laughed. "I'll talk it flat, thanks. Fits better with being kidnapped by pirates."

He brought the glass to where she sat on the sofa, legs curled under her, and handed it to her, their fingertips brushing at the transfer, sending little charged sparks up his arm.

The thrill of the win.

Because it was certain he would win her over to his plan. He had waited over thirty years for his revenge— there was no way it would be jeopardized by the whim of a reformed rich girl.

"Are you hungry?" he asked after she had taken a few sips and set the glass on the end table.

"Not now, thank you." When she wasn't paying attention to them, her default manners were everything one would expect from a high-bred young lady.

He wondered if she knew that.

"I would like to know where I'm being kidnapped to, though," she continued, her questions mild and off-hand as she stared out at the sea views around them.

"Calla, on the Sidran coast."

She filed the information away, the process as obvious to him as if he was the one doing it.

Known for his ability to read people, for cutting through the layers of deception and power-grabbing to discern the path of his advantage with uncanny and unparalleled accuracy, he had never encountered anyone as transparent to him as Helene.

Watching her, it was as if he could read her thoughts even as they formed in her mind. He wondered if it drove her crazy that her face showed her thoughts so clearly. He bet it did. He could picture her as a younger woman, practicing in the mirror, trying to hide her reactions.

The thought made him smile. He was willing to bet

she had been adorable—purely earnest in an effort to change something that was fixed.

"Why Calla?" she asked, and in the question he heard layers.

"My home," he said, unable to restrain the pride in his voice. He had been born a duke's heir and had everything stolen from him. Then he had picked himself up, and climbed his way back to the very same position by his own strength and means. His title had been a gift from the Sidran king. None of his peers could say the same. It was unheard of.

Perhaps it was why his inner compass was so strong. He'd braved paths, both on land and sea, that other men had feared to tread—attack, loss, poverty—and not only lived to tell the tale, but also used them to catapult his way from their dark recesses to the very top. By himself. By trusting his instincts and inner guide and no one or nothing else. Growing up in the Sidran capital poor would have taught him that hard lesson, if witnessing his father's betrayal and resulting loss of everything hadn't already drilled it into the very fabric of his being.

He required Helene's participation in what was the most important campaign of his life, career and retirement, but trust was not a requirement, neither hers nor his. Compatibility, which they had in spades, and agreement, which she had given, were all that was required from her. Now that both were secured, it would only be a matter of time before they were well on their way.

However, as he took in the incredibly dangerous, barely clothed woman in his cabin, he had to admit that there was an unexpected flavor beneath revenge, and it was turning out to be a bit more…complex than he'd anticipated.

Challenge, he'd expected—she was one of the most dangerous and accomplished women in the world. Her vow was certainly a dangerous hurdle, but he was confident he could seduce her and had come to terms with the idea of making love to the daughter of a man he loathed long before setting his plan in motion—he would not have been the first man to turn the lights out and close his eyes for the greater good.

What he hadn't been prepared for was how good it would feel—not the achievement of his revenge, but its execution.

He hadn't anticipated she would feel like a live wire in his hands.

He hadn't planned on caring whether or not she was impressed with what he'd grown from the ashes of his life. But as his home came into distant view through his cabin's portholes, he realized it was the case nonetheless.

Calla—his little bay, purple-blue in the twilight, and it's palatial manor, set farther inland in the harbor, visible high above the high-tide line and built into the craggy savannah forest cliffs. Here was a fortune he had built himself.

Though he could not see them yet, ships, he knew, were docked farther into the harbor, safe and sleepy in their moorings, peacefully undisturbed. He'd worked hard to ensure his home was lovely, prosperous and pretty.

And with his ship's incredible speed, it was only a short time later that he sent the command to set anchor.

His personal assistant met them, boarding immediately with the change of clothing he'd ordered for Helene. With just seven days for his seduction, he didn't want any of it to be uncomfortable...even just for the duration of the drive to Caline, his ducal manor.

Visible from the docks, Caline, his home, jutted out from the hillside overlooking the bend in the river and the entire city of Calla, high above the city. Reaching it by foot was an uphill undertaking along an ancient trail under the best of circumstances, even if the journey was breathtakingly beautiful. Attempting it at the end of a long day, which had included an unexpected bout of sparring with one of the world's best soldiers and running headlong into her unexpected little vow, was not, however, the best of circumstances, and so he called a car for them.

Tonight he would wine and dine her in the privacy and seclusion of home, before he took her out to charm her with his city.

Helene's expression, however, upon opening the delicately packaged garment box brought by his assistant, did not suggest his seduction was off to an auspicious beginning.

She held up a simple dress—blue, flowing and long. Her lips pursed and she drew her eyebrows together, her opinion obvious, and he had to hold back his laugh.

"Not your style?" he asked, unable to keep the amusement from his voice. She had revealed multiple facets in their short time together, but this was the first he was seeing the spoiled daughter.

But she was not in the mood to be more revealing, or had recalled her manners, it seemed, because she just flared her nostrils and looked around, for a place to change he presumed.

Indicating the door that led to his closet, he held both his smile and comment. Whatever she didn't like about the dress, he wouldn't press. His seduction efforts stopped at comforting a woman over her clothing.

Clothes were a means to an end, not meant for emotional investment.

And, like everything he'd seen her in, when she returned draped in the clean hanging of the dress, she was beautiful.

His assistant had included a pair of strappy leather sandals, as he'd instructed. She couldn't arrive barefoot.

As he'd anticipated, the sandals were forgiving for his guess on size. Unlike the dress she'd worn upon their meeting, this was made of breezy cotton—local, if he was not mistaken—and would allow her far greater freedom of movement. She should be relieved.

She did not look relieved.

As lovely as she was, Grecian and elegant, he was reminded of his younger sister, Nya, on the occasions their mother had forced her to dress up.

He almost laughed, but held back, and instead offered her his arm. "Shall we?"

For a moment, he wondered if she would take it, but she did not disappoint, shrugging away whatever displeasure she had with her attire to rest her arm on his. As usual, there was a jolt on contact.

He led her onshore and into the sleek black car that waited for them.

They rode in a comfortable quiet and he realized it was the first truly settled stretch of time they'd had since their meeting. In fact, when he thought back, it was the first settled stretch of time he could remember in years. It seemed like peace might finally be his in less than seven days. What would that feel like? He was ready to find out.

They pulled up the hill and into the curved stone driveway at Caline's entrance. She marveled as they exited the car, but he did not slow for a tour—they would have time for that tomorrow. Tonight was about rest, relaxation and recuperation, completely free of pressure. He wanted her supple and easy and off her guard before he set to work.

After they'd shared a kiss that had her redefining the word, Hel had expected Drake to launch a full-blown-seduction onslaught, assuming he would waste no time, or his newfound advantage, in his effort to budge her from her vow. Because an advantage was certainly what he'd proved he had with that kiss—he had an advantage strong enough to rip her from the shore and cast her out to sea. So she would need to remain on her guard, to take seriously the threat he posed to her defenses, as mesmerizing as he was.

She had mentally prepared for it throughout the nerve-racking ride to the manor—nerve-racking not because the drive was treacherous or road conditions dangerous, but because the effect he had on her was amplified by being in a dark, comfortable confined space together. She would need to avoid kissing, and touching, at all costs.

If this was attraction, it was a wonder anyone got anything done. The relentless drive of her mind to focus on the object of her interest certainly explained some of her cousin's more asinine behavior when it came to his wife.

But she sensed none of that from Drake.

In fact, he was behaving as if the matter had gone from his mind entirely.

He had not tried to impress her with his manor, though the glimpses she'd caught had impressed her nonetheless as he'd all but marched her through the grand manse to a small, secluded balcony, the archway leading into it picturesquely framed by blooming flowering vines and soft twilight. Centered in the picture, as if intended for a still life or a movie scene, was a lovely round table, set for two with wineglasses, bread, cheese, charcuterie and fruit. Her stomach growled.

Drake laughed, "I had a feeling you would be hungry. We'll eat. After that, I've kept our evening simple—massages, followed by rest. Tough as you are, you've had a lot to process today." His smile was warm, friendly, with no trace of teasing fire.

The juxtaposition from his demeanor earlier—flirtatious, wild—was enough to put her off balance. Hot and cold, the unfamiliar territory was disorienting to say the least.

She was no more grounded after dinner. Yes, they'd shared a wonderful meal, enjoying surprisingly easy conversation, and a camaraderie she hadn't experienced since her academy days. But he hadn't directed so much as a flirtatious glance in her direction since they'd arrived in Calla.

True to his word, massages followed dinner, but he surprised her with no setup attempt, with each of them receiving their massages in serenely appointed private spa rooms.

And afterward, rather than pouncing when her mind was mush and her muscles relaxed postmassage, she was greeted by a friendly staff person who showed her to a peaceful room that looked out over the harbor. And she was its only occupant.

The next morning, the same kind staff member led her to breakfast, this time in another lovely dining area, with an enclosed sun porch that had views into the river canyon.

"Did you sleep well?" he asked.

For a moment, she simply took him in. He looked like he had rested, and well. His smile was as bright and sunny as the morning, his clothing fresh, his skin as alluring and velvet smooth in the daylight as it had been through the afternoon and evening before.

His eyes danced, observing her in the simple dress she'd found laid out for her this morning. Two days in a row in dresses and she was contemplating going nude. If he didn't have such an unpredictable effect on her and his wager didn't sit between them, she just might have.

This dress was a spaghetti-strapped maxi in corn-flower-blue, shapeless but nicely draping...if one went for that kind of thing. Hel did not, and her face must have said so. She wore the sandals she had been given the evening before and knew objectively that the ensemble was lovely, the picture of a young woman on holiday. Still, it remained, indisputably, a dress.

"Fantastic, thank you. And you?" She refused to rise to the challenge in his eyes and mention the dress.

Gaze laughing, he said, "Very well. It's so much easier to rest knowing your dreams are on the brink of coming true."

Hel snorted, "I would think that might make it harder to sleep."

He brushed the back of her hand as he reached for the butter and said softly, "Maybe it's just your calming influence."

Hel laughed out loud. No one had ever called her influence calming. Her father had called it an embarrassment, a shame, unnatural, defiant, upsetting, disgusting and all manner of other things, but never calming.

That Drake did, as untrue as it was, soothed feathers she hadn't realized were ruffled. She might not be calm, but that had never made her unpleasant. It was nice to know someone beside her mother thought so.

"So what's on the agenda for today? A romantic beach walk? Dinner and a movie? A private boat ride down the river?"

His habitual smile only grew in the face of her sass.

"Hardly, I wasn't born common." He winked, but his words were an eerie echo of her father...and yet, from Drake, they were silly rather than cutting. "I thought we would play tennis."

She started. She couldn't remember her last game of tennis, and in truth, a match sounded...wonderful.

"After our rather active day yesterday, I thought it'd be a good way to get the kinks out," he said, putting words to her thoughts exactly.

Light, fun, easy—tennis would be perfect. And separated by a net, she wouldn't have to worry about touching.

He instructed his staff to find more appropriate attire for her and they met on the court twenty minutes later.

She'd been told all they'd have was a classic white skort and simple white halter top, but she had suspicions the close fit and short length were more intended for the enjoyment of Drake than her mobility on the court.

The match started out fast and strong. Drake had an incredibly powerful serve and precise aim. Hel was light on her feet, with a reach to boot, and the combination kept them evenly matched.

As he served for his last point, Hel was struck by his arresting physique. The man was truly a work of art, all power and heat, and it was all she could do to keep up. Something he only proved true with his serve. Diving toward the far left corner when she'd been positioned on the right, she barely missed the ball with the edge of her racket, cursing when both her body and the ball made contact with the court.

Drake was at her side in a moment, leaning over her, backlit by the sun, concern on his face.

"Are you all right?" he asked, gently probing her exposed skin.

His touch was featherlight and gentle, not in the least sexual, and yet her body reacted as if they were already in bed together, skin prickling, instantly sensitized to every caress, even just that of the warm, dry air of Calla. Their eyes locked, blue and brown meeting on a shore as old as man and woman, holding both of them at a standstill.

Secrets and deep emotions churned behind his gaze, and though she feared where such an undertow might carry her, she was tempted to dive in, anyway.

Eyes dropping to his lips, she found herself wetting her own and swallowing, suddenly thirsty, though not, she realized, for water.

She wanted him to kiss her again, she wanted him to look at her with that teasing flirtation that tempted her to forget who she was just on the chance he might let her run her fingers down his skin.

She wanted to see the look in his eyes she'd seen when they kissed—electric, intense, a little surprised. Looking up at him, far from home and completely at the mercy of the Big Bad Wolf, she had the horrifying realization that she wanted him to seduce her, and that meant she was in way over her head.

His plan was unfolding perfectly. They'd parted ways, the air charged between them, at the tennis court, and the look in her eyes had been undeniable. After an evening of rest, and a leisurely morning and afternoon, she was exactly where he wanted her: hungry for more.

The enchantment of the Calla night market was famous throughout Sidra. With its abundance of hand-painted paper lanterns and string lights, the dancing aromas of fresh-cooked local food, roasting meats and hot, sweet treats, and his talented artisans, farmers and craftspeople on display, it would be a seduction of the senses in itself.

He had worked hard to turn Calla into the prosperous, cheerful port town it had become—it could do work for him in return.

Hel smiled a blinding aristocratic smile at every vendor she met.

Somewhere along the way, she collected a patterned woven basket, which was overfilled with other free offerings from vendors as they made their way through the market.

She mesmerized everyone she encountered, despite the language difference. It wasn't a shock that she caught attention—she was movie-star beautiful and had a presence about her, was utterly confident and relaxed.

What surprised him, though, was the effort she put

into it. She went out of her way to be kind to everyone she met, trying offered foods and dutifully examining every item and tasting every morsel she was presented with.

After encountering her as a fighter and then a sarcastic captive, he was mildly surprised—and a little impressed—to witness her as a gracious traveler.

But he didn't fail to notice the almost imperceptible sigh of relief and easing of her shoulders as they exited the market. She had put on a good show, but the effort had tired her, more so than any of their battles of strength and will had, which he would not have expected. The woman had incredible reserves of energy.

Together they walked along the Tela River, outside of the market now, along the quieter row of long-established, high-end riverside restaurants. Later, after dinner, a car would meet them to take them back to the manor.

Cobblestone streets and whitewashed mud-brick walls dominated here, but bright pops of color in the forms of painted buildings and trees exploding with blossoms ensured the eye had a full buffet of delights.

The Tela was a cool whisper at their side, quiet and calm, before it opened softly into the harbor, having made its long slow curve through the city and its mad rush through the semi desert canyon valley, where wild goats and deer came down the steep cliffsides to drink from its banks.

The restaurants along the river were among the most popular and expensive in the city, their special coastal cuisine famous throughout the entirety of Sidra.

As Drake understood it, reservations were a must, and hard to come by, but he wasn't worried. Being the man who had made it all possible had its perks.

He secured them a lovely mosaic-topped bistro table facing the night-darkened Tela, her waters inky and slick, small eddies catching the flicker of streetlamps to glisten and sparkle.

They sat on either side of the table, separated by a tasteful flower arrangement, elegant, largely rounded, long-stemmed wineglasses, a bottle of the local red and a pitcher of fresh water, picturesquely dripping condensation in the warm breeze. Drake spoke to their server.

In Sidran, his smooth baritone undulated and danced with a warmth it lacked in his mother tongue, his second language alive with the love and welcome he'd found far from home. He knew Helene didn't speak it, but appreciated the reprieve from speaking in the formal and reserved language of his early youth.

The server lapped up their presence like a flower in the sun, his demeanor that of a proprietor eager to impress an important guest. Some things required no translation.

Their dinner, however, did.

Still smiling, Drake turned to Helene. "He says he's preparing each of his specialties, which he will serve over three courses. I tried to rein him in, but as you'll undoubtedly realize on your own, any attempt to ward off Sidran hospitality is absolutely futile."

Helene smiled and for a moment he forgot why they were there, forgot that she sat across from him at a table in Calla because he had less than six full days to convince her to give up the deathbed vow she made to her father. For a moment, she was simply the bright star of a woman he was having dinner with…and that was a kind of loosening of the reins he couldn't afford.

"I haven't gone to dinner in a long time," he admitted before he could stop himself. Eyebrows drawing together, he frowned. Verbal slips were not something common in his experience, not with his kind of control. Something about her disarmed him, though—lured, or perhaps hypnotized, him into taking his hands off the wheel, at least for a moment. It was all the more pressing that he remain diligent.

A frown crossed her own expression like a cloud, then she said, "Neither have I. Not since the academy."

That surprised him, though his research had already told him as much.

He understood being dedicated and driven, more than most, but by his age he'd learned the value of R & R. Any sailor worth his salt knew that they were certain limits the body could not overcome. The need to recharge was one of them.

"That's a long time," he said.

She nodded, taking a bite and savoring it. Everything from the fork to the swallow was slow and sensual, then she added, "I joined the royal guard straight out of the academy, and quickly realized I wanted to make captain. I had to sit for another set of exams for that, which isn't my strong suit, and pass a more rigorous physical exam. Doing all of that while on active duty didn't leave much time for socializing."

"You made captain a long time ago," he challenged. "What has your excuse been since?"

"Touché," she said, lifting a glass to him. "I made captain and everything was wonderful—the agony and uncertainty of dating far from my consciousness—until the king was assassinated and suddenly I was a brand-new monarch's chief defense."

He noted she said, "the king," and "new monarch"

rather than "my uncle," or "my cousin," when she could have said either. She took pains to distance herself from her royal connection.

"Why do you do that?" he asked.

"Do what?" she said, startled out of her assassination pity party.

He almost laughed. "Refer to your family by their titles?"

She stopped mid bite, her expression as if she'd never considered the question. Setting down her fork, she stared into the distance while she thought, and he took the opportunity to do his own gazing. Candlelit shadows danced across her face, her skin smooth, expression alive. He wouldn't have to close his eyes and think of revenge with her. In fact, the idea of seeing her at all was becoming far more than a transactional idea.

Which meant he needed to recenter his head on his mission. His goal was revenge and the end of the d'Tierrza line. They shared the same goal—therefore, she should cooperate with him and his revenge was as good as won.

When she spoke, her voice was quiet and tinged with melancholy. "I don't want to reflect badly on them."

In his chest, his heart missed a beat. A goal like that would make for a lonely world…and he could imagine where it originated. What might have begun as a war of vengeance was turning into one of liberation. All she had to do was say yes.

"I'm not sure it's possible for Helene Cosima d'Tierrza to reflect badly on anyone. Did you know you revert to impeccable manners when you're tired? That's how I know you need to rest, when you don't have the energy to be outrageous."

She laughed, as he'd hoped she would, before inclining her head. "Thank you for the pep talk, I think."

"Thanks for going on a date with me," he said, and winked. "So tell me about your friends? If you refer to your family by their titles and haven't gone out to dinner in over a decade?"

"No, you go first. Tell me about growing up in Sidra."

He looked away, breaking their eye contact. "You don't want to hear that story. It's long and not very interesting. Your turn."

She rolled her eyes and let out a little chuckle that sounded suspiciously like a sigh. "I'm only letting you get away with that. And I eat dinner with my best friends almost every day, thank you very much. When I have free time, I like to spend it alone."

"Chatting with statues of your father?" he teased, not buying the image at all.

She snorted but conceded, "Chatting with statues of my father. There's only one, you know."

He shuddered theatrically. "That there is even one…"

She cringed. "You're right. My mother and I always say we'll have it removed."

"What's stopping you?" he asked, curious how a woman who could hate her father so much could keep such a substantial reminder of his presence around. Particularly when she had all the money and resources she could want.

She looked thoughtful for a long moment before answering. "I think it reminds us both of what we survived."

Dark words to come from a daughter.

Drake wondered, if the child they would have together turned out to be a daughter, what she would say about him when she grew up. Nothing that Helene had to say about her own father, he vowed.

"I never thought I'd have to ask this, but why did you hate your father?" he asked.

Dominic d'Tierrza had been a hateful man, every new bit of information Drake unearthed about him that much more damning, and yet he still wondered at the kind of thing that made a daughter despise her father.

Helene smiled and Drake immediately recognized it for the clever and beautiful deflection it was.

Waving her hand airily, she said, "Pick any ten possible reasons off the list and it'd be enough, wouldn't it?"

Leaning back in his chair, he took her in, the blue dress bringing out the color of her eyes, a wonderful fit for her willowy frame, and yet somehow hanging awkwardly on her. "But I think it's more specific than that."

Shaking her head, she looked out over the dark river and said, "Sadly, no. Just a lifetime of monstrosity the likes of which you unfortunately know."

Again, he saw the deflection. By drawing the focus to his grievance with her father she hoped to refocus the conversation away from her own.

But he was more interested in what she was hiding.

"That I do," he said gravely. "But perhaps mine is not the most egregious?" He spoke casually, as if they were considering the future of a sports team.

Something sharpened in her eye, the look dangerous if used as a weapon. She hedged. "The game of comparing egregiousness never goes anywhere. Suffice to say, there were many reasons to hate my father."

"Agreed. And what was yours?"

She smiled, but if anything, the glint in her eye had

sharpened further. "Like a dog with a bone. Is that where the name 'Sea Wolf' comes from?"

He shook his head. "No. Why did you hate your father, Helene?"

Snorting, she said, "Do you really want to know?"

He nodded, though he knew she wouldn't tell him now.

"He murdered my uncle and tried to murder my cousin because he was in love with my aunt and wanted me to quit my job." She kept her inflection the same, almost bored, as if none of it was important to her and, while he knew it wasn't truly the reason she hated her father, it was true, and it hurt her.

Outwardly, he remained the same, while inside, his mind and pulse raced. This fact—that her father had been behind the plot to assassinate the former King of Cyrano—was incredible international intelligence and she'd handed it to him over a dinner table by the river.

Her cheeks were flushed, and he knew she knew the implications of what she'd just said, just as he knew she was testing him with it.

From their brief time together he'd gleaned that she was loyal, dedicated to those she loved, committed to her duty and willing to be lethal in its execution. Her father's actions would have compromised every one of those core values.

But she'd hated her father long before that. She was testing him, baiting him to see if he could be distracted from digging too deep where things were too sensitive.

Like attracted like, and just like his, hers was a mature hatred, barrel-aged in a human heart for years.

Their lives had been intertwined mirrors, each marred by the scar of Dominic d'Tierrza, without either of their knowing. She was testing to see if she could distract him, like she did everyone else, even if she didn't realize it.

She wanted him to, and he wanted her off balance, so he didn't press. When it was clear he wouldn't, the light of a real, if rueful, smile lit her expression, and she said, "So when do we eat? I'm starving?"

As if the restaurant staff could hear her, they began to bring out their food. As promised, the chef had gone all out, sending succulent bites of lamb, savory vegetables, crispy fried calamari, fresh regional fish served raw with citrus slices and a melon-ball salad with no less than four different types of melons. And this was merely the appetizer course.

She'd gotten her distraction…for the moment.

Helene took bites, oohing and aahing when appropriate, humming her pleasure after each bite, though, in truth, he wondered if she truly tasted anything.

She was being a good sport about his seduction, but since their moment on the tennis court, he had yet to truly ensnare her.

He shared stories of Calla's history and his family, and asked her about her life and work, but knew he was no closer to moving her than he had been when they'd disembarked from his ship.

The chef sent out the soup and salad, followed by a resplendent dinner course, and for the moment, both he and Helene were sidetracked by the flash and flare of spicy and sweet.

When they could stuff themselves no more and the server asked if they would like to see the dessert selection, both shook their heads emphatically, waving their hands in surrender.

"I couldn't," Helene exclaimed, her glow only enhanced from overindulging.

"No, thank you," Drake said to their server, but with a smile and the promise to return and save room for dessert the next time.

The car waited for them along the river plaza, then took them up the ancient cobblestone streets of Calla toward Caline and the further pampering that awaited them there. Drake's attack plan was always direct and relentless—he didn't stop until his objective was achieved. The seduction of Helene would be no different.

Anticipating the timing, he had ordered dessert be readied following their visit to the bathhouse and massages. That should give them plenty of time to digest.

At that point, if they weren't restored enough by pure decadence, he would show her to her room and she could sleep.

And women complained that men didn't know their true needs.

This woman had the carefree aura of the soldier that didn't know when to quit. He'd had men like that under his command before.

They were assets—as long as they were managed to prevent reckless burnout.

The driver pulled into the curved entryway and parked before coming around to open the door for them.

Drake stepped out first, offering Helene his hand, a broad smile stretching across his face at the opportunity to show her more of his manor, Caline.

She raised a slender platinum eyebrow at his offered hand and took it, sapphire eyes twinkling.

Inside, he pointed out dining rooms, party rooms

and libraries on their way to his private rooms, more invested than he'd like to be in what she thought of it all.

She was used to luxury, had been weaned on it, in fact, and he watched her for her reaction. Unlike the ducal estates they had both been born to, he himself had pulled Caline and Calla from the brink of collapse and ruin. He'd rebuilt and grown them with his own labor, pockets and efforts, dragging the entire estate to a level of class that he had been accustomed to. But would she think so? Would she see that, and taste it, and feel it, as she wandered the suite designed to be his sanctuary? He wanted her to.

Situated high and center in the manor, his suites featured full landscape views of Calla, from its busy bay entrance, to the rich, fertile farmland inland and upriver.

Like the great medieval structures of Europe, Caline was built from stone.

Counting his office, bathrooms, closets, workout room, meditation space, living area and large bedroom, his suite consisted of ten rooms, including a set of guest rooms where Helene would sleep—until she slept with him, that was—and comprised the greater portion of the wing.

His sister was housed elsewhere in the structure, a floor below, her rooms with river and farm views but nothing of the sea.

While she loved him, she didn't share his love of the sea and hated waiting and watching for him to come home like some tragic figure from a dirge…at least in her words. Since it had become just the two of them occupying the manor, Caline felt cavernous. Strange and echoing and far too big for a pair of adult siblings even though they'd been just three before.

His mother had had a big presence, though, dying her gray hair silver-white and keeping it in long decorated braids, wearing daring patterns and prints, unafraid to be seen, confident she'd be admired—Amira Andros had been his model for how to navigate the world. She'd had to be after they'd lost his father.

Then it had been just him and Nya and his mother. And now it was just him and Nya, the last of the Androses. Unless, of course, Helene was agreeable.

In his common room, the decor was simple, but each and every item was of the highest quality, from his leather sofa, to the sleek built-in entertainment centers, which blended seamlessly with his still, watery aesthetic. And while no one would think to describe the room as sea-themed, there were hints of his passion and calling everywhere in the space—an original from Picasso's Blue Period, an intriguing piece of smooth, polished driftwood to bring a piece of his private island, Yancy Grove, to Calla, a subtle wave of Chihuly glass in the same swirling blues and grays of the Mediterranean during a storm, low-profile furniture and vast windows filled with open sky. Everywhere he went, he took the sea with him.

"It's lovely," she whispered, voice low.

Caught off guard by the husky thickness of her voice after going so long without words, he started.

"Thank you," he said, inclining his head. "I take my sanctuaries seriously."

A soft smile, gentle and distracted and completely new to him, lifted the corners of her lips. "I can imagine…"

A wicked grin lit his expression "What else can you imagine?"

He hadn't meant to tease her, to flirt or lure. Not yet. But then he'd watched her explore his space and see him in it.

She snorted. "Not what *you're* imagining," she retorted.

"And what's that?" he asked, keeping his face as innocent as his question was leading.

"I think we both know," she said, lifting an eyebrow.

He shook his head. "I haven't the slightest idea what you're implying."

"I'm sure."

"Bathhouse? Another massage? Dessert?"

Her mouth dropped open. "I can't believe you can even think of dessert yet. I'm still so stuffed I can barely move. But…" Her eyes took on a speculative look.

"What?" He asked, eager for her to make another request of him, eager to once again give her what she wanted—the surest means to unlocking a heart that he'd yet to find.

Looking around, she said, "I'd love to play a game of poker."

It was the last thing he expected her to ask, and absolutely perfect. Innocent that she was, she didn't realize the doors she was opening, but he did. That she'd chosen a tool he loved so well—poker—felt like a sign that things were looking up for his little plan.

Snapping his fingers, he smiled. "Done. Anything else?"

She nodded, plucking the fabric of her dress between her thumb and forefinger. "How can I get rid of this dress?"

CHAPTER FIVE

"EASILY," HE SAID with a smile.

He could get her whatever she wanted.

Much like her father had always been, Drake was a king in his kingdom. Hel was increasingly wondering what was going on with her. It wasn't the first time she'd seen the similarities between Drake and her father—in their complete dominance, in their utter assuredness in their own way, in their ability to reduce her to emotions and reactions. And yet she was here with him, had chosen to go along, was challenging him even now to sit with her, get closer and more personal than they should, play a game that acted like a superconductor to sexual tension.

Outside, she had the wherewithal to make a joke about her dress.

Inside, her blood thrummed like a live electrical current rather than something as mundane as human ichor.

She was playing with a box of matches beside a powder keg—walking a delicate tightrope while the metaphoric wind kicked up.

But really, she hated dresses.

Sending word to the staff through his watch, he looked up at her and her breath caught, but he just asked, "What are you looking for and what size?"

"Tank top and shorts, and a small, please," she said.

He relayed her request and asked also for a deck of cards, then said, "That will be everything, thank you."

He might have had his aristocratic life stolen from him, but he certainly hadn't lost any of its nature. And for that, she was grateful. That anything remained of him after what her father had done was a wonder. That he was still—as more and more memories resurfaced, jogged loose from her time with him—so much the same young man she'd once known was nothing short of miraculous. That must have been what it was that so captured her attention about his eyes—they revealed that the same honorable, brave and kindhearted boy she'd looked up to as a child remained in the man.

Faster than she would have assumed possible, they had not only the cards, but also the change of clothes.

Her instructions had been taken quite literally. Drake handed her a plain white tank top in lovely soft cotton and a pair of black shorts. Both items were of high quality and very small.

Entering the bathroom he'd pointed out to her, Hel quickly stepped out of the dress, replacing it with the top and shorts.

Both fit, though that fit would be better described as high-performance workout wear than loungewear.

The shorts were the crevice-creeping type and the tank top hit her just below the belly button, but they were better than a dress. In these, at least, she could move.

She stepped out of the bathroom and found him waiting for her, coffee table and cushions set up for their game.

Eyes locking with his, she couldn't miss the appreciative light that lit in his gaze as he took in her attire, or do anything to stop the strange tightening of her skin in reaction.

He hadn't brought up their kiss, or the fact that she'd punched him, or their moment on the tennis courts, or really any of their physical encounters, nor had he made any further moves, all of which implied that, despite the obvious wine-and-dine attempt and his words to the contrary, he respected her vow.

Now, she just needed to stop feeling disappointed by that fact. It was a good thing—it meant she could relax and actually enjoy this unplanned vacation by smashing the gorgeous man at her side in poker.

He might have had seduction on his mind with the picturesque market and decadent dinner, but to Hel, the true seduction was the downtime. He'd told her to treat the week as an enforced vacation, and that's what she planned to do.

Not that she intended to cooperate with her own seduction. She simply hadn't had the opportunity to relax in so long.

She couldn't remember when. And while they would be worried back home, undoubtedly, she had absolute faith that her friend and fellow guard Jenna could handle her absence.

She also couldn't remember the last time she'd played poker. It was one of the things she missed about what she now realized were her carefree days at the academy. Back then she hadn't seen things in such a positive light.

They played Texas Hold'em. He dealt. She made no comment, and merely smiled when he began handing out cards.

He lifted an eyebrow and smiled back, a wild and mischievous charge thrumming between them.

Sixty hands and two hours later, while she hadn't smashed him, it was clear who the real shark was.

"Merciless," he said, tired, but relaxed in a way he hadn't been at any other point in the evening.

It was all she could do to keep her eyes off him.

The velvet cream darkness of his skin was unlike anything she had ever encountered, and she found herself filled with the most curious urge to reach out and touch it, to run her fingertips lightly along his jaw, his arm, along the edge of his hip and down his thigh...

"Now, now, Helene. What are you thinking?" His grinning question interrupted her with a start and she let out a small gasp.

His dark gaze shot to her lips, moistened and parted, and for a second, they were caught together.

And then they weren't. Then she was crossing the table and sitting on his lap, a ghost in the shell of her body that moved like a strange automaton, driven by a primal code.

He seemed to have respect for her vow.

She, it seemed, didn't.

A part of her observed from a place of panicked remove, trying in vain to put a stop to the chain of events.

The rest of her made the first move. Or was it the third move? She'd lost count. It didn't matter. It was too late to turn back.

She kissed him and he smiled into it, opening to her exploration with smooth ease, every inch her match.

For a woman who had always considered herself a solitary issue, it was a novel concept—to fit together with another human being so perfectly it seemed only divine design could have created it. Or at the very least, the longest odds the galaxy had ever seen, that random chance would construct two tiny specks, meant to join, in the infinite vastness of the entire universe.

With the exception of Queen Mina and her cousin, whose random stars had truly aligned, she didn't even believe in love like that. To feel it, alive and beating, and turn away felt like sacrilege.

Though to call resisting what was between them—mired in murder and vengeance and dangerous gambles as it was—sacrilege felt a little self-aggrandizing, no matter that the pressure of her lips against his was exquisite torture she never wanted to end.

Her body was an unyielding weapon, her very form a tool she kept in smooth order, yet now it was in charge, begging for his touch in all the silent ways women's bodies knew how...even when the woman did not.

Her breasts pressed into his chest, growing heavier, her nipples pebbling on contact. Her breath became erratic—deep, then shallow, then catching—as his fingertips trailed down her neck and farther to cup each soft peak in his hands.

She moaned when his thumbs found her nipples, running lazy circles around them while he took control of her mouth. Her breasts ached beneath his manipulations, the lightest touches making her gasp.

Her lips parted, her body yearning and straining toward him without her knowledge, a hot, heavy and needy siren song she didn't know she was singing.

With a growl he swept her up, and she wrapped her legs around his waist. Carrying her to his bed, he lay her down on her back, before pulling back from their kiss.

"I want to see you."

His command was rough, but she only smiled, shaking her head, a teasing gleam lighting her eyes. Whatever controlled her now was more daring than she, because when she opened her mouth and spoke, her voice was thick and heavy and laden with things she had never done before, even if her honor insisted as she replied, "My vow."

He leaned down over her, coming to kiss the sensitive spot behind her ear, and whispered, "There's so much ground to explore between here and breaking it…"

She shivered beneath him—her curiosity was as piqued as her pleasure.

Kissing a trail down her neck, he found another treasure trove of nerve endings along her collarbone, his hand reaching for the hemline of her T-shirt. Lifting it, his knuckles brushed along the smooth, taut skin of her abdomen, and she shivered, the sensations rippling across her skin in erotic waves.

She wore no bra and he palmed her breast without a barrier. She arched into his hand with a breathless gasp. Pulling back, he made quick work of removing her top before taking off his own shirt. Her eyes widened, lighting with greedy hunger as the tip of her tongue moistened her lips.

No longer able to tolerate the space between them, Helene pressed into him, skin-to-skin, her body responsive and needy. And then his mouth returned to her breasts.

While he feasted, his hand traveled back down the plane of her belly and farther, reaching beneath the waistband of the shorts she wore.

She was as hot and wet as a tropical hurricane, and though she didn't know where the knowledge came from, she knew that traveling through the eye of this storm would be one amazing ride.

But she was trusting him not to take them too far.

He slid his finger inside of her and her entire body clenched around him, motionless and tight for a moment, before she fell back in a heap of pulsing woman, her inner walls throbbing and squeezing around his finger, while she moaned and shuddered.

He showed her no mercy, pressing and circling the sensitive bud, overseeing it all every time the waves seemed to slow.

Only when she could truly take no more did she fall back against the bed, boneless.

He grinned down at her as she was lying there, catching her breath.

And then he set to work pulling her shorts down over her hips.

She remained boneless as he did, lifting her hips only when he was ready to slide them down. She smiled at him, the expression slightly askew and silly.

"I'm not sure you're going to be able to get much more out of me." Her words were giddy, dazed and confused.

Expression wolfish, he said, "Oh, I think you'll be surprised." His lips touched the supple skin of her stomach.

Tensing, her hand fluttered to his shoulder, and he smiled against her skin. He paused, kissing and teasing her torso, exploring the sensitive skin beneath her breasts and along her rib cage, experimenting with touch and sensation until she forgot all about her earlier tension. And when her mind was thoroughly lost in the chills undulating across her skin, he resumed his journey, gently kissing his way to her core.

When he arrived, she stilled, her senses intent and alert, desperate to know what would come next, but no longer hesitant. She was in too deep for that now.

His lips made contact and she cried out his name, her hips flying off the bed. In response, he gripped her, his fingers pressing into the firm flesh of her thighs and behind, easily catching and holding her weight in his hands.

Then he ran his tongue around the outer edge of her opening, slowly, deliberately, agonizingly slow, and when his circle was completed, he plunged his tongue inside her, and she dove over the edge.

Her body convulsed like a storm, hot waves of her pleasure pulsing, while her breath came in ragged gasps. His kiss had shaken her to her core. This—this had shattered her into a million pieces and melted each and every one of them.

Congealing back into her former self, she couldn't stop the goofy grin.

He hadn't been lying. There was a long stretch between celibacy and not pregnant, and it seemed like a week of enforced vacation with Drake might be the perfect time to explore it. His eyes—easy, warm and cocky, as always—suggested he was up for the adventure.

She just had to remember that he was also up for crossing that outer boundary. He was exciting and thrilling and more beautiful with every passing moment, but like all of the aristocratic men she'd known in her life, he had an agenda.

An agenda that had nothing to do with her and everything to do with her name and her father.

The thought cast a shadow over her lingering pleasure as she sat up. Sliding off the bed and pulling up her shorts, she marveled that so much could shift without getting completely undressed.

In fact, he was fully clothed, if disheveled.

Which was convenient, as someone chose the moment to swing the door open exuberantly.

Hel quickly scanned the newcomer, noting that she was a statuesque young woman with deep umber skin whose proportions presented serious competition to Queen Mina's newly famous curves. The young woman's hair was deep black and hung to her waist in hundreds of tiny braids. Each one was perfect and glossy, many of them decorated with thin golden rings and tiny gold cuffs that sparkled where they caught the light.

It was little Nya, all grown up and gorgeous. And, based on the stunned expression on her face, she had not been expecting her brother to be entertaining company.

"I— Oh, goodness. I'm so sorry!" she gasped.

Hel blushed—she wouldn't have been able to help that if her life depended on it, to her shame—but she didn't cringe or flinch in the face of being caught. She'd never be a spy, but she'd learned how to make up for her weakness by being better than everyone else at her job. And, as long as they weren't deadly, she'd learned to see embarrassments and stumbling blocks, such as being caught playing with fire when your honor was on the line, as opportunities to learn and grow.

This situation, for example, was an excellent reminder of just how quickly things burned out of control when touching got involved.

Touching was most definitely not safe, not when the mere brush of skin set them off like it did.

Hel shook her head, opening her mouth to say that she should be the one to apologize, when Drake cut her off, turning to Nya with frustration in his voice. "Helene, Nya. Nya, Helene. Helene and I have some serious matters to come to a conclusion on and not much time to do it so I am taking her to Yancy Grove. We'll sail on the *Ibrahim*."

"Now? It's past eleven o'clock at night," Nya pointed out.

Hel, to whom this was also news, lifted an eyebrow.

"Yes, immediately. We'll be gone no more than a week, Nya. Stay out of trouble."

It was a clear dismissal, and his sister, desperate to get out of the room, was going to heed it. She smiled the same half smile her brother had and said, "I always try," then shot Hel a final apologetic wave and left the room.

The room was quiet, neither of them speaking, the weight of what they'd done heavy and delicious all at once, until Hel couldn't take it anymore.

Forcing a half smile, she tilted her head, brought a hand to her chin and pondered. "I wonder what she wanted." She had always been happy to play the clown if it meant lightening the mood, a trait she'd learned from her mother.

Just as it'd always worked with her mother, Drake smiled at her, the expression warmer and more rooted than her attempt had been, and he reached a hand out to her.

She didn't know whether it was because of the incredible adventure of the day they'd shared, or because she knew they'd been heading in a direction she'd had no control over and was still shaken from it, but she took it.

For a moment, she thought he might pull her close, but then he released her hand to grab a jacket from a closet.

"You're going to need another layer when we get down to the harbor."

Smiling, she slipped the high-quality, but much-too-large waterproof jacket over her body, swimming in it ridiculously like some kind of haute couture runway model.

"You're always trying to get me in a dress," she teased.

He laughed. "I will deny it to my dying breath. We both know I am trying to get you *out* of your dress."

Cheeks heated, Hel laughed, her heart lighter than it had been since before his sister had come in.

A few minutes later, a car was driving them back down the long hill from Caline, into the lovely streets of Calla.

There, Drake led her by the hand to an exquisite sailboat docked at the end.

Gleaming silver and wood and fiberglass shone in the growing moonlight. It was large enough that it likely boasted all the necessary amenities for a long trip, but small enough for a single man to manage on his own. It was freedom fabricated.

In the sweeping script at its bow was the name of his father, *Ibrahim*. Hel suspected this boat meant more to him than even the larger *Nya II*, which he'd used to... borrow her.

Standing on the dock at his side, wonder at his sailboat a wedge in her throat, she searched for the shield of her nonchalance. "So. We're going to Yancy Grove, are we?"

He laughed, seeing through her act in a way no one

else ever had, not even those closest to her. "We are. Yancy Grove, my secluded private island."

Hel raised an eyebrow. "You have a private island? What happened to the poor sob whose inheritance was stolen?"

Again his laughter rang out, skipping across the lapping waves like a perfectly smooth stone. Shaking with it, he asked her, "Now what kind of self-respecting pirate would I be if I didn't have a private island where I stash my booty?" he asked.

Watching him, his deep brown eyes flashing in the moonlight, the sound of the water lulling her into dropping at least some of her shields, something strange and delightful fluttered in her throat and she smiled at him, then repeated his question, "What kind of pirate indeed?"

And when he jumped on board and reached a hand out to help her up, Hel surprised herself once again by taking it.

CHAPTER SIX

DRAKE STEERED HIS beloved *Ibrahim* out of Calla Bay, which rested so quiet now that no one in their right mind would have believed it had once been a chaotic playground for modern-day pirates.

Hel sat on the dash to his right, her long legs curled up beneath her as she watched the night dark sea blur into the stars ahead. Impossibly hungry again, she chewed an apple that she had found upon searching the galley after they'd set off.

She had offered him one, but he had declined.

As an admiral, he had been in command of many ships, and as a sailor before that had long become used to sailing with company, but it was a novel experience sailing with a companion. Especially on the *Ibrahim*. This was his private vessel.

"I told you, you don't need to stay up," he repeated.

She crunched into her apple, then replied, "And miss sighting land on my very first pirate island? No way."

He chuckled.

"Well, it's lucky for you, then, that we'll arrive at Yancy Grove in less than an hour."

She let out an exaggerated sigh. "Good. I was afraid we might have to sleep *here* tonight."

This time he laughed outright. She spoke like the *Ibrahim* was a tin can, rather than a sixteen-foot luxury yacht, personally designed to meet his every whim and provide the highest level of comfort.

He loved the boat only slightly less than his late mother and his sister.

"No. Our accommodations will be regrettably more stationary for the night."

"You say regrettable, I say acceptable," she retorted and he reflected that it was a good thing they were alone, with no possibility of interruption, for more reasons than seduction.

She was far too good at putting him at ease. It was becoming a struggle to remember that it wasn't mutual admiration that held them together.

He watched her while she watched the stars, her strange moonglow even brighter in contrast to the pure black of the starlit sky.

She fit there, sitting on his dash bathed in the lights of the night, as solemn and motionless as a freshly carved and diamond-painted masthead.

She was certainly as unearthly beautiful as the mermaids and Valkyries that graced the bows of so many antique boats, including some he'd had the pleasure of sailing. *La Sirenita*, *Tristan's Wake*, *Cassiopeia*… Each one was a grand dame of his past. Helene and the children they would have were his future.

A future he'd been dreaming of since the day he'd washed up on shore, choking salt water and sand, remade and reborn out of the ashes of personal tragedy, though he'd only realized that was true when they'd lowered his mother into the ground, the land welcoming her solid and firm and eternally far from home.

It hadn't been right, that his family had been the one to suffer while a criminal lived in splendor. It wasn't right and he was determined to balance the scales. Helene was the key to that, in a plan that required he remain removed and rational. He must maintain control.

His grip tightened on the helm but his voice was even when he said, "It's a shame your first sight of Yancy Grove will be at night. Moonlight doesn't do it justice."

She looked at him over her shoulder, the move somehow erotic despite the fact that nothing about her demeanor spoke of sex.

Still draped in his jacket and once again barefoot, she should have looked like a child in adult's clothing. Instead, she was a creature of endless limbs, the quintessential irascible waif. For a woman of her height, to achieve the effect was no small feat.

"What's it like?" she asked, her words direct, like her cerulean stare. It was a trait he liked about her.

For a moment, he was lost in the sea of her eyes. Then he answered, "Long, creamy stretches of near-white sand." His gaze took in her limbs hungrily, recalling the supple lengths of milk-pale skin pressed against his head while he feasted on her. His trousers tightened, but he continued his perusal, his gaze trailing up to meet the incredible gemstones of her eyes. "The water is crystal clear," he added. "Ranging from the deepest sapphire-blue to turquoise." Then he looked up, eyes locking on the starlit strands of her short silver-blond hair. "The surf shimmers, glittering both day and night, whether it laps beneath the sun or moon."

Her breath held as he paused, her attention fixed on his lips.

His mouth quirked up. All he had to do was get her

alone and give her enough time to stare at him and she seduced herself. The fact that he got the distinct impression this was a new phenomenon for her wasn't hard on the ego. Even if it made other things hard.

Each encounter with Helene had been electrifying, unprecedented and edifying. Helene was an innocent, not simply to physical pleasure, but romance, as well. And, he suspected, attraction in general. It was clear in the way she threw herself wholly into the throes of the moment. How she was caught, mesmerized by her own reaction to him. How there was a vulnerability in her approach that existed in nothing else he'd seen her do.

Existed for him alone.

A tremor went through him at the thought, strange and tangled and possessive, but there was no time for it. No time for poetry and no time for… There was no time for any of it. His future was on the line. Justice was on the line.

He licked his lips, and she swallowed and he told himself the rush that surged through his veins was triumph rather than a trap. "Amongst the dunes," he said, voice thick, "palm trees sway in the breeze. Tall, slender, supple…" he continued, his voice dropping, luring her to lean closer.

She took the bait, scooting her body closer to the helm, and he continued. "In the sunlight, its beauty is nearly blinding, it's so bright and crisp."

She had turned around to face him, still cross-legged, attention snared. "When did you find it?"

Drake smiled at the memory. "By accident, a long time ago. We were retreating."

A little laugh escaped her. "I wasn't sure the term was in your vocabulary…"

His smile widened, as he let her see hints of his bite in the expression. "I said it was a long time ago. And as it turned out, our retreat turned into the discovery and claiming of a heretofore unknown island, as well as the opportunity to stage an ambush and collect our first prize...on behalf of King Amar of Sidra, of course."

"How efficient."

He inclined his head. "I try."

"And humble, too."

He shrugged, about as humble as a house cat. "It doesn't pay to get ahead of yourself..."

"Certainly not," she agreed, rolling her eyes. "How lucky that you stumbled upon a completely uninhabited, previously undiscovered island. In the Mediterranean."

He laughed at her dry words. "I never said undiscovered, I said unknown—to Sidra. It falls just this side of the edge of Sidran waters, hence being left alone by the rest of the sea, but it's use predates the establishment of Sidra. Until my men and I landed there was no modern record of its existence. After our report, an official review revealed that the island had been used as an ancient military port but had fallen out of use after the country's first wave of modernization."

"Hmm-m-m..." She stretched out the hum of the *M* and he felt the thrum of the vibration all the way in his bones. "Ancient military outpost. So, structures?"

He nodded, pleased with her quick mind. "Yes. And a bit more glamorous than what the men and I were used to as professional sailors. Ancient generals had it good."

She grinned, and in it he sensed her solidarity with those ancient military men, even though they wouldn't have recognized her place among them.

He was under no such illusions. Having encountered

her in action, he knew without a doubt that the woman at his side was a warrior, through and through. She didn't just live—she attacked existence. She had been that way as a child, he recalled now, as more and more memories of her as a girl returned, visions of her long hair trailing behind her as she trailed behind him.

The long hair was gone. The girl, however, was surprisingly alive in the woman at his side.

The heir to his greatest enemy.

The memory of Dominic d'Tierrza brought along with it the usual surge of rage—it was the beast that had hunted him from the moment he'd washed up on that shore thirty years ago. One he would be free of with the achievement of his vengeance.

All he needed to do was get the agreement of the tall, bright and deadly woman at his side. A part of him resented that he needed even that much. But he was making progress…

He guided them through the slight change of direction that would take them on the current that led to Yancy Grove. The more dominant current, which veered north sharply, took ships out of sight of the island.

Then he reached out to take her by the back of the head and draw her closer. Her eyes widened but she merely watched him, body taught, ready to strike should he push her further than she wanted to go.

The knowledge of her coiled strength, more than a match for his own, did not deter him in his intention. She was strong, but he was dominant and relentless.

Her hair felt like cool silk slipping through his fingers, her skin beneath it faintly chilled.

She stared him directly in the eyes as the space between them disappeared, her lips parting slightly as their inevitable contact neared.

And then she was gasping, pulling back abruptly, her eyes widening into blue saucers.

Turning quickly, the sight that met him had him letting out a breath of relief.

No enemies or obstacles graced the horizon, just Yancy Grove rising in the night.

Like the woman at his side, even in the darkness, Yancy Grove glowed.

Against the backdrop of the black sky, the island was an endless stretch of moonlit sand, speckled with palm trees and dune grasses, their silhouettes stark against the white cliffs. From the cliffs, a fortress rose, carved out of the very hillside to tower multiple stories above it. The whitewashed stone walls, arched windows and gorgeous natural accents were vibrant and visible— both at a distance in dim lighting.

Simultaneously ancient and timeless, the fort at Yancy Grove was beautiful and beautifully defensible.

If love at first sight was the instantaneous knowledge that your heart had found its home, then that was what Drake had experienced as he'd scrambled on the beach and looked up at the cliffs that long ago day.

He felt the same strange calm to this day that had fallen upon him that moment when Yancy Grove had come into sight. Calla was his pride, but Yancy Grove was his joy.

Helene's eyes were glued to the island growing on the horizon.

"It's stunning," she whispered.

He stood taller, his chest expanding at her praise.

Like Calla, with Yancy Grove, Drake had taken what fortune he had been given and run with it.

Bit by bit, he had modernized and updated the fort, retrofitting it with all of the modern conveniences he'd become accustomed to as the Duke of Calla, as well as the high-tech security and telecommunications capabilities he demanded as retired admiral Drake Andros and internationally known privateer, the Sea Wolf.

Yancy Grove began their relationship, opening her arms wide and succoring him as a pup, and he maintained it, caring for her with the ardent devotion of a young lover.

"We will dock and walk up to the fortress. I do not keep a staff here as this is my private getaway."

Her reply was droll. "I think I can handle a walk."

He laughed. "We'll see if you're still singing the same tune when you see the hill." He joked, but in truth, he was impressed with her. The only child of his greatest enemy she may be, but the woman had stamina. She had kept pace with him through every unexpected hurdle the day had thrown at her, including him. He was man enough to acknowledge that there had been a number of times throughout the day that she hadn't merely kept pace, but had surpassed him.

Noting her proud bearing and the light of excitement in her eyes, he didn't think she was anywhere close to her edge, either. Not for the first time, she reminded him of a bolt of lightning masquerading as a human, not powered by an internal battery like poor unfortunate mortals, but the source of power herself.

He docked the *Ibrahim*, meticulously preparing it for rest before he and Helene disembarked. The island was silent, the warm breeze a permanent and welcome friend, carrying the scents of sea and salt.

They also walked in silence, her long legs easy match for his stride. She was tall and strong, and yet undeniably a woman, even in the darkness, dressed in his clothing, feet youthful and bare.

"You've got a thing against shoes," he observed.

Startled out of stargazing by his statement, she looked down at her feet before looking back up to him, a lopsided grin turning her classic beauty impish. "I think it might just be the barefoot sea-faring life for me."

She had a siren in her blood. He was sure of it. That or she was some kind of mystical creature, a selkie, a shield maiden, a mermaid given legs. What else could explain the way his jacket flowed around then hugged the firm lines of her lithe legs, or how when she smiled, her wide coral lips revealed a mouthful of pearlescent teeth, charming and sharp at the same time, ready to take a bite out of whatever life threw at her.

That light in her eyes was an unquenchable thirst for adventure and it could make it all too easy, if he allowed it, to lean over and set off a series of aches that began below the belt and ended with his plans embedded in her womb.

She had been drawn from a sailor's dream, but like all the great sea tales, she sprang from the loins of hell. And every time he touched her, she opened like a flower created only for him.

"I find it hard to picture you this way full-time," he lied.

She brought a hand to her heart. "You mock my dreams!"

He couldn't stop his smile, even knowing she'd commanded it from him as they rounded the curve that led to the fort's entrance.

This time, she didn't gasp at the encounter, but stopped in her tracks, mouth dropping open.

He laughed, pleased more than he cared to examine at her reaction to the project of his heart.

If the fort at Yancy Grove was breathtaking at a distance, it was a masterpiece up close. Lit up against the night sky, its walls were blinding white, butter-smooth and hand-painted for over a century, the layers of paint freshened regularly. Smooth curves dominated the architecture, with abundant built-ins tucked away for every possible convenience: reading nooks, sea-view benches, dining alcoves, boundless bookshelves. Vibrant patterned pillows and cushions in intricately designed handwoven cases fit wherever one might imagine lounging and gorgeous rugs in one-of-kind patterns adorned gleaming hardwood floors, lending softness and color to the crisp beauty of the interior. The floors were such a deep rich brown they were almost black, and shone to the point of reflection.

An assortment of embroidered and beaded slippers waited for them in the foyer. Drake reached for a rare plain tan pair while Helene looked back and forth from the sparkling interior to the slippers.

Finally, she said, "I'm going to ruin your slippers."

Drake laughed. "Don't worry about it. There's plenty more where those came from. They're meant for company, donated afterward if the condition is still good. I buy enough from a shoreline family to keep them in the black for the year."

With the matter settled, she reached greedily for a

pair in royal blue, embroidered with gold threading in the shape of sea birds.

She clearly had a thing for blue. And the sea.

The thought brought a smile to his lips.

She would adore the island in daylight.

Their feet adorned, he led her on a tour of the converted fort, locating each of the necessary items, including the four luxurious spa bathrooms, outdoor shower, both kitchens and all three kitchenettes. Then he showed her the superfluous stuff—the saunas, the workout room, the home theater, each of the six guest rooms, both libraries, the various patios, the war room, the wine cellar and, finally, all eleven indoor pools.

The pools were the gems of Yancy Grove, the features of true brilliance amongst a sumptuous sea—diamonds on a silk cushion. Unlike indoor pools common to million-dollar homes, these were hand-hewn, like the walls, literally built into the room, seamlessly integrated and oriented—either starring in or supporting the overall design of the room. Each pool was accented with features to complement its intended use, whether soaking, sky viewing, swimming, drinking, or playing. Seating, places to balance glasses, long wide lanes and broad wall cutouts were common sights among the pool rooms, as were intricate hand-tiled mosaics featuring dazzling designs made from brilliant ceramics and glittering gemstones.

"Amazing," she breathed, eyes glued to the design before her. It was the last of the pool rooms, and his favorite. This pool was designed for stargazing, its mosaic a celebration of the heavens, boasting an incredible blue ombré sky dotted with stars of golden filigree, arranged in imitation of the view above, constellations and all.

A curved archway opened up to the great yawning sky, the pool's edge drawing nearly to its gate. Alongside the pool were long cushioned benches, their fabrics and designs subdued and minimal compared to the rest of the rooms—whites and pale blues repeated in simple patterns. Made from the same material as Turkish towels, each pillow's interior was waterproof with absorbent, moisture-wicking cases, ensuring comfort as one drifted between soaking and lounging in the moonlight.

"I want to get in," she said, her eyes hungry as she took in the clear water.

He laughed, gesturing toward the pool with an open palm. "By all means." He was fine letting Yancy Grove and the sea do the work of seducing her for him. They had stolen his heart long ago.

She looked at him then, her brow furrowing. "I don't have a suit."

He shrugged. "Haven't we moved past modesty by this point?"

She quirked up a golden eyebrow in response and said, "Interesting that a man with slippers available in every size and eleven pool rooms does not have spare swimming attire."

Grinning unapologetically, he said, "You got me. Ah, well then. I suppose I must tell you about the storage closet full of an assortment of guest clothing."

Laughing, she crossed her arms in front of her chest and nodded. "I suppose."

He gave her directions and she was off, her one-track mind focused on its goal, and he smiled after her.

Though he had researched her thoroughly, she was turning out to be different than he had expected—transparent one moment and inscrutable the next, electric fire and cold logic, utterly a soldier to her core. Unlike her father, she was courageous, committed, willing to risk herself for anything greater, or, perhaps, anything at all.

Following her lead, he exited the star pool, heading for his own rooms rather than the guest closets.

The air in the room was still, hushed and undisturbed since his last visit to the island, only weeks before. Quickly finding a pair of trunks, he slid them on, not caring of the style or design, instead more eager to get back to his target, so to speak.

He found her in the star pool, already in the water. To no surprise, she had chosen a blue swimsuit. Deep navy, it was a simple bikini, of high quality, because that was all he bought, handmade and local. It fit her well, highly adjustable as it was, being mostly comprised of string.

As she had aboard the *Ibrahim*, she watched the stars above, her back to him, her skin pale and shining, the swatch of dark, thick, water-resistant fabric stretching across the toned cheeks of her derriere, held in place by perfect ribbons tied at either side of her hips.

If there was a part of him that was forever young, it was the part that rose up to whisper to him how easy it would be to pull one of those strings, to free the gallant cloth from its tremendous burden of covering her creamy curved behind.

"You didn't say the pool was heated," she said on a moan, breaking into his prurient thoughts.

Nothing about her demeanor indicated that she had become aware of his reentrance, yet she knew he was there.

Smiling, he answered, "It didn't seem important to you either way."

Turning around with a smile, she froze him in place with a look. "I was willing when it was cold water. I am compelled now that I know it is warm. I am never leaving." She drew her words out like a purr and he felt himself stir, even as something in him cautioned that he had tested her far enough tonight.

Ignoring the voice, he smiled, his mouth and tongue working, though his mind was still mildly stunned by the sight of her breasts pushing against the small triangles of fabric, as determined in their effort to press the bounds, it seemed, as their owner. It was her smile, though, unguarded and bright, transporting him to times before he'd learned the world was hard—times he thought he'd long ago forgotten—that truly held him in place. "I'll have to keep that preference in mind," he muttered, trying but unable to shake off her glamour.

He wasn't sure how it happened, but she made him laugh. Regularly. Not the laugh he was in control of— his father's loud, booming, carefree laugh that he'd mimicked his whole life—but the genuine amusement of a man.

"Why do you call it Yancy Grove?" she asked.

The answer was as easy as it was painful. "We named it for our friend who didn't make it back from its discovery."

The frown that furrowed Helene's face, shadowing her eyes in the process, was one of understanding. "I'm sorry."

Drake shook off the sympathy. "It was a long time ago. Yance, Malik and I graduated from the naval academy and entered the king's navy the same year. It was Prince Malik's first command. We were outgunned by a human trafficker and Yance was hit and we were boarded."

Helene's eyes widened. "You lost the ship?"

He shook his head. "I didn't say that. We were boarded. We fought them off, but Prince Malik was nearly killed and ended the battle unconscious. I led the retreat. The luck of the sea was with us that day, but even though we discovered the island, we lost Yancy. We buried him in the fort's courtyard grove and named the island in his honor."

Moving quietly through the water, she came to his side and placed a hand on his shoulder. "I'm sorry." The blue of her eyes, as tempestuous as the ocean, was deep and serious, and he was once again reminded that a soldier hid beneath the pretty mask.

Not just a soldier. A commander. Someone who could understand this particular pain. The kind that gnawed and ate at you from the inside, clawing to get out but too tender for the light.

"I miss him still," he said. "But that was a long time ago. Long before duty called Malik back to the capital and I retired."

"You mentioned he was a prince?"

He smiled, a teasing glint coming to his eyes. "Helene, are you angling for an introduction?"

Her snort in response was the furthest thing from being blue-blooded he could imagine, and yet, coming from her, the noise was upper-crust. "Spare me. I just wanted to make sure I got it right and you were talking about hobnobbing with Prince Malik of Sidra."

"More fishing with every word…"

She splashed him again until he raised his palms. "Yes. Prince Malik. Though we only call him that when he's being particularly pretentious."

Helene smiled again, the real one she'd graced him with before—the one that stopped him in his tracks. "It can be so trying to pal around with royalty."

This time Drake snorted. "You must know from experience, niece and cousin to kings, as you are."

She didn't bother to deny it. "Where else would I come off making a statement like that?"

"Odd sentiment for a royal guard."

Rising to on her back, she let her long body bob in the water while she stared at the stars above. As mesmerized as she appeared by the heavens, he, too, could not seem to take his attention from her. "Not all royalty is created equally," she said. "Zayn, the cousin you mentioned, is as insufferable as you might imagine—intelligent, handsome, excellent at everything—but Mina is different. She was born common, didn't even know she was going to be wed to the king until the day of their wedding."

"A similar story to your own near-engagement," Drake observed, earning a splash from her foot.

"Before becoming queen she was a scientist," she continued.

He was surprised despite himself. "An usual occupation for a future monarch."

Helene smiled, the expression private and protective. "She is an unusual queen."

"You're proud to protect her."

The fact was evident in her voice.

"I am. Zayn is a good king, and my best friend, but Mina... Mina is a gift to the nation. There's only one other person I trust to keep her safe."

Drake quirked an eyebrow. "Somehow I don't imagine that's her husband."

Helene snorted as if the notion was absurd. "Not round-the-clock, no. He's got too many responsibilities for that. He loves her, fiercely, but I meant Moustafa."

"Moustafa?"

"We share guard duty."

"Shared."

Again, she snorted, and added, "*Share.* While this has been a lovely diversion, in slightly less than six days, I'm going back to work."

Unbothered by her conviction, he offered a small, smug smile. "We'll see."

"We will indeed." Face turning serious, she added, "My father was a bad man, I know it. I've spent my whole life cleaning up the messes he left, only to have new ones swoop in from the sea." Her blue eyes sparkled for him as she spoke and he found himself hypnotized. "I cannot bring your father back or give you your life back, but I am committed to restitution and reparation without breaking my vow."

She made a picture and it eviscerated him—glistening pearly skin, tropical sea-blue eyes, her body barely restrained by straps and swatches of navy fabric of her bikini, unarmed and absolutely unbothered by that fact, and assured in her ability to make the world more just.

Dominic d'Tierrza was dead. His daughter was very much alive. And, having no idea just how close she was to being devoured by the Big Bad Wolf, heedless of just how vulnerable she was to his seduction, she was unwavering in her sweet and brave commitment to right the wrongs of the past. And in that way she made him question himself, question the path he'd chosen, for the first time since Helene had come apart beneath him. Should he continue? Was it right?

His research had revealed her rebellion. It hadn't revealed her innocence. It hadn't revealed the open sensitivity of her responses, or her utter helplessness to them. It hadn't revealed that touching her would fill him with a sense of reverence and honor.

Experience had shown him he had the upper hand when it came to passion. That she was both good and innocent demanded he tread lightly with that power, rather than take advantage of the fact that she came alive at the barest touch. And he would. His revenge didn't demand he lose his honor, just that he not lose his focus, or his heart.

He was old enough to know that once lost, hearts were unrecoverable, and that love, like water, could find a way through even the tightest seams.

A life at sea had taught him that fighting water was the fastest pathway to a watery grave. Like water, no matter the resistance, love got in whether you wanted or not. His father, his mother, his sister, Yancy, Prince Malik—he loved them all. And, for the most part, it was loving all of them that had led to his greatest heartbreaks. What lay between Helene and himself was, and should remain, about triumph and overdue justice, not tender feelings and heartache.

Where love traveled, pain followed, and for the first time in his life, he was ready to celebrate without enduring.

But the waters of love were drawn to the kind of strong physical attraction between them. Whether she realized it or not, he knew the dangers implied when bodies fit together like theirs seemed to.

And while her inexperience was clear, she wasn't clumsy, but merely eager, her energy and attention bright with wonder at what came next. Her enthusiasm alone was a heady aphrodisiac, rousing him to heights he couldn't remember reaching with any other woman.

His balls tightened at the thought, as if he was the one that was brand-new to all of this. And therein was the danger.

Though there was a first time with every new partner, there was something singular to what happened when he and Helene touched.

Either way, wisdom and experience aside, he wasn't the only one with power when they came together… even if she had no idea what to do with it, or even that she had it in the first place.

CHAPTER SEVEN

HE HADN'T SPOKEN a word since she'd made her statement, but his eyes had communicated a world's worth of data. Heat, anger, passion, desire and more danced across his endless brown gaze.

His arms had fallen out of their habitual crossed position, revealing the massive stretch of his muscled chest. His smooth, deep brown skin, decorated with a surprising arrangement of tattoos, well-placed and balanced on his body, and dusted at his pecs with faint curling hair, cried out to be touched, stroked.

He was more attractive in swim trunks than any man had a right to be. Out of trousers, his legs were thick, as defined and muscled as his chest, and incredibly powerful, even standing at ease in the pool as they were.

His shorts were the perfect length that it seemed only one man in a million could find—not so long he looked like he might still live with his mother, not so short he seemed like he had something to sell.

As tall as she was, it was rare for a man to make Hel feel small, but standing beside him, craning her neck to remain in the trap of his stare, she was hyperaware of how broad he was in comparison to her own narrow frame.

And if she wanted to keep her vow, if she didn't want to be putty in Drake's hands for the second time this evening, she needed to think of anything else.

Desperate, she reached for something she thought might get him talking, and get that look—intense, possessive and as tangible as a hand at the nape of her neck would have been—off his face. That look that felt like the home that she'd been waiting for her whole life.

"You told me how you got a private island, but how does a poor exile become a foreign-born aristocrat?" she asked. And she wanted to know. It was an incredible feat, particularly following the trauma her father had inflicted.

"Calla was a gift from King Amar for saving his son's life."

"A duchy is a pretty grand gift, even for saving a son. How old were you?" The idea of a king granting a young man a duchy was as medieval to her as Cyrano was thought to be throughout Europe.

Drake gifted her with one of his cocky smiles.

"Twenty-six, and, at the time, Calla was not without its…challenges. King Amar needed a man with naval experience he could trust to take care of the kinds of problems that Calla had, and when I came along, he wasn't going to look a gift horse in the mouth. Even if it was a twenty-six-year-old hothead who'd seemingly come from nothing."

She whistled. "What could you take care of as a young whippersnapper that had stumped a king?" she challenged.

Coming closer, his grin was wide, without a hint of irony. "Pirates."

"I should have known," she groaned.

"Calla had been in the possession of the crown for a number of years following the stripping of titles of the previous duke. By the time I came along, however, they'd turned it into a disaster. Caline was uninhabitable, the bay choked with debris and toxic algae, the arable cropland lying fallow and without irrigation, and everywhere you looked, pirate factions made it impossible for regular people to build lives."

It sounded like a scene from a movie.

"Calla?" Hel asked, astounded. That sounded nothing like the warm and welcoming city she'd experienced.

He nodded. "It took most of the money I earned in the navy, all the way through being an admiral, but once I dealt with the pirates, new residents moved into the area, bringing new commerce along with them. It was only a matter of time before word spread that Calla was once again one of the most highly desirable locations in all of Sidra, and instead of draining my accounts, she began to return on my investment. Tenfold."

Hel smiled. He was proud and he'd earned it. Unlike herself or her cousin or any of the other aristocrats she knew, Drake had built that himself. Not his father or grandfather before him. There was another difference between him and her father. He'd truly created the legacy he was proud of, and in all of that, had not let success corrupt him. He knew hard work and was willing to do it himself—it was a rare trait among the men she'd come of age alongside.

But he clearly didn't need to hear that from her. He had arrogance enough to fill a room. Even one with an open wall to the wide star-filled sky.

Hel shivered, something deep and warm moving inside of her, but she kept her tone light when she finally spoke. "Impressive. A duchy can be a real drain on the pocketbook."

He chuckled, as she'd hoped he would, and the sound warmed her heart. Though she refused to succumb to his charm, she'd make sure she did as right by him as she possibly could.

And she promised to remember the conviction even after they were done luxuriating in the most glorious pool she'd ever been in.

"You never told me why you hate your father so much," he said as if they'd been on the subject.

If he'd meant to throw her off balance with the non sequitur, he was going to be disappointed. She answered without missing a beat. "I did. He was a terrible man, and an actual criminal who terrorized my mother and I."

"Terrorized how?" he persisted.

Looking away, Hel kept it casual. "Yelling, belittling. Hitting before I learned self-defense."

Drake clenched and released his fists, but was even-toned when he asked, "Where was your mother through all of this?"

Instantly protective, Hel's spine straightened. "Being yelled at, belittled and taking the brunt of the hitting until I learned self-defense." Their bond was tied up in more than just the stuff of mothers and daughters.

He pressed, "She didn't keep you safe."

Hel let out a dry, joyless laugh, almost more of a cough than any sound of pleasure. "She couldn't."

"But it still bothers you."

"Not that."

"What?"

When he simply waited for her to respond, she let out an exasperated breath. "She loved him," she finally said.

Drake frowned and she understood his confusion. History was full of powerful men who were bad husbands and evil men yet somehow remained secure in the love of their wives. Though, of course, the d'Tierrza story couldn't be so straightforward. If that had been the case it'd have been a simple thing of rebelling against them both and being done with it. Her relationship with her mother was all the more complicated for the incredible love that bound them together.

"Through it all?" he asked after a long pause, and she was astounded once more by his remarkable perceptiveness. A man didn't come from nothing and make it all the way to the top without being perceptive.

In response, she let out a weary sigh and shook her head, sharing because he had shared so much and, though she'd only now realized it, because she respected him. "No. Not even love was strong enough to overcome his evil." She hugged her arms around herself, hoping to regain some of the liquid warmth the pool had provided before the chill of telling her deep dark secrets had begun to seep into her bones. "She loved him from the moment she saw him. She was still a teenager, and he was actually pursuing my aunt Barbara—she was the prettier one." The aside dripped with bitter hindsight.

"But Barbara ran away with the prince instead…"

Hel nodded. That part of the story was well known. Her aunt Barbara had become the queen and her mother the duchess, now dowager, of Tierrza.

With a long, slow blink, Hel picked returned to the tale. "My mother thought he was so handsome and dashing. He courted Aunt Barbara by the storybook, and my mother ate it all up from the stands—hook, line and sinker. She was only seventeen—young and bright, and too naive to see the obvious rot at his core. They weren't even married yet, the first time he hit her. They'd been engaged for a month. The dress he'd instructed her to wear to an event was damaged the day of, so she changed at the last moment without telling him. She said he gave her a light slap, a little thing really, and that he'd been merely irritated, not enraged. She said at first she was stunned but wrote it off, since it was an important event. He was under a lot of stress. She wrote it off every time after, too. Until I turned sixteen."

After the silence stretched between them, he said, "I would not have thought it possible, but your father was more evil than even I realized."

Helene laughed, the sound not so much joyous as it was the sound of having spent years coming to terms with the fact. "He was." Her father had been an atrocity in so many people's lives, and there would never be enough she could do to make up for it. That kind of ill karma could only be addressed by total annihilation, and the only way she knew how to do that was to ensure that she was the end of the line.

Catching her chin and lifting it, Drake's warm brown eyes enveloped her, lulled her the same warm water, or a cozy blanket did, safety of a different kind than self-defense provided. "So what happened when you were sixteen?"

His voice was deep and soft, and the warm water of the pool lapped at her legs. The space was intimate, made sacred by the dark confessions she'd already made.

She said quietly, "When I was sixteen, he married me off."

Confusion danced across Drake's gaze. The situation had been scandalous, but very public knowledge. "I read about that," he said carefully.

Hel looked away, wrapping her arms around herself, chilled despite the heated water. "It was later annulled."

She had known her father disdained her before that. After, she'd known it was worse: he didn't care about her at all. He only cared about the name d'Tierrza. She was merely a tool, intentionally created and crafted to enhance the family dynasty.

Drake searched her face, the full force of his incredible intensity focused on her, and she wished she could create some barrier between them, some way to satisfy him with a simple answer.

But he wasn't easily distracted.

"What happened?" he persisted.

Balling her hands into fists at her sides, Hel took a deep breath and then intentionally released them. "Nothing happened. Because I didn't let it. I had begun studying self-defense and parkour—mainly because he abhorred women with manly pursuits—and if I hadn't…" She met his eyes again, the icy distance in them still the only true defense she had against the indisputable proof of her father's feelings toward her… and the fact it never stopped hurting. "They wanted to force me and wanted to ensure there could be no annulment—the property deal the marriage secured was too important to both families. I was lucky. I escaped my, 'fiancé,' and my mother helped me run away to the academy. We made sure everything was high-profile enough and we made it public enough that there was nothing my father could do, and my fiancé was too embarrassed to have had his butt kicked by the teenage girl he'd tried to force himself on to tell anything but the official story."

An inferno raged in the deep wells of Drake's eyes, but he was utterly controlled, utterly terrifying.

On her behalf.

She had no idea what that meant.

She cleared her throat. "So, yeah. Real bad guy."

"A monster," he agreed.

Hel nodded.

"You're his daughter." He was unflinching without cruelty and it still burned.

Hel's eyelids fluttered closed. When she could speak, she agreed, "Unfortunately."

And there would never be enough she could do to make up for it.

When she opened her eyes, he was watching her with a serious frown, which somehow only emphasized the boy still hidden in his face.

"You are your father's daughter, but you are not your father, and you are not responsible for his actions," he said.

Her smile was a small and weak thing. "It sure doesn't feel that way."

"Only you can set that burden down."

"I'm strong enough to carry it."

He surprised her when he asked, "But are you strong enough to put it down?" His words were heavy with the weight of the bigger question between them.

She shook her head. "Strength isn't always a good thing."

He frowned, his eyes seeing something far away from the moment they shared. "But it's necessary, none-theless. There is something poetic in the fact that the strength he gave you would become part of the weapon to destroy him—because whether or not you adopt my plan, you have already defeated him." He shook his head and added quietly, "My father wasn't strong."

Hel frowned. "Your father was heartbroken. No one was more loving or loyal than Uncle Ibrahim." The familiar address rolled off her tongue as smoothly as if it hadn't been nearly thirty years since the last time she'd uttered it.

Looking away, turning to the stars overhead, shining bright through the open viewing wall of the pool room, Drake said, "And he used that as an excuse to break. He left my mother alone, in a strange land, to care for two children in poverty. She had no skills for that…"

And he didn't want to say what it had required of her, because he loved his mother. That much was obvious.

"But you've made up for it now. I imagine she enjoys the good life all the more for having watched her son build it from the ground up…with his own hands."

Instead of the glint of pride that she saw in his eyes whenever he spoke of his accomplishment, Drake closed his eyes with a dry clearing of his throat. "She did."

Did. Hel's chest squeezed. "What happened?"

"Breast cancer."

"What?" She'd heard him—of course, she had—but the detail didn't fit with the narrative. How could a woman who had survived such incredible trauma and upheaval, whose life had had all the highs and lows of a long-running television drama, fall to such a quotidian evil as cancer?

Hel would have had an easier time accepting an anvil falling from the sky than the reality that the woman of her memories and Drake's description, one whose light had burned indefatigable, had been snuffed out, betrayed by her own body.

Hel's heart broke for Drake and Nya and Amira, whom she would never reunite with now, no matter how things worked out with her son. The family would have had no skills for the kind of life they found themselves in. But they had endured.

She thought of herself before the rigors of military training and her stubborn will had broken her of the helplessness bred into her by the lap of luxury. What a hard lesson that would have been to learn, and to be forced into it, rather than to have willingly selected it.

They had survived Hel's father, the loss of Ibrahim and poverty. They held, through it all, and long enough for Drake to play Atlas, raising them up through seeming strength of will alone.

Hel would have thought whatever fates existed would have been satisfied with all of that for one family story. But she was apparently destined to be wrong where the fates were concerned.

As if strangely affirming her thinking, Drake said, "My father's love left our family more than half-drowned on a beach. My mother's will brought us back to life. Or, most of us, anyway. And then she died of cancer."

The subtext was clear—whatever had happened to Ibrahim, it was Hel's father who had killed him. Uncle Ibrahim, it seemed, wasn't the type who could come back from being betrayed by someone he loved and trusted so much.

Drake was more like his mother, then—granite-tough and as gorgeous as marble. He was lucky.

Hel's own strength, as he'd noted, came from more tainted sources. She said, "My mother isn't so strong."

The corner of Drake's mouth lifted, a mischievous glint coming to his eye. "I can remember a few times she was strong enough to be downright scary…"

The boyish lightness in his tone shed lines of care from his face, hooking his beauty even deeper into Hel's psyche. She knew that even after this encounter, he would be her standard of male perfection. "I never said she wasn't a mother," she said. "As a mother, she can put the fear of god into your soul. But outside of that, she's…gentle."

"Then she is lucky to have you to protect her."

His words weren't what she had expected to hear, but as they made their way into her heart, something hard and angry cracked and broke, the pieces shaking away to reveal healthy, vibrant emotion beneath.

"Thank you," she said, though it wasn't nearly enough. If she was the type to cry, a tear might have slipped free as she realized, oddly safe and protected by his presence and their isolation, just how hard it had been to carry the shame. And maybe, in this unusual place, she could acknowledge just how much she resented the fact that her mother's weakness meant she had had to bear it alone.

But for this moment, close together and secluded, she could lean into him, the soft smoothness of his skin on hers a sensation far more electrifying than the comfort she might find with her mother, and all the more powerful for it.

Marriage and children might not be her destiny, but if they had been, if she had had the chance to put together an imagined husband, he would have been remarkably like the man she was with now—strong, upright, determined, resilient and committed to justice.

Pulling back, unwilling to lean too hard, to get too used to the support, she was struck by his beauty.

His gaze dropped to her parted lips and her breath caught. The look in his eyes took on an intense focus that hadn't been there a moment before.

He was going to kiss her again, and as her body strained closer to him ever so slightly, she realized she was going to let him again. She was going to let him, because she *was* strong enough to set it down—her vow, her father, all of it.

She could set it down for Drake.

Their lips met with the shocking electric intensity that was fast becoming an old friend. He was a warm front meeting her cold, the force of their coming together creating a private hurricane of bodies pressed together, his plundering tongue the eye of the storm.

Her long fingers danced across his back and down his arms, freed, uninhibited and empowered to be surprisingly gentle. Everywhere he pulsed warmth and strength—the thrum of blood in his veins beneath his skin, his hands, exploring her body, the growing length of him, separated from her by just the thin fabric of his shorts and her bikini.

Water lapped at their legs, its quiet splashes licking up only to drip down her inner thighs as the mingled sound of their heavy breathing echoed and swirled throughout the pool room like steam in a sauna.

His roughened sailor's palms came to rest at her lower rib cage before caressing her in an upward motion, his thumbs brushing under and along the outer edges of her breasts, exposed on either side of her bikini top. Her skin tightened at the contact, shivers trailing their way outward from her spine to the tips of her extremities, chasing the breath out of her lungs as if at the end of breath lurked bliss. Her sigh was pressure released in pleasure, escaping her swollen lips to weave them together before she even recognized the sound as her own.

He growled in response, the sound a rumble originating somewhere near where their hips ground against each other before it vibrated up through his torso to become pure possession in his kiss.

She moaned into him, giving him more of her weight, more of her need, more of her.

He answered by running his hand down her side to catch her thigh, lifting it in a smooth motion, bringing them even closer, core to nuclear core. And still, it wasn't enough. She still wanted more.

Greed was a new experience.

When resources were infinite, there was no want or lack to breed greed. But here, between them, she met limits for the first time—a limit in how close she could press, a limit in how she could assuage the growing chasm inside that cried out for more even after being given more than it had ever been given before, a limit in her ability to join with him, as if the brand-new concept the primitive voice inside whispered to her was not only possible, but also imperative. They could become one, it promised. If she was brave enough, their essence could unify, creating a new entity, greater than the sum of their perfectly suited parts.

It was a fascinating lure. Truly tempting, in a way none of the tepid stolen kisses of her past had been. It wasn't possible to be a beautiful, rich, female royal without having had her fair share of unwanted advances. Before she'd become strong enough to fend them off in other ways, she'd learned that the best response was simply to reveal to the absolute chill of disinterest their efforts inspired in her. But the truth was, until Drake, she had never been tempted.

His kisses made her forget herself, lose her sense of time and place. There was no upper hand under the command of his lips.

And she couldn't get enough.

Neither, it seemed, could he. With another growl, this one dogged by frustrated need, he scooped up her other thigh, unbalancing her as he took her weight easily, holding her body—hot, slick and wet—tight against his…all without breaking his kiss.

He was strong. Stronger than she was, she noted, though she usually didn't think in terms like that. Strength was nothing against determination—unless that strength was a volcano rising from the sea, threatening to engulf her in its molten waves. He was overwhelming, and she realized she wanted to be overwhelmed, but only by him.

Without breaking the kiss, he carried her to the edge of the warm pool, placing her there gently, as if she was something delicate and fragile, rather than the same woman he'd sparred with only yesterday morning.

Standing between her parted thighs, he brought his hands up to cup her jaw, his touch reverent as he tilted her face up toward his to plunder the depths of her mouth further. And then his fingers were in her hair, massaging her scalp as his lips made mush of her mind.

Everything in her strained toward him, reaching for that elusive union her body insisted was their ultimate destination. Her breasts ached, longing for what she didn't know, while everywhere her skin flushed and burned.

His lips followed his hands, tracing her jawline to find her earlobe, where he bit her softly before whispering something long and lovely in Sidran. And then all the air, and her wits, rushed out of her at the same time, every ounce of her focus zeroed in on the point where his thumbs pressed against her aching nipples.

Blue triangles of swimsuit separated them, but she felt the contact as acutely as if she had been nude, each rosy peak exposed beneath the dark sky.

And then he was rolling the hard pearls between his thumb and forefinger, his palms joining in the sensual explosion, cupping and lifting her breasts, and she was arching her back, pressing herself farther into his hands.

Snaking an arm around her waist to hold her, he kissed down her neck, pillaging the ivory column all the way, his free arm working its way behind her back and pulling the string that held her top in place.

He made quick work of the string around her neck, tossing the top to the side as he pulled back to feast on the sight of her bare breasts. The look in his eyes said he was ravenous for a sustenance only she could provide. In that instant, she felt what it was to be a font—a source of life, beauty and wonder—rather than an embattled soldier with grim purpose.

It felt like earning wings.

His hot mouth locked around the needy peak of her nipple and she soared, the sensation breaking free in the form of his name on her lips, the syllable a drawn-out cry of pleasure. Her legs squeezed around his waist of their own volition, the movement a subconscious flirtation, drawing him nearer to the untapped power source at her core.

Her movement set off a tremor of reaction through his body that she felt deep within her own. She marveled that she had the ability to make this incredible man shake. The thought went straight to her head, light and bubbly even as it was tremendous, like standing on the edge of a skyscraper.

Her breath came in shallow pants as he devoured her, switching to the other breast only when he'd completely ravished the first, his free hand quickly coming to replace the spot where his mouth had been.

She was putty in his hands, his to play with and mold, pliable and unguarded in a way she hadn't been since long before the days they'd chased each other through the flowers as children.

He didn't waste the opportunity.

His tongue traced lines of fire around her breasts, driving her mad in a tempest of temperature and taste and tightening. His beard and teeth gave an edge to every sensation, the combination of sandpaper and silk keeping her spinning.

And then he said her name.

It was more of a breath than even a whisper, but it shot through her, lacy and lithesome as it was, rolling off his tongue with hushed reverence.

"Helene."

No one called her that. Hel. D'Tierrza. Duke. Captain. Not even her mother, who preferred the term *daughter* most of the time.

Hel had always hated *Helene*, fussy and formal, perfect and composed—everything she stood in opposition of.

Until now. The moment he said it, his tone worshipful, his lips soft against her skin as he spoke, she was transformed.

Helene had the power to bring this god of the sea to his knees. It was the knowledge, from wherever it arose, that he could weather her most powerful storms, and be strong, steady and, most of all, kind.

Rock-hard and warm beneath her hands, he was living, throbbing, ready proof that maybe she was wrong, that maybe, just maybe, incredible strength could come without cruelty.

And whether it was due to that seismic realization or the onslaught of his sensual attack, her body began to tremble. What had begun as faint tremors grew into stronger, more insistent rolling waves, threatening to carry her out to sea, relentless in their increasing strength as her power to resist waned.

"Show me," he demanded, his voice guttural, all the more commanding for playing her like a maestro at his instrument. "Show me how you fall apart."

She wanted to fight. She wasn't the kind of woman who complied easily—she was famous for it—and yet her body strained toward his, the gnawing hunger coalescing where she shamelessly pressed against him.

Yet still she resisted.

She might retreat, but she didn't surrender.

"Do it now," he said, and he took one nipple in his mouth at the same instant as he pinched the other and she exploded into a brand-new galaxy—herself, her energy, her very life bursting into a vast collection of stars, planets and memories, spread out before her for an endless second.

His palm scraped lightly down the long plane of her

belly, branding her as his as surely as a cattleman's mark. Then the tips of his long fingers slipping beneath the top edge of her swimsuit and stopped.

He pulled back, commanding her gaze. He was beautiful—his brown eyes burning in low light, his incredible physique harnessed and focused entirely on her, his glorious erection obvious—and he was absolutely not going any further without her signal.

And even though none of it was for her, not marriage, and certainly not children, just for tonight, in this magical place so far from her regular life, she wanted to pretend it was. Disheveled and thoroughly taken, her lips swollen and sensitive, her deepest core throbbing and hungry, aching, craving and insistent that there was more despite his thorough gorging, she nodded.

CHAPTER EIGHT

SLIDING HER BLUE bikini down revealed the trim triangle of white-blond curls, a treasure he was desperate to cup, hold, slide his finger along the seam of and slip inside… Muscles straining, he refrained. Instead, he brought his fingertip back up to the center point between her eyebrows and trailed down, skin lightly touching skin, all the way down, over her chin, down her neck, between her breasts, past her belly button, only to stop at the beginning of that triangle. She sucked in her breath on a soft hiss, her skin tightening, back arching. Her skin was soft and sensitive for a woman who made a living of being hard.

Moonbeams streaming in through the sky-view wall lit and outlined her perfection—her nipples, dusky rose and proud, her breasts, soft and pliant, each one his perfect handful, her waist, slender and long, the rounded swell of her hips and muscular curvature of her backside, each line an artist's, emphasizing her form with shadow and highlight.

Rock-hard and throbbing, the tip of his manhood was damp in anticipation of her, as if it knew this was her first time, knew that even though he would take care of her, that he would ensure she was as wet the ocean floor before he entered her, that she would need all of that and more to ease his entry.

He was a lot to take for the first time, but he had no doubt she could handle him—all of him—like a custom-made sheath. A captain learned to trust his instincts, and his instincts were screaming that he had found his Penelope. But unlike famous Odysseus, he would not ask her to put her life on hold. He would set her free.

But not until he'd heard her beg. If she was going to make his dreams come true, he was going to blow her mind.

While she still shook, he took her further under his command, gripping her hips on either side, strong fingers digging into the taut flesh. Adjusting her position, he sat her on the edge of the pool and spread her legs, an open buffet for his feast.

Languorous and love-drunk, she was unprepared for the onslaught. He attacked directly, no longer content to resist the siren song of her scent.

She tasted like citrus, snapping him back to the bright bergamot that infused the private courtyard air outside his childhood bedroom in Andros, a sensory pleasure long-lost—she tasted like home. Even when he'd tasted her for the first time, the knowledge hadn't surprised him, as if some part of him had known the moment he'd laid eyes on her, watching her argue with the ghost of her father.

He could have told her there was no use arguing with that man.

But then he wouldn't have her here, slick and hot and sumptuous.

She screamed his name as his tongue teased the crease at her core.

Her fingers found his shoulders, her hands strong and capable, and she held onto him like a life raft when, in fact, he was the storm.

He couldn't remember ever being this hard, this eager, this close to the edge from little more than the sound of her pleasure and a taste.

Of course, he couldn't remember a taste quite like her before, either. And as she bulldozed the competition in his record book, he was taken aback at what was happening to him. She was mesmerizing him, luring him into a dazed stupor with every passing and savored second he spent with his hands on her, his mouth on her… and if he went further, if he steered them into a union, as was his undeniable plan, she would wreck him.

What was happening between them, what blossomed, was as far from the careless encounters of a sailor on leave as a lake from the ocean. This was the stuff of forever, and deeper connection, and baring real emotions. Everything paled in comparison to Hel because he had never felt this for another woman. Their bodies told him what their battle-weary hearts resisted: this was the stuff of love.

It was too late to change course now, though. Sometimes the only way out of a storm was through it.

He was ready for the tempest when she came apart the second time, lapping her up like a fool in the rain. Her thighs clenched around his head and he smiled against her, glorying in each and every one of her unintentional reactions, each reflexive tightening and release, each pulsing wave that carried her away with as much surprise as joy.

She would carry this memory of him with her forever. He'd make sure it was unforgettable.

He held her there, helpless to both his attack and her pleasure, until her hips relaxed in his hands and the pulses of her climax slowed, her breathing jagged and airy.

Again, he knew she thought she was done, wrung out. It was written in the boneless fall of her body, the dazed glimmer in her eyes.

Humming a long "mmmmm" against her, he began to trail kisses upward again, over her stomach, before stopping to shower her breasts with more attention. In no time at all, her soft sighs grew heavier, elongated and interspersed with drawn-out pauses, moments of time standing still.

While he kissed the plump underside of her breasts, his hand returned south, finding the heat of her core. Fingers once again playing along her entrance, his thumb found the little bud at the top that held the key to it all and pressed with gentle firmness, before beginning the alternating dance of pressure and release that would push her over the edge yet again.

If anything, she was more responsive. And why should he be surprised? Her body was a well-honed machine—of course, she responded to practice like a master. She was a true wonder.

He slipped one long finger inside as she moaned and her inner muscles clenched around him so hard he groaned, sweat beading on his forehead. It was absurd—she couldn't be this tight and hot and not kill him. Her body was a vise around his finger, so snug the thought even flitted across his own mind. Would he fit?

He had always laughed the concern away in the past, as confident in the engineering of nature as he was in his endowment, but now, when it mattered more than it ever had, he doubted.

Would she be ready? Could she take him? He didn't want to hurt her.

He slipped another finger in, stilling both digits to allow her time to adjust and stretch.

A tremor radiated from her center outward and he shuddered, unsure if he would make it for the first time in his life. His control had been ironclad the night three older friends had taken him to a house of ill repute to make a man of him.

Tonight, it threatened to break with each silken compression.

Would he survive it?

Whatever the answer, the time was at hand. Knowing throbbed in him as hard and hot as he was.

Rising over her, he was filled with an unfamiliar wave of possession. Eyes glittering, she stared up at him, unflinching and hungry despite having been sated time and again. She belonged to him and no one else.

She would let him in, and him alone. He could offer her a part of himself and never fear betrayal.

Without words, her body whispered the most tempting lure of all. *You can trust me*, it promised, and the incredible thing was, he believed he could.

The revelation was heady and powerful.

Reaching an arm between them, he gripped himself, already cloudy with his excitement. Then he ran his sensitive head along the same hot seam that his fingers had traced earlier, torturing them both with the electric waves each movement set off.

Breath catching, her fingers squeezed into his shoulders, when he paused at her entrance, pressing just slightly, holding there, breath, time, life itself on pause for the space of a heartbeat, before continuing the sweet agony of the caress.

She whimpered beneath him, hips lifting unconsciously inviting him deeper.

Where the strength came from, he could not say, but he held fast.

She pressed against him, body rooting for the next level of pleasure she sought if her mind didn't yet know what it wanted and needed.

Maintaining the game was excruciating. He knew he could plunge into her at any moment and she would scream in relief, the fullness her body instinctively knew it craved achieved, but he did not.

Her sighs and moans became puffs of frustration and her eyes flew open, irritation as clear as the blue in her gaze. Faint pink danced across her cheeks, flushed and glowing as she was, and it was all he could do to hold the line.

His shaft virtually wept for release, but he denied them.

She shifted her hips, opening wider, giving him greater access. He groaned, muscles taut and screaming, body screaming, throbbing, screaming, but continued to tease.

Another noise of frustration and then the word he had been waiting for, breathlessly uttered and slipping between her plump lips.

"Please."

It was a whole sentence when she said it. She needed something from him, didn't know what it was, but trusted him to interpret her impassioned plea and give it to her.

"Please, Drake," she said again, his name an intoxicating addition.

And he could hold back no longer.

He plunged into her in one stroke, using all his strength to hold still, and he strained under the assault of sensations. Heat, grip, slick and pulsing. Fully sheathed, her body held him like a vise. They stayed like that, still joined, while the veins in his neck bulged. She might kill him, but he would die happy.

And then she began to stir and it was only iron will that stopped him from embarrassing himself.

Tentative at first, soon she was exploring the feel of him with her characteristic boldness. And when he knew he could take no more, he took charge, setting a slowly building rhythm. He knew the instant the smooth friction snared her attention, baiting her down the path of falling part yet again.

When another hot wet wave engulfed him, he knew she was close. Close enough to increase his pace, diving and driving her harder and deeper, her increasing moans telling him everything he needed to know about her enjoyment. And when even that wasn't enough, when he had to push harder, deeper, she kept pace without lagging, her energy more than enough to match him, her strength promising him he couldn't break her.

His name was her last word, called out like a dying woman before her body tightening stole the very breath from him, before she broke into a thousand searing convulsions. The realization that would be burned into his soul from this moment forward was his last coherent before he was tossed to sea himself, pounding to the very depths of her before breaking into a million little pieces.

He came to with his arm wrapped around her, holding her upright in the curve of his arm, her legs dangling in the pool.

She radiated the contentment they both felt, bodies joined and humming in tune, the physical evidence of the way things had changed.

Because things had changed.

He was unwilling to look at the most profoundly intimate sexual encounter he'd ever had and pretend otherwise.

His mother's words, her ever-optimistic mantra, whispered in the back of his mind. *You never know what flowers the manure will turn up.*

His arrangement with Helene might not have grown from love, but the potential for it was there. That much was as clear as the blue of her eyes. That he could love, not merely tolerate, the daughter of Dominic d'Tierrza was a testament to the power of the emotion, the idea so foreign that the possibility had never once occurred to him all of his plotting—not even after seeing her and realizing the task might not be so onerous as he'd once imagined. Only now.

It was a delicious if unexpected icing on the cake he'd finally gotten a slice of—because if her actions were any indication, and this matter was one in which action was as good as word, she had agreed to be his accomplice, his partner in justice. Even when his mind and body were tempted to float away in favor of examining emotions other than triumph, reticent emotions that lurked beneath the surface, entirely unconcerned with obsession and revenge, and all the more powerful for it.

Those emotions were best left for times after they'd worked through their shared business.

Her vow had been thoroughly burned to ashes.

His children, his name, would replace d'Tierrza on the map.

That victory had come wrapped up in the most phenomenal package he'd ever had the pleasure of opening, was more than a cherry on top.

If they had not already achieved his ultimate goal of seating his children on the d'Tierrza throne, it would certainly be a pleasure to try again. And again.

The incredible had occurred: he'd gotten his cake and got to eat it, too. He'd turned tragedy into triumph so monumental that he was on the verge of pinching himself. He couldn't stop the smile that stretched wide as he pulled her close and nuzzled his face in her hair, drawing in the fresh scent of her, before shifting her gently. Her noise of protest had him wincing, tightness squeezing his chest as he pulled back. He'd been lost in thought when he needed to see to her comfort.

"It's time to get you out of this pool. I'm sure you're wrinkled all over by now."

She groaned, the sound a tremor quaking through her body. He felt it like a knife edge along the oversensitive line where they were still connected. He slid out of her slowly, careful to go easy, knowing she'd be sore nonetheless.

More groaning came from her, but he could tell it was merely on principle now. He was surprised to find it…cute.

For the briefest second, he wondered if she was some kind of sleeper agent, the ultimate coup de grâce of Dominic d'Tierrza's grand evil schemes, even while he knew it wasn't possible.

A move like that would have required that he understand things like love, and need, and the cruel choices of the heart.

To the world's great fortune, Dominic had not been aware of exquisite agonies of the warmer emotions. If he had realized love could burn like fire, he would have seen his daughter as a weapon, instead of merely a pawn. That he had done even that, and that it was only her own ingenuity that had kept her safe from his machinations, was repulsive enough.

But as childhood images of her flashed through his mind, he wondered if perhaps Dominic had understood more about his daughter's potential than he'd ever let on.

In his memory, it was as if she had always been there, a constant companion at his side, carried around to protect and encourage and goad and draw smiles from, rather than a woman with whom he'd only recently become reacquainted.

He gave his head a shake to free it from the cobwebs of melodrama. It was time to get out of the pool and away from his gorgeous linchpin.

But first he drew her closer again.

She softened against him, her eyes closing on an exhale.

Just like that, they fit together—as naturally as if they had been made to comfort one another.

They stood together in the pool without words as the sun made its debut, its light dancing across the black waves of the sea, bursting free to bring blue to the sky.

Helene opened her eyes in the growing light, the pool room sparkling, and he watched the realization dawn on her that the room's nighttime performance had been mere sleepwalking, that it truly woke with the dawn, its bright white walls near blinding, its mosaics glittering like paintings rendered with multifaceted gemstones. The room itself was a treasure chest, the water of the pool crystalline turquoise, the beautiful cushions of fabrics and pillows even more stunning by day.

"Are you hungry?" he asked, enjoying the irritation that flickered across her face at being asked such a mundane question after all they had shared.

"You're always trying to feed me," she grumbled.

"You're too skinny," he insisted, to her outrage.

She crossed her arms in front of her chest.

"On a normal day, I eat three thousand calories!" she said.

"So you say," he said, shrugging. "Your frame speaks for itself, however."

Her eyes narrowed, glittering in the light as jewel-toned as the mosaics beneath their feet.

Her statement was ruined, however, when Hel's stomach grumbled.

Squinting in the ever-brightening room, he turned a grin her direction and said, "You're hungry. And tired, I'm sure, after our little adventures. We'll eat, rest and then we'll return to Cyrano to destroy your father's legacy."

From the pool room, it looked as if the sun had bleached out every color except for blue on the island, the palm fronds mostly silhouetted against the sand and sea.

She nodded, eyes wide blue orbs in her moon-pale face reflecting the impossible blue of the sea in the distance, as well as the topaz-clear waters of the pool. Her cheeks had pinkened again, making her look like a porcelain doll...but he knew she was far from fragile.

Lifting himself from the water, he wrapped a towel around his waist before reaching out a hand to assist her.

Taking it, she followed his lead, wrapping her towel to hang low around her hips, and he shook his head, his smile growing. Most women would have covered their whole bodies.

Helene wasn't most women.

He walked them out of the room, toward the kitchen.

The compound on Yancy Grove was impressive, considering its foundations were historic, if not ancient— he didn't know for certain because accurate structural dating of the original foundations was less important than privacy.

Over the years he had improved the existing ruins, maintaining structural integrity wherever he could, and made sure that every element of new architecture blended stylistically with what remained.

The result was like traveling back to the times of the great African kings. Wide walkways lined with fragrant blooming vines created the boundaries for smoothly tiled hallways. Cleverly placed arched cutouts in the walls encouraged the sea air to dance through the buildings, cooling as they went, as well as ensuring there wasn't a poor view to be had. The complex of buildings was loosely rectangular, arranged around a central courtyard with a massive, three-tiered fountain in its center. The fountain was classic with simple flowing lines and flourishes rather than ornate carvings with waterspouts. Palm trees and flowering shrubs grew wherever there was space, giving everything a feeling of overgrowing paradise, newly discovered, like the day they'd stumbled upon it so desperately.

Flat-roofed buildings had staggered heights, architecturally anchored by the domed roofs of each corner building, which created spaces for rooftop dining, as well as a rooftop shower and soaking pool.

Between the pool room and roofs, he could spend every moment in the open air should he want to, just like his days at sea, as if the island itself was his ship.

There was no retiring from the sea.

He led Helene through the perfumed corridors between the pool room, into the smaller of the kitchen and dining rooms. Yancy Grove was structured so that it could accommodate his whole crew and their immediate families should the need arise, but it was also comfortable to reside in alone. After all, that was how he spent most of his time on the island.

In the kitchen, he indicated that she should take a seat at the counter-island bar chair, while he prepared them a meal, the significance of what had just transpired heavy and unspoken between them.

"You cook?"

He lifted an eyebrow. "I like to eat."

She grinned. "So do I, and I don't know the difference between a sauté pan and a boiling pot."

"At the very least you know what you don't know," he said dryly.

She laughed, watching avidly as he sprinkled seasonings. "What are we having?"

"Lightly seared ahi steaks."

"Sounds delicious. You don't have staff here?"

Eyeing her, he said, "Your pampered lifestyle is showing, princess."

Hel made a rude gesture with her hand in response. "I don't need staff. I just expected you would have them."

"And why is that?"

It was Hel's turn to be dry. "You're a double duke."

Her words landed like cold darts. She was right, though he had never truly thought of himself as Duke Andros. That had been his father most of the time and his stolen birthright otherwise.

Instead of the elation he had felt earlier, the knowledge came with a strange sense of emptiness. What was there now that he had achieved his greatest dream?

But to Helene, he said, "I started out as a humble sailor."

Helene rolled her eyes. "Then became an admiral and a duke."

He shook his head, grin flashing. "No. I was a duke before I was an admiral."

"And impossible even before that," she retorted.

Still grinning, he gave her a little salute before taking the platter of steaks out to the grill. Minutes later he returned to the kitchen, seared ahi ready to serve.

He set the table for the two of them easily, laying out island-grown dates and figs, as well as fresh goat cheese, bread and olives, brought from the mainland by his staff during their once-weekly trips.

He finally answered her question as she joined him in the bright sky-lit breakfast nook. "I don't keep regular staff here because I like the privacy. I only have guests when I want them."

But he found he didn't mind sharing the space with Helene.

He had been observing her from the moment he'd seen her in the d'Tierrza courtyard, catching the unguarded moments between her forced nonchalance when her expression was fierce, earnest and so transparent he could read her thoughts like a marquee.

That this woman could be the product of Dominic d'Tierzza was unbelievable.

An entire world had gone up against Dominic d'Tierrza, and as far as Drake could tell, the only one who had walked out even remotely whole was the woman eating at his side. As incredible as it was, and despite the fact that he would have carried out his plans regardless of who she was, respect and affection for her had taken root in their short time together. He hadn't intended or thought it even possible, but, beyond their incredible sex, he truly liked her.

Or maybe plotting revenge for thirty years had finally pushed him over the edge.

After breakfast, they agreed to rest, though he wasn't sure how much sleep he would be getting.

Hours spent with Helene were akin to plugging in to a live wire. He was electrified.

He showed her a set of rooms she could use, equipped with their own bathroom and shower, and left her there while he found a change of clothes for her in the supplies closet.

After laying them on the bed, he left the room to take his own shower and rest.

As energizing as her company was, he ultimately fell asleep quickly. Being in the military for so long had taught him to take advantage of opportunities to sleep when he could.

Hours later, he woke, fully alert the moment his eyes opened, another holdover from a career in the service. He was hyperaware of the absence of Helene.

He found her, equally alert, when he rapped on her door. She looked rested, though he wasn't certain how he could tell, having never observed her looking tired.

He had never met another woman who embodied the word *indefatigable* so well, something he appreciated as buoyant as he was feeling.

"How did you sleep?" he asked, smile wide and warm. He was eager to begin planning the next stage now that he had secured her cooperation, but he had the sense not to start when she'd only just woken up.

Seeing her again, though, after their time in the pool, had his blood thrilling again, his pulse as jumpy and eager as a little boy with a big present.

Impossibly, she was even more beautiful. They had slept much of the day, which was to be expected after almost sixty hours of near constant activity. It was past the normal dinner hour, but still bright enough outside that he considered a late dinner alfresco. And after that, they could christen another pool room.

He loved that she was so at ease in the water.

Her smile was coral magic. "Wonderfully, thank you."

His mouth quirked up at those impeccable manners. Blue-blooded-ness really was her default, for all that she was a soldier.

"Are you hungry?"

"Trying to feed me yet again?" She quirked up an eyebrow.

"Can I help it if I was raised right?"

She smiled and for an instant he simply let himself appreciate the way the smile warmed him. He was driven, determined and unstoppable. It was easy to forget he was also a man. A man who wanted to hold his woman, for just a breath, before they got back to work.

"I'm not hungry, but I would like a walk on the beach," she said.

"Then a-walking we will go. There are spare sandals where the slippers were." He offered her his arm and she smiled at him, cheeks tinged with pink, and took it.

They walked together, arm in arm, while he marveled at the lightness between them. She was a royal guard, a consummate professional, and he was a retired admiral turned privateer specializing in hunting down traffickers, and together, they were in the business of revenge, and yet there was a lightness to being around Helene…as if alongside work, there could be play.

"Do I need sandals on a deserted island?" she asked, a light in her eyes.

He shook his head. "You have something against footwear?"

She laughed, stretching her arms wide. "I don't like being hemmed in. I told you. It's the barefoot-and-free-seafaring life for me now."

He snorted. "More like the barefoot-with-babies life for you now. At least temporarily."

Laughing, she said, "Well, not right away! I've got to get back to work eventually, and now that I've broken the seal, there's so much to explore before babies…"

He stopped, still smiling. "There's no rule that says we have to stop exploring when you're pregnant. But we should begin right away if we want the best chances. The process of marriage and unifying titles is lengthy and should be begun immediately, as well. It's hitting the ground running and a lot all at once, but in the long run, it's just two to three years…"

Stopping beside him, Hel frowned, a sense of warning, like a frigid gust, blowing through the languorous tingles that had been pulsing in her body ever since the pool room. "I can't get pregnant now," she said. "It's not the right time with my job."

He smiled. "While we both know you're far from decrepit, at your age, it's best we don't waste time."

Hel snorted, "Calling me old now? Hardly. I'm in fantastic shape. And we certainly have options if that traditional way didn't work out." She blushed, her body still tender and alive with doing things the traditional way. "Kids and marriage will need to wait, if only temporarily," she assured him with a grin, then added, "but in the meantime, we can keep practicing…"

But the flirty grin she expected didn't flash across his face. Instead, his eyebrows came together, shadowing his eyes, bringing turbulence to his expression. "How long?" he asked, his voice rough and salty, older than she'd ever heard it.

Taking a step back, she wrapped her arms around herself. She was chilled, whereas before she'd felt loose and easy. "I don't know. A year, maybe two? It's not long to wait."

"I could say the same to you and science would be on my side," he said, crossing his arms in front of his chest.

A strange pressure filled her lungs, making her breath come thick and heavy.

"It's just not a good time. There is the royal wedding, and my mother will expect a full wedding before we start announcing grandchildren."

"We'll elope," he said, as if that made everything easy.

Hel's head began to throb, the sensation of tightening, an ever-intensifying squeezing spreading throughout her whole body, familiar for all that she couldn't place it.

"My mother will want a wedding."

He scoffed. "It's not your mother's nuptials. What she wants is irrelevant."

And then Hel knew. She knew where she'd felt this before. She knew why she had the urge to fight—to kick and scream and do exactly the opposite of what he wanted from her. His words were an echo of her father.

"I want a wedding. I want to wait until the timing is better before *I* have children. That means after the royal wedding, and after our wedding, and maybe even after a honeymoon," Hel retorted, her hands coming to rest on her hips as her temperature kicked up with each word, despite the cool sea breezes. "You've asked me for my entire life, to abandon my own quest for justice, to have your children, and I have, in a matter of days, which is a remarkably quick turn of fashion, I'd say. I'm just asking you for a year, at most, two. I gave you my word."

"In my experience, the word of a d'Tierrza isn't worth a lot."

She lifted an eyebrow, danger slipping into her voice. "I am not my father. You either trust me or you don't."

His eyes narrowed, equal ferocity coming to his expression. "I can't say that I think much of your conviction, based on my personal experience. In fact, in my experience, you've only been able to hold out, for what was it you mentioned? A matter of days."

The color drained from her face. "Excuse me?" she asked, her head cocked at a stiff angle, her body rigid with the pain each successive word launched.

She had been so mature. So reasonable about the whole thing. She had been flexible and open, willing to alter her course in the name of honor.

She made choices with her eyes open, knowing what

and why he wanted. So why did his words feel like darts? Why did she feel such a deep aching in the center of her chest?

It couldn't simply be sex, could it? Yes, he had been her first and she knew how easy it was to entangle sex with emotion, but they were both adults. She was mature enough to realize the two didn't automatically go hand in hand.

So why did it hurt when he threw what she'd given him at her like that? Why did it hurt, that he dictated careless of her needs, wants and desires? Why did she feel like a child all over again, simultaneously wanting to strike and to please him? Why did she feel like ten times a fool at the same time, blithely walking into her mother's fate—that of the tragic, foolish and abused woman—when she'd sworn to herself it would never be hers?

"I'm just saying the evidence of your ability to keep your word is sadly lacking." His words were flat. Dismissive. Distinctly unimpressed.

The rising heat in her body dissipated like a popped balloon.

He had gone past anger.

Lust and longing would not make a pawn or a slave out of her—she wouldn't allow it. She had been caught up, ensnared and foolish enough to falter once, but never again. And it started immediately. She would never let a man dictate to her, no matter what she'd given him. Never.

She stood still, her body's readying itself reminiscent of the surf being pulled out to sea before a tsunami. It was quiet, eerie, all wrong, though it would have been hard to immediately pinpoint why. "Take me home. Immediately."

* * *

For a moment he just stared. She couldn't be serious. She had broken her vow. She had agreed to his plan. She was dedicated and honorable. She wasn't backing out now. "What? That's absurd."

"Take. Me. Home. Now. I say no and it's over."

His ears roared like the inside of a conch shell. This was not happening. She'd already given up her vow. She couldn't go back now. They'd gone too far. The roaring took on a tunneling quality. "Did it occur to you," he said, proud of how steady and even he kept his voice, "that it might already be too late?"

Horror filled her eyes, transforming into two bottomless pits of sapphire, and the expression was a knife in his gut. "The odds of human conception in any given encounter are rather low, so while, yes, it occurred to me, I was not so naive as to jump to that conclusion."

"I wouldn't be so quick to assume averages would apply to the two of us," he said, the words tasting bitter on his tongue. She, like everything else in her hands, became a weapon.

She rolled her eyes. "Right. I might be pregnant because the big bad Sea Wolf looked at me. That's a pretty high opinion you have of yourself. But why should I be surprised?"

The flare of his temper was as unwelcome as the realization that he wasn't entirely in control—of himself or the situation.

It was a novel experience.

"What's that supposed to mean?" he asked, pleased with his low and even tone.

Anger danced in her eyes. "Why should I be surprised that a man like you thinks he's somehow above

everyone around him, that the air he breathes is so rar-
ified that it gives him the right to make decisions for
everyone around him?"

His eyes narrowed, his glare warning her to quit
while she was ahead.

She didn't back down. "Why should I be surprised
when I have known that man my whole life?"

He didn't explode, though his anger at being compared to her father by her was as deep and thick as the
molten lava waiting to burst forth from below the earth.

With the words out, unable to be taken back, she eyed
him warily with an expression that he would have said
was tinged with sadness had it graced any face other
than hers. She burned too hot for something so cold
and wet as regret.

He returned her regard from a remove, a distance
that was entirely invisible separating them, and separating him from what he said.

"He'd be dead and gone if you didn't work so hard
to keep his memory alive, Helene. He died years ago
and yet you talk to him like he's alive. In fact, Helene,
he is. You keep him alive with every breath you take.
You look in the mirror and deep in your eyes, you know
the person who looks back is him, and no matter what
you do to offset his evil in the world it won't matter
because as long as you exist to do battle with him, he
lives." And if his words applied to himself, too, it didn't
matter, because he had scored his point.

Pain lanced her expression, but the tears that glistened in her eyes did not fall. Instead, she jutted out
her chin at a stubborn angle and he was instantly sent
back, the image of her now superimposed over the dusty

memories his mind had stored of her from when they'd been children together.

Coltish even as a young child, Helene, he recalled, had been nonstop energy from sunup to sundown, absolutely determined to keep up with her older playmate. Absolutely determined that no one—certainly not a twelve-year-old boy—would dominate her.

He felt an undeniable déjà vu comparing his images of the child Helene to the woman who stood before him.

"I said I'd give you seven days, but I've made my mind up already. I will not be a part of your plot. I will not be your pawn. I promised myself on the steps of the academy that I would never let a man like my father control me, ever again. I meant it. Not him, and certainly not you. Take me back to Cyrano. I want to go home now."

His eyes blazed rage at her, impotent as it was, as the plan he'd waited thirty years for went up in flames, laced with an even sharper pain, an underlying and relentless acid ache that started in his chest and radiated outward, as if his heart was being slowly eaten alive. And it was worse since there had been more than mere revenge between them, because, whether she knew it or not, the potential for something real existed between them.

Like a child with no thought to the devastation of her words, she carelessly compared him to his greatest nemesis while simultaneously tearing at the new, dangerous and delicate thing that beat in his chest, the thing that wanted to please her.

He smiled, though the expression felt as dry and brittle as a barking cough. "Certainly," he said. He kept his voice firm and cool, though for the life of him, he could not recall words cutting his mouth so sharply on the way out.

He had trusted her. Trusted her to keep her word, to go along with his crazy idea, and the sting he felt at her betrayal was stronger than anything he'd felt since discovering his father's suicide or his mother's cancer, or even what he'd felt as he held Yancy as he'd died. When she'd given herself to him, she'd agreed, she'd taken his hand and he'd dared to hope.

She had given him her body, and he'd mistaken it for something more, trusting the breaking of her vow to speak for her. Replaying the events, it was obvious trusting was where he had gone wrong. Who knew better than he that even the most reliable constants could abandon you when you most needed them?

He didn't know what he was doing anymore. That much was clear. He couldn't trust people—not with his thoughts, not with his emotions and certainly not with his hopes and dreams. Trust was a luxury of the privileged, and even then, only few.

But he would not take back his words. He'd meant what he said when he told her he didn't force women. When one made it a policy to only speak the truth, there was nothing to ever take back.

Once again he looked out over the Mediterranean, squinting against the bright sun shining on the bright white sand and bright cerulean sea, the wheels of his crystalline mind turning.

Following the shoreline, observing the palm trees swaying gently in the breeze that were rooted atop small grassy dunes dotting the swaths of almost antiseptically white sand, it occurred to him that she might be right.

Perhaps he was like her father, as ravenously hungry and driven by greed. He had everything and more that a hard-scrapping poor boy could dream of, and he had the strength and resilience he would have been denied had the silver spoon he was born with not been ripped from his mouth.

Recognizing it did nothing to soothe the roar inside, but it underscored Helene's point.

He was used to the abyss, had grown comfortable with its unceasing demand for nothing less than the total annihilation of his enemies.

It wasn't her black hole to bear. Was even, his conscience warned as it threaded its way to the surface of his mind to remind him, wrong to ask of her.

To insist that a daughter—rebellious or not—actively plot to destroy her father. How far away from Dominic d'Tierrza was that, really?

The fact that he didn't have an answer for the question didn't sit well with him.

Nor had it settled any better later, after he'd shut down Yancy Grove and led her back to the dock.

He boarded the *Ibrahim* behind her and prepared for the journey. He showed her her accommodations, and this time, she took him up on the offer, pleading tiredness.

He didn't comment that she had woken from her nap more vibrant and bright than he'd ever seen her. There was no need to call her out on it when he was the one she was running away from. Besides, as glorious as her moonglow remained, her light had begun to fade. Faint circles edged her eyes and her shoulders slumped as she'd thanked him for the room and closed the door.

It would take approximately twelve hours to return to Cyrano from Yancy Grove. They had plenty of fuel and ample supplies—he believed in being prepared, though he had not planned to return to Cyrano so soon.

Strange, how he had not set foot on the island in over thirty years and now was readying to return for the second time in less than thirty-six hours.

His last trip had had a very specific purpose and, by proxy, had an extremely firm time limit. This time he had neither constraint, and yet the journey was colored with an air of finality. His grand revenge, his life-long quest, his quest for the holy grail, had concluded, if not exactly to his specifications.

And what did he have to show for it?

Twelve hours of silent questioning and one more sunrise later, he spotted land. Having joined him at the helm, Helene watched quietly as Cyrano grew larger on the horizon.

When she spoke, the first time since he'd left her at her cabin door, she said, "So we're going through Andros?"

Something old and seismic shifted across his heart, a feeling so deep and timeless he could no more interpret it than shifting sands. He gave a brief nod. "We're going through Andros."

Muffling the motor, they stealthily approached Andros's sleepy port.

Andros was too small to be bustling, but was an important specialty port due to its deep waters. More charming than even Calla, Andros was like nowhere else on earth.

Drake steered them through the latticed network of limestone caves quietly, tucking into a shadowed cove with familiar ease. It was not the first time he'd returned to Andros since his family's exile.

Located on the rainy side of Cyrano, Andros grew lush forested hillsides and verdant farms. The west-

ern-most edge of Cyrano's "Great Green Spot," a phenomenal patch of agricultural territory responsible for
growing the bulk of the food produced on the island,
Andros was a small, productive duchy that generated
dependable and respectable income, had little to no
trouble and the happiest citizens in all of Cyrano...ac-
cording to a popular magazine survey.

Helene had been its steward for the past two years,
and in that time, he knew, she had dutifully cared for it.

But it was Drake's stolen home, the cozy hills welcoming him, speaking to him through his blood and
bones, rather than his head and eyes.

Leading Helene along a narrow path toward the main
residence, he ran through his plan. It was basic and
would see to her safe return, without putting him in
the uncomfortable position of having to explain things
to the authorities.

He trusted her, as foolish and novel as the experience was, to keep her word, and more, to stand by him
should he face legal action. In a matter of days, she had
swept in like a hurricane, devastating thirty years of
planning in one fell swoop, and yet he could not hold
it against her.

He had set out to seduce her, but he feared, in the
end, she might have seduced him.

The path he took them on led to a hidden doorway
built inexplicably into the hillside. He reached for the
handle as if he had every expectation that it would be
open, and it did.

Inside was a dark corridor, lit with flickering exposed light bulbs.

Confident in the confirmation of his memory, he led

them down the corridor, around a corner and up a small darkened stairway that led to another door.

This door was locked. Drake pulled out a key, the action practiced, and the door opened into a completely innocuous storage closet.

Behind him, Helene's voice was filled with wonder. "It's some kind of smuggler's tunnel."

Drake shot a grin at her. "Exactly. It was built during the war of the city-states of the midcentury." The intimate pride in his voice was undisguisable. Like Calla, Andros was his home. But Andros was also more than that—it was his birthright, his childhood kingdom.

That he'd been forced away from it because of her father was a knife in the chest that never stopped throbbing. Or hadn't, at least, until he'd swooped in and stolen Helene d'Tierrza into his life.

He should be the current Duke of Andros. He had created in Calla what he missed so sorely, and yet leading them through staff corridors, deftly avoiding being seen, he could not deny it was still a mere facsimile of the home he craved. Like Yancy Grove, Calla was a lovely getaway. Andros was home, the place he was most at ease, even when surrounded by enemies with his plans in tatters.

They came to another doorway—this one he listened at first.

After seconds stretched into minutes of taut silence, his ear glued to the doorframe, he held two fingers up to signal quiet, then retrieved the same key he'd used on the earlier door.

As before, it worked easily. Drake stepped through, followed by Helene.

They stood in another quiet room, a pantry, though

it was obvious from the lack of dust and tidily stacked dry goods that this room was in regular use.

"Through that door is the kitchen. The day staff will be in there. They'll be able to make arrangements to get you back to the capital."

She nodded, looking up at him, her eyes full of things she had to say.

She opened her mouth, then closed it and shook her head, then opened it again. "I'm sorry," she said.

They weren't the words he wanted to hear. Though what he hoped she would say he had no idea. Pulling her into his arms, he rested his nose on the top of her hair and drew in a long inhale. Then he tilted her chin, angling her face toward his one last time. Running his thumbs below her eyes and along her cheekbones, he leaned closed, pressed his lips against hers and kissed her goodbye.

And then, without speaking, he turned and left. If he had stayed a moment longer, he wouldn't have been able to leave at all.

CHAPTER NINE

A WEEK AND a half later, Hel was in the worst shape of her life.

Despite being in the comfort of her own bed, and the warm bosom of most of her dearest friends and family, she'd slept horribly and felt sicker and sicker with each passing day since leaving Drake in Andros.

Once she'd made herself known, it was a simple thing to get dropped off at a public location, from which point she called the palace first and her mother second. Everyone accepted her story of escaping her unknown kidnapper and returning—how could they not? She was Helene d'Tierrza, captain of the queen's guard, indefatigable and unbeatable.

And right now, she was a strange shade of grayish green. Strange, because she hadn't experienced a second of seasickness through her adventure with Drake, and yet was feeling all of its symptoms now.

She wondered if there was such a thing as land-sickness, and if so, if one could suddenly develop it after having spent a short time sampling the seafaring life.

Real or not, it certainly wasn't helping her track down what had happened with Moustafa.

All that she'd been able to discern was that her

cousin, in a move that made absolutely no sense to her, had sent the queen to the summer palace and placed Jenna on a leave of absence the very same day Drake had abducted her.

Zayn had quickly followed behind Mina, traveling to the summer palace and conducting business from there through Hel's absence. Though he had personally called to tell her how glad he was to know she was safe, and they'd spoken at length about her supposed escape, she had not known at the time to speak to him about Moustafa.

Mina, too, between being at the mercy of Roz for wedding planning and being completely in the dark as to what had led Zayn to reprimand Jenna, had been unable to explain the situation.

Trying to untangle the mess with a hollowed-out and aching hole where her heart should have been, and a nagging and persistent sense of nausea, was presenting her with an entirely new kind of endurance training.

Thankfully, though she never would have imagined thinking this, Mina was gone. The fact that Hel was not on official duty was a shocking saving grace. Normally, her work energized her. It was the thing she lived for, but now, the thought of it made her stomach roll.

Being a guard had given her something real and lasting to do for the first time in her life, a sense of duty and responsibility that the charity rebellions of her youth had lacked—the sense of independent self she'd been so desperately seeking. It had shored up her wobbly, childish hope to undo the ill her father wrought in the world, and made it a full-fledged adult goal and given her the power to enact it.

And, for a short time after the nightmare of her engagement, it had been the only reason she got out of bed and got dressed every day.

Becoming a guard and making a promise to protect those who needed it was the reason she didn't just let the Tierrza duchy fall into disrepair in order to tarnish her father's legacy. The neglect would have been satisfying, but that satisfaction would have come at the expense of her tenants and the people who depended on her.

Being a guard was the reason she had female friends. She and Moustafa had been partners for nearly seven years, graduating together from the royal security academy. They were an unlikely pairing—the priory girl and the rebel heiress. After her cousin, the king, Jenna Moustafa had quickly become Hel's second-best friend in the world.

And from the moment she had watched Dr. Mina Aldaba, now Queen Mina d'Argonia, proud and disheveled academic that she'd been, walk through the chapel doors to become queen not long ago, she'd known she'd gained her most important responsibility and another dear friend.

Knowing that Mina was safe under the protection of the specially trained summer-palace security unit was a deep relief.

Even if it left Hel with nothing but time on her hands and too much to think about, an upset stomach and no idea where her partner had gone.

Tracking down Moustafa was the obvious best choice of her options. But short of calling her family, which she was hesitant to do, she had exhausted her resources with no luck.

And knowing that her resources were…considerable, that pointed to Moustafa actually being with her family.

Hel felt like an idiot. If anything truly terrible had happened to Jenna, her family would have been hounding Hel's heels like Cerberus.

Jenna's family was large, ever-growing, it seemed, and deeply interconnected. They were absolutely wonderful, incredibly tight-knit, insatiably nosy and unparalleled at ferreting out information. Hel liked to tease that the terrier spirit was what made Moustafa such a good guard. It was also the reason Hel had avoided calling. It wasn't wise to call on the Moustafas with heavy secrets on your heart.

But now that the idea had occurred to her she was certain that was where Jenna would be. The Moustafas were members of a long-rooted religious minority in Cyrano. They believed in big families, which made living close in the capital a challenge. Jenna herself came from a farm on the outer edges of a suburb that bordered the city.

Satisfied with at least that one thing in her world, Hel rolled onto her stomach, hoping the pressure might ease the persistent nausea.

"Darling, are you all right? Liza said you weren't feeling well. And do you mind putting a shirt on?"

Hel's mother, Seraphina d'Tierrza, stood at the entryway of her quarters, wearing, notably, loungewear. Seraphina d'Tierrza did not wear loungewear. Her hair, also, was not as it usually was, perfectly coiffed without a strand out of place. Instead, it was tousled and pulled back into a messy French twist, strands falling loose around her face, which itself looked…tired, rather than its typical perfect polished pearlescent.

Sitting all the way up, and then regretting the motion, Hel sent her mother a weak smile. "Just a stomach bug," she said. "And what's the point?"

Seraphina eyed her for a moment, her deep blue gaze drifting down to her daughter's exposed breasts before traveling back up to her face. "Helene Cosima d'Tierrza. The point is that once a daughter has breasts, her mother doesn't want to see them. Now put this on. I want to talk to you." Mildly indignant, ever proper, and eternally loving, Hel's mother held out a hand that held a blue cotton T-shirt.

Hel pulled it over her head, unable to ignore the comfort of the soft, thin material, despite the fact that her skin had become so sensitive lately that she'd taken to going shirtless in her room just to ease the chafing.

Her mother knew her well, though.

The shirt was made from the softest cotton, had no tag, was lightweight and breathable. Everything she looked for in a T-shirt, and the only thing she could stand right now.

Joining her daughter on the bed, Seraphina pushed the bangs out of her eyes, tucking them behind her ear the same way she had since Hel had been a little girl and her hair much longer.

Searching her daughter's eyes with her own matching pair, Seraphina said, "Tell me your symptoms."

Hel shook off the concern. "I'm fine. Really. Just a bit off. I'll be right as rain in no time." She smiled the same smile—the one that said, "Don't worry, everything's fine, I'm strong"—that she'd been giving her mother since she was in elementary school.

This time, however, Seraphina wasn't to be put off. "Your symptoms," she repeated firmly.

Hel sighed before offering her mother a brisk run-down. "Primarily nausea, but also elevated temperature, sensitive skin, mild vertigo." She tried the smile again. "Just your garden-variety flu."

Her mother closed her eyes and took a breath, then opened them again. "Helene. You're pregnant."

Sapphire blue locked with sapphire blue, and Hel had the strangest sensation of panic rising in the back of her throat, slick and oily. She fought the nausea and shook her head. "No. No. That's not possible."

Seraphina nodded, her expression a strange blend of happiness and sadness. "I suspected it when you asked Liza to tone it down on air fresheners."

Still shaking her head, Hel said, "It can't be…"

Seraphina smiled, her expression turning soft and distant. "I was the same. Couldn't stand artificial scents and so, so sick. Everyone told me it was a sign you would be a girl."

Beneath her, the bed trembled. Until she realized it didn't. She was trembling, like a leaf in the wind.

She was pregnant.

If she'd broken her vow before, she'd eviscerated it now. The line would not end with her. A part of her wanted to laugh, and laugh, and laugh, and laugh, and not stop laughing until they took her away somewhere.

Pregnant and alone. Her father would have hated that, so there was at least a small silver lining.

Sitting as near to her as she was, it was an easy thing for her mother to pull her into her arms as she asked quietly, "What happened, Helene?"

Hel realized what her mother thought and pulled quickly back to look her in the eyes. "Nothing like that," she said, palms waving. "Nothing like that," she repeated, looking away.

Her mother let out a long sigh, dread shedding from her shoulders, and Hel was grateful she could at least reassure her on that front.

"Are you sure you're right?" Hel asked. Obviously, the only way to be truly sure would be to take a test, but she trusted her mother.

Seraphina gestured toward her T-shirt-clad chest. "If I hadn't already suspected I would have after your exhibition."

And just like that, the bubble of horrified tension in her chest burst, and Hel surprised herself by laughing, but not the hysterical laughter that had threatened earlier. The laughter of release.

Her mother's subtle humor had always tickled her funny bone in a way nothing else could, and it felt good to laugh, especially in the face of having absolutely no idea what she was going to do, but knowing her mother would be there with her, every step of the way. There was a lot wrong with the world, but some things would always be right. And she would have Drake's baby, to raise and love, freely and openly, with a fireplace and not a whisper of murder or revenge.

"So…" Seraphina's words trailed off.

Helene looked up at her, head tilted.

Seraphina cleared her throat. "I know young people do things differently these days, but do you know who the father is?"

Hel's stomach sank, another wave of nausea choosing that moment to overtake her.

Drake.

He would want to know that his wildest dreams had come true after all.

For an instant, Hel was filled with the urge to protect him, to keep his name a secret and protect both him and her mother from the truth, because once she said his name, she would have to reveal the whole story to her mother.

But she couldn't hold it in.

"Drake Andros."

Once again, confusion flickered across Seraphina's expression. "What an odd coincidence," she said.

Hel shook her head. "Not a coincidence…" she said. And then she told her mother the whole story.

When she was done, her mother looked aghast, face tilted to the ground, shaking her head to herself with an unfamiliar, sad smile on her face. "I never thought I would see the day."

"What day?" Hel asked, sitting up. "The day your daughter came home unwed and pregnant?"

Her mother cast her a mischievous smile. "There was a time when *that* was my greatest fear," she said.

Hel rolled her eyes with a laugh. Her mother had never had anything to worry about and she'd known it, despite Helene's show for the public. They had always been close, and there wasn't anything Hel couldn't tell her mother. Which did not explain the persistent sense of dread that grew with each of her mother's words. They'd been a team so long that Hel knew when she was about to say something she didn't want to hear.

"No," Seraphina continued. "I never thought I'd see the day you fell in love. And with Drake Andros, no less."

For a moment, time stopped.

"What?" Hel repeated.

Her mother frowned, confusion darkening in her eyes. "You did say Drake Andros was the father, correct?"

Hel shook her head and said, "No. I mean yes. He is. But that's not what I meant. The other part. What'd you say?"

Understanding dawned on Seraphina's face and with it, the brittle casing hiding the truth inside of Helene cracked, breaking open at the painful compassion in her mother's expression.

Hel shook her head. "No."

"I'm afraid so, my darling."

"No," Hel said, as if repeating would make her mother's words go away, rather than worming their way inside of her until they burrowed so deep, to deny them would be to deny herself.

"I think so, my dear."

It couldn't be. She couldn't be in love with a man who tried to dictate, manipulate and force her major life decisions—it didn't matter how kind or observant or compassionate he was. She couldn't be with a man who wasn't above simply taking what he wanted, who pushed until he got his way, no matter how generous or dedicated he was. She couldn't love a man that refused her because she wouldn't bow to his will.

She couldn't be in love with a man like her father. It all started with love. All the years of hurt and disappointment of trying to please and then trying to displease—it had all started because her mother had foolishly loved her father.

Hel refused that life for herself and her child. "No. I said no."

It was her mother's turn to shake her head. "Real love is not really a matter of choice, my sweet. At least that's what your aunt Barbara said," she added with a shrug.

But it was all far too serious to shrug.

Expression pained, Hel grabbed her shirt at her chest and twisted, as if the motion might make some difference against the growing pressure in her chest. "No. No. That's not for me."

Because if it was true, it would make her like her mother had been so long ago. It would make her blind and weak when she had worked what felt like her entire life to be strong.

A bittersweet smile flickered across her mother's face. "You don't have to take it. But I think you should."

"What?"

"Don't let your chance at love get away, Helene. Don't let you father take that from you, too."

"But..." Hel shook her head, unable to get the words out.

Her mother waited, patient and steady.

She looked away. "You loved him, and look what it did to us."

"Oh, Helene." Her mother's utterance of her name sat heavy between them, bearing the weight of a thousand feelings, most of them tangled and dark. Seraphina closed her eyes and took a shuddering breath. As she exhaled, tears slipped from between her eyelids.

She stayed like that, breathing, still though she shook, for a while before she spoke. "Oh, Helene. Helene. Helene. Helene. I should have told you. Oh, my sweet, I should have told you so long ago. When you were so little and would ask me so many questions, I couldn't bear to tell you the truth. And later, well, I guess there were no more questions. But no, my darling, I never loved your father. He slapped any delusions of that out of me that night so soon after our engagement."

Hel opened her mouth. "But you said..."

Seraphina gently pressed her fingers against her daughter's mouth. "I told my daughter a fairy tale to spare her a nightmare. I was infatuated with your father, the way young girls are wont to get, but that is a far cry from real love. What I sense you have with Drake."

Hel shook her head. "It's not possible."

"I'm afraid so, my greatest love. You wouldn't be having his baby if you didn't love him." Her mother patted her knee, a grin lightening her features. "You're not that kind of girl."

Hel snorted. "I'm no kind of girl."

Seraphina smiled, wide and soft. "There's my girl. And speaking of girls, I'm certain you're having one."

Hel brought a palm to rest lightly on her stomach, hoping to settle the disturbed butterflies that fluttered there. She was pregnant. That she had passed even an instant with that not being the foremost concern on her mind spoke volumes.

It suggested she loved him.

If that was the case, other things began to make sense: the precision with which her mind recorded every detail about him, the way her body was drawn to his, the way she'd run away from him.

Her heart rate picked up, sweat beading at her brow.

She had done everything in her power to ensure that she didn't end up like d'Tierrza women before her—just another entry in the annals of aristocratic girls played out as pawns to advance the aims of their grand families.

She had thought she'd been the rebel heiress, a duchess and the captain of the queen's guard, that she'd refused to marry so many times that no one would bother trying any longer. And that she'd taken a vow of chastity to give him his ultimate comeuppance, that she'd done it all to frustrate and thwart her father's will and desire at every turn, but that wasn't right. She'd done it all because he terrified her. He terrified her so much she'd done everything in her power and imagination to keep safe from him. She'd lived in the public eye, endeared herself to the most elite security force in the country, and guarded her heart, the most dangerous thing of all, ingeniously ensuring that she'd never fall for a man like her father.

"Helene? Are you all right, Helene?"

Hel stared into the face that was a sneak peek into her future. She was taller than her mother, but otherwise her spitting image.

"I love him," she said dumbly, as if, as with her pregnancy, her mother could be the one to confirm for her.

Heart in her eyes, Seraphina opened her arms wide, and Hel fell into them, silent sobs raking her sinew-and-bone frame.

She loved him and it was too late. They'd already said their goodbyes in the dusty light of the pantry, the salt and pepper in his beard and hair layered wisdom and gravitas over his foundation of sheer male perfection, and she knew he'd thought through everything— word, deed and action—before making a move.

He was autocratic and driven, but he was still the best man she had ever met.

She had broken her vow for him, and he had broken her understanding of the limits of joy and love and pleasure in return. And so she'd pushed him away.

Her heart squeezed, but even with her mother, she didn't cry. D'Tierrzas didn't cry. According to her father, d'Tierrzas struck.

But she would not add insult to her open heart by allowing this moment to be the one that turned her into her father.

She was cut from a different kind of cloth. The kind attracted to hard men. It seemed she was more like her mother than she realized.

She was the kind of woman who loved hurt. Strange, how often the two feelings danced together within her, as if they were each other's favorite partners.

Love made her vulnerable.

She couldn't breathe.

And to top it all off, she was pregnant.

CHAPTER TEN

SHE WAS AS beautiful asleep as she was awake, Drake noted, as he slipped into Helene's room long after she'd settled into the movement and breathing patterns of deep sleep.

She had been even more attractive in her street clothes earlier that day, all legs and platinum and blue, absolutely thirst-quenching when the only thing he wanted was a long drink of water.

That had been his first thought when she'd popped into view.

There was just something sexy about knowing all that dangerous and deadly power was wrapped up in something as innocuous as blue jeans and tennis shoes.

His second thought was that she was a liar. By omission, yes, but a liar nonetheless. But he'd already known that.

Now, looking at her, he thought she was a beautiful sleeping liar, clad only in a T-shirt.

He had trusted her and she had turned out to be as treacherous as her father had been.

Moving in silence, he traversed her room with ease. Taking in the design as he went, he scanned the space for whatever revelations it might have to share about the woman he couldn't stop thinking about.

It should have come as no surprise to him by this point, but her taste was exquisite.

As she did in everything, in her quarters the color she gravitated toward was blue.

Varying shades of the color could be found all around—pillows, throws, piping, art…and beneath that, crisp, clean white. The combination was as refreshing as a cool breeze, an elegant nod to the sea and the sky without an overt beach theme.

He had entered by climbing the trellis that framed the side of her balcony, then opening the French doors into her bedroom.

The trellis was a silly feature, obviously a security risk.

Inside the room, her large bed was tucked into its own nook, ensconced, cozy and separate from the other areas.

The great room was dominated by a large blue braided area rug, which was circular, and, if he wasn't mistaken, homemade.

It blended seamlessly with the rest of the room. In fact, it seemed as if the rest of the suite had been designed around it. The incongruity of its quality, everyday cotton, when compared to the incredible sophistication of the rest of the room snagged his attention.

But he wasn't here to ponder braided rugs. He was here to kidnap the mother of his unborn child, who slept the peaceful sleep of the innocent in her bed alcove, her breathing deep and even.

The soundness of her sleep would have concerned

him had it not been an expected and direct side effect of the reason he was here in the first place.

Helene was pregnant.

Walking away from her in Andros had been about as much as he'd been able to manage in the two and a half weeks since they'd parted. Instead of returning to Calla, he'd remained in Cyrano, first staying in Andros, until it became too far away and he returned to the private docking in Tierrza that he'd first used to present his wild scheme to Helene.

How incredible, that he'd achieved everything he'd set out to do—that that wild plan had come so powerfully into fruition. Like so many grand achievements, reaching it paled in comparison to the hope and expectation—it hadn't been enough. Arriving at its summit brought no satisfaction, merely the new vantage point from which to see the next, bigger, even more elusive goal. This time, it was her love.

He'd realized it while living out of the *Ibrahim*—he'd made an art out of keeping tabs on her. Observing her comings and goings, noting her pallor, her altered sleep patterns, her visit to the doctor in which she had walked in confidently and been led out of by the hand by her mother. The intensity of his focus, the need to drink her in every day. He wasn't done where Helene d'Tierrza was concerned—he'd never be done until he'd secured not just her body, but her heart.

Watching her as he had been had also made it clear that she was pregnant. That she hadn't told him—and wasn't planning on telling him, if her behavior had been any judge—was something he would bring up with her after they'd discussed other, more important matters.

Standing over her, moonlight streaming in through the windows that encircled the bed, it was all he could do to not throw her over his shoulder and haul her out of there like a caveman of old.

Sensing him, she shifted in her sleep, her body angling toward him, her lips parted, breath catching at the same time. In sleep, her full bottom lip quivered, coral temptation.

Still sleeping, her cheeks flushed, the softest pink, faded in the moonlight but still high and bright along the angled bone structure of her face, contributing to the overall effect of her glow, illuminating the space around them in what felt like holy light.

He wanted to shake his head free of the flowery thoughts—he had never been a man for poetry—but could not seem to staunch the flow, despite her secrets.

Leaning down, he caught her soft, sleeping lips with his own.

Her mouth was its own sweet homecoming, more and more addictively familiar with every taste.

Unsurprisingly, her bed was firm, the give going only skin-deep, but comfortable nonetheless, steady and secure and just soft enough to be welcoming.

She softened into him on a sleepy sigh, her arms coming around his neck, the silken length of her skin brushing along his as they went, charged beneath the surface like lightning coated in velvet.

Pulling back far enough, he looked into her remarkable eyes. She was awake, her stare as cool as deep and alert as a well, and full of welcome.

Trailing a line of kisses along her jawline, around her ear and down her neck, he laid his sensual trail from her face south, pressing his lips along her collarbone, before trailing down the valley of her chest, and farther still, until he reached his treasure.

She tasted like salt and summertime, and his mind overlaid the moment with memories of licking sweet melted juice off his fingertips beneath a hot sun, infusing her flavor with the rush of forgotten freedoms and untethered joy.

She had been his from the moment he'd seen her throw her champagne glass at her father's statue, and he was territorial—even if she didn't believe it was real. And he sensed that was true. That despite all they had been through together, despite the fact she carried his child, she expected to return to life as normal when all was said and done—another grand adventure over and gone.

Breaking apart, once again at his mercy, he proved yet again that she was wrong.

He would prove it to her as many times as it took, as many times as she had to shatter beneath his hands, his mouth, his body, in order for the idea to take root and sprout.

Still ruthless and restless, he made his way back up to her mouth, possessing her once more, absorbing her lingering gasps in his kiss.

He was hungry for her, his body demanding satisfaction even as his eyes drank in the sight of her. It had been a matter of weeks and he felt as starved for her as if it had been years, and that was a power she had over him. A power he didn't want her to see in his eyes for fear of what she'd do with it.

When she opened her eyes, he was caught in their blue web.

"Where'd you come from?" she asked, voice thick.

Turning from her, taking in the room, anything but her, he said, "I never left."

She nodded. "And you've been tracking me?"

"Yes," he said. He saw no reason to deny it.

"You came in through the trellis?" she asked.

He nodded.

Rubbing her neck, she yawned. "That's crazy. I never sleep that hard."

His narrowed eyes shot to her, but her own were closed as she stretched her neck. It would have been a good opportunity for her to tell him.

She didn't.

His stomach churned and he looked away again.

Following his gaze, unaware of his inner turbulence, a grin stretched across her face, her chin taking on the arrogant tilt he had learned to find both maddening and delightful, and she said, "That was my first win against my father."

He lifted an eyebrow at the rug. There were at least a hundred shades of blue in it, its huge round form taking up a remarkable amount of space.

She laughed, a little breathless in her pride, even now, what he imagined was a long time later.

"You made it?" he asked.

She nodded. "It took two hundred and sixty-eight T-shirts and an entire summer to secretly complete. I got the idea online and when I showed my parents, my father said, 'Playing with garbage is for trash, Helene.' Mother and I redesigned my entire suite around it."

It was a small battle, but he could tell it was meaningful. "How old were you?" he asked.

She looked out the window in an evasive move that was obvious. "Ten."

At his side, his fist clenched, though he had intended not to react. "A big project for someone so young."

She turned to him then, wearing a real smile, unguarded and true, as opposed to sarcastic and unbothered, and it hit him like a blow to the solar plexus. Resisting the urge to go to her, he frowned, but the expression did nothing to dim her light.

"My mother said something along those lines. She loved it," she said. Her voice always softened when she spoke about her mother. A phantom of sadness flashed across her clear blue eyes, but when she spoke, her words echoed his earlier thoughts. "I'm the only one who's ever been able to stand up to him."

He wondered if she realized how often she slipped into present tense when speaking about her father.

Haunting his daughter was just another sin to add to Dominic d'Tierrza's long list. Not for the first time since he'd learned of the man's death three years ago, Drake wished him back to life, just for the chance to be the one to destroy him. Now that his plan had been achieved, however, he would have to settle for stealing his legacy.

But not without settling things with his daughter first. She'd earned that much.

"It's no small feat."

He could see her blush, even through the darkness.

With forced lightness, she chuckled. "No one had ever accused me of having small feet."

Laughing softly, his voice playful in a way even those closest to him wouldn't recognize, he said, "Oh, really?"

"I bet you never thought death wore a size-eleven heel," she said.

He snorted. "My death doesn't wear heels at all. My death is a kindly elderly lady who prefers house slippers and nodding off peacefully in front of the television."

She laughed. "You're fooling yourself if you think that's true. You're a pirate, for crying out loud."

"Privateer," he corrected. "I have legal authority to take every prize I bring in."

She quirked an eyebrow. "*Every* prize?"

This time he laughed, perfectly picking up on her meaning. "Perhaps not *every* prize," he acknowledged. "But, one small deviation does not a pirate make one. I am a respected retired navy admiral. I have earned my rest and my peaceful passing. Unlike some of us, I'm content to go gently into that good night. I somehow get the impression you're more the down-in-a-fiery-blaze type."

Helene shook her head exaggeratedly. "Absolutely not. I'm more the disappear-in-a-transatlantic-flight type."

"Not you," he countered. "Too subtle. You're more direct than that."

"Speaking of direct… Why are you here?" she asked, bringing it all crashing back to reality.

He was here because she was carrying his child and keeping it from him. He was here not just to devour her, but to take her heart, as well.

"You're pregnant," he said. She wasn't the only one who could be direct. "What are the odds?"

The color drained from her face, the pallor quickly bolstered by her lip curled in disgust as knowing dawned on her face. "And you're here to collect for your revenge?"

He placed a finger on her lips, shaking his head with

a smile. "No. You're pregnant, and I am in love with you. And I'm going to marry you, whether that means I have to accidentally kidnap you or not."

As it had the first time she'd gotten a look at him, her mouth dropped open, and while it wasn't words, he had to smile at the expression on her face, a wide grin stretching across his own. As it had that not-so-long-ago day, appreciation and hunger lit her eyes.

Today, though, she didn't run. Today, she sat up, leaned into him and gently laid her palms on either side of his face. She looked at him closely, as if memorizing his face, then took one long slow blink, opened her eyes and said, "I love you, Drake Andros."

Something shifted within him—was knocked over, cracked and grew bigger. And for the first time in his life, Drake Andros, the exiled duke, scrappy sailor, deadly admiral, vengeance reaper and feared privateer was satisfied.

Wrapping her in his arms, he held her with all the joy that sneaking into her room late at night prevented him for shouting.

And in the end, it turned out he didn't have to kidnap her.

When she finally stopped crying, and after she finished showing him exactly how much she meant it, she took his hand and followed him down the trellis.

CHAPTER ELEVEN

SHE STILL COULDN'T believe they were getting married.

She'd slept for thirteen hours straight once they'd arrived in Calla and woken with a thirst unlike any she'd ever had before. Even the strange realities of pregnancy felt brighter, since she was facing the future with the man she loved at her side.

And now, she sat on her private balcony, situated off the suite, viewing the sea. The same staff person that had helped her before had delivered her wedding attire, which was lying out on the bed in the room behind her.

She was taking her mother's advice, and even Drake's—she wasn't giving her father another moment of her life. He was dead and she was going to live, not in penance for his sins, but because she deserved happiness after surviving him.

She and Drake did together.

As unorthodox as it was, he'd planned their entire elopement, down to ordering something special for her. She'd expected something ridiculous, only to be stunned by what she found.

Her bridal attire was made of exquisite, featherlight linen, comfortable and loose-fitted while remaining flattering. She'd appreciated the way the wide cut of the pants and the long brightly embroidered sleeveless tunic gave the illusion of added length to her already wiry frame. She loved the ensemble on sight, knowing it would look elegant on her without restricting her movement in the least. The cut emphasized how slim she was in the middle, and the assists she had, while the lovely embroidery, with various shades of blue, from cornflower to aqua to navy to sapphire, distracted from the fact that she had more hard angles than curves. And when she had seen herself in it in the mirror, she gasped, because, despite the fact that she had been draped in bespoke couture since before she could walk, it was the first time she'd ever worn something that had so obviously been selected with her in mind. Not her role, her utility, or her power—just her. Her personality, her thoughts and her needs. The flats that accompanied it, supple, flexible strappy things that moved with her feet, yet were delicate and pretty at the same time, were further evidence that the mind behind the ensemble had taken in every single detail about her since their meeting, observing and tending to her each and every need.

And it wasn't a dress.

In fact, her wedding was shaping up to be nothing like what she had imagined it would be. Granted, she had been six years old the last time she'd imagined her wedding, but even the rough outline she'd formed in early childhood had taken place in Cyrano surrounded by friends and family.

Instead, she was to meet her groom where he was waiting for her on a boardwalk by the sea in his lovely harbor city, their nuptials attended only by the officiant and the witness he'd brought to the island for the event. That nuptials were to occur at all, intimate and private or not, was truly a shift in fate.

But when she arrived, even that expectation turned out to be off.

Rather than the small group of strangers she'd expected, standing on the pier was her mother, as well as King Zayn and Queen Mina.

Tears glistened in her mother's eyes.

Zayn, as always, looked bored. "It took you long enough, cuz."

Hel opened her mouth to retort back, but before the words came out a pair of long, golden-brown arms pushed the king out of the way.

"I told you not to be antagonistic!" Irritation colored the woman's voice as the owner of the arms stepped aside to get a better look at her.

"Mina." Hel's sense of relief at seeing the queen, safe and sound, was smaller only than her joy and surprise at having one of her dearest friends, with her heart of a gold and brilliant mind to match, at her wedding.

Hel felt recharged merely standing in the warmth of her hazel gaze.

Crossing to her with long-legged strides, Mina drew Hel into a warm, summer-scented embrace.

Smiling her bright, far-too-open smile—the one Hel despaired of her ever learning to guard—Mina said, "I missed you."

"I missed you, too. A lot to catch up on."

Mina said dryly, "That's an understatement," and Hel laughed.

"We came here as soon as someone was sure it was safe for me to leave the summer palace." Mina rolled her eyes and thumbed in the direction of the king, but

Hel was in agreement with Zayn. She wouldn't have approved of Mina remaining in the capital without both of her regular guards.

"Where's Moustafa?" Hel asked, noting her partner's absence.

Guilt dimmed Mina's smile, made it tight. "When it rains, it pours, eh? I'll catch you up on that, later. For now, we have more pressing matters. Namely—you getting married."

Instincts on alert, Hel wanted to know more about Moustafa, but had a feeling that was a story she was going to have to wait on. Zayn and Drake eyed each other with barely restrained hostility, which she supposed had to do with a combination of the kidnapping and Zayn being the only living male relative she had remaining. Her cousin was nothing if not traditional.

After hugging her mother and once again exclaiming with Mina, the small group took their places. Hel's mother walked her down the aisle toward Drake, who, true to his word, looked for all the world like a man marrying the love of his life.

They said goodbye to everyone on the pier when Drake made the announcement that they would be taking their honeymoon at Yancy Grove.

What she thought was going to be a nightmare had turned out to be a dream.

Leading her down the docks, he took her not to the *Ibrahim*, but to yet another one of his personal fleet: the *Andros*.

The *Andros* looked like something out of a top-secret operation: all black, opaque, sleek and sharp enough to cut a diamond, this boat was made for speed and sex.

They'd use it for both.

The cabin's wing door opened with his voice command, lifting out of the way for him to walk them down the steps into the spacious interior.

From the outside, the *Andros*'s antireflective exterior and aerodynamic design gave the impression of smallness, but it was a false one. Black was such a slimming color. The Andros was outfitted with a captain's suite, full gourmet kitchen, guest suite, lounge, library and sky-lit, central-navigation room.

He passed all of it without comment, intent on getting her into his bed.

As it always was, the energy between them was electric. Snapping and crackling, it was a constant reminder that he would never be able to contain her, that she was lightning, meant to strike.

If that had been her mission, she had accomplished it, achieving proximity to him he couldn't think of anyone else reaching on the eve of her disappearance.

He had taken her. She had taken his world by storm.

He would take her now, tonight, as many times as she could handle before they expired.

And it wouldn't be enough.

Fortunately, they had the rest of their lives.

Finally, after the eternity of time it had taken them to get there, he lay her on his bed.

Her eyes were the sea—blue, deep and greedy, sparkling and glittering as they caught every glimmer of the low light in the room. She was beautiful, ethereal and deadly, like an ocean creature—a thing of beauty and danger.

But she posed no more danger to him—the worst had happened. She had harpooned his heart and he was caught. Destined to bleed out when she removed her weapon, or be taken as her prize—doomed either way.

It was a sailor's fate to drown at sea, though, and if he was going to go, he vowed he would plumb her all of her depths before.

She was stunning in the clothing he'd had made for her. He watched her move with fluid ease, her attire attuned to her in form and function for the first time since he'd known her. She was fluid grace, her body in motion a thing of beauty, like a racing thoroughbred or foreign sports car.

Slipping an arm under her back, he lifted her mouth to his. She opened for him without resistance. Offering everything up for his plunder with a moan and he took it, before she had the chance to take it back.

Unzipping her tunic, he followed the line of her spine all the way down, curving his palm over the swell of her behind in one smooth motion before bringing his hand back out to slip the shirt over her shoulders.

Beneath the tunic, her moonstone skin glowed.

Her bra was blue, made of supple silk, and hand-sewn. He had not been an expert on ladies' underthings prior to outfitting her. He was now.

If it concerned her, it necessitated expertise.

She lifted her hips so he could slide the trousers over and down her hips, freeing legs as long and lithe as a river snaking to the sea.

Her panties were lacy boy-shorts, with a tiny bow front and center, also blue.

Taking a moment to simply soak her in, he marveled at her pearlescent skin, silky smooth and clear as a cloudless night, and her slender, well-muscled limbs, each one honed and strong, an elegantly designed weapon at her disposal.

But nothing was so powerful as the mind and soul behind her appearance. The knotted net that had ensnared him. He'd realized it the moment he'd watched he walk away and realized nothing else mattered, not revenge, not justice, if she wasn't there to share his life. He was entirely at her mercy.

So he balanced the scales now by making her beg here.

Her panties followed the path of her trousers.

He brought his palm to her hip, driven with unexpected urgency and strength to run his hand down the incredible silken length of her thigh. Had he ever met a woman with softer skin? He couldn't recall.

It was as if every woman that he had ever known had disappeared from his consciousness, their memories cleaned and cleared from his mind in order to make room for her, for this.

She shared herself with him alone, it seemed only fair, he be born again, every woman created in her image. And though he'd sworn excruciating slowness, he could no longer resist the urge to taste. He covered one rose peak with his mouth and reveled in the sound of her moans echoing in the cabin.

Her legs were quivering before he moved to the other side with his attention, and, after only a few moments of attention, she was falling apart in a symphony of cries and gasps he felt as if they were his own.

Returning to earth and emboldened by pleasure, she met him with the fierce intensity she brought to everything, incorporating everything she'd learned from each of their previous kisses.

The effect was as powerful as a nor'easter, enough to rip everything he'd ever known about the meeting of lips out by the roots and unmoor his understanding of the limits of human joining.

He shuddered, desperate to once again be inside of her, desire and need swirling, raising the inner alarm that he was entering dangerous territory, the space where implacable goals were set.

He wanted her in every way, all at once.

With a small shake of his head, he broke their kiss gently, drawing his focus back to pleasing her, noting how easily she tempted his control, her responses a siren call luring him to pillage and plunder when restraint was required.

Because for all her worldliness, the billionaire heiress and tabloid duke, eternal darling of the gossip rag, was still a relative innocent.

For a little while longer, at least.

He was a pirate, after all.

Sweet summer child that she was, she had so much to learn. His grin showed enough teeth to warn any girl that she might be dealing with a Big Bad Wolf, but she was too drunk on pleasure to take note. All the better to eat her.

She moaned and gasped in response, each sound punctuated by a small tremor, each one unique, never repeated and utterly intoxicating.

He was harder than he'd ever been in his life, and she had no idea of the sweet misery she was causing in him. She was lost in the storm, and just as he directed, mindless to his agony of wanting her.

And if it hurt, it felt that much sweeter to have her melting in his hands, this powerful woman completely his to do with what he wanted, an amazon, unconquerable but for him. He traced her soft outer lips, running his fingertips along her slightly parted, slick, opening with smooth caresses. She pressed her hips against his hand, instinctively grinding against him as he teased the sensitive bud at the top. He slid a long finger between her swollen lips and along the inner edges of her opening, and she cried out his name.

He let out a low growl, the sound rumbling up from the place inside of him that knew he would never, ever let another even try for.

The thought became the voice inside demanding he claim her, make her his irrevocably. Her body trembled, the tremors racking through her telling him all he needed to know about how close she was the edge.

In truth, they had not even begun the feast there was to be had between their bodies. If anything, this sweet heaven—the melody of her moans, her taste electric on his tongue—was merely the first of a long train of delectable experiences that were to be experienced with her. And if he got too carried away with the images flashing through his mind, they were going to carry him away to bingeing rather than savoring. They would have time for all of it.

It was his pleasure to be both for her—the anchor that held her there, safe, protected, guided through unknown waters, as well as the gale force that swept her away, the hurricane that broke her apart and remade her.

But if he remade her, she, too, ripped him apart and put him back together as she wanted him—devoted and unable to ever deny her, he would spend the rest of his life reminding her of that fact.

Later, after they'd exhausted their bodies and he'd

fed her and they'd sat together at the helm, beneath stars that were vast enough to swallow even the greatest distrust, companionable in a way he'd never experienced with anyone else, he looked into the eyes of the daughter of his greatest enemy and said the words he once had such a hard time admitting.

"I love you."

And the joy in her face was like the sunrise, though dawn was still hours away.

EPILOGUE

IT HAD BEEN one month since Hel and Drake had relocated back to Cyrano. Nya had decided to remain in Calla, having spent most of her life in Sidra.

Tierrza was no more. As they'd plotted, Hel and Drake, with the help of the King and Queen of Cyrano, had unified their titles and lands under the name Andros and relocated the seat of the duchy to the port that Drake knew like the back of his hand.

With Hel on enforced maternity leave—enforced by Seraphina, Mina, Zayn and Drake—the queen had returned to the summer palace, temporarily relocating until her security situation was resolved. She insisted it was for the best, as it gave her and Roz the undisturbed time they needed to plan a wedding that was to go down in Cyrano's history books.

As Hel had suspected, when she finally tracked down Moustafa, she learned her friend had returned home to her family. It continued to be shockingly hard to gather details about what had happened with Jenna in her absence, but she and Drake would be making the trip out to the Moustafa farm to find out once and for all in a matter of days.

She had a great deal to catch up her partner on.

Prior to returning to the summer palace, the queen had made the suggestion to offer Drake a position in the national security council of Cyrano as a naval security adviser. Hel was ecstatic when Drake accepted the position, ensuring that, after the baby was born, she would indeed be able to return to her position as the captain of the royal queen's guard.

And for the first time since the event had begun, after sitting down together, Drake, Hel and Seraphina had decided to retire the annual Dominic d'Tierrza gala, conceiving of a new event and charity named the Ibrahim Andros Foundation.

Hand in hand with her husband, assured by her doctor that there was an end to morning sickness in sight, and free from her father's ghost for the first time since before he'd even died, Helene finally threw in the towel.

Together, they'd beaten him, and now they had the rest of their lives, free to enjoy, happily ever after, together.

* * * * *

WAYS TO
RUIN A ROYAL
REPUTATION

DANI COLLINS

To my fellow authors in this trilogy,
Clare Connelly and Tara Pammi.

Writing is a strange beast, and can be lonely at times,
but when a fun project like this one comes along,
it reminds me I have water-cooler colleagues
who know exactly how my work day is going.

I can't wait until we can get together
to celebrate these books in person!

CHAPTER ONE

"RUIN ME."

Amy Miller blinked, certain she'd misheard Luca Albizzi, the king of Vallia.

She'd been reeling since she'd walked into this VIP suite in London's toniest hotel and discovered who her potential client would be.

Her arrival here had been conducted under a cloak of mystery. A call had had her assistant frowning with perplexity as she relayed the request that Amy turn up for an immediate consultation, now or never.

Given the address, Amy had been confident it was worth pandering to the vague yet imperious invitation. It wasn't unheard-of for managers of celebrities to conceal a client's identity while they brought Amy and her team into a crisis situation.

Amy had snatched up her bag and hurried across the city, expecting to meet an outed MP's son or an heiress being blackmailed with revenge porn.

The hotel manager had brought her to the Royal Suite, a title Amy had not taken seriously despite the pair of men guarding the door, both wearing dark suits and inscrutable expressions. One had searched through her satchel while the other inspected the jacket she had nervously removed in the lift.

When they opened the door for her, Amy had warily entered an empty lounge.

As she set her bag and jacket on a bar stool, the sound of the main door closing had brought a pensive man from one of the bedrooms.

He wore a bone-colored business shirt over dark gray trousers, no tie, and had such an air of authority, he nearly knocked her over with it. He was thirtyish, swarthy, his hair light brown, his blue eyes piercing enough to score lines into her.

Before she had fully recognized him, a hot, bright pull twisted within her. A sensual vine that wound through her limbs slithered to encase her, and yanked.

It was inexplicable and disconcerting—even more so when her brain caught up to realize exactly who was provoking this reaction.

The headlines had been screaming for weeks that the Golden Prince, recently crowned the king of Vallia, would be coming to London on a state visit. King Luca had always been notorious for the fact he was powerful, privileged and sinfully good-looking. Everything else about him was above reproach. According to reports, he'd dined at Buckingham Palace last night where the only misstep had been a smoky look of admiration from a married duchess that he had ignored.

"Call me Luca," he said by way of introduction, and invited her to sit.

Gratefully, Amy had sunk onto the sofa, suffering the worst case of starstruck bedazzlement she'd ever experienced. She spoke to wealthy and elite people all the time and never lost her tongue. Or her hearing. Or her senses. She refused to let this man be anything different, but he was. He just was.

She saw his mouth move again. The words he'd just spoken were floating in her consciousness, but his gorgeously deep voice with that Italian accent evoked hot humid nights in narrow cobblestone alleys while romantic strains of a violin drifted from open windows. She could practically smell the fragrance of exotic blossoms weighting the air. He would draw her into a shadowed alcove and that full-lipped, hot mouth would smother—

"Will you?" he prodded.

Amy yanked herself back from the kind of fantasy that could, indeed, ruin him. *And* her. He was a potential client, for heaven's sake!

A cold tightness arrived behind her breastbone as she made the connection that she was, once again, lusting for someone off-limits. Oh, God. She wouldn't say the king of Vallia reminded her of *him*. That would be a hideous insult. Few men were as reprehensible as *him*, but a clammy blanket of apprehension settled on her as she realized she was suffering a particularly strong case of the butterflies for someone who potentially had power over her.

She forcibly cocooned those butterflies and reminded herself she was not without power of her own. She could turn down this man or this job. In fact, based on this off-the-rails attraction she was suffering, she should do both.

She would, once she politely heard him out. At the very least, she could recommend one of her colleagues.

Why did *that* thought make this weird ache in her diaphragm pang even harder?

She shook it off.

"I'm sorry," she said, managing to dredge the words from her dry throat. "Did you say someone is trying to ruin you? London Connection can definitely help you defuse that." There. She almost sounded like the savvy, confident, cofounder of a public relations firm that her business card said she was.

"I said I want *you* to ruin me."

You. Her heart swerved. *Did he know?* Her ears grew so hot, she feared they'd set her hair on fire. He couldn't know what had happened, she assured herself even as snakes of guilt and shame writhed in her stomach. Her parents and the school's headmistress had scrubbed out that little mess with all the alacrity of a government cleanup team in a blockbuster movie. That's how Amy had learned mistakes could be mitigated so well they disappeared from the collective consciousness, even if the stain remained on your conscience forever.

Nevertheless, her hands clenched in her lap as though she had to physically hang on to all she'd managed to gain after losing everything except the two best friends who remained her staunchest supporters to this day.

"Our firm is in the business of *building* reputations." Muscle memory came to her rescue, allowing her voice to steady and strengthen. She said this sort of thing a million times a week. "Using various tools like media channels and online networking, we protect and en-hance our clients' profiles. When a brand or image has been impacted, we take control of the narrative. Build a story." Blah, blah, blah.

She smiled while she spoke, hands now stacked palm up in her lap, ankles crossed. Her blood still sizzled be-cause, seriously, he was positively magnetic even when he scowled with impatience. This was what a chiseled jaw looked like—as though a block of marble named "naked gold" or "autumn tan" had been chipped and worked and shaped to become this physical manifestation of strength and tenacity. Command.

"I know what you do. That's why I called you." Luca rose abruptly from the armchair he'd taken when she'd sat.

He paced across the spacious lounge. His restless movement ruffled the sheer drapes that were partially drawn over the wall of windows overlooking the Thames.

She'd barely taken in the decor of grays and silver-blue, the fine art pieces and the arrangements of fresh flowers. It all became a monochrome backdrop to a man who radiated a dynamic aura. He moved like an athlete with his smooth, deliberate motions. His beautifully tailored clothes only emphasized how well made he was.

He paused where the spring sun was streaming through the break in the curtains and shoved his hands into his pockets. The action strained his trousers across his firm behind.

Amy was not an ogler. Men of all shapes, sizes and levels of wealth paraded through her world every day. They were employees and clients and couriers. Nothing more. She hadn't completely sworn off emotional entanglements, but she was exceptionally careful. Occasionally she dated, but even the very nice men who paid for dinner and asked politely before trying to kiss her had failed to move her.

Truthfully, she didn't allow anyone to move her. She preferred to keep her focus on her career. She'd been taught by an actual, bona-fide teacher that following her heart, or her libido, or that needy thing inside her that yearned for someone to make her feel special, would only leave her open to being used and thrown away like last week's rubbish.

But here she was acting like a sixth-former biting her fist because a particularly nice backside was in her line of sight. Luca wasn't even coming on to her. He was just oozing sex appeal from his swarthy pores in a passive and oblivious way.

That was ninja-level seduction and it had to stop.

"I'm asking you to reverse the build," Luca said. "Give me a scandal instead of making one go away."

She dragged her attention up to find him looking over his shoulder at her.

He cocked his brow to let her know he had totally and completely caught her drooling over his butt.

She briefly considered claiming he had sat in chewing gum and gave her hair a flick, aware she was as red as an Amsterdam sex district light. She cleared her throat and suggested gamely, "You're in the wrong part of London for cheap disgrace. Possibly hire a woman with a different profession?"

He didn't crack a smile.

She bit the inside of her lip.

"A *controlled* scandal." He turned to face her, hands still in his pockets. He braced his feet apart like a sailor on a yacht, and his all-seeing gaze flickered across her blushing features. "I've done my research. I came to *you* because you're ideal for the job."

Whatever color had risen to her cheeks must have drained out of her because she went absolutely ice cold.

"Why do you say that?" she asked tautly.

His brows tugged in faint puzzlement. "The way you countered the defamation of that woman who was suing the sports league. It was a difficult situation, given how they'd rallied their fans to attack her."

Amy released a subtle breath. He wasn't talking about *her* past.

"It was very challenging," she agreed with a muted nod.

She and her colleagues-slash-best friends, Bea and Clare, had taken on the case for a single pound sterling. They'd all been horrified by the injustice of a woman being vilified because she'd called out some players who had accosted her in a club.

"I'm compelled to point out though—" she lifted a blithe expression to hide the riot going on inside her "—if you wish to be ruined, the firm we were up against in that case specializes in pillorying people."

"Yet they failed with your client because of *your* efforts. How could I even trust them?" He swept a dismissive hand through the air. "They happily billed an obscene amount of money to injure a woman who'd already been harmed. Meanwhile, despite winning, your company lost money with her. Didn't you?"

His piercing look felt like a barbed hook that dug deep into her middle.

Amy licked her lips and crossed her legs. It was another muscle memory move, one she trotted out with men in an almost reflexive way when she felt put on the spot and needed a brief moment of deflection.

It was a power move and it would have worked, buying her precious seconds to choose her words, if she hadn't watched his gaze take note of the way the unbuttoned bottom of her skirt fell open to reveal her shin. His gaze slid down to her ankle and leisurely climbed its way back up, hovering briefly on the open collar of her maxi shirtdress, then arrived at her mouth with the sting of a bee.

As his gaze hit hers, his mouth pulled slightly to one side in a silent, *Thank you for that, but let's stay on task*.

It was completely unnerving and made her stomach wobble. She swallowed, mentally screaming at herself to get her head in the game.

"I would never discuss another client's financial situation." She would, however, send a note to Bea advising her they had some confidentiality holes to plug. "Can you tell me how you came by that impression, though?"

"Your client was quoted in an interview saying that winning in the court of public opinion doesn't pay the way a win in a real court would have done, but thanks to *Amy* at London Connection, she remains hopeful she'll be awarded a settlement that will allow her to pay you what you deserve."

Every nerve ending in Amy's body sparked as he approached. He still seemed edgy beneath his air of restraint. He dropped a slip of paper onto the coffee table in front of her.

"I want to cover her costs as well as my own. Will that amount do?"

The number on the slip nearly had her doing a spit take with the air in her lungs. Whether it was in pounds sterling, euros, or Russian rubles didn't matter. A sum with that many zeroes would have Bea and Clare sending her for a cranial MRI if she turned it down.

"It's...very generous. But what you're asking us to do is the complete opposite of London Connection's mission statement. I'll have to discuss this with my colleagues before accepting." Why did Clare have to be overseas right now? Starting London Connection had been her idea. She'd brought Amy on board to get it off the ground, and they usually made big decisions together. Their latest had been to pry Bea from slow suffocation at a law firm to work for them. Bea might have specific legal concerns about a campaign of this nature.

"I don't want your colleagues," Luca said. "The fewer people who know what I'm asking, the better. I want *you*."

His words and the intensity of his blue eyes were charging into her like a shock of electricity, leaving her trying to catch her breath without revealing he'd knocked it out of her.

"I don't understand." It was common knowledge that the new king of Vallia was nothing like the previous one. Luca's father had been… Well, he'd been dubbed "the Kinky King" by the tabloids, so that said it all.

Amy's distant assumption when she had recognized Luca was that she would be tasked with finessing some remnant of Luca's father's libidinous reputation. Or perhaps shore up the cracks in the new king's image since there were rumors he was struggling under the weight of his new position.

Even so… "To the best of my knowledge, your image is spotless. Why would you *want* a scandal?"

"Have I hired you?" Luca demanded, pointing at the slip of paper. "Am I fully protected under client confidentiality agreements?"

She opened her mouth, struggling to articulate a response as her mind leaped to her five-year plan. If she accepted this assignment, she could reject the trust fund that was supposed to come to her when she turned thirty in eighteen months. Childish, perhaps, but her parents had very ruthlessly withheld it twice in the past. Having learned so harshly that she must rely only on herself, Amy would love to tell them she had no use for the remnants of the family fortune they constantly held out like a carrot on a stick.

Bea and Clare would love a similar guarantee of security. They all wanted London Connection to thrive so they could help people. They most definitely didn't want to tear people down the way some of their competitors did. Amy had no doubt Bea and Clare would have the same reservations she did with Luca's request, but something told her this wasn't a playboy's silly whim. He looked far too grim and resolute.

Coiled through all of this contemplation was an infernal curiosity. Luca intrigued her. If he became a client… Well, if he became a client, he was absolutely forbidden! There was a strange comfort in that. Rules were rules, and Amy would hide behind them if she had to.

"I'll have to tell my partners something," she warned, her gaze landing again on the exorbitant sum he was offering.

"Say you're raising the profile of my charity foundation. It's a legitimate organization that funds mental health programs. We have a gala in a week. I've already used it as an excuse when I asked my staff to arrange this meeting."

"Goodness, if you're that adept at lying, why do you need me?"

Still no glint of amusement.

"It's not a lie. The woman who has been running it since my mother's time fell and broke her hip. The entire organization needs new blood and a boost into this century. You'll meet with the team, double-check the final arrangements and suggest new fundraising programs. The full scope of work I'm asking of you will remain confidential, between the two of us."

His offer was an obscene amount for a few press releases, but Amy could come up with a better explanation for her friends later. Right now, the decision was hers alone as to whether to take the job, and there was no way she could turn down this kind of money.

She licked her dry lips and nodded.

"Very well. If you wish to hire me to promote your charity and fabricate a scandal, I would be happy to be of assistance." She stood to offer her hand for a shake.

His warm, strong hand closed over hers in a firm clasp and gave it a strong pump. The satisfaction that flared in his expression made all sorts of things in her shiver. He was so gorgeous and perfect and unscathed. Regal.

"Now tell me why on *earth* you would ask me to ruin you," she asked, trying to keep her voice even.

"It's the only way I can give the crown to my sister."

CHAPTER TWO

LUCA RELEASED HER hand with a disturbing sense of reluctance. He quickly dismissed the sexual awareness dancing in his periphery. Amy Miller had a scent of biscotti about her, almonds and anise. It was going to be incredibly distracting to sit with her on the plane, but she was now an employee and he finally had a foot on a path that would allow his sister to take the throne. His entire body twitched to finish the task.

"Eccellente," he said in his country's Italian dialect. "Let's go."

"Go?" Amy fell back a half step and blinked her sea green eyes. "Where?"

"I'm needed in Vallia. We'll continue this conversation on our way."

He glimpsed a flash of panic in her expression, but she quickly smoothed it to show only professional calm.

"I have to take your details first. Prepare and sign the contract. Research—"

Impatience prickled his nape. "I want a secure location before we discuss this further."

"My office is secure. We don't have to go to Vallia." She made it sound like his home was on another planet.

"It's only three hours. My jet is waiting."

Amy's pretty, glossed mouth opened, but nothing came out.

Luca had had his doubts when she had first come onto his radar. He didn't trust anyone who seemed to enjoy being the life of the party, and her job involved nonstop networking with spoiled, infamous attention-seekers. Her online presence was filled with celebrity selfies, club events and influencer-styled posts. It all skated too close for comfort to the superficial amusements his father had pursued with such fervor.

Along with awards and praise from her colleagues, however, she came highly recommended when he'd made a few discreet inquiries. In person, she seemed levelheaded and knowledgeable—if aware of her ability to dazzle with a flick of her more-blond-than-strawberry locks and not the least bit afraid to use such tactics. She was mesmerizing with her peaches and cream skin. Her nose was cutely uptilted to add playfulness to her otherwise aristocratic features, and there was something intangible, a certain sparkle, that surrounded her.

But the very fact she entranced him kept him on his guard. He was long practiced at appreciating the fact a woman was attractive without succumbing to whatever lust she might provoke in him. He was *not* and never would be his father.

Even if he had to convince certain people he was *enough* like him to be undeserving of his crown.

"But—" She waved an exasperated hand. "I have other clients. I can't just drop them all for you."

"Isn't that what I just paid you to do? If you needed more, you should have said."

"You really don't know what my work is, do you?"

She frowned with consternation before adding in a disgruntled voice, "I'll have to shift things around. I wish you'd made it clear when you called that you expected me to travel. I would have brought a quick-run bag." She moved to the leather satchel she'd left on a stool at the bar.

"Are you a PR rep or a secret agent?" Luca asked dryly.

"Feels like one and the same most of the time. At least my passport is always in here."

He eyed her slightly-above-average height and perfectly proportioned curves. Amy wore nothing so pedestrian as a skirt suit. No, her rainbow-striped dress was styled like an ankle-length shirt in lightweight silk. She'd rolled back her sleeves to reveal her bangled wrists and left a few buttons open at her throat and below her knees. It was a bohemian yet stylish look that was finished with a black corset-looking device that made him want to take his time unbuckling those five silver tongue and eye closures in the middle of her back. Her black shoes had silver stiletto heels that glinted wickedly, and the shift of filmy silk against her heart-shaped ass was positively erotic.

Not her, Luca reminded himself as a bolt of want streaked from the pit of his gut to the root of his sex. He was woke enough to know that objectifying women was wrong, that women who worked for him were always off-limits, and that grabbing anyone's backside without express permission was unacceptable—even if she'd gawked at his own like she'd wanted to help herself to a handful.

When he'd caught Amy checking him out a few minutes ago, he'd considered scrapping this whole idea in favor of suggesting he refile his flight plan so they could tour the king-size bed in the other room.

Luca didn't place nascent physical attraction over real world obligations, though. Whether it looked like it or not, allowing his sister to take his place was the greatest service he could do for his country. He wouldn't be swayed from it.

If that left room in his future to make a few less than wise decisions with a woman who attracted him, that was icing. For now, he had to keep his mind out of the gutter.

Or rather, only go there in a very shallow and deliberate manner.

Look at the bar Papa set, his twin had sniffed a few weeks ago when he'd been relaying his frustration with the Privy Council's refusal to allow him to abdicate. *You have a long way to sink before they would even think of ousting you in favor of me.*

Luca didn't want to put the country into constitutional crisis or start firing dedicated public servants. He only wanted to make things right, but there were too many people invested in the status quo. He'd tried cultivating a certain incompetence as he'd adopted the duties of king, pushing more and more responsibilities onto Sofia to show she was the more deserving ruler, but the council dismissed his missteps as "adapting to the stress of his new role." They hovered more closely than ever and were driving him mad.

Sofia's casual remark had been effortlessly on the nose, providing Luca with the solution he'd been searching for. He needed to sink to that unforgivable depth in one shot, touch bottom very briefly, then shoot back to the surface before too much damage was done.

Amy Miller was uniquely positioned to help him make that happen, having bailed countless celebrities out of scandals of their own making.

She was helping herself to items from the hospitality basket, dropping an apple and a protein snack into her bag before adding a water bottle and a bar of chocolate.

"I'll deduct this from your bill," she said absently as she examined a lip balm before uncapping it and sweeping it across her naked mouth. She rolled her lips and dropped the tube into her bag. "I'll buy a change of clothes from the boutique in the lobby on our way out."

"We don't have time for a shopping spree. I'll make arrangements for things to be waiting for you when we arrive."

"I'm hideously efficient," she insisted. "Shall I meet you at the front doors in fifteen minutes?" She plucked the black motorcycle jacket off the back of the stool and shrugged it over her dress.

Something in that combination of tough leather over delicate silk, studded black over bright colors, fine blond hair flicked free of the heavy collar and the haughty expression on her face made him want to catch her jacket's lapels in his fists and drag her close for the hottest, deepest kiss of their lives. His heart rate picked up and his chest heated.

Their eyes met, and they were close enough that he saw her pupils explode in reaction to whatever she was reading in his face.

Look at the bar Papa set.

"Car park. Ten minutes." He pushed a gruff coolness into his tone that made it clear he was not invested in her on any level. "Or the whole thing is off."

She flinched slightly, then gave him what he suspected was a stock keep-the-client-happy smile, saying a very unconcerned, "I'll risk it."

It was cheeky enough to grate, mostly because it lit an urgency in him, one that warned him against letting her get away. He started to tell her that when he said something, he meant it, but she was already gone.

Amy fled the suite. She had reached the limit of her ability to pretend she was cool with all of this and desperately needed to bring her pulse under control, especially after what had just happened.

What *had* just happened?

She had found an excuse to escape his overwhelming presence, dragged on her jacket, glanced at Luca, and a crackling surge of energy between them had nearly sucked her toward him like a tractor beam pulling her into an imploding sun. For one second, she'd thought he was going to leap on her and swallow her whole.

Much to her chagrin, she was a teensy bit disappointed he hadn't. In fact, she was stinging with rejection at the way he'd so quickly frozen her out, as if he hadn't handpicked her to make his worst nightmare come true.

As if she'd been obvious in her attraction toward him and he'd needed to rebuff her.

As if she had consciously been issuing an invitation—which she hadn't!

She was reacting on a purely physical level and was mortified that it was so potent. So *obvious*. She didn't understand why it was happening. Even before all her PR management courses, she'd had a knack for being dropped into a situation that demanded swift, decisive action and turning it around. Now it was her day job to create space for clients to freak out and sob and come to terms with whatever drama might have befallen them. She was adept at processing her own reactions on the fly, but today she was shaking and wishing for a paper bag to breathe into.

Luca was the diametric opposite of everything she'd ever encountered. He wasn't a boy from the council flats who'd stumbled into stardom and didn't know how to handle it. He'd been raised to be king. He was a man of impeccable reputation who wanted her to engineer his fall from grace. Instead of his looks and wealth and privilege getting him into trouble, he needed her to make that happen for him. *I want* you, he'd said.

He'd made it sound as if he saw her as exceptional at what she did, but there was that niggling fear deep in her belly that she'd been chosen for other, bleaker reasons.

Even as she was texting Clare and Bea from the lift, informing them she was leaving town with an important new client who'd offered a "substantial budget," she was stamping her feet to release the emotions that were accosting her.

There was no tricking herself into believing Luca Albizzi was a client like any other. He wasn't. Not just because he was a king. Or because he radiated more sex appeal than a whole calendar of shirtless firefighters. He was…magnificent.

He was causing her to react like a— She pinched the bridge of her nose, hating to admit it to herself, but it was true. She was behaving like damned *schoolgirl*.

That would not do. She was older and wiser than she'd been back then. Infatuation Avenue was firmly closed off. Men were no longer allowed to use her very natural need for affection and companionship as a route to taking advantage of her. Besides, he was a client. Their involvement had to remain strictly professional. It *would*, she vowed.

As the lift doors opened, Clare texted back that she would run things remotely. Bea promised to email their boilerplate for the contract. Neither protested her disappearing, darn them for always being so supportive.

Amy hurried to the boutique. Thankfully, she was blessed with a body that loved off-the-rack clothing. It took longer for the woman to ring up her items than it did for Amy to yank them from the rod. She didn't need to buy a toothbrush. She always kept the grooming basics in her shoulder bag since she often had to freshen up between meetings.

She was catching her breath after racing down the stairs to the car park when the lift bell rang. Luca's bodyguards stepped out. One checked as he saw her hovering, nodding slightly when he recognized her. An SUV slid to a halt, and Luca glanced at her as he appeared and walked across to the door that was opened for him.

"I didn't believe you could find what you wanted in less than an hour." His gaze dropped to the bag she swung as she hurried toward him. "Your ability to follow through on a promise is reassuring."

"Reassurance is the cornerstone of our work. I'm not being facetious. I mean that." She let his bodyguard take her purchases and climbed into the vehicle beside Luca, firmly ignoring the cloud of the king's personal fragrance, which may or may not have been a combination of aftershave, espresso and undiluted testosterone.

Whatever it was, it made her ovaries ache.

As the door shut and the SUV moved up the ramp

into the daylight, Amy withdrew her tablet from her satchel, determined to do her job, nothing more, nothing less.

"I was going to look up some background information unless you'd rather brief me yourself?"

He pressed the button on the privacy window, waiting until it was fully shut to ask, "How much do you know about my family?"

"Only the—" She pursed her lips against saying *sketchiest*. "The most rudimentary details. I know your father passed away recently. Six months ago? I'm very sorry."

He dismissed her condolence with an abbreviated jerk of his head.

"And your mother has been gone quite a bit longer?" she murmured gently.

"Twenty years. We were eleven." The flex of agony in his expression made Amy's attempts to remain impervious to him rather useless.

"That must have been a very hard loss for you and your sister. I'm so sorry."

"Thank you," he said gruffly, and something in his demeanor told her that even though his mother's death was two decades old, he still mourned her while his grief over his father was more of a worn-out fatalism.

"And Princess Sofia is…" Amy looked to her tablet, wishing she could confirm the impressions that leaped to mind. "I believe she's done some diplomatic work?" Amy had the sense it was far more substantial than a celebrity lending their name to a project.

"Sofia is extremely accomplished." His pride in his sister had him sitting straighter. "She began advocating for girls when she was one. We both studied political science and economics, but when I branched into emerging technologies, she pursued a doctorate in humanities. More recently, she played an integral part in the trade agreements in the Balkan region. She's done excellent work with refugees, maternal health and global emergency response efforts."

"I had no idea," Amy said faintly. Her parents had disinherited her and she'd come a long way from a hard start, but women like his sister made her feel like a hellacious underachiever.

"She's remarkable. Truly. And has way more patience for politics that I do. I don't suffer fools, but she's willing to take the time to bring people around to her way of thinking. We both know where Vallia needs to go, but my instinct is to drag us there through force of will. She has the temperament to build consensus and effect change at a cultural level. She's better suited to the role, is arguably more qualified and, most importantly, she's an hour older than I am. The crown should be hers by birthright."

"Wow." If her voice held a touch of growing hero worship for both of them, she couldn't help it. "It's rare to hear a powerful man sound so supportive and willing to step aside for anyone, let alone a woman. That's so nice."

"I'm not 'nice,' Amy. Shake that idea from your head right now," he said tersely. "I am intelligent enough to see what's obvious and loyal enough to my country and my sister to make the choice that is right for everyone concerned. This has nothing to do with being *nice*."

He was using that voice again, the one that seemed intent on warning her that any designs she might have on him were futile.

Message received, but that didn't stop her from lifting her chin in challenge. "What's wrong with being nice? With being kind and empathetic?"

"I'm not advocating cruelty," he said with a curl of his lips. "But those are emotions, and emotions are hungry beasts. Soon you're doing things just so you *feel* kind. So you have the outside validation of people believing you're empathetic. Ruling a country, doing it *well*—" he seemed to pause disdainfully on the word, perhaps criticizing his father's reign? "—demands that you remove your personal investment from your decisions. Otherwise, you'll do what appeases your need to feel good and lose sight of what's ethically sound."

She considered that. "It seems ironic that you believe giving up the crown is the right thing to do when your willingness to do what's right makes you ideal for wearing it."

"That's why my sister won't challenge me for it. She refuses to throw Vallia into turmoil by fighting for the right to rule, not when I'm healthy, capable and wildly popular. From an optics standpoint, she can't call me out as unsuited and install herself. She has to clearly be a better choice, recruited to save the country from another debacle."

"Why was she passed over in the first place? Primogeniture laws?"

"Sexism. Our father simply thought it would make him look weak to have a woman as his heir. He was too selfish and egotistical, too driven by base desires to see or do what was best for Vallia. When it was revealed my mother was carrying twins and that we were a boy and a girl, he declared the boy would be the next king. Even though Sofia was born first, making her the rightful successor, the council at the time was firmly in my father's pocket. No one pushed back on his decree."

"Does that council still have influence? Can't you simply abdicate?"

"I've tried." Impatience roughened his tone. "Once I was old enough to understand the reality of my position, I began to question why the crown was coming to me." He pensively tapped the armrest with a brief drum of his fingers. "Our mother knew Sofia was being cheated, but she worried that pressing for Sofia's right to inherit would cost her what little influence she had. She used her mandate of raising a future king to install a horde of conservative advisers around us. They genuinely wished to mold me into a better king than my father was, and they are extremely devoted to their cause. That isn't a bad thing, given the sort of people who surrounded my father." He side-eyed her.

Amy briefly rolled her lips inward. "I won't pretend I haven't read the headlines." Countless mistresses, for instance, sometimes more than one at a time. "I don't put a lot of stock into gossip, especially online. Paparazzi will post anything to gain clicks."

Even if Luca's father had been into polyamory, it was merely a questionable look for someone in his position, not something that negated his ability to rule.

"Whatever you've read about my father is not only true," Luca said in a dark voice, "it is the whitewashed version." His voice rang as though he was hollow inside. "When he died, I brought up crowning my sister despite the fact I've always been the recognized successor. It was impressed upon me that Vallia was in too fragile a state for such a scandal. That we desperately needed to repair our reputation on the world stage and I was the man to do it."

"It's only been six months. Is Vallia strong enough to weather you renouncing your crown?" she asked skeptically.

"It's the perfect time to demonstrate that behaviors tolerated in the previous king will not be forgiven in this one. A small, well-targeted scandal that proves my sister is willing to make the hard decision of removing me for the betterment of our country will rally the population behind her. I need something unsavory enough to cause reservations about my suitability, but not so filthy I can't go on to hold positions of authority once it's over. I don't intend to leave her in the lurch, only restore what should be rightfully hers."

"What will you do after she ascends?" she asked curiously.

"Vallia's economy has suffered from years of neglect. Recent world events have not helped. Before the duties of a monarch tied up all my time, I was focused on developing our tech sector. We have a small but exceptional team working in solar advancements and another looking at recovering plastics from the waste stream to manufacture them into useable goods."

"Be careful," she teased, noting the way his expression had altered. "You almost sound enthusiastic. I believe that's known as having an emotion."

His gaze clashed into hers. Whatever keenness might have briefly brimmed within him was firmly quashed, replaced by something icy and dangerous.

"Don't mistake my frankness for a desire to be friends, Amy," he warned softly. "I'm giving you the information you need to do your job. You don't know me. You can't. Not just because we'll never have a shared frame of reference, but because I won't allow it. I've lived in the shadow of a man who made everything about himself. Who allowed himself to be ruled by fleeting whims and hedonistic cravings. If I thought my desire to go back to reshaping our economy offered anything more than basic satisfaction in pursuing a goal, I wouldn't do it. It's too dangerous. I won't be like him."

They were coming into a private airfield and aiming for a sleek jet that had the Vallian flag painted on the tail. A red carpet led to the steps.

Amy squirmed internally. He might not have emotions, but she did. And she was normally well-liked. It bothered her to realize he not only didn't like her, but he didn't want to. That stung. She didn't want to feel his rebuff this keenly.

"Developing a rapport with a client is a way of building trust," she said stiffly. "Given the personal nature of this work, and how I live in my client's pockets through the course of a campaign, they like to know they can trust me."

"I've paid top price for unquestionable loyalty. I don't need the frills of bond-forming banter to prove it."

Keep your mouth shut, she warned herself.

"Lucky you. It's included with every purchase," she blurted cheerfully.

The SUV came to a halt, making it feel as though his hard stare had caused the world to stop spinning and her heart to stop beating.

"Dial it back," he advised.

She desperately wanted to tell him he could use a laugh. *Lighten up*, she wanted to say, but the door opened beside her. He was the customer and the customer might not always be right, but they had to believe she thought they were.

She buttoned her lip and climbed aboard his private jet.

Did he feel regret at taking her down a notch? If Luca allowed himself emotions, perhaps he would have, but he didn't. So he sipped his drink, a Vallian liquor made from his nation's bitter oranges, and watched her through hooded eyes.

He told himself he wasn't looking for signs she'd been injured by his cut. If she was, she hid it well, smiling cheerfully at the flight attendant and quickly making a work space for herself. She made a call to her assistant to reassign various files and eschewed alcohol for coffee when offered, tapping away on her tablet the whole time.

She seemed very comfortable in his jet, which was built for comfort, but she was relaxed in the way of someone who was not particularly impressed by the luxury. As though she was familiar with such lavishness. Took it for granted.

She catered to celebrities so she had likely seen her share of private jets. Why did the idea of her experiencing some rock star's sonic boom niggle at him, though? Who cared if she'd sat aboard a hundred yachts, allowing tycoons to eyeball her legs until she curled them beneath her like a cat while tracing a stylus around her lips as she studied her tablet? It was none of Luca's business if she traded witty barbs with stage actors or played house with playwrights.

He was absolutely not invested in how many lovers she'd had, rich, poor or otherwise. No, he was in a prickly mood for entirely different reasons that he couldn't name.

He flicked the button to bring down the temperature a few degrees and loosened his tie.

"I'm sending you the contract to forward to your legal department." Amy's gaze came up, inquiring. Professional, with a hint of vulnerability in the tension around her eyes.

Perhaps not so unaffected after all.

A tautness invaded his abdomen. He nodded and glanced at his phone, sending the document as quickly as it arrived. Seconds later, he realized he was typing her name into the search bar, planning to look into more than her professional history. He clicked off his phone and set it aside.

"How did you get into this type of work? The company is only two years old, isn't it? But it won an award recently?"

"For a multicountry launch, yes. Specifically, 'Imaginative Use of Traditional and Social Media in a Coordinated International Product Launch Campaign.'" She rolled her eyes. "These types of awards are so niche and specific they're really a public relations campaign for public relations." She shrugged. "But it's nice to have something to brag about and hopefully put us at the top of search engines for a few days."

"That's how your firm came to my attention, so it served its purpose."

"I'll let Clare know." She flashed a smile.

"Your partner." He vaguely remembered the name and photo on the website. The dark-haired woman hadn't projected the same vivacity that had reached out from Amy's headshot, compelling him to click into her bio and fall down an online wormhole of testimonials.

"Clare is one of my best friends from boarding school. London Connection was her idea. She came into some money when her father passed and wanted to open a business. I worked the social media side of things, organizing high-profile events and managing celebrity appearances. Once we were able to expand the services beyond straight promoting into problem-solving and crisis management, we exploded. We're so busy, we dragged our friend Bea from her law firm to join our team." Her face softened with affection. "We're all together again. It's the best career I could have imagined for myself."

"Boarding school," he repeated. That explained how Amy took to private jets like a duck to water. She'd probably been raised on one of these. "I thought I detected a hint of American beneath your accent. Is that where you're from?"

"Originally." Her radiance dimmed. "We moved to the UK when I was five. I went to boarding school when my parents divorced. I was just looking up your foundation. Do I have the name right? Fondo Della Regina Vallia?"

"That's it, yes."

"I have some ideas around merchandise that would double as an awareness campaign. Let me pull a few more details together." She dipped her attention back to her tablet, corn-silk hair falling forward to curtain her face.

And that's how it was done. Replace the thing you don't want to talk about with something that seems relevant, but actually isn't.

Amy Miller was very slick and not nearly as artless and open as she wanted to appear.

Rapport goes both ways, he wanted to mock, but he didn't really want to mock her. He wanted to know her.

Who was he kidding? He wanted to know what she *liked*. She was twenty-eight, and at least a few of the men photographed with her must have been lovers. Maybe some of the women, too. What did he know? The fact was, she was one of those rare creatures—a woman in his sphere who attracted him.

His sphere was depressingly empty of viable lovers and historically well guarded against them. His mother had surrounded her children with hypervigilant tutors, mentors and bodyguards. It had been the sort of blister pack wrapping within a window box frame that allowed others to look in without touching. He and Sofia had been safely admired, but never allowed out to play.

Mostly their mother had been trying to protect her children from learning the extent of their father's profligacy, but she'd also been doing what she could for the future of Vallia. There'd been a small civil war within the palace when she died. Luca and Sofia's advisers had collided with their father's cabal—men who had had more power, but also more to hide.

In those dark days, while he and Sofia remained oblivious, deals had been struck that had kept everyone in their cold war positions. Their father's death had finally allowed Luca and his top advisers to carve the rot from the palace once and for all. Luca had installed his own people, and they all wanted to stay in the positions to which *they* had ascended—which was how he'd wound up in this predicament.

And the reason he was still living a monk's existence.

He had no time and was monitored too closely to burn off sexual calories. At university, potential partners had always been vetted to the point that they'd walked away in exhausted indifference rather than run the gamut required to arrive in his bed.

As an adult moving through the hallowed halls of world politics and visiting allied territories, he occasionally came across a woman who had as much to lose by engaging in a loose-lipped affair as he did. They would enjoy a few private, torrid nights and part ways just as quickly and quietly. The few who had progressed into a longer relationship had been suffocated by his life, by the inability to make the smallest misstep with a hemline or a break with protocol without suffering cautionary lectures from his council and intense scrutiny by the press.

Luca didn't blame women for walking out of his life the minute they saw how little room there was to move within it.

Amy would die in such a confined space. She was too bright and vivacious. It would be like putting a burning light inside a cupboard. Glints might show through the cracks, but all her heat and power would be hidden and wasted.

Why was he dreaming of crawling in there with her? Imagining it to be like closing himself within the cradle of a suntan bed, surrounded in the sweet scent of coconut oil and a warmth that penetrated to his bones.

He dragged his gaze from where the barest hint of breast swell was peeking from the open buttons of her dress and set his unfinished drink aside. Best to slow down if he was starting to fantasize about a woman he'd hired—to *ruin* him.

He bet she could ruin him. He just bet.

His assistant came to him with a tablet and a handful of inquiries, and Luca forced his mind back to who he was and the obligations he still had—for now.

Perhaps when this was over, he promised himself, he would be able to pursue the iridescent Amy. Until then, he had to remain the honorable and faultless king of Vallia.

CHAPTER THREE

AMY'S FATHER USED to joke that he had oil in his veins and a rig where his heart ought to be. His great-grandfather had hit a gusher on a dirt farm in Texas, and the family had been filling barrels with black gold ever since. Her father was currently the president of Resource Pillage International or whatever name his shell company was using these days. He had moved back to Texas shortly after the divorce, remarried, and was too busy with his new children to call his eldest more than once or twice a year.

Amy's mother came from a family of bootleggers, not that she would admit it. *Her* great-grandfather had been born when Prohibition ended. The family had quickly laundered their moonshine money into legal breweries throughout the Midwest. Two generations later, they had polished away their unsavory start with a chain of automobile showrooms, fashion boutiques, and most importantly, a Madison Avenue advertising firm.

Amy's mother had taken the quest for a better image a step further. After pressing her husband to move them to London, she had traded in her New York accent for an upper-crust British one. Since her first divorce, she had continued to scale the social ladder by marrying and divorcing men with names like Nigel who held titles like lord chancellor.

Amy had to give credit where it was due. Her mother had taught her that if reality wasn't palatable, you only had to finesse the details to create a better one. *Of course I want you to live with me, but boarding school will expose you to people I can't.* And, *Delaying access to your trust fund isn't a punishment. It's a lesson in independence.*

People often remarked how good Amy was at her job, but she wasn't so much a natural at repackaging the truth as a lifelong victim of it. Case in point, her mother's first words when Amy answered her call were, "You wish to cancel our lunch Wednesday?"

As if Amy had been asking for permission.

Amy reiterated what she'd said in her text. "I had to run out of town. I can't make it."

"Where are you?"

In a car with the king of Vallia, winding up a series of switchbacks toward the remains of a castle that overlooked the Tyrrhenian Sea.

"I'm with a client."

"Who?"

"You know I can't tell you."

"Amy, if he won't let you talk about your relationship, it's not going anywhere." Perhaps if her mother had worked at the family firm instead of choosing "heiress" as her career, she would know that Amy's job was not a front for pursuing men with fat money clips.

"Can I call you later, Mom? We're almost at our destination."

"Don't bother. I can't make lunch, either. Neville—

You remember him? He's the chargé d'affaires to Belgium. He's taking me to Australia for a few weeks."

"Ah. Lovely. Enjoy the beach."

"Mmm." Her mother sniffed disdainfully. She was more vampire than woman, eschewing sunshine in favor of large-brimmed hats and absorbing her vitamin D through high-priced supplements. "Behave yourself while I'm gone. Neville is ready to propose. I wouldn't want to put him off."

Seriously, Mom? It's been ten years. But her mother never missed an opportunity to remind her.

Amy's stomach roiled with suppressed outrage, but she only said through her teeth, "You know me, all work and no play. Can't get into trouble doing that."

"You wear short skirts to nightclubs, Amy. That sort of work is— Well, I'm sure I can persuade Neville to introduce you to someone if you manage not to mess this up for me."

Could Luca hear what her mother was saying? He'd finished his own call and pocketed his phone. This town car was the sort that made the drive feel like a lazy canal ride inside a noise-canceling bubble.

"I have to go, Mom. Travel safe." Amy cut off the call, which would result in a stinging text, but she wasn't sorry. She was hurt and angry. Bea and Clare always told her she didn't have to talk to her mother if it only upset her, but Amy lived in eternal hope that something would change.

"Everything all right?" Luca was watching her with a look that gave away nothing.

She realized she had huffed out a beleaguered sigh.

"Fine," she lied sunnily. "Mom's off to Australia."

"You didn't mention any siblings earlier. Are you an only child?"

"The proverbial spoiled kind. I had one of everything except a brother or sister, which is why my friends are so special to me. Will I meet your sister?"

There was a brief pause that made her think he knew she was deliberately turning the question around to avoid delving into her own past.

"She's traveling, due home later this week," he replied evenly.

They were driving past the shell of the castle. As they came even with a courtyard bracketed by two levels of arches in various states of disintegration, she glimpsed a young woman in a uniform leading what looked like a group of tourists. They all turned to point their phones at the car's tinted windows as it passed.

Seconds later, when they halted to wait for golden gates to crawl open, Amy glanced back, curious.

"The castle is a heritage site," Luca explained. "Open for booked tours. The island of Vallia was a favorite summer destination for Roman aristocracy. The palace is built on the remains of an emperor's villa. You'll see what's left in one of the gardens." He nodded as the palace came into view.

"Wow."

At first glance, the imposing monument to baroque architecture, ripe with columns and domes and naves, was almost too much. Amy could hardly take in everything from the serpentine balcony to the elaborate cornices to the multitude of decorative details like seashells and ribbons. Stone angels held aloft what she presumed to be Vallia's motto, carved into the facade.

"This is amazing."

"You can accomplish a lot when you don't pay for labor," Luca said, mouth twisting with resigned disgust. "Vallia was a slave trading post through the Byzantine era. Then the Normans used them to build the fortress while they were taking over southern Italy." He nodded back to the castle. "They sent the slaves into the fields to grow food, and the first king of Vallia used them again to build this palace in the late 1600s, when the Holy Roman Emperor established the kingdom of Vallia."

Despite its dark history, she was in awe. The white stone of the palace was immaculately tended and blindingly beautiful. The gardens were lush, the windows reflecting the blue skies and colorful blooms.

"It's not showing its age at all."

"My father had it fully restored and modernized."

"The workers were paid this time, I hope?" It was out before she thought better of it.

Luca's expression hardened. "A livable wage for honest employment, thanks to efforts by my sister and I, because he couldn't be dissuaded from doing it. Hardly the best use of Vallia's taxes, though."

Amy managed to bite back her observation that he didn't sound as though he had been super close with his dad.

They stepped from the car, and the comforting warmth of sunbaked stones radiated into her while a soft, salt-scented breeze rolled over her skin. The palace was set into terraced grounds facing the sea, but the view stretched east and west on either side. Flowers were bursting forth in splashes of red and yellow, his country's colors, in the gardens and in terra-cotta pots that sat on the wide steps. New leaves on the trees ruffled a subtle applause as they climbed toward the entrance.

A young man hurried to open a door for him.

Entering the palace was a step into a sumptuous garden of white marble streaked with pinks and blues, oranges and browns. Ornate plasterwork and gold fili-gree climbed the walls like vines, sweeping in curves and curls up to the sparkling crystal chandeliers. The fresco painted on the dome above had her catching at Luca's arm, it made her so dizzy. Amid the cerulean skies and puffy clouds and beams of sunlight, the an-gels seemed rather...sexual.

They weren't angels, she realized with a lurch of her heart. That satyr definitely had his hand between the legs of a nymph.

A man cleared his throat.

Amy jerked her gaze down to see a palace sage of some type, middle-aged, in a dark suit. His gaze was on her hand, which still clutched Luca's sleeve.

She let it fall to her side.

"Amy, this is Guillermo Bianchi, my private secre-tary. Guillermo, Amy Miller. She's with London Con-nection, a public relations firm. She'll assist with the foundation's gala."

"I received the email, *signor*." Guillermo nodded as both greeting and acknowledgment of her role. "Wel-come. Rooms have been prepared and appointments arranged with the team."

"Thank you. Er...*grazie*, I mean."

"Amy will join me for dinner in my dining room while she's here."

Guillermo gave an obsequious bow of his head that still managed to convey disapproval. He asked Amy to accompany him up a wide staircase beneath a massive window that allowed sunlight to pour in and shoot rainbows through the dangling chandelier.

She looked back, but Luca was already disappearing in another direction toward a handful of people waiting with tablets, folders and anxious expressions.

Amy went back to gawking at the opulence of the palace. She'd grown up with enough wealth to recognize hand-woven silk rugs and antiques that were actually priceless historical artifacts. She lifted her feet into a slight tiptoe when they reached a parquet floor, fearful of damaging the intricate artistry of the polished wood mosaic with her sharp heels. She could have stood upon it for hours, admiring the geometric designs.

This whole place was a monument to ancient wealth and abundance that stood on the line of gaudy without quite crossing it.

After a long walk through a gallery and down a flight of stairs, she was guided into a lounge that was a perfect mix of modern and period pieces. It had a wide gas fireplace, tall windows looking onto a garden with a pond, and Victorian furniture that she suspected were loving restorations. Everything in the room was the height of class—except the pornographic scene above the sofa. Amy blinked.

"The previous king commissioned a number of reproductions from Pompeii," Guillermo informed her in bland, barely accented English. "I've ordered tea and sandwiches. They'll be here shortly. Please let the maid know if you require anything else."

Amy almost asked whether the sofa was a pullout, but he was already gone.

She poked around and discovered this was a self-contained flat with a full kitchen, a comfortable office with a view to the garden, and two bedrooms, each with more examples of Pompeii's salacious artwork.

Her meager luggage was waiting to be unpacked in the bigger room alongside a handful of clothes that were unfamiliar, but were in her size. There was a luxurious bath with a tempting, freestanding tub, but she only washed her hands.

A three-tiered plate arrived full of sandwiches, savory pastries and chocolate truffles, and was accompanied by coffee, tea and a cordial that turned out to be a tangy sweet liquor meant to be served with the soda water that accompanied it.

She did her best not to reveal she was completely bowled over, but she was only *around* wealth these days. London Connection was doing well, but they were reinvesting profits and using them to hire more staff. Amy had conditioned herself to live on a shoestring after being expelled from school. She'd been unable to take her A-levels and had had to sell what possessions she'd had at the time—mostly designer clothes and a few electronics—to set herself up in a low-end flat. She'd come a long way since then, but the maid probably had a higher net worth than she did.

Amy asked her to set the meal on the table outside her lounge. The patio overlooked a man-made pond full of water lilies where a weathered Neptune rose from the middle, trident aloft. Columns that were buckling with age surrounded the water. This must be the ruins of the Roman villa that Luca had mentioned, she thought.

Between the columns stood statues that looked new, though. Huh. The gladiator had a bare backside that rivaled Luca's, and the mermaid seemed very chesty.

After the maid left, Amy gave in to curiosity. She set aside her tea to walk out for a closer look.

"My father's taste was questionable," Luca said behind her. "To say the least."

She swung around, but had to look up to find him. He stood on a terrace off to the right that she surmised was the best vantage point to admire the pond. He wore the clothes he'd had on earlier, but his jacket was off again and his sleeves were rolled back. His expression was shuttered, but once again she heard the denigration of his father's waste of taxpayers' money.

"I thought I wouldn't see you until dinner." She had been looking forward to reflecting, putting today's events into some sort of order in her mind. Now she was back to a state of heightened awareness, watching his long strides make for a set of stairs off to the left. He loped down them and came toward her in an unhurried stride that ate up the ground easily.

"I don't want any delay on your work."

"Oh, um." Her throat had gone dry, and she looked longingly back at her tea. "I was about to sit down and brainstorm ideas, but I'm having trouble understanding why you'd willingly give up all of this." She waved at her small flat. His private quarters were likely ten times more luxurious and grand. Looking up, she suspected his was that second-level terrace that looked out to the sea unobstructed.

"Allow me to enlighten you." He jerked his head at the pebbled path that wove through the columns around the pond, indicating they should walk it.

She started along and immediately came upon a soldier performing a lewd act with a nymph, one that made her cheeks sting with embarrassment. It grew worse when she darted a glance at Luca and discovered him watching her reaction.

Her heart lurched, but he didn't seem to be enjoying her discomfiture. If anything, his grim expression darkened.

"Oh, those Romans," she joked weakly.

"My father commissioned them. He could have used the funds in a thousand better ways. My first act once I was crowned was tax relief, but I couldn't offer as much as was needed. Our economy is a mess."

Their footsteps crunched as they wound between the columns and wisteria vines that formed a bower, filling the air with their potent fragrance.

The statues grew increasingly graphic. Luca seemed immune, but Amy was as titillated as she was mortified. She was mortified *because* she was titillated.

Even more embarrassing was a stray curiosity about whether Luca would have the strength to have free-standing sex like that, arms straining as his fingertips pressed into her bottom cheeks. His shoulders would feel like marble beneath her arms where she clasped them tightly around his neck, breasts mashed to his flexing chest as her legs gripped around his waist. They would hold each other so tightly, they would barely be able to move, but—

"Do you know why Vallia needs a queen, Amy?"

"No," she squeaked, yanking her mind from fornication.

"Because the king of Vallia is this." He nodded toward the statuary. "A sex addict who never sought help. In fact, he used his position to take advantage of those over whom he had power."

The butterflies in her stomach turned to slithering

snakes that crept up to constrict her lungs and tighten her throat.

Amy knew all about men who took advantage of their position of power. It was adding a razor edge of caution to every step as they walked among these erotic statues.

Luca was a client, which made her feel as though she had to defer to him, but he wasn't forcing her into an awkward situation for his own amusement. She might be blushing so hard the soles of her feet hurt, but he was radiating furious disgust. He was trying to explain why he was so committed to her doing this odd job for him.

Not that kind of job, Amy! She dragged her gaze off the woman whose hands were braced on a naked gladiator's sandals as he sat proudly feeding his erection to her.

"You're not like him," she managed to say. "Your father, I mean."

"No, I'm not," he agreed, jaw clenched. "But I have to make at least a few people believe I could be. Briefly." He glanced from the narrow shadow of the trident on a stepping-stone to his watch.

She followed his gaze and said with delight, "It's a sundial! Half-past oral sex and a quarter till—" She slapped her hand over her mouth, cheeks flaring so hotly, she thought she'd burn her palm. "I'm sorry." She was. "I use humor to defuse tension, but I shouldn't have said that. This is a professional relationship. I'll do better, I promise."

She was still stinging with a flush of embarrassment that boiled up from too many sources to count— the situation, the blatant thing she'd just said, the lack of propriety on her part and, deep down, a pang of anguish that she was giving him such a terrible impression of herself when she wished he would like her a little.

His mouth twisted. "You'll have to say a lot worse than that to shock me. The Romans themselves couldn't hold a candle to some of the obscene things my father did."

He veered down a path to a small lookout that was mostly overgrown. A wooden bench faced a low, stone wall, but they had to stand at the wall to see the blue-green water beyond.

Compassion squeezed Amy's insides as she sensed the frustration rolling off him.

"I've worked with a lot of people trying to keep scandals under wraps. It's very stressful. I can only imagine the pressure you've been under since you took the throne."

Luca made a noise that was the most blatantly cynical sound Amy had ever heard.

"For my whole life," he corrected her grimly. "As long as I can remember I've been trying to hide it, fix it, compensate for it. I've had to be completely different from him despite looking exactly like him while training for his job. A position he made seem so vile, there is absolutely no desire in me to hold it."

At his own words, he swore under his breath and ran a hand down his face.

"That sounds treasonous. Forget I said it," he muttered.

"This is a safe space. It has to be." Amy had long ago trained herself not to judge what people revealed when they were in crisis. "Are you still under pressure to hide his behavior? If there are things you're worried could come out, I might be able to help manage that, too." She looked to where the array of erotic statues was shielded by shrubbery. "I could put out confidential feelers for a private collector to buy those, for a start."

"That's well-known." He dismissed the statues with a flick of his hand. "There's no point trying to hide them now."

His jaw worked as though he was debating something. When he looked at her, a cold hand seemed to leap out of his bleak gaze and close over her heart.

"The way he died may yet come out," he admitted in a voice that held a scraped hollow ring, one that held so much pain, she suspected he was completely divorcing himself from reality to cope with it.

"Do you want to tell me about it? You don't have to," she assured him while her heart stuttered in an uneven rhythm. "But you can if you want to."

His father's death had been reported as a cardiac arrest, but there'd been countless rumors about the circumstances.

"My sister doesn't even know the full truth."

It was all on him and the secret weighed heavily. Amy could tell.

She wanted to touch him, comfort him in some way. She also sensed he needed to be self-contained right now. It was the only way he was holding on to his control.

"If you're worried there are people who might reveal something, we could approach them with a settlement and a binding nondisclosure," she suggested gently.

"That's already been done. And the handful of people who knew where he was that night were happy to take a stack of cash and get away without a charge of contributing to manslaughter, but they're not the most reliable sort." He searched her gaze with his intense one. "Frankly, I wish he'd hired prostitutes. They would have acted like professionals. This was a party gone wrong. There were drugs at the scene. Nasty ones."

"Here? In the palace?" That was bad, but she'd cleaned up similar messes.

"In the dungeon."

She didn't school her expression fast enough.

"Yes. *That* kind of dungeon." His lips were snarled tight against his teeth. His nostrils flared. "I wouldn't normally judge how people spend their spare time, but if you rule a country, perhaps don't allow yourself to be tied up and flogged by a pair of women who get so stoned they don't know how to free you when your heart stops. Or who to call."

Amy caught her gasp in her hand. Talk about making a traumatic situation even more distressing for all involved!

"Luca, I'm so sorry." Her hand went to his arm before she realized she was doing it.

He didn't react beyond stiffening under her touch.

She'd seen clients shut down like this, doing whatever they had to in order to carry on with their daily lives. It told her exactly how badly his father's behavior had affected him.

"Look, I have to ask before we go any further. Are you sure you're not just reacting to what you've experienced? I'd want to wash my hands of this role if I were in your shoes. That's understandable, but what you've asked me to do is not a decision you should make in haste."

"It's not one incident, Amy. It's everything he stood for. All of the things I've learned he was capable of, now that I'm privy to it. It's appalling. There was a thorough cleaning of house once I took the throne, but how can I claim to be righting his wrongs if I ignore the very basic one where he installed me as monarch instead of my sister?"

The flash of a tortured conscience behind his searing blue eyes tempted her to shift her fingers in a soothing caress. She moved her hand to the soft moss that had grown on the stone wall and scanned the view through the trees.

"And no one will listen to this extremely rational argument? Let you turn things over without drastic measures?"

"My supporters see Sofia as an excellent spare, but they are extremely attached to keeping me exactly where I am. Our constitution doesn't allow an abdication without proper cause. Even if I was incapacitated, I would keep the crown and Sofia would rule as a regent until I died. I've exhausted all other avenues. This is what's left. I have to prove myself a detriment to the country. An embarrassment that can't be tolerated because I'm too much like my father after all."

"Okay. Well…" She considered all she'd learned, formally and informally. "Most scandals fall into three categories—sex, drugs and corruption. It sounds like your father had his toe in all of those?"

"He did."

"It's hard to come back from embezzlement or political payoffs. I wouldn't want to tar you as a crook, especially if you're planning to take an active part in improving Vallia's economy afterward."

"Agreed."

"Drug scandals usually require a stay in a rehab fa-

cility and ongoing counseling. Addiction is an illness, so there's a risk you'd be expected to continue to rule. It's also very complicated to manage image-wise. There has to be sincere, visible effort, and it becomes a life-long process of proving sobriety. There's always a certain mistrust that lingers in the public eye. The world expects a recovering addict to trip and is always watching for it. I would prefer not to use a drug scandal."

"So that leaves us with sex." His mouth curled with dismay.

"Yes. People love to act outraged over sexual exploits, but they all have their own peccadillos to hide so they tend to move on fairly quickly."

"It can't be anything harassment related or exploitative," he said firmly.

"No," she quickly agreed. "I couldn't defend that, even a manufactured charge. London Connection is always on the victim's side in those cases. It will have to be something compromising, like cheating or adultery." She tapped her chin in thought.

"That would mean courting my way into a relationship with someone in order to betray her. I don't want to use or hurt an unsuspecting woman."

"Something that suggests you have a streak of your father's tastes, then?"

"I'm won't be tied up and spanked. That's not my thing."

"Like anyone would believe you're a bottom. I'm sorry!" She hid her wince behind her hand. "These are habits of a lifetime, trying to be funny to keep a mood light."

After a silence that landed like a thump, he drawled,

"I'm definitely a top." The firmness in his tone underscored his preference for dominating in bed.

Which caused the most inexplicable swoop in her stomach. Runnels of tingling intrigue radiated into her loins, much to her everlasting chagrin.

When she risked a glance up at him, she saw humor glinting in his eyes along with something speculative that noted the blush on her cheekbones.

Her heart swerved, and she shot her attention to the sea while her shoulders longed for the weight of his hands. Something wanton in her imagination pictured him drawing her arms behind her back by the elbows while he kissed the side of her neck and told her not to move.

While he held her. *Claimed* her.

Her scalp tingled in anticipation and she refused to look down, deeply aware her nipples were straining against the soft silk of her dress, swollen and tight and throbbing with lust.

"Perhaps…um…" Her voice rasped and her brain was wandering around drunk in the dark. "Something with role-play?" she suggested tautly.

"Leak a photo of me wearing pointy ears or dressed like one of those gladiators?" He thumbed back toward the path. "No, thanks."

He would so *rock* a leather sword belt. She licked her lips. "Voyeurism?"

"Hidden cameras? Gross."

"What if you, um, did something questionable in public?"

"Caught with my pants down? Like a flasher?"

"*With* someone."

"Mmm." He grimaced as he considered it. "It has

potential, but it means compromising someone else, and naked photos are forever. Keep going."

"You're really hard to please."

"You'll get there," he chided.

A fluttery excitement teased through her.

"Group sex?" she suggested, then realized that might be *too* reminiscent of his father.

Luca's gaze held her own in a way that made her stumbling heart climb into her throat.

"I prefer to give one woman one hundred percent of my attention," he stated. "And I refuse to compete for hers."

So dominant.

Bam, bam, bam went her heart, hammering the base of her throat while the rest of her was slithery honey and prickly nerve endings.

"The only thing left is tickle fights and foot fetishes." She turned her gaze to the water, nose questing for any hint of breeze to cool her blood. She was boiling inside her own skin.

"I like a pretty shoe," he allowed in a voice that angled down to where her silk dress fluttered against her ankles. His voice climbed as his attention came up. "Quality lingerie is always worth appreciating."

He could see the sea-foam green of her lacy bra cup peeking from the open buttons at her chest; she was sure of it. Could he also see she was fighting not to pant in reaction? Why, oh, why was she responding to him so strongly?

"But it's hardly a crime to admire a beautiful woman, is it?"

Was that what he was doing? Because she was pretty sure she was being seduced.

"I want to do something *bad*, Amy."

She choked on a semihysterical laugh, fighting to stay professional and on task while imagining him— *Don't*, she scolded herself. *Don't imagine him doing anything, especially not making babies with y*—

"Oh! Baby daddy!" She leaped on it, pointing so hard toward him, she almost poked him in the chest. "A woman claims to be pregnant with your baby."

His brow went up toward his hairline. "That sort of extortion died when DNA tests came along, didn't it?"

"That's why it would be taken seriously." She spoke fast as she warmed to it. "Women don't make the claim unless they've actually slept with the potential father. Here's what I like about this idea." She excitedly ticked off on her fingers. "It's a very human mistake that still makes you seem virile, and you'll take the honorable steps to accept responsibility. But, because she's not suitable as a queen, it opens the door for your sister to question your judgment and take over."

"It won't work." He dismissed it flatly. "If I conceive a baby while I'm on the throne, my honor would demand that I marry her. That child would become the future ruler of Vallia and my sister would be sidelined forever."

"There is no baby." Amy opened her hands like it was a magic act. "We'll keep the timeline very short. We leak that a woman approached you and *thinks* she's pregnant. You take the possibility seriously, but even while the scandal is blowing up, she learns it was a false alarm. She wasn't actually pregnant. That way the trauma of a pregnancy loss can be avoided. The scandal will be about you taking reckless chances with your country's future. Your sister can call you irresponsible and take the throne."

His brow was still furrowed. "There's no actual woman? I'm the only name in the press? I like that."

"I think you need a living, breathing woman." She wrinkled her nose. "Otherwise the public will search forever for this mystery woman. You'd have people coming forward for generations, claiming to be your long-lost descendant. No, you need someone you conceivably—ha-ha—could have met and slept with. Perhaps a reality star or a pop singer. Let me go through my contact list. I'm sure I can find a few women who would be willing to do something like this as a publicity stunt."

He cringed.

"You hate it?" She had been so proud, convinced this was a workable plan.

"I don't love that I have to use someone, but if she's in the know from the beginning and getting something out of it, I can live with it. This sounds effective without being too unsavory." He nodded. "Run with it."

CHAPTER FOUR

A DISTANT NOISE INTRUDED, but Luca ignored it and continued indulging his lascivious fantasy of Amy's dress unbuttoned to her waist, held closed only by the wide black corset-style belt. Her lacy green bra and underwear would hold the heat of her body and have a delicious silky abrasive texture against his lips and questing touch. She—

"Signor?" His private secretary and lifelong adviser cleared his throat very pointedly, forcing Luca to abandon his musing and focus on the fact that Guillermo was standing in his office, awaiting acknowledgment.

"Yes?" Luca prompted.

"About Ms. Miller's work with the charity…" Guillermo closed the door.

"Is she shaking things up? Because that's what I hired her to do." If she appeared to be an impulsive, misguided decision on his part, all the better.

Guillermo's mouth tightened before he forced a flat smile. "The palace PR team is perfectly capable of handling this last-minute promotion of the gala. In fact, the foundation's board could carry the event over the finish line without any help at all so I'm not sure why Ms. Miller is necessary."

This was the sort of micromanaging Luca had suffered all his life and would have burned to the ground if he'd been planning to remain king. Given their lifelong relationship, Luca could also tell Guillermo smelled an ulterior motive and was digging to find it.

"The board of directors are my mother's contemporaries," Luca said. "They're committed and passionate, but at some point, adhering to tradition only demonstrates a lack of imagination. We're there."

"Have you seen Ms. Miller's contemporaries? Her online presence is very colorful." It wasn't a compliment.

"She's well-connected and understands how to leverage that community."

"But to *whom* is she connected, *signor*? That is my concern. She's photographed with a lot of men, often in relation to a drug charge or the like."

"It's her job to mitigate scandals."

"Are we certain she's not actually the source of them?" Guillermo wasn't being an alarmist. Their previous head of PR had been an enabler to the former king's vices. "Even if she's aboveboard, she wishes to pitch the directors on having the foundation's logo embroidered onto pajamas to be sold as a fundraiser. She thinks celebrities could be encouraged to post photos of themselves wearing them. Might I remind you, *signor*, of your standing instruction that all those associated with royal interests project a more dignified profile than we've seen in the past? Have I missed an announcement that your attitude has changed?"

"You know it hasn't," Luca said flatly. "I'll have Amy tell me about the pajama idea over dinner and judge for myself."

Guillermo didn't take the hint that he was dismissed. "Is dining with her a good idea? She's very familiar. She makes frequent jokes."

Dio aiutami, his patience was hanging by a thread. "Off with her head, then."

"I'm merely pointing out that if she were a true British subject, she might understand the role of a sovereign, but she was born in America—"

"She has the gall to be an American? What *will* we do?"

"*Signor*, I wouldn't want her levity or imprudence to cast any shadows upon you."

"A moment ago, she was too colorful. Would she not cast rainbows?"

"She is already rubbing off on you if you're not taking my counsel seriously. Ms. Miller is a poor fit for any palace endeavor," Guillermo insisted.

"On the contrary, Amy understands influence and image better than you or I ever will. That's why I hired her." Luca was genuinely annoyed by his secretary's snobbish dismissal of a woman who was a font of problem-solving ideas. She had quickly grasped the pros and cons of his unusual request and shaped a workable plan in the shortest possible time. She was the type of person he loved to hire. Instead, he was surrounded by stodgy relics who started their day by shooting protocol directly into their veins.

"I'm sure her *image* is what influenced you," Guillermo sniffed.

"What are you implying?" Luca narrowed his eyes.

"Only that she's very beautiful. The sort of woman who might charm and distract a man from his duties. Impact his judgment."

"I hadn't noticed," Luca lied flagrantly, adding with significant bite, "But if you're having trouble seeing past the fact she's attractive, I'll work with her personally. Safer for all."

"*Signor*, I am perfectly capable of working with her."

"But I'm not?" Luca was down to his last nerve. "I am thirty-one and the king. It's time you trust me to know what I'm doing." *As I nuke my own life...but needs must.*

Do you? Guillermo didn't say it, but the words echoed around the room all the same.

"You're dismissed."

Guillermo closed the door on his way out with a firm click.

Luca hissed out a disgusted breath. Guillermo wasn't stupid. Or wrong. If he'd been a true detriment to the family, the palace, or Vallia, he wouldn't hold the position he did.

Luca was resolved, however, in giving up the crown. The part where he was all too aware of Amy's attributes wasn't part of the plan. He was crossing certain lines if only within his own mind, imagining how snugly silk and lace would sit against Amy's skin. It reinforced temptations that were already difficult to resist.

And much as he was willing to appear fallible, he didn't want to do anything that would sit on his conscience—like make an unwanted pass at an employee. Dignity and responsibility had been his watchwords all his life. He had never had room for even those small human mistakes that Amy found so forgivable.

Her accepting nature was as disarming as her sense of humor and sparkling beauty. He'd signed the contract she'd sent him so he knew she was legally bound to keep his secrets, but he was still unnerved at how easily he'd told her about his father. The night of his father's death had been horrific and something he'd expected to take to his grave—even though it sat inside him like a boil.

Lancing that poison had been a profound relief. Maybe she was onto something about building rapport with her clients.

He choked on a fresh laugh as he recalled her blurted joke. *Half-past oral sex and quarter till—*

What had she been about to say? Doggy-style?

So inappropriate, considering their professional relationship, but damned if he wouldn't recall that remark every time he looked at the sundial in future. And laugh instead of wanting to bash it apart with a sledgehammer.

He'd fought noticing how the graphic statues were affecting her as they walked through them. She'd been curious, as anyone would be. They were meant to be sexually provocative. He'd seen her blushes and lingering looks and the way her nipples had poked against the cups of her bra beneath the layer of her silk dress.

He'd had his own stiffness to disguise. In another life they might have had an entirely different sort of conversation among those athletic examples of libidinous acts, one that might have ended in an attempt to emulate—

Stop. He couldn't let himself do this. He had *hired* her. To ruin him.

And their conversation on how best to go about that had been some of the most amusing banter he'd enjoyed in ages.

Guillermo was right. Amy could be very dangerous to him on a personal level.

Even so, he glanced at his watch and decided he was hungry for an early dinner.

* * *

Amy eyed the slim-fit chive-green pants and the madras patterned jacket in pink and green and gold that she'd bought from the hotel boutique. They would work for tomorrow's meeting with Luca's gala committee, but it wasn't a formal enough outfit for dining with a king.

She debated between the two tea dresses in the closet. One was a pale rose, the other a midnight blue. Both were exceedingly good quality, elegant and pretty, but so demure as to bore her into a coma while looking at them. That pastel pink with the long sleeves would make her skin look sallow, and its sweetheart neckline would have her begging for an insulin shot.

She tried on the blue. It had a round collar, cap sleeves and a sheer overlay on the A-line skirt. She was tempted to put her own leather corset belt over it, but tried the belt off the pink dress. It was a narrow plait with a spangled clasp that added some pop against the blue.

She ignored the closed-toe black patent leather pumps and put on her own silver-heeled stilettos. Then she pushed all her bangles so they sat above her elbow. She couldn't hide the tattoo on her upper arm and shoulder, so she underscored it.

Her hair was in a topknot with wisps pulled out at her temples. Simple eye makeup made her new crimson lipstick all the more dramatic. She was ready to face Luca.

She hoped.

The young man who escorted her—was he a footman?—glanced at her in the various reflective surfaces they passed. She wasn't falsely modest. She knew she attracted the male gaze. Even before her curves had developed, her mother had coached her to play up her femininity and keep the men around her happy and comfortable.

Manipulate them, was what her mother had meant. Trouble was, she'd taught Amy to hunt without teaching her to kill. Thus, Amy's first experience had been to successfully stalk a predator and become his prey without even realizing what was happening.

But she wouldn't think about that right now. The footman was letting her into an office that held a small lounge area and a scrumptious king.

"Amy," Luca greeted.

The impact of his presence, of a voice that sounded pleased to see her, was a blast of sensual energy that made all the hair on her body stand up.

He was freshly shaved and wore dark pants with a pale blue shirt. Both were tailored to sit flawlessly against his muscled frame. Funny how she almost wished he wore a jacket and tie so this would feel more formal. She wasn't sure why she wanted him to put up armor against her, but it would have made her feel safer.

Not that she felt *un*safe as the door closed, leaving them alone. She just wanted him to put up barriers because she couldn't find any of her own. She suddenly felt very raw and skinless as she faced him.

So she turned her attention to the old-world decor, the fine rugs and carved wooden columns. No overtly sexual images in here. It was decorated in a combination of modern abstracts, contemporary furniture and a few period pieces. His desk had to be three hundred years old. It was all very beautiful and…impersonal.

He hadn't moved in. Not properly. He might have erased his father's presence, but he'd made no effort to stamp the space with his own. He'd been planning his abdication from the day he was crowned.

When she looked at him, she caught him staring at her tattoo.

"You really don't care for convention, do you?" he said.

Her toes tried to curl, reacting to the conflicting mix of approval in his tone with the suggestion of disapproval in his words.

"Does that bother you?" she asked, voice strained by the pressure in her chest.

"Some." He poured two glasses of white wine and brought them across the room to offer one. "This is our private reserve. If you don't care for it, I have a red that's not as dry."

"I'm sure it will be fine." She accepted it, and they touched the rims of their glasses before she tried the wine. It was icy and very dry, but complex with a fruit forward start, a round mouth feel and a brief tang before its soft finish. "This is lovely. I'll take payment in cases."

His mouth twitched. He nodded at her shoulder. "Do you mind? I saw online that you had one, but I didn't see what it was."

She angled slightly so he could examine the inked image of a bird flying free of a cage suspended from a branch of blossoms.

"Colorful," he murmured. Something in his amused tone was drier than the wine. It made her feel as though he was making a joke she didn't understand, but his thumb grazed her skin, blanking her mind while filling her body with heat. "It must have taken a lot of time."

"Four hours. It hurt so much," she said with a laugh

that was shredded more by her longing for another caress than any memory of pain. "It's too on-the-nose and was a foolish expense since I was broke at the time, but my mother had always threatened to disinherit me if I got a tattoo. Since she'd gone ahead and done that, I saw no reason to wait."

"The same mother you spoke with in the car today? The one who spoiled you because you were an only child?"

"Yes. But then she stopped." She wrinkled her nose. "I'd rather not talk about my parents. It's a complicated relationship."

"That's fine," he said mildly. "But you *can* talk about them if you decide you'd like to. This is a safe space," he added in a sardonic tone that threw her own words back at her.

She choked back saying it didn't feel like it and said, "Good to know." She gulped wine to wet her dry throat. "Do you have any?"

"Tattoos?" He snorted. "No." He sipped his own wine, then walked his glass to an end table and set it down. "I was also forbidden to get one, but that didn't bother me. I've never had much appetite for rebellion. My father thought being king gave him license to do whatever the hell he wanted despite the responsibilities that come with the title. I was taught differently."

"By your mother and her team."

"Yes. And his behavior impacted her. She had mental health struggles. That's why the foundation exists. She started it because she understood the hurdles people face when seeking treatment. She passed away from an unrelated condition, but I often think her depression affected her…" Agony tightened his expression. "Her will to fight. She loved us, but she was very disillusioned. Humiliated by my father's conduct. Or lack thereof," he said with a twist of his lips. "He was completely indifferent to the effect he had on her. Not oblivious. He simply didn't care. If anything, he was spiteful about it. He didn't *want* to be a good husband or father or ruler. He set out to prove he didn't have to conform or put anyone's needs above his own. As a result, I find rebellion a selfish and unattractive behavior."

"Ouch," she said blithely as she set aside her own wine, fighting not to let him see how deeply that knife had plunged.

"I didn't mean to suggest you're selfish. I was speaking of the characteristic in general."

"Oh, but I was," she assured him. "I was a self-involved brat until such time as that luxury was denied me." She'd been hurt and feeling abandoned by her parents after they'd divorced and shuffled her off to boarding school. She'd made demands for things she didn't even want in a clichéd cry for the love and attention she really craved.

Her behavior had spiraled from there and yes, Amy carried some of the blame for what had happened with the field hockey coach. She had known what she was doing was wrong, but so had he. And he'd been a man of twenty-nine while she'd been an eighteen-year-old student in his class.

"I didn't always direct my independent streak in the best way," she admitted. "But it annoys me that pushing back on how girls and women are 'supposed to' behave is considered rebellion. That's what I was really fighting. My mother was always saying, 'Don't speak up. You have to fit in.' She buys into this silent agreement with society that women aren't supposed to draw attention to ourselves because it pulls the spotlight from the really important people. Men," she stated with a scathing eye roll.

"Ouch," he said ironically.

She bit her lip, quelling her smile.

He was shaking his head, but taking her remark with good-natured amusement.

She liked him, damn it.

Best to focus on why she was here. "Can I show you the women I've identified who might be willing to ruin you?"

"I thought I was already looking at her," he drawled.

Amy faltered in retrieving her phone.

He sobered. "That was a joke."

"I know. I didn't realize you knew how to make one." She shakily breezed past her tiny betrayal of a guilty conscience and brought her phone to him. "These are celebrities I know well enough to approach. I am neither confirming nor denying they are clients."

"Noted."

They stood so closely, she could feel the heat off his body and detected the mellow scent of his aftershave. He picked up his wine and she heard him swallow as she began to thumb through images, providing a brief biography for each.

"German car heiress trying to start her own fashion line. Country music star, American, won an award for a song about her messy divorce. This is a cousin of a British ambassador. She has a popular online cooking series."

Luca rejected them all just as quickly. "Too young. No one will believe I listen to American country music. Where would I have met an online chef?"

Six more went by and Amy clicked off her phone. "You're being too picky. *No one* will be perfect. That's the point."

"If I don't believe I'm attracted to her, no one else will." He set aside his glass again.

"What kind of woman do you want, then?" she asked with exasperation.

His gaze raked down her face and snagged on her mouth, then swept back to her eyes. The heat in the depths of his blue irises nearly set her on fire before he looked to a corner.

Amy caught her breath, swaying on the skinny heels of her shoes. She had really hoped this attraction was only on her side. It would have made this a silly infatuation where she was reaching out of her league and had no chance.

It was a lot harder to ignore when she knew he felt the same. The space between them seemed to shrink, drawing them in. Her gaze fixated on the tension around his mouth.

"I…" She had no words. She should have moved away. "I thought you were…" She thought back to that dismissive rebuff he'd given her in London. "Indifferent to me."

His lips parted as he exhaled roughly. "You do speak your mind, don't you? I *want* to be indifferent." The air crackled between them. "But I'm not."

What was she supposed to do with that? She could only soften with helplessness. He had to be the strong one.

As they both fell silent, she felt the pull of an invisible force. He moved in such small increments, she thought she imagined that he was drawing closer; but he was suddenly so close that a prickle of anticipation stung her lips. She dampened them with her tongue.

"Amy." It was a scold that rang with defeat. His hand found her hip as though to ground them both as his head dipped and he covered her mouth with his own.

Sensation burst to life in her. His lips were firm and smooth and confident. Smothering in the most delicious way as he angled and fit and claimed her. Devastated her.

How long had it been since she'd kissed a man? Really kissed one with hunger and passion and a hand that went to the back of his head, urging him to ravish her?

His arm banded across her lower back, dragging her in so her body was plastered to the hardness of his. They rocked their mouths together, pressing tighter, opening wider, exploring deeper.

A moan left her throat and she wound her arms around his neck, clinging weakly as she lost herself to the delirium. No one had ever made her feel like this. Never, ever.

Suddenly he took her by the shoulders and set her back a step. The regressive light in his eyes stopped her heart before he ruthlessly leashed whatever animal was alive inside him.

His hands dropped away as he turned to stand directly in front of her.

"Sì," he barked and the door opened.

Oh, God. Someone had knocked and she hadn't even heard it. She dropped her face into her hands.

She recognized Guillermo's voice, but stayed exactly where she was, hidden by the wall of Luca's back as she tried to gather her composure.

The men exchanged words in crisp Italian and the door closed again.

"There's a call I must take." Luca's arm reached past her to snag his wine. She heard him finish it in one gulp. "I'll be tied up for hours. Your meal will be delivered to your room."

She nodded jerkily and made herself lift her head and turn to face him. She cringed as she saw him, saying remorsefully, "My lipstick is all over your mouth."

He swore and swiped the back of his hand across his lips, noted the streak of red and swore again, this time with resignation.

"I shouldn't have done that. I'm sorry." A muscle in his cheek ticked.

Her stomach clenched around the pang his regret caused her.

"I know better, too." Her voice rasped and the backs of her eyes were hot. "I'll go."

"Amy."

She turned back.

Compunction was still etched across his face, but he held out a handkerchief. He touched her chin, urging her to lift her mouth. In a few gentle swipes, he cleaned the edges of her lips.

He then used the same soft linen to wipe his own mouth. He dropped his hand and let her examine his work. All trace of their kiss was gone as though it had never happened.

She nodded, too empty to feel anything but despondency. She swallowed a dry lump from the back of her throat, turned and left.

CHAPTER FIVE

Luca took the call regarding a handful of Vallia's elite military serving overseas on a humanitarian mission. No one had been injured, but there'd been an incident that required he draft a statement and follow up with calls to overseas contacts.

By the time the whole thing was put to bed, it was long past time he should have been asleep himself.

"Take the morning off," he told Guillermo as he rose from his desk.

"Signor." Guillermo had an uncanny ability to inject a host of meaning into that single word. This one held appreciation for the sentiment, protest that the extra sleep wasn't necessary, caution and concern and a waft of smugness that he'd been right to warn Luca against Ms. Miller.

"I'll speak to the Privy Council in the morning," Luca said, meeting Guillermo's gaze with an implacable one. "You needn't make any reports to them on this evening. At all."

Guillermo's mouth tightened. "As you wish. Sleep well."

Luca didn't. He got slightly drunk while roundly berating himself even as he stood on the terrace off his bedroom, overlooking the Roman pond surrounded by sexual gymnastics.

If Amy had been wandering around there like a lost ghost, he would have had a reason to go out to see her, but she hadn't given him one.

Kissing her had been such a stupid thing to do. A mistake. Mistakes were something else he'd never had the appetite for. He'd been so scrutinized all his life, so quickly corrected for the tiniest errors, he had little tolerance for imperfection, especially within himself. He was the Golden Prince, after all.

And Amy was...

The image of her tattoo came into his mind, oddly pretty and feminine despite the jailbreak it depicted. He had wanted to clasp his hand around her warm arm and set his mouth against the ink. Taste her skin and kiss that small, pretty bird that he instinctively knew had been as chirpy inside that cage as she was outside it.

What kind of woman do you like, then?

Not anyone like her—with her cheeky remarks and hair that looked like it had already been mussed by raunchy sex. Not someone who didn't so much get under his skin as draw him out of his own. One who made him want to shake off his restraints, self-imposed and otherwise.

One with whom he'd already broken a cardinal rule of keeping his hands to himself.

He managed to sleep a few hours, then got an early start on his day. He met with his Privy Council, spoke briefly with his sister who was distracted as she wrapped up a diplomacy conference in North Africa, then made his way to the meeting of the gala committee.

Amy was holding court and faltered when he entered.

She was like a tropical bird in pinks and greens and gold. Beautiful, if projecting an air of delicacy that he hadn't expected. There were hints of shadows beneath her makeup and a wary fragility in her smile.

"Your Highness," she greeted.

"Continue," he said, waving everyone to stay seated while he remained on his feet at the back of the room. "I want to hear your pitch on the pajamas."

"I'm almost there." She glanced at her slide presentation and finished talking about the recruitment of influencers. She switched to photographs of elegant satin pajamas.

"Sometimes we want to call in sick to life." Her apprehensive gaze flicked to him and her laser pointer wasn't quite steady as she circled the pajama shirt. "Sometimes we need to feel safe and cozy as we navigate personal challenges. Asking celebrities to model the foundation's merchandise isn't about making mental health struggles seem glamorous. Yes, it's a fundraiser and some people will be motivated to buy the pajamas because of who wore it best, but we're also promoting self-care. We're saying it's okay to have a pajama day."

Amy paused for reaction, seeming to hold her breath.

Heads turned to gauge his reaction. One voice said pithily, "There's no way to have them printed before the gala."

"No," Amy agreed. "The campaign would be announced at the gala with an opportunity for those attending to place preorders. People love to be on the ground floor of something new. When they received their pajamas, it would bring the foundation back to their minds. In a few months, you could offer a new color and send out reorder forms. Later in the year, you could host a low-key pajama party."

"*That* doesn't sound very dignified," someone murmured.

"I like the central message," Luca stated firmly. "And it offers flexibility moving forward. My vote is to go ahead. Amy, I'd like to meet with you on another matter when you've finished here."

The attitude in the room changed as Luca left. A few old guard on the council were sitting as though perched on a pin, but they were the type who didn't like change. The rest had been hiding their interest for fear of offending them. Now that Luca had granted royal assent, several people had excited questions and seemed eager to carry the campaign forward.

Amy contributed as best she could, but she was having trouble concentrating. She'd nearly fainted when Luca walked in. She had half expected him to announce she was off the case and should catch the first flight back to London. Last night had been a rough one full of self-recriminations—and not just because their kiss had been so improper.

Was it, though?

Or was she searching for a way to rationalize her own poor judgment?

She wasn't an impressionable student any longer. She was an adult and their kiss had been completely consensual, but Luca did have power over her, most of it financial. He also had enough influence politically and socially to destroy London Connection if he wanted to call her out as offering sex to entice his business or some other twist of the truth.

Was it naive of her to believe he would never do such a thing? She barely knew him, but she didn't believe that he had it in him to act so dishonorably.

No, the real power Luca wielded was his ability to make her cast aside common sense.

As she'd ruminated alone last night, over a meal she'd barely touched, part of her had been tempted to tear up their contract, pack up and disappear in the dead of night.

It would cost her a nonperformance fee and impact her own reputation as dedicated and reliable, but Amy had suffered through hard times before. She wasn't as vulnerable and cushioned from reality as she'd been when she'd first been expelled, either. She didn't *want* to start over, but she knew how to do it. And she had modest savings set aside for exactly the sort of emergency that would arise if she turned her back on Luca as a client.

Amy wasn't a quitter, though. And she didn't want to believe she was so weak she could fall under a man's spell and ruin her own life in the process. Not again.

Eventually, to quiet her mind, she had gone back to working on the gala presentation and the other, private assignment. If Luca decided to fire her for lacking professionalism, so be it. She, at least, would carry on as if she still had the job.

Which, it turned out, wasn't any easier than being fired. It meant facing him again. In front of a crowd. She had tried to sound knowledgeable and unaffected by the memory of their kiss while her ideas were picked apart and his laser-like gaze watched her every move.

Now the meeting had broken up and a footman was leading her back to the private wing of the palace. He showed her into a different room from last night, this one a parlor in colors of olive and straw and pale, earthy reds.

"The king will be with you shortly," he said before he evaporated.

Amy took a cleansing breath and allowed the open doors to draw her out to a small, shaded courtyard. It was full of blooming roses exuding fragrances of lemon and raspberry, green tea, honey and cloves. She felt like a bee, incapable of deciding which to sniff first.

A small round table was set with snow-white linens and a splendiferous table setting fit for—well. Duh.

She studied the gold pattern on the china plates and the scrolls of what had to be real gold applied to the glasses. A yellow orchid blossom sat on the gold napkin ring. The flatware was gold, too. Intricately patterned and heavy and engraved with the Italian word for—

"Caught you," Luca said, startling her into clattering the gold knife back into its spot.

She sent him an admonishing look while his mouth curled into an amused smirk.

He was so effortlessly perfect. Lean and athletic, confident in his own skin, moving as an intrinsic part of the beauty and luxury that surrounded him.

"I was trying to make out what it said," she grumbled. "My Italian needs work."

"The setting was commissioned for my grandparents' wedding by my great-grandmother." He touched different pieces of cutlery as he translated the various words etched upon each. "Respect, honesty, trust, loyalty. The foundation of a strong marriage."

Don't read anything into it, Amy ordered herself, but couldn't help the way her pulse quickened and her cheeks grew warm with self-consciousness.

"My grandmother always used it when she had private luncheons with her women friends." He touched a fork to minutely adjust its position. "So did my mother."

"What a lovely tradition." Her heart twisted as she realized she was being very firmly friend zoned. "It puts a literal spin on women coming together to dish the dirt, doesn't it? I'm honored you would share it with me."

"I'm sure it made the women feel privileged to hear palace gossip from the queen herself, but if we're being honest?" He gave the knife with *Lealtà* scrolled upon it a sardonic nod. "I think it was also a reminder that the secrets she revealed were meant to be kept."

"The qualities of any good relationship, then." Amy spoke with casual interest, but her veins stung with indignation. She wasn't going to tell anyone that they'd kissed, if that's what he was worried about. "I've signed a nondisclosure contract," she reminded him, chin coming up a notch. "You don't have to drive it home with a golden spike."

"I thought you'd think they were pretty," he said in a blithe tone that disconcerted her because why would he care what she thought about anything? "The dishes and the courtyard."

"They are," she allowed, feeling awkward now. Privileged and entrusted.

He nodded past her and staff approached to seat them. Wine was poured, and as they took their first sips, her gaze clashed with his over their glasses. His expression was inscrutable, but the impact of looking him in the eye caused her to rattle the rim of her glass against her teeth. Her throat contracted on the wine, so she choked a bit, which she tried to suppress. The burn of alcohol seared a path behind her sternum.

An antipasto course was served. The staff didn't leave so they spoke of general things. Luca asked about the rest of her presentation, and Amy managed to say something lucid.

"What drew you to public relations as a career?" he inquired.

"Dumb luck. I was serving drinks at a pub. They had a band coming in, and I put it on my social media feeds. My circle was quite posh from school, daughters of celebs and such. One was a girl from a movie that was a cult favorite. She came out, and it turned the pub into that summer's hot spot. Another pub asked me to put them on the map, and word got out on the music circuit. Instead of serving drinks, I started planning and promoting events. The more people I knew, the more I got to know."

"I presumed you'd taken a degree, not learned on the job."

"I've since taken a vocational qualification." She didn't have to elaborate on why she hadn't gone to uni. Rice and fish were served, delicately spiced with saffron and scallions.

While they enjoyed it, he told her some more history about the palace and his country.

By the time they'd finished with a custard tart topped with whipped cream and fresh berries, they had discovered they both enjoyed mind-teaser puzzles, horseback riding—though they found little time to pursue it—and shared a fascination with remote places on Earth.

Amy had forgotten who he was and why she was here. This had become the most effortless, enjoyable date she'd been on in ages.

Then Luca told the server, "We'll take coffee in my drawing room," and Amy crashed back to reality. This wasn't a date.

She found a smile and said, "Coffee sounds good."

A few minutes later, they walked down the hall to the room where they'd kissed last night. The drapes were open, allowing sunshine to pour into the expansive space, but it still felt intimate once the espresso had been served and they were alone.

She understood the expression "walking on eggshells" as she approached the sofa. Each step crushed something fragile underfoot. Should she acknowledge last night? Express regret and move on? Ignore it completely and see if he brought it up?

"I saw your press release this morning," she said, deciding on an oblique reference to the phone call that had pulled them apart last night. "I'm glad things weren't more serious."

After a brief pause, he drawled, "You ought to defuse bombs for a living."

"I do," she replied mildly, obeying his wave and sinking onto the cushion. "Proverbial ones." She felt as though a sizzling string was running toward a bundle of dynamite sitting beneath her.

She added a few grains of raw, golden sugar to her coffee. He took his black.

"It's fine if we're not going to talk about it," she said in the most unconcerned tone she could find, sitting back and bringing her cup and saucer with her. "I respect boundaries. Yesterday's evidence to the contrary," she added with a wince of self-recrimination. "I don't make a habit of behaving so unprofessionally."

"My behavior was wildly inappropriate, given my

title and the fact I've hired you. I want to be clear that I expect nothing from you beyond the work I've commissioned from London Connection. If our contract is something you'd prefer to dissolve now, I would understand."

Weren't they the most civilized people on the planet? And why did it make her feel as though she was swallowing acid?

"We bear equal responsibility."

"Do we?" He sounded so lethal, it struck her as an accusation. Her heart lurched.

"I'm not a victim." Conviction rang in her tone. She refused to be one ever again. "I don't think you are, either. Are you?" It took everything in her to hold his gaze and not shake so hard she'd spill hot coffee on her knee.

"No. On the contrary, I can have nearly anything I want." He smiled flatly. "It's up to me to exercise control and not take it."

"You didn't take anything I wasn't giving. I'm not afraid to tell you no, Luca. I've done it before, I can do it again." *If I want to*. The problem was, she didn't really want to.

His expression shifted into something close to a smile, but his exhalation gave away his annoyance.

"What?" she asked caustically.

"It makes you even more attractive," he said bluntly. "That toughness inside that angelic persona you project. I find it infinitely fascinating. Which I shouldn't tell you, but we're past pretending we're not attracted to each other. Better to name the beast."

Was it? Because something ballooned in her chest, cutting off her airways. She really was going to freak out and spill hot coffee all over herself.

"It's not like we can do anything about it," she reminded him. "You're about to publicly tie yourself to another woman."

His expression shuttered, and he didn't sound pleased as he said, "True."

"I think I've found a good fit." Amy forced herself to plow forward.

"Oh?" Luca sat back, projecting skepticism. Reluctance, perhaps?

"She's an actor." She leaned forward to set her coffee on the table. "She plays a spy on that cold war series that's streaming right now. Even if you haven't seen it, people would believe you might have. It's very popular, and they film all over Europe so it's feasible you would have been in the same city at some point. We could say you were introduced by a mutual acquaintance who remains nameless. She's very pretty." Amy flicked through her phone for the woman's image.

Luca took the phone long enough to glance at it before handing it back. "Why didn't you suggest her yesterday?"

Amy almost said, *Because she's very pretty.*

"I don't know her that well. We met at a club a few weeks ago." Amy had provided a shoulder while the woman poured her heart out over a man she was having trouble quitting. "I reached out last night with a very superficial mention of a potential 'unique opportunity.' She said she'd take a meeting. I'm waiting to hear where and when."

"How much do you think she would want?"

"That's why I think she would be a good fit. Obviously, she should be compensated, but I don't think she'll care about money or publicity. She generates plenty of both on her own. But when we met, she said something that leads me to think she would find it useful to be seen as being committed to a man of your caliber."

His brows went up in a silent demand for more info.

"Romantic troubles. I don't want to gossip out of turn. I'm sure she would be more forthcoming if you formed a liaison."

He hitched his trousers as he crossed one leg over the other, looking toward the windows with a flinty expression.

Amy bit her lip, well practiced in giving a client time to process her suggestions. In this case exercising patience was especially hard. She was eager to please, but was so aware of their kiss—their mutual attraction—that it twisted her insides to suggest he even pretend to see another woman.

After a long minute, he said, "I hate this."

Her heart lurched.

Did he hate that he was sabotaging his own reputation? Or that he'd behaved badly with her and the repercussions were still coloring their discussion?

Or was he harboring a secret regret, the way she was, that they had to relegate their kiss and any potential relationship firmly offstage?

"I have to do this," he said, bringing his gaze back to hers in an ice-blue swing of a scythe. "You understand that? I don't have a choice to put it off or..." His hand scrolled the air and it sent an invisible lasso looping around her, strangling her. "I can't chase what I want at the expense of what is right. I couldn't even offer you— It would be *once*, Amy. Nothing more. And the window for that is already closing."

Amy supposed his words were a compliment, but

they slapped like a rejection. Through the fiery agony, she reminded herself that she was respecting boundaries and nodded acceptance. "Don't worry about me. My job comes first."

"Same." His mouth twisted in dismay. "She sounds like a good option. Meet with her. Keep my name out of it until we're further along."

"Of course." She ignored how heavy it made her feel. "I'll have her sign confidentiality agreements before I pitch it, and I'll gauge better whether she's a good fit before you're mentioned at all."

"When will you see her?"

"I've asked for tomorrow afternoon." Her heart was pounding so hard, her ears hurt. "Do you want a slower rollout? If she turns it down, we'll have to find someone else."

"I want my sister installed as quickly as possible," he said decisively, rising.

"I think we're on the right track." She rose too, getting the message that this meeting was over. "I'll finish up my gala work while I wait to hear."

He nodded and she started to leave.

"Amy," he growled, sounding so deadly, her breath caught.

She swung around.

He wore a look of supreme frustration. His hands were in his pockets, but were fisted into rocks.

"It would only be once," he repeated grittily.

Such a bright light exploded within her, she was ignited by the heat of a thousand suns.

"Once is better than never." She ran into his arms.

CHAPTER SIX

HE CAUGHT HER, barely rocking on his feet. His arms wrapped tightly around her, holding her steady even as he hesitated. His lips peeled back against his teeth in a moment of strained conscience.

"It's just once," Amy blurted in a bleak urgency that awakened old ghosts inside her. The wraiths slipped and swirled in cool trails of guilt, hissing, *You shouldn't. You know you shouldn't. Nothing good will come of this.*

"Just once," he echoed in groaning agreement as he claimed her mouth with his own.

She'd been in a state of deprivation since last night. Relief poured through her as he dragged her back to where they'd left off. White heat radiated from his body into hers, burning away her cobwebs of misgivings. This was nothing like that tainted, ancient memory from years ago. It was sweet and good and right.

Amy felt safe and cherished in these arms that could crush, but didn't. His mouth rocked across hers, seducing and ravaging, giving as much as he took. He stole soft bites of her tingling lips, and the heat in his eyes sent shimmering want through her limbs.

"Will anyone come in?" She wasn't ashamed of what they were doing, but she dreaded another discovery.

"No," he murmured, adding, "But let's make sure."

He moved as if they were dancing, smoothly pivoting her before he caught her hand and swirled her toward an unassuming door. It led to an anteroom and from there they entered a massive bedroom.

This was the king's chamber, a mix of the palace's opulence and Luca's spare, disciplined personality. Huge glass doors led to a terrace that overlooked the sundial and the sea. The glass was covered in sheer drapes that turned the light pale gold. The marble floor was softened with a thick rug in shades of gold and green, the ceiling painted a soothing blue between the white plaster and gold filigree. There was a fireplace and a comfortable sitting area, and a button that he touched caused all the doors to click.

"We have complete privacy now. Even the phone won't ring."

He turned to her and she stepped into his arms with a sigh of gladness, wanting to be swept away again into that place where second thoughts were impossible.

He cupped her face. His spiky lashes flickered as he scanned her features.

"What's wrong?" she asked, uncertainty creeping in.

"Absolutely nothing, but if we only have today, I'm damned well going to take my time and remember every second."

"Oh," she breathed. His words dismantled her at a very basic level. She wasn't that special. Didn't he realize that? She was actually tarnished and broken. What she was doing right now with him was akin to stealing.

But as the pad of his thumb slid across her bottom lip, she whispered, "I want to savor you, too." She lifted a hand to touch his hair, startled to find the strands so soft and fine when it looked so thick.

He adjusted their stance so their bodies aligned perfectly. His feet bracketed hers, and his thighs were hard against her own. He was aroused, the stiffness of him undeniable against the part of her that was growing soft and damp and ripe.

She slid her arms around his strong neck. His touch slipped under her jacket so his hands splayed across her back while they crashed their mouths together.

Something wanton in her wanted—needed—to know he was as helpless against her as she was against him. She arched, inciting him with a grind of her hips against that alluring ridge of hardness, seeking the pressure of him *there*.

Lust exploded between them. His whole body jolted, and his arms tightened before he backed her toward the high bed.

Her thighs and bottom came up against the edge of the mattress. He held her there, pinned against the soft resistance while his legs went between hers. Now he was the one who gave muted thrusts, his gaze holding hers, watching as she released a soft mew of helpless, divine pleasure. She felt herself dissolving.

"Good?"

He had to know it was. She couldn't even speak, only nod and brace her hands on the mattress behind her, arching to encourage his rhythm, sharp heels liable to snag his expensive carpet and who the hell cared because this was the most incredible experience of her life. Every breath was filled with his scent. All of her muscles were shaking with sexual excitement.

His hands swept forward and opened her jacket so he

could roam his hot palms over the lime-green camisole she wore. A tickling touch danced across her chest and shoulders as he spread the jacket to expose all of her torso. The hot caress of his hands enclosed her breasts.

She groaned and he caught that with his mouth. His thumbs worked over her nipples through the layers of silk and lace. His tongue brushed against hers, and she groaned again as the coiling pleasure in her center became a molten heat. An unstoppable, screaming force.

She had wanted to push him past his own control and here she was losing hers, fists clenched in his bedspread, hips bucking with greed.

When he lifted his head, she dragged her eyes open, dreading how smug he must be at doing this to her, but she saw only a glow of barely leashed lust in his sharp gaze. He was with her, deep in the eye of the hurricane.

"What do you need?" His voice was a rasp that made her skin tighten. "This?" His head dipped and his mouth was on her breast, fingers pulling aside her camisole and the cup of her bra. His touch snaked across her nipple before he exposed it and enveloped her in the intense heat of his mouth.

A lightning bolt of pleasure went straight to where they were fused at the hips and she groaned, moving helplessly against that lethal shape lodged in the notch of her thighs. Acute sensations were taking over, heat and pleasure and a need so great she couldn't resist succumbing to it.

As he pulled on her nipple, a muted climax rose and broke and cascaded shimmering sensations through her.

Ragged noises left her lips as his hand replaced his mouth, tucking inside the cup of her bra to hold her breast as his mouth came back to hers, tender yet rough, soothing, but determined to catch all of her moans.

The pleasure continued to twist inside her, sweet and delicious and teasingly unsatisfying. She was more aroused than ever. Ready to do *anything*, which caused a twinge of anxiety as she weakly sank onto her back on the mattress, legs still dangling off the side, essentially offering herself to him.

He stayed hovering over her. He could persuade her to do anything right now, she acknowledged. He stood with his thighs between her splayed ones, his thick erection pressed indelibly to the swollen, aching flesh between her legs.

He could have lorded her abandonment over her, especially because she was lifting her hips in a muted plea.

He looked wild, though. Barbaric in the most controlled way possible. If he was an animal, he was the kind that might chase his mate to ground, but he would kill *for* her before he'd allow her to be harmed in any way.

Amy might have reached past that veil of savagery if she'd wanted to, but as he raked his hand down the front of his shirt, tearing the buttons loose and baring his chest, she was lost. He was pushed to the limits of his restraint, and she was bizarrely reassured since she had no ability to resist him, either.

His shirt landed on the floor, and he popped the button on the fly of her new green trousers. His hand swept up, urging her to lift her arms. He lifted her jacket up and threw it off the far side of the mattress. She left her arms up so he could sweep the camisole up and away, as well.

His nostrils flared at the sight of her bare belly and pale breast overflowing the dislodged cup of her green bra, she arched to tease him with the sight, inviting him to skim his hand behind her back to find the hook.

He whisked away the bra, then traced each shadow and curve of her torso, claiming her with tickling touches and firm flicks of his thumbs. He bent to nuzzle her skin with his lips, pooling his hot breath in the hollow of her collarbone before taking a blatant taste of each pouting nipple, leaving them erect and gleaming.

The zipper of her pants gave with a snap as his hands raked them down her hips.

She didn't protest the damage. She was too caught up in the urgency he was projecting. It was mesmerizing to see the intensity in him as he dragged her pants down her legs and gave each cuff a yank to pull them free of her shoes.

"I can take them off."

"I don't want you to," he said, voice distant, fingertips sliding across the sensitive skin on the top of her feet and encircling her ankles. "I want to do this."

He set the shoes on his shoulders as he lowered to his knees beside the bed.

She strangled her groan of helplessness with the back of her wrist, lost before he'd even touched her.

He delicately moved side the damp silk of her panties. His touch traced between her folds, making her groan again and twist in tortured anticipation. In the self-conscious knowledge he was looking and touching and—

She gasped as his mouth grazed the inside of her thigh, then the other one. He slowly, slowly kissed toward her center.

She shifted her feet so she could urge him with a heel in his back—forgetting the sharp shoe until he laughed starkly and said, *"That's* what I wanted."

His hot chuckle was her only warning before his mouth was on her and she nearly came off the bed. No restraint in him now. He claimed her unabashedly, tasting, teasing, learning, then mercilessly pleasuring her until she had her thighs locked to his ears.

"Luca. Luca." She lost all inhibition, fist knotted in his hair and hips lifting to meet the swirling pressure of his tongue.

This time her orgasm shattered her. It was one crescendo after another because he made it so, continuing to pleasure her as each wrenching burst of joy contracted through her. He didn't stop until her weak, quivering thighs fell open.

Then he rose to survey the destruction he'd caused. She was in pieces before him, stomach quivering, limbs weak. She was no longer autonomous. She belonged to him.

Which made the way he paused as he hooked his hand in her knickers somewhat laughable, but she lifted her hips in silent consent. Satisfaction came into his stark features then, along with an undisguised possessiveness. His gaze swept down her nudity as he drew the wisp of green off her ankles.

His gaze came back to hers, glints of untamed desire in his fiery blue eyes.

That primeval heat called to her. Drew her to sit up on the edge of the bed and reach a hand to the back of his neck to drag him into kissing her.

His hands went down her bare back and cupped her bottom as he thrust his tongue between her lips, flagrantly making love to her mouth. She sucked on his tongue and blindly fumbled his fly open, then slid her hand inside the elastic of his boxer briefs to clasp the thickness of his shaft and trace her touch to caress his wet tip.

He tangled his hand in her hair and kissed her so deeply, she could hardly breathe, especially when his hand arrived at her breast, reawakening all her erogenous zones as he delicately pinched her nipple.

She squeezed him in reaction, and that seemed to be his snapping point.

He lurched back and shoved his pants down, taking his underwear at the same time. His shoes were toed off and he was naked in seconds, reaching to the nightstand drawer.

She should have removed her own shoes, but she was too caught up in watching his deft movements. He smoothed a condom into place and moved to stand before her.

Her bones softened and she melted onto her back.

Intense pleasure was stamped into his expression and his hands went over her, claiming hip and waist and breast and belly and the tender heat between her thighs as he spread her legs to make room for himself. His elbow hooked under one of her knees and he pushed her farther onto the bed so he could get his knee onto the mattress between her own.

His gaze snagged on her shoe where her leg was draped over his arm. "Perhaps I do have a fetish after all."

He lined himself up against her entrance and watched her face as he began to press into her.

She bit her lip.

He paused.

"Don't stop," she gasped. "It just so good."

Her eyes were wet with some emotion between joy and intense need, her sheath slick and welcoming his intrusion with shivering arousal. She couldn't touch enough of him—shoulders, chest, straining neck, the fine strands of his hair on his head.

He made a noise that was a mangled agreement and let his weight ease him deeper, sliding all the way in and coming down onto his elbow so he hovered over her. Her one leg was hooked high on his arm. His free hand tangled in her hair and his mouth covered hers.

She wrapped her arms around his neck and arched her back, signaling how eager she was for the feel of him moving over her. Within her.

He began to thrust.

It was mind-bendingly good. She brought her free leg up to wrap around his waist and felt his knees bracket her backside. He rocked them and pushed his arm under her lower back, lifting her hips so he could thrust more freely. With more power.

The new angle caused his next thrust to send a hot spear of intense pleasure through her, one that had her tearing her mouth from his to cry out with tormented joy.

His mouth went to her ear and he sucked on her lobe while their heat and energy built. Their lovemaking turned raw and primal, then. The room filled with their anguished grunts of growing tension and clawing need.

"I need you deeper. Harder," she begged, pulling at his hair.

He caught her other leg and released his full strength,

holding back nothing as he drove her higher and higher up the scales of what she could bear.

"Don't stop," she demanded. Pleaded. "Luca! Luca!"

"Let go. You're killing me," he growled, holding both of them trapped on a precipice with his rhythmic, powerful thrusts. "I won't come until you do and I *need* to."

His jagged voice pulled at her while his hard body shifted over her, his mouth taking hers. He surrounded her so fully, there was barely any place he didn't touch. Didn't claim. She was all his. At the mercy of his unconstrained sexual heat.

He slammed into her and rocked against her swollen, delirious flesh. The universe opened into an expansive void. For an infinite moment, they were suspended like stars in the universe, caught in the peak of supreme perfection for all eternity.

Then his tongue touched hers and reality folded in on itself. Orgasm struck like a hammer, and she was moaning against his own noises of supreme gratification while waves of culmination rolled over them, again and again.

Luca woke to the sound of the door locks releasing.

He kept his head buried in his pillow, willing himself to let her go.

"Just once" had turned into twice. Twice was not a slip of control. Twice was unabashed self-indulgence. He had deafened himself to his internal voices of caution and abandoned himself to sheer lust. It had been incredible.

And disturbing to realize he was so capable of immersing himself in base desire. He was not so far above his father as he liked to believe. He was just as capable of pursuing immediate gratification.

When sexual exhaustion had crept over them, he'd thrown himself into a hard nap so he wouldn't have to face this reckoning—which was another facet of abandoned responsibility. On the few occasions when he had made a mistake, Luca always confronted and corrected it. He didn't play denial games.

Sleeping with Amy was definitely a mistake. He'd known it even as her name had left his lips after their lunch. He should have let her walk away.

At least he was doing it now. She was making it easy for him by slipping away while she thought he was sleeping. He would make it easy for her by not trying to stop her, even though his shoulders twitched with the need to come up on his elbows. *Wait*, hovered unspoken on his lips.

What time was it? Beyond his lowered eyelids and the mound of the pillow, he had the sense that daylight was fading. He didn't look. He held still with belated but ruthless control, waiting to hear the door close behind her.

The sound came from the wrong side of the room. The air moved. It tasted cool and carried the scent of the sea. He lifted his head and glanced toward the terrace.

The sight of her knocked his breath out of him.

Amy, bare-legged and shoeless, strawberry blonde hair streaked with gold wafting loosely down the back of his rippling shirt, was backlit by one of Vallia's signature sunsets.

A trick of air and water currents beyond their west coast caused wispy clouds to gather on the horizon at the end of the day, providing a canvas for dying rays.

As the air cooled, the sea calmed to reflect sharp, bright oranges that bled toward streaks of pink and purple while indigo crept in from the edges. Couples came from around the world to photograph their wedding against it.

Luca rose and was outside before he'd consciously thought to join her. He was *drawn*. That power she exerted without effort should have scared the hell out of him, but he was too enchanted by the expression on her face when he came alongside her.

She had moved to the northern end of the terrace and was looking back toward the castle ruins where the colors of the sunset were painting the gray stones bronze and red, throwing its cracks and crevices into dark relief.

He joined her and took in her profile with the same wonder she was sending toward the castle. Her mouth was soft, eyes lit with awe. Her creamy skin held the magical glow off the horizon.

"This is so beautiful. I've never seen anything like it."

"Me, either." The compliment was meant to be ironic, but his voice was lodged in his chest where thick walls were fracturing and tumbling apart.

He gave in to the compulsion to draw her into his arms. His hand found the curve of her bare backside beneath the fall of his shirt, and he reveled in the way his caress fractured her breath.

Let her go, the infernal voice inside him whispered. It was more of a distant howl, like wolves warning of the perils that stalked him if he continued to linger with her.

But she was fragrant and soft and shorter without her heels. She sent him a smoky, womanly smile as she realized he was naked and traced patterns at the base of his spine that tightened his buttocks with pleasure.

Her expression grew somber. Vulnerable. "Thank you for this. I haven't been with anyone in a long time. I needed to know I could be intimate with a man and not lose everything."

Tension invaded his limbs. Not jealousy or possessiveness, but a primitive protectiveness that tasted similar. His arms unconsciously tightened, wanting to hold on to her because he understood from her remark that she was afraid of being caged again.

She was reminding him this couldn't be anything more than this one day.

He knew it as well as she did, but he moved his hand into her hair and gently dragged her head back, mostly to see if she'd allow it. They'd grown damned familiar in the last couple of hours, and he wanted that small show of trust from her.

Her lips parted in shock while lust hazed her gaze.

A self-deprecating smile tugged at the corners of his mouth. "I should hate myself for enjoying this as much as I do." Her capitulation. The surge of virility it gave him that she allowed him to dominate her this way. He was an animal, just the same as everyone else. He had never wanted to admit that. "Sex was *his* thing. It's hard for me to give in to desire without thinking there's something wrong with me when I do." He had never told that to anyone. He'd barely articulated it to himself. "It's probably best that today is all we have." Otherwise, they might destroy one another.

With absolute gravity, she said, "There is nothing wrong with the way you make love."

They should be exchanging playful banter, preparing for a lighthearted parting. Instead, he kissed her, hard. He wanted to imprint himself on her.

The wolves were continuing to howl, but he let himself absorb the fullness of the moment. The way her nails dug into his scalp as she pressed him to kiss her more deeply, the way her tongue greeted his own… This was all they had. This moment. This kiss.

That's all it should have been. But as the fine hair on her mound tantalized his erection and her toes caressed the top of his foot, his heart pounded hard enough to crack his sternum. "Once more?" he asked through his teeth.

She was as powerless to this force as he was and didn't bother trying to hide it. "Once more," she breathed.

With a savage smile, he pressed her toward the doors. "Get back in my bed then."

Amy woke in the early morning, naked and alone in her bed in the guest suite. She stretched and let out a sigh that was both enjoyment of the luxurious thread count and a half moan as her sore muscles twinged. She was glowing with the lingering sensuality of their lovemaking, but beneath it was despondency.

Once had not been enough, even when it turned into an afternoon and evening.

Yesterday was all they would have, though. One golden memory. She worked for Luca. She had an assignment to complete, one she had neglected because they'd been so wrapped up in each other. She'd stolen from his room near midnight like Cinderella, shoes in hand, jacket held in front of her to hide her broken fly.

A footman had escorted her, but she trusted he wouldn't say a word.

She was starving and desperate for coffee, so she rose to find the French press in the kitchen. There was cheese, fresh berries and yogurt in the refrigerator, too. Perfect.

She set them out and started the kettle, then went in search of her phone. It was still in her jacket pocket from last night, still set on Do Not Disturb from when she'd joined Luca for lunch. They'd skipped dinner, which was why she was ready to gnaw her own arm.

Still yawning, she touched her thumb to unlock her phone and it flashed to life with notifications. She had several alerts set for her own name since she was often attached to press releases for clients, but this wasn't a press release.

It was about her client. And *her*.

The photos showed her and Luca with the sunset behind them, and each headline slanted them into a different, damning light.

Like Father, Like Son! one headline blared.

The king of Vallia continues a tradition of depravity by seducing his new hire, socialite Amy Miller of London Connection, who caused a stir in the late queen's foundation with her publicity campaign for an upcoming gala…

Victim or Villain? the next asked while the photo's angle revealed her seductive profile and Luca's riveted expression.

The Golden Prince is dragged into the gutter by a gold digger…

Crown Jewels on Display! screamed the most tawdry headline.

They'd blurred the photo, but she knew he'd been naked and fully aroused.

"Oh, Luca," she whispered.

How had something so perfect and unsullied become…this?

As her unblinking eyes grew hot, Amy sank onto the sofa, crushed by the magnitude of this development. Her stomach churned while her brain exploded with the infinite agonies that were about to befall her—the sticks and stones and betrayals and blame.

Her life would disintegrate. Again.

And, just like last time, she had no one to blame but herself.

CHAPTER SEVEN

"Photos were published overnight, *signor*. They are… unfortunate."

"Of *who*?" It was a testament to how thoroughly Amy had numbed his brain that he didn't compute immediately that it was, of course, about the two of them.

Guillermo thrust a tablet under his nose.

Luca's head nearly exploded. The foulest language he'd ever uttered came out of his throat. "Where the *hell* was security?"

"They went up to the castle as soon as they realized they had a stray hiker, but he had already departed."

The guards wouldn't have sensed any urgency. Despite the regulations against visiting the ruins without a guide, the odd tourist still made their way up there, usually photographing the silhouette of the palace against the sunset. Since the lighting was so poor at that time of day, and all the private rooms faced the sea, the chance of compromising a royal family member was low. The paparazzi who'd made the trek had never struck pay dirt because even Luca's father hadn't been stupid enough to stand naked on the *one* visible corner of the terrace.

"We presume it was taken by an amateur," Guillermo continued stiffly. "Given the photo's quality and the fact it was initially posted to a private account. The images have since been reposted by the tabloids with... As you can see."

Unspeakable headlines.

Golden Prince: Feet of Clay, Rod of Steel?

At least they'd blurred his erection, but they'd set his image beside a grainy one of his father in a miniscule swimsuit.

King of Vallia Inherits the Horny Crown

When he saw *Another Molesting Monarch*, he thought he might throw up.

"The PR team is discussing damage control. I've made arrangements for Ms. Miller to return to London."

Luca barely heard him. For his entire life, he had kept to the straight and narrow and the *one time* he had stepped out of line, he was caught and being compared to his father in the most abhorrent way—

Wait. His heart clunked its gears, shifting from reflexive shame and fury to a glimmer of possibility. This was bad. But was it bad *enough*?

This wasn't the scandal he'd wanted. Amy was being derided as badly as he was, but his heart lurched into a gallop as he suddenly spotted the finish line after a marathon that had gone on for two decades.

"She'll be mobbed in London," Luca said, his mind racing. "She doesn't go anywhere until I've spoken to her. PR doesn't take steps without my input."

Guillermo's mouth tightened, but he moved to the door to relay that instruction.

Luca drummed his fingers on his desk. This was far messier and more degrading than he'd wanted it to be, but he would owe London Connection an efficiency bonus if it worked.

It had to work. He would *make* it work.

"Has my sister been informed?"

"A secure line has been established." Guillermo nodded at the landline on Luca's desk. "The Privy Council is divided on how to react." He looked like he'd swallowed a fish hook. "Some are alarmed and suggesting a review of the line of succession. I did try to warn you, *signor.* I *strongly* suggest Ms. Miller be returned to London—"

"I'll speak to my sister." With a jerk of his head, Luca dismissed him.

"I can't believe you did that," Sofia said. There was no ring of outrage or remnants of the secondhand embarrassment they'd both suffered after their father's various exploits. No, there was a far deeper note of stunned comprehension in her tone.

Luca bit back trying to explain it wasn't how he'd meant for this to happen. It was worse and he was genuinely embarrassed, but this was their chance. They had to run with it.

Also, focusing on his goal allowed him to sidestep dealing with the fact he was now the poster boy of depravity.

"You have no choice but to take this to the nanny panel," he said gravely, using their childhood reference to the ring of advisers, now the Privy Council, which kept such a tight leash on both of them. The same ones who had insisted Luca take the throne despite Sofia being entitled to it by birth.

"My travel is already being arranged. I'll meet with them the minute I'm home. I've drafted a statement that I'll release the minute we hang up." She paused, then asked with soft urgency, "Are you *sure*, Luca? Because I'm taking a very assertive stance on this. I don't want to undermine you."

"Sofia. Be the ruler you *are*. It's what is best for Vallia. Don't worry about me."

"Impossible. You're my one and only brother." She took a steadying breath. He thought she might be choking up with emotion, but she was well practiced in keeping a cool head. She cleared her throat. Her voice was level as she continued. "I have questions that can wait, but I plan to make the case for you to stay on as my heir provided you're willing to express your sincere regret and assurance that nothing like this will ever happen again?"

Which part? Being caught naked with a woman? Trysting with an employee? Or making love to Amy in particular?

Some nascent emotion, a grasping sense of opportunity, rose in him, but he firmly quashed it before it could become a clear desire. An *intention*.

Their "just once" might have turned into three times, but their connection was exposed to the entire world, and it was completely inappropriate. *He* didn't want to be labeled the sort of man who took advantage of women in his employ.

"You have my word," he said, feeling a tear inside him as he made the vow.

"*Grazie*. I'll see you soon. *Ti amo*," Sofia said.

"I love you, too." Luca hung up and a cool chill washed over him, like damp air exhaled from a dark cave. It was done.

* * *

Amy hadn't stopped shaking, even after a hot shower and too many cups of scalding coffee. The fact that she couldn't seem to leave this room, let alone this palace or this country, didn't help at all.

"I'll pay for the taxi myself," she beseeched the maid, Fabiana.

"It's not my place to call one, *signorina*." Fabiana set out ravioli tossed with gleaming cherry tomatoes and pesto. It looked as scrumptious as the fluffy omelet Amy had ignored midmorning, the focaccia she'd snubbed at lunch and the afternoon tea of crustless sandwiches and pastries she'd disregarded a few hours ago.

There was only room in her stomach for nausea. Her whole world was imploding, and she couldn't even reach out to the best friends who had got her through a similar crisis in the past. Her Wi-Fi connection had been cut off while she'd still been reeling in shock.

Then an ultra-calm middle-aged woman had appeared and identified herself as the senior Human Resources manager for the palace. She was genuinely concerned and had urged Amy to "be honest" if her night with Luca had been coerced in any way.

Amy had insisted it was consensual, but she now wondered if she'd strengthened Luca's position and hindered her own.

She was cold all over, sickened that she'd let this happen and angry with herself because she knew better. She had been fully aware of the potential dangers in sleeping with him, and she had gone ahead and put herself in this awful position anyway.

"My instructions are to ensure you're as comfortable

as possible," Fabiana was saying. "Is there anything else I can bring you?"

"Hiking boots," Amy muttered peevishly. She had already asked a million times to speak to Luca. She'd been assured he would see her as soon as he was available.

Fabiana dropped her gaze to the bedroom slippers Amy was wearing with yellow pajama pants and a silk T-shirt. "I wouldn't recommend trying to leave on foot. Paparazzi are stalking the perimeter. Security is very tight at the moment."

Amy hugged the raw silk shawl she'd found in the closet and wrapped around her shoulders. "Restore my Wi-Fi." It wasn't the first time she'd asked for that, either.

"I've passed along your request. I'll mention it again." Fabiana gave her yet another pained smile and hurried out.

Amy was so frustrated, she stomped out the doors of her lounge to the garden patio.

A security guard materialized from the shrubbery. He'd been there all day and once again held up a staying hand. "I'm sorry—"

She whirled back inside.

She needed to get back to London. She needed to know exactly how bad this was. How could she control the damage to London Connection if she was cut off like this?

She ached to talk to Bea and Clare. What must they be thinking of her? She'd told them she was dropping everything for a big fish client with a substantial budget and an "unusual request." Would they question her tactics in getting Luca's business? They had stood by her last time, but they would be fully entitled to skepticism of her motives, especially since her actions were jeopardizing their livelihood along with her own.

Amy's mother was likely having fits, too. Even without a call or text, Amy knew what Deborah Miller was thinking. *Again, Amy? Again?*

She felt so helpless! Crisis management was her bread and butter. She ought to be able to *do* something. As she paced off her tension, she took some comfort in methodically thinking through her response.

In any emergency, there were three potential threats to consider. The first was physical safety. This wasn't a chemical spill. Innocent bystanders weren't being harmed. She forced herself to release a cleansing breath and absorb that tiny blessing.

The second threat was financial loss. She sobered as she accepted that she would take a hard hit from this. There was no way she was taking Luca's money now. That meant all of the expenses for this trip along with the travel home were hers. She had reassigned several of her contracts to other agents at London Connection so she had lost a substantial amount of income. There would be costs to salvaging London Connection's reputation and, since this was her mistake, she would bear that, as well.

How would she pay for it all?

Here was where panic edged in each time she went through this exercise. She was standing hip deep in the third type of threat. Her credibility was in tatters.

She looked like a woman who slept her way into contracts and had no means to spin that impression. In fact, somewhere in this palace, a team of professionals exactly like her was deciding how to rescue Luca from this crisis, and Amy knew exactly the approaches they were taking—deflect the attacks on him. Blame her. Claim she had seduced him. Say she had set him up for that photo to raise the profile of London Connection.

Heck, the headlines she'd glimpsed before losing her connection had already been suggesting she'd had something to gain. They only had to build on what was already there.

What if they found out she had a history of inappropriate relationships?

Her stomach wrenched so violently, she folded her arms across it, moaning and nearly doubling over.

Luca wouldn't hang her out to dry like that. Would he?

Of course, he would. The teacher, Avery Mason, had. The headmistress and her own parents had.

In a fit of near hysteria, she barged out of her suite to the hall.

She surprised the guard so badly, he took on a posture of attack, making her stumble back into her doorway, heart pounding.

She was so light-headed, she had to cling to the doorjamb. She sounded like a harridan when she blurted, "Tell the king I'll set my room on fire if he doesn't speak to me in the next ten minutes. Punch me unconscious or call the fire brigade because I *will* do it."

The guard caught the door before she could slam it in his face. He spoke Italian into his wrist. After the briefest of pauses, he nodded. "Come with me."

Now she'd done it. He was taking her to a padded cell. Or the dungeon.

Yes, that kind of dungeon.

She sniffed back a semihysterical laugh-sob.

He escorted her through halls that were familiar. She

was being taken to Luca's office. The scene of their first criminal kiss. And their second.

People filed out as she arrived, but she didn't make eye contact. She stared at the floor until she was told to go in. She went only as far as she had to for the door to close behind her.

"Will you introduce us, Luca?" a woman asked.

Amy snapped her head up to see only Luca and his sister were in the room.

Luca was as crisp and urbane as ever in a smart suit and tie, freshly shaved with only a hint of fatigue around his eyes to suggest he'd had a long day. His gaze sharpened on her, but Amy was distracted by his twin.

Sofia Albizzi was a feminine version of Luca, almost as tall, also athletically lean, but with willowy curves and a softer expression. Where the energy that radiated off Luca was dynamic and energizing, Sofia's was equally commanding but with a settle-down-children quality. She wore a pantsuit in a similar dark blue as Luca's suit. Her hair was in a chignon, and she offered a calm, welcoming smile.

Amy must look like a petitioning peasant, slouched in her shawl and slippers, hair falling out of its clip and no makeup to hide her distress. She felt *awful* coming up against this double barrel of effortless perfection. She wanted to turn and walk back out again, but Luca straightened off the edge of his desk.

"Your Highness, this is Amy Miller. Amy, my sister Sofia, the queen of Vallia."

"Queen?" Amy distantly wondered if she was supposed to curtsy.

Sofia flicked a glance at Luca that could only be described as sibling telepathy.

"My new title is confidential," Sofia said. "Only finalized within the last hour. There will be a press release in the morning. I hope I can trust you to keep this information to yourself until then?"

Amy choked on disbelief. "Who could I tell? You've cut off my online access."

"We did do that," Sofia acknowledged. "The prince said you understand the importance of limiting communication during a crisis, so we can project a clear and unified message."

Prince. He'd been dethroned. *By her.* She was definitely going to faint. Amy blinked rapidly, trying to keep her vision from fading as she looked between the two.

Sofia came toward her, regal and ridiculously attractive while exuding that consoling energy. "I appreciate how distressed you must be, Amy. It's been a trying day for all of us, but I hope you'll allow us to show you the best of our hospitality for a little longer? And not frighten staff with threats of setting the palace on fire?"

Emotion gathered in Amy's eyes, beleaguered humor and frustration and something that closed her throat because she suddenly had the horrid feeling she had disappointed Sofia. Not the way she consistently disappointed her mother. She wasn't being held to impossible, superficial standards. No, Sofia simply projected a confidence that Amy was better than someone who made wild threats. *Let's all do better,* she seemed to say.

Luca was right. She was an ideal ruler.

But there was no comfort in being the instrument that had installed her on the throne, not when it had cost her the life she'd worked so hard to build.

"I want to go h-home." She was at the end of her thin, frayed rope.

"Our people will arrange that soon," Sofia began, but Luca came forward with purpose.

"I'll walk you to your room."

Sofia shot him a look, but Luca avoided her questioning gaze and held the door for Amy.

From the moment the photos had emerged, he had been buried in meetings, phone calls and demands for his attention. He felt as though he'd gone twelve rounds, taking hits from every angle.

It was *not* in his nature to throw a fight. Keeping his mouth shut while his sister called for an HR investigation had been particularly humiliating. To protect the integrity of that report, he hadn't spoken to Amy.

While they'd awaited a determination on whether Amy had been harassed by Luca, other factions had proposed throwing her to the wolves of public opinion to save Luca's reputation. Several voices on the council had tried to cast him as the victim of a scheming woman, eager to make excuses for Luca's lapse in judgment so they could maintain the status quo.

Sofia's supporters had been equally quick to question what kind of queen Amy would make, forcing Luca to declare his intentions toward her.

"We seized a moment, that's all." He hated to reduce her to a one-night stand, but it was what they had agreed and it was better for her to be seen as collateral damage, not a contributor.

"The media storm will rage forever unless we take decisive action," Sofia had pressed. "No matter how we attempt to explain it away, the photos will be reposted every time the king of Vallia is mentioned."

"I've become synonymous with our father," Luca said grimly, hating that it was true, hating that this was the only way, but he threw himself on the proverbial sword. "I won't have his transgressions pinned on me." On that he wouldn't budge. "Vallia's queens have always been bastions of dignity and honor. If I step aside, that's what you'll have again."

That had been the turning point. Discussions had moved from if to how.

Luca had spared a thought to ensure Amy's comfort, but he hadn't allowed memories of last night to creep in. It would have destroyed his concentration.

That fog of desire was making him light-headed now, but he continued to fight it. He had sworn his misstep wouldn't be repeated. His libido might have other desires, but tomorrow his sister would take the crown and Luca would once again become the Golden Prince, honorable to a fault.

Nevertheless, he owed Amy an explanation for how things had played out today.

"It's standard protocol to shut down all the open networks and allow only secure messaging when incidents occur," he told her as they walked. "And I wanted to shield you from the worst of what's happening online."

"I understand." She nodded jerkily, looking like a ghost.

A pocket of gravel formed in the pit of his gut, a heaviness of conscience he wasn't familiar with because he so rarely made mistakes.

"I assumed you would have an idea what was going on behind the scenes."

"I did." She was nothing but eyes and cheekbones and white lips, her profile shell-shocked.

It hit him that she did know—all too well. He wanted to stop and touch her. Draw her into his arms. Kiss her and swear he wasn't pinning the blame on her.

He settled for following her into her suite.

"I couldn't bring you into the discussions today. I realize, given our contract, that you expected to be consulted, but I had to sideline you. It was best to let the process play out through normal channels."

"You think I'm upset because I feel 'sidelined'? I wish I was a footnote! Why didn't you tell me we were exposed out there? Did you *plan* this?"

"Of course not!" He hadn't given thought to anything but *her* last night. Did she think he would walk outside naked for anyone else? He was still uncomfortable with how immersed he'd been in their mutual desire. "It was a fluke. For God's sake, Amy. How could I plan it?"

"A fluke?" she scoffed. "You just happened to pick *me* to come here and take on the task of *ruining* you. You just happened to kiss me and take me to your room—" She cut herself off, shielding her eyes in what could only be described as shame.

The rocks in his belly began to churn.

"When I heard the door, I thought you were leaving." He started forward, drawn by her distress. "I didn't know you were going outside. I didn't *take* you out there."

As soon as his feet came into her line of sight, she brought up her head and stumbled back, keeping a distance between them.

That retreat, coupled with the trepidation in her face, was like a knee to the groin.

He held very still, holding off a pain that he barely understood. It was new, but so acute he actually tasted bile in the back of his throat.

"I'm not going to touch you if you don't want me to." He opened his hands in a gesture of peace.

"I don't want you to scramble my head again," she muttered, arms crossed and brow flexing with anguish. "This wasn't supposed to happen, Luca. No one was supposed to know about us. You made me think that's what you wanted."

"It was." But affirming it made his mouth burn. "Look, I know this wasn't the way we planned it, but once the photographs were out there, I had to seize the opportunity. This is what I hired you to do."

"You did *not* hire me to sleep with you. I won't take money for it," she said jaggedly.

He was insulted by her implication. "I hired you to ruin me. You have."

She gasped if he'd struck her. Her hurt and distress were so clear, his arms twitched again to reach for her.

"I honestly thought you would understand this was the incident I needed," he said. "I'm not clear why you're so upset."

"I was supposed to find someone who *wanted* the attention. Someone prepared for it." She kept pulling at her shawl until it was so tight around her, the points of her shoulders and elbows looked as though they would poke holes in the raw silk. "I was supposed to control the message to minimize the damage. It wasn't going to be ugly exposure where a woman's reputation is torn to shreds."

When her gaze flashed to his, there was such agony in the green depths, his heart stalled.

"My team won't crucify you," he swore, and started to take a step forward, but checked himself. "I won't allow it. I'm taking responsibility. This was my slipup—"

"I slept with a client, Luca!" Her arm flung out and the shawl fell off her shoulder. "I compromised him so badly I caused a *king* to be *dethroned*. It really doesn't matter what you or your team say. People will come to their own conclusions."

He briefly glimpsed her tattoo before she shrugged the shawl back into place.

She was shaking so hard, he started to reach for her again and she stumbled back another step.

"I won't touch you." He couldn't help that his voice was clipped with impatience. "But I'm worried about you. Sit down. Have you eaten? I told them to make sure you had food."

"I'm not a dog!" she cried, eyes wild. "You don't get to hire someone to check if I have food and water and call it good. Although, at least I would have got a proper walk today instead of being held like a prisoner."

"That—" He squeezed the back of his neck. "I realize you're angry, but stop saying such ridiculous things."

"Oh! Am I overreacting?" She shot him a look that threatened to tear his head from his shoulders. "You know nothing about what I'm going through. *Nothing.*"

"So explain it to me," he snapped back. "Because I don't see this as the disaster that you do. You said it yourself. People love to clutch their pearls over a sexy escapade. I'm the one who's naked in that photo, not you! Are you upset that *we* happened?" It took everything in him to ask that. It wasn't an accusation, he really needed to know, but he braced himself. "Are you feeling as if I took advantage of you? Like you couldn't say no last night?"

HR had interviewed her. She'd reported that Amy had confirmed their involvement was consensual. Even so, Amy's chin crinkled. Her eyes welled.

His heart lurched and he couldn't breathe.

"I should have said no." Her shoulders sagged. "I knew it was a mistake and I want to take it back." She buried her face in her hands. "So badly."

That sent a streak of injury through him because the thing that unnerved him most was how little he *didn't* regret sleeping with her.

As the dominoes had fallen today, he'd disliked himself for playing manipulative palace politics the way his father had. He'd met the disillusioned gazes of mentors and advisers and understood he'd fallen miles in their estimation. He loathed feeling fallible.

He had suffered through all of that to correct a thirty-one-year-old wrong and, unpleasant as proceedings had all been, at least he had the extraordinary memory of *her* to offset it.

Even now, as he saw how devastated she was over their exposure, he couldn't make himself say he was sorry. Did she remember how much pleasure they'd given each other?

He pushed his hands into his pockets so he wouldn't try to remind her.

"The announcements will be made tomorrow. I'll step down, and Sofia will be recognized as the rightful ruler. My coronation ceremony was scheduled to happen before our parliament sits in the autumn. It will be revised for her, but she's taking control immediately.

Let the dust settle on some of this before you assume you'll take the fall for it."

She snorted, despondent, and turned her back on him. She looked like a tree that had been stripped bare. She was a hollow trunk swaying in the dying winds of a storm.

Was she hiding tears?

His guts fell into his shoes and his heart was upside down in his chest. He wanted to take her in his arms, hold her and warm her and swear this would be okay. *Come to my room.* He kept the words in his throat, but they formed a knot that locked up his lungs so his whole torso ached.

"When can I go back online? Bea and Clare are probably frantic." Her voice was a broken husk.

"My people have provided them with a statement."

That had her whirling around to face him, eyes shooting fires of disbelief that were quickly soaked by her welling tears. "You don't speak for me, Luca. You don't get to tell your side without giving me a chance to tell mine!"

"It's only a standard 'not enough information to comment—'"

No use. She disappeared into the bedroom and slammed the door on him.

CHAPTER EIGHT

AMY TOSSED AND TURNED and finally quit fighting her tears. When she let go, she cried until her eyes were swollen and scratchy, then rose and set a cool, wet cloth over them. Her stomach panged so hard with hunger, she dug up cold leftovers the maid had left in the fridge.

It was almost two in the morning. She didn't know if the guard was still in the garden and didn't check. Her one brief thought about trying to run away was stymied by exhaustion.

She crawled back into bed and didn't wake until mid-morning when her phone came alive with alerts and notifications. Her internet access had been restored.

Tempted as she was to post *I'm being held against my will*, she was quickly caught up in reading all the news updates, emails and texts along with listening to her voice mail.

She brought her knees up to her chest, cringing as her mother's message began with an appalled "For God's sake, Amy."

Beyond the bedroom door, she heard the maid enter the suite, but kept listening to her mother harangue her for making international headlines "behaving like a trollop."

It wasn't the maid. Her heart lurched as Luca walked into the bedroom with a tray. He was creaseless and stern, emanating the scent of a fresh shower and shave.

Amy was nestled in the pillows she'd piled against the headboard, blankets gathered around her. She clicked off her phone mid maternal diatribe and dropped the device.

"You really have been demoted, haven't you?"

He stilled as he absorbed the remark, then gave her a nod of appreciation. "Nice to have you back. I was worried. Especially when I was told you didn't eat a single bite yesterday. That changes now." He touched something on the tray and legs came down with a snick.

"Your spies don't know what I do when no one is around." She was dying for coffee, though, so she straightened her legs, allowing him to set the tray across her lap.

"They're spies, Amy. Of course, they do." He sat down next to her knees and poured coffee from the carafe into the two cups on the tray.

"Are you really having me watched?" She scowled toward the ceiling corners in search of hidden cameras.

"No." His mouth twitched. "But I'd be lying if I didn't admit to concern over how you might be handling the restoration of your internet connection. You were very angry last night." He sipped his coffee. "Anything we should know about?"

She followed his gaze to her phone, facedown and turned to silent, but vibrating with incoming messages.

"I've been reading, not responding. My social feeds are on fire. In times like this, you find out very quickly who your real friends are." A handful of clients were ready to die on a hill defending her. Others were asking about terminating their contracts. "Bea and Clare have asked me to call when I can. They won't judge, but I don't know what to tell them. The rest of the office is used to being left in the dark with certain clients or actions we take on their behalf. They're reaching out with thoughts and prayers, but I can tell they're dying of curiosity, wondering if this is a stunt or if I'm really this stupid." Her hand shook as she dolloped cream into her coffee. "Our competitors are reveling in my hypocrisy, of course, crossing professional lines when I'm usually defending victims of such things. They'll dine on this forever, using it to tarnish London Connection's integrity and my competence."

"London Connection won't be impacted." Luca's expression darkened. "I've set up the transfer. That will keep things afloat until you're able to right the ship."

"I told you not to pay me." She clattered her cup back into the saucer, spilling more coffee than she'd tasted. "I won't accept it. Taking money for this makes me feel cheap and dirty and stupid. Don't make me refuse it again, Luca."

He set his own cup down with a firm clink while he spat out a string of curses and rose to pace restlessly. "You did what I hired you to do," he reminded Amy as he rounded on her. "I want to compensate you."

"I ruined *myself.* I ruined my friends' livelihood."

"Quit being so hard on yourself."

"Quit being so obtuse! Just because I don't run a country doesn't mean my actions don't have consequences." She snatched up her phone and tapped to play her mother's message from the beginning, increasing the volume so Luca got the full benefit of her mother's appalled disgust.

"For God's sake, Amy. You've really done it this time, behaving like the worst sort of trollop. Neville is putting me on a plane back to London. He doesn't want to be associated with me. I've had your father on the phone, too. How can I tell him you're reliable enough to take control of your trust when you do things like this? You really never learn, do you?"

Amy clicked it off so they didn't have to hear the rest.

"I thought you were already disinherited."

"My father has control of a trust fund that was set up for me when I was born. I was supposed to start receiving income from it ten years ago, but I was expelled from school." She didn't tell him why. "They decided I wasn't responsible enough. I was supposed to assume full control at twenty-five, but my career promoting high-society parties online wasn't deemed serious enough. Daddy moved the date to my thirtieth birthday, eighteen months from now. Apparently, that's now off, as well." She threw her phone back into the blankets.

Luca swore again, this time with less heat, more remorse.

"I don't care." It was mostly true. "I've learned to live without their financial support. But when I took your contract, I had a fantasy of finally telling them to shove it. I wanted to prove I'd made my fortune my own way, which was pure pride on my part. Looks like I've got more time to make that dream come true. Problem solved," she said with facetious cheer while bitterness and failure swirled through her chest.

Why was life such a game of chutes and ladders? Why did she always hit the long slide back to zero?

"I had no idea." He came back to sit on the bed.

"Why would you?" She wrapped her cold hands around the hot cup of coffee, ignoring that it was wet down one side. She couldn't help fearing her earlier mistake with Avery Mason would emerge. It had been covered up, and all the key players had more reason to hide it than expose it, but it was still there, lurking like a venomous snake in the grass.

His firm hand gripped her calf through the blankets. "You have to let me help you, Amy."

"Luca." She jerked her leg away. "If you offer me that money one more time, you're going to get a cup of hot coffee in the face. It will turn into a whole thing with your bodyguards, and I'll wind up Tasered and rotting in jail. Not the best path to saving my reputation so leave it alone."

He didn't back off one iota. He found her leg again and gave it a squeeze. "Are you really prone to arson and violence?"

"No," she admitted dourly. "But after my own parents left me fending for myself at eighteen, I've become hideously independent. The worst thing you could have done yesterday was leave me alone like this, helpless to solve my problem."

"Because it's not your problem," he insisted. "That's why I didn't ask you to solve it." He shifted so he was looking at the wall, elbows on his knees, hands linked between them. He sighed. "I didn't see how much damage this would do to you. I want to help you fix it, Amy. Tell me what I can do."

She sank heavily into the pillows. "If I had a clue how to fix it, I would have busted out of here and done it already."

"Let me talk to your parents. I'll take responsibility, patch things up."

"Pass. There's too much water under the bridge there…" Her nose stung with old tears she refused to shed. "And I don't want someone to talk them into forgiving me. I want them to want to help me because they love me." She was embarrassed that they didn't and turned her mind from dwelling on that old anguish since it would never be resolved. "I'm more worried about London Connection. I might have to resign."

"You're not losing your career because you did your job," he said forcefully.

"No one can know that, though, can they? To the outside world, I got involved with a client and caused him to lose *his* job. No one is going to hire the sordid one-night stand who caused a king to be overthrown. If I resign, London Connection can at least say they cleaned house in the same way that Vallia is dumping you."

"That's rubbish." He rose again, all his virile energy crackling around him like a halo. "You're not a martyr and you're not a tramp. You're not something that needs to be swept under a rug or out a door. The answer is obvious."

"A tell-all to the highest bidder?" she suggested with a bat of her lashes.

"Pass," he said with flat irony. "No. Once Sofia is clearly established as Vallia's queen, you and I will take control of our narrative, as you like to say. We'll reframe our affair as a more serious relationship."

"You want to keep sleeping together?" Shock echoed within her strained words.

He wanted that so badly, he had to stand on the far

side of the room so he wouldn't crowd her or otherwise pressure her into it. "Appear to, at least. I understand if you'd prefer to keep things professional."

"Because we're so good at *that*." Her chuckle was semihysterical.

He took perverse comfort from the helplessness in her choked laugh. He wasn't the only one who felt this irresistible pull between them.

"I'm just saying, now that I fully grasp how our affair complicates things for you—"

The noise she made drew his glance.

"Do I *not* understand?" He narrowed his eyes, noting the flush that had come into her cheeks, the glow of disgrace in her eyes. "Is there more?"

She bit the corner of her mouth and dropped her gaze. "There are things in my past I only share on a need-to-know basis. Right now, you don't need to know."

She set aside the tray and flung back the blankets. She wore a silk nightgown that rode up her bare legs as she slid her feet to the floor.

"Don't you have a throne to abdicate?" she asked.

He swallowed and forced his gaze upward to the suppressed turmoil in hers.

She was trying to throw him off with a glimpse of her legs and her air of nonchalance.

He couldn't pretend he wasn't falling for the diversion. Sexual awareness instantly throbbed like a drumbeat between them. His feet ambled him closer before he remembered he was trying to give her space.

"I do have a title to renounce," he confirmed, gaze drawn to the way oyster-colored lace coyly pretended to hide her cleavage. It took everything in him to only caress her pale skin with his eyes. "Then I have a gala to attend. *We* do."

"I'm not convinced our continuing to see one another is the best way forward." Her head shake was more of an all-over tremble.

He closed his fists so he wouldn't reach for her. "If you go scurrying home in disgrace, you really will be painted as the scarlet woman who toppled a kingdom. If you stick around and attend the gala where the new queen will speak to you, the whole thing will be reduced to a family squabble between my sister and I. You made arrangements to be here for two weeks, didn't you?"

"Yes, but—"

"You don't have to decide this instant. Let me finish my business, then we'll talk more. Away from the palace," he said. "We'll shop for a gown for the gala. Do you prefer Paris or Milan for evening wear?"

"The Glam Shed," she said haughtily, giving her hair a flick. "I quid pro quo promotion campaigns for red carpet rentals."

"I'll pretend that was a joke and make arrangements for Milan. It's closer than Paris and I have a cottage in Northern Italy. We can talk there about how we'll portray our relationship." For the first time in a very long time, he could be with a woman openly with few distractions. He wanted to take her there right now.

Perhaps she read that urgency in him. She flashed him a nervous look, but there was no fright in the depths of her pretty green eyes. Only a vacillating nibble of her lip and another, slower study of his chest and upper arms.

She was going to be the death of him, teasing him so unconsciously and effortlessly.

"Cottage?" she asked skeptically.

He tilted his head. It was an understatement. "A castle on a private island in one of the more remote lakes. The key word is 'private.' We can let this furor die down before our attendance at the gala stirs it up again."

"Are you sure you want to continue associating with me?" she asked anxiously.

She couldn't be that obtuse.

"I want to do a damned sight more than 'associate.'" He snagged her hand with his own and brought her fingertips to his mouth, dying to taste her from brows to ankles, but he had places to be. And he was trying not to take when she was vacillating and vulnerable.

She caught her breath and looked at him with such defenseless yearning, he gave in and swooped his free hand behind her waist to draw her close.

She suddenly balked with a press of her palm to his chest. "I haven't brushed my teeth."

"Then I'll kiss you here." He set his open mouth against her throat, enjoying the gasp she released and the all-over shiver that chased down her body. By the time he'd found the hollow beneath her ear, she was melting into him with another soft cry.

The slippery silk she wore was warm with the heat of her body as he slid his hands to her lower back and drew her closer, inhaling the scent of vanilla and almonds from her hair.

"Luca." She nuzzled his ear and nipped at his earlobe.

His scalp tightened and a sharp pull in his groin threatened to empty his head of everything except the rumpled bed behind this wickedly tempting woman. One quick tumble to hold him. That's all he wanted.

"Give me a few hours," he groaned, lifting his head, but running his touch to her delectable bottom, tracing the curve and crease through the silk as he drew her into the stiffness her response had provoked. "We'll pick this up later."

She searched his gaze, still conflicted.

He kissed her, quickly and thoroughly, tasting coffee as he grazed her tongue with his.

"Eat something," he ordered, then released her and adjusted himself before he left to end his brief reign.

Amy ate. Then she took her time with a long bath and a quiet hour of self-care where she painted her toenails and plucked her brows and moisturized every inch of her skin. She ignored her phone and let the sickening feeling of having her privacy invaded recede while she considered what to tell her best friends.

She was always honest with Bea and Clare, but aside from emailing a promise to call as soon as she could, Amy hadn't found the right way to explain what had happened between her and Luca.

They would know they were being put off, but Amy would touch base with them as soon as she decided whether she would agree to Luca's suggestion.

He had a point that appearing to continue their affair would soften the photo from being a lurid glimpse at a king's downfall to a private moment between a loving couple, but they weren't a loving couple. They were barely a romantic couple, having only met two days ago.

It shocked her to realize that. They'd shared some very personal details with one another. She'd never talked about her expulsion or her parents' rejection of her so candidly. For his part, Luca had entrusted her with the secret of his father's death. On a physical level, they had opened themselves unreservedly.

That meant they had the seeds of a close relationship, didn't it?

Oh, Amy, she chided herself. She had made the mistake of believing physical infatuation meant genuine caring once before.

Her stomach curdled. She hadn't shared *that* part of her story with Luca, had she?

Her affair with Avery Mason wouldn't come out, would it? Aside from Bea and Clare, who would never betray her, the story had never been confirmed. If any of the catty girls from back then had wanted to take Amy down by repeating that morsel of vague gossip, they would have done it by now. They'd had plenty of opportunities while Amy had been posting photos of herself with movie stars and fashion designers. Even if someone did decide to bring it up, they had no proof. It would be a very watery accusation that would quickly evaporate.

Avery could say something, obviously, as could his mother, but Amy didn't believe either would. There was no value in destroying their own reputations, and Amy's parents were equally determined to keep it a private matter. Her mother much preferred to use it as salt in Amy's wounds, dropping it as an aside to blame Amy for her own tribulations like being dumped by her latest paramour.

That would let up once she realized Amy was still seeing Luca, of course.

There was a bonus! Amy paused the hair dryer to drink in a fantasy of her mother groveling for an invitation to meet Amy's beau, once she believed her daughter had a real future with royalty.

Which she didn't. Amy's soaring heart took a nose-dive. Even if they slept together again, their relationship was still about optics. Nothing more.

She ignored the streak of loss that cut through her chest and returned to yanking the brush through her hair as she dried it, ruthlessly scraping the bristles across her scalp as an exercise in staying real.

Luca wasn't a sociopathic lothario like Avery, but he was a man. The wires between heart and hard-on weren't directly connected. No matter what she did, she had to protect her own heart so it might be better if she and Luca only pretended to be involved.

She didn't want to pretend, she acknowledged with a twist of remorse wrapped in wicked anticipation. Despite the fact that sleeping with him had pulled the rug out from under her hard enough to topple her entire life, she wanted to make love with him again. She wanted to run her hands across his flexing back, feel his lips against her skin. Play her tongue against his and lose herself to the grind of his hips—

Whew! Had the AC cut out? She fanned her cheeks and opened the door to let the humidity out of the bathroom.

Fabiana was packing the clothing that didn't belong to her into a suitcase that was also not hers. "The prince will be ready to travel shortly. He asks that you join him at the helipad in one hour? I've set out your lunch."

A few hours later, Amy was in Milan's fashion district, enjoying a crisp white wine with bruschetta. Luca was beside her, speaking Italian into his phone.

"That looks like it would suit you," he said as he ended his call and pocketed his phone. He nodded at the model on the catwalk.

"I like the train, but I prefer the neckline on the blue." She pointed at the model posing toward the back. "The gala isn't black tie. Could I wear something like that fade?"

"Wear whatever you want," Luca assured her, picking up her hand and touching his lips to her knuckles. "I'm indulging the woman who has captured my heart. I want the world to know it."

Her own heart flipped and twittered like a drunken bird even as she reminded herself it wasn't real. Nevertheless, she leaned in and cut him a sly look that he would recognize as her rebellious streak coming to the fore if he knew her well enough.

"Anything? Because I would love something very avant-garde."

Luca's indulgent nod said, *By all means.* "Control the narrative. Tell them what to talk about."

Amy looked to the designer. "What do you have that says, 'space opera'?"

The woman lit up with excitement and rushed into the back with her models.

Soon Amy was being fitted for a dress that hugged her curves while stiff, saucer-like ruffles gave the impression of a stack of dishes about to fall. The glittering sequins reflected prisms in every direction and a matching hat with a polka dot veil completed the dramatic look.

When she was back in her own clothes, she came upon Luca saying something about Vallia to an attendant. Parcels were being taken to the car.

"That's casual wear for the island," he said. "The rest will be sent to Vallia with the gown for our other events."

"What other events?"

"Cocktail parties. Ribbon cuttings. I'm making an award presentation in Tokyo after the gala."

Then what? There was a small cloud of anxiety chasing her. She had a career to get back to, and she had never aspired to be any man's mistress. She'd cleared a block of time to work with Luca so she still had a few days to consider all her options, but no matter if she only pretended or was really his lover, it wouldn't last.

They left the design house, but word had leaked that they were in Milan. They were chased back to the helicopter, soon landing on a blessedly remote and quiet island.

They disembarked into what could only be described as a fairy-tale setting. A wall of craggy, inhospitable mountains plunged down to the jewel-blue lake. A quaint village sat on the far shoreline. A handful of boats dragged skiers in their wake, keeping their distance.

Luca told her the castle had been built as a monastery in the fifth century. It had a tall, square bell tower in the middle of one outer wall, but the rest was only three stories. The ancient stone walls were covered in moss and ivy. A pebbled pathway led them from the helipad, winding beneath boughs that smelled of Christmas pine and fresh earth and summer vacation.

"No vehicles, just a golf cart for the luggage and groceries by boat," Luca said, pointing into a man-made lagoon surrounded by stone walls as they passed. Two fancy looking speedboats were moored there alongside a utilitarian one that was being unloaded.

They entered through what had once been a scullery room. It was now a very smart if casual entryway with hooks for their jackets and a box bench where they left their shoes.

This was why he called it a cottage, she supposed. It was homey and he exchanged a friendly greeting with the chef as they passed the kitchen, nodding approval for whatever menu was suggested.

"The sun is beginning to set. He asked if we wanted to eat something while we watch it from the terrace or view it from the top of the tower?"

"The tower sounds nice."

He relayed her preference, and they climbed to the belfry where no bell hung.

"I have no plans to ring it, so why replace it?" he said as he led her up a heart-stoppingly narrow spiral of stairs that took them to the roof. "This has been inspected. We're safe," he assured her.

"I forgot my phone," she said with a pat of her pockets. "I want photos!"

She went to the corners of the roof, more awed by the view each direction she looked. She paused to watch where the sun was sinking behind one peak, leaving a glow of gold across the surrounding mountaintops. The air was clean and cool, the height dizzying enough to make her laugh.

"You must have loved coming here as a child. How long has it been in your family?"

"I bought it for myself when it came on the market a few years ago."

"Oh. That's interesting." She glanced at him. "Why?"

"Because it's beautiful and private." His tone said, *Obviously.*

"You didn't buy it to hide your women here?"

"Like a dragon with a damsel? Yes, I've lured you

here and you can't leave until your hair grows long enough to climb down. No, Amy. What women are you even talking about?"

"I don't know. The ones you have affairs with. Discreetly. On private islands." She turned to the view because this was a conversation they had to have, but she didn't know how.

"Actually, this is where I hide from those legions of women, to rest and regain my virility," he said dryly. "I've allowed my sister to stay here, but you're the only person I've brought as my guest, female or otherwise."

"Ever?" She moved to another corner.

"Why is that so surprising? Exactly how many lovers do you think I've had?"

"Enough to get really good at sex," she said over her shoulder, as if she didn't care. She did care. A lot more than she ought to.

"*You're* really good at sex." He came up behind her to trace his fingertips in a line down her back. "Should I ask how many men you've been with?"

"How do you know it's just men?" She swung around and threw back her head in challenge.

He didn't laugh. Or take her seriously.

"You really do have to work harder to shock me," he admonished. "I honestly don't care what you've done or with whom so long as it was consensual and safe enough that I don't have to worry about my own health."

Her heart faltered. She wondered if she could shock him with the deplorable thing she'd done with her teacher, but he set his hands on the wall on either side of her waist, crowding her into the corner. Now all she could see was his mouth, and her thoughts scattered.

"I'm *very* interested in what sort of history you'd *like* to have. With me. What do you want to do, Amy?"

"Nothing kinky," she warned, reflexively touching his chest. "Just normal things."

"Normal?" His smile was wide, but bemused. "Like tennis and jigsaw puzzles?"

"Yes," she said pertly. "And read books to one another. Austen preferably, but I'll allow some Dickens so long as we have a safe word."

"Nicholas Nickleby?" The corners of his mouth deepened. "Tease. Will you sleep in my bed and continue to ruin me for every other woman alive?"

It was flirty nonsense. Banter. But she was incredibly sensitive to words like "ruin."

She swallowed. "I don't want to be your downfall, Luca. I don't want…"

He sobered and brushed a wisp of hair away from her cheek. "What?"

She didn't want to get hurt. Not again.

"I don't want to get confused about what this is." She touched a button on his shirt. "It's just an affair. Right? For a couple of weeks? To, um, take the worst of the poison out of what's going on out there?" She jerked her chin toward the world at large.

He backed off, equally somber. "We barely know each other," he reminded her. "I'm not saying I don't take this seriously, but I can't promise anything permanent. I've never had the luxury of contemplating a future with anyone. Marriage has always been something I would undertake with a woman vetted by a team of palace advisers." His mouth twisted and he dropped his hands to his sides, fully stepping away. "I still have to think that way until Sofia marries and produces our next ruler."

"So you're offering an affair." She hugged herself. "That's fine, but I need to be clear on what to expect since we'll be pretending it's…more."

After a long moment, he gave a jerky nod. "Yes," he agreed. "Just an affair."

And wasn't that romantic.

She looked to where the sun had set and the sky was fading. The glow of excitement inside her had dimmed and dulled, too.

"We should go down while we still have light," she suggested, more to pivot from how bereft she suddenly felt.

He looked as though he wanted to say something, but stifled it and nodded.

He went in front of her, promising to catch her if she missed a foot on the narrow, uneven steps. It was dizzying and nerve-racking, and she clung tightly to the rope that was strung through iron rings mounted to the wall, thinking the whole time, *Don't fall, don't fall*.

But she feared she probably would.

CHAPTER NINE

LUCA WAS RESTLESS and prickly. He blamed the fact he was at a crossroads, having given up the throne, but not yet having found his place in the new order. The work that typically dominated his thoughts now fell to his sister, and the mental vacuum allowed him to dwell on the public's reaction to his fall from grace.

And the woman who had caused it.

They weren't dressing for dinner, but Amy had disappeared to call her business partners, leaving him to nurse a drink and contemplate how completely she seemed to have shut down once he'd pronounced that this was only an affair.

Did she want it to be more? Did he?

He felt as though he'd disappointed her with his answer. Hurt her. That frustrated him. He'd been as honest as possible. Up until that moment, she'd been her bright and funny self. An amusing companion who made him feel alive in ways he had never experienced.

Damn but that was a lot of feelings. He didn't do feelings. They were messy and tended to create the sort of disaster he'd been scrupulously trained to avoid. He'd accomplished what he wanted by giving in to his lust for Amy, but it was time to go back to being his circumspect, disciplined self.

Which meant he shouldn't have a real affair with her, but the mere thought of denying himself when she was willing caused a host of feelings that were more like a swarm of hornets inside him. Which was exactly why he shouldn't indulge—

He swore aloud and set aside his drink as though he could set aside his brooding as easily. Filtering through his texts and emails, he picked up one from an old friend, Emiliano. They had met through their shared interest in emerging tech. Emiliano had since increased his family's fortune by developing tools for facial recognition software.

News bulletin says you're in Milan? I'm at my villa on Lago di Guarda. Join me if you want to escape the fray.

His villa was a comfortable and well-guarded compound.

Luca texted back.

Grazie. We're fine, but I'll be in touch about the solar tiles we discussed last year.

Luca moved on, but Emiliano promptly texted back.

Sounds good. The invitation is open anytime. Tell Amy I said hello.

Just like that, Luca's agitation turned to a ferocious swarm of stinging jealousy.

Jealousy was the most childish of all emotions, but

he was bothered and even more bothered by the fact he was bothered. He was having feelings about his feelings, and it was annoying as hell.

Amy returned wearing a concerned frown.

"Is everything all right?" he made himself ask, trying to overcome his sudden possessiveness.

"Clare's overseas and Bea has gone off with a client," she said with a perplexed shake of her head. "When we talked her into joining us, it was purely for legal support, but she got roped into working directly with Ares Lykaios. You would have seen his name on our website. He's our biggest client. We owe him for putting us on the map."

"I know who he is." And there was no reason Luca should feel so threatened that he would ask, "Would you rather be in her place right now?" He hated himself for it.

"A little. Bea must be out of her depth. He's tough and assertive, and Bea's shy by nature. It's always been our dynamic that she helps me work through my internal rubbish and I play her wingman in the external world. She might not know how to handle Ares."

"But you do?"

Her air of distraction evaporated and she narrowed her attention onto him. "He's a client whose professional needs dovetail with the services I offer. Why? What are you suggesting?"

"Nothing," he muttered, disgusted with himself.

"You meant something," she accused. "I don't have personal relationships with clients, Luca. That's why you no longer are one."

"Is Emiliano Ricci a client? Is that how you know him?" Her expression blanked with surprise, then she shrugged. "Not that it's any of your business, but no. He's not. Why? You said you didn't care what I'd done or with whom."

"I don't," Luca insisted, pacing the lounge. "You were lovers, though?"

"I met him on a weekend cruise for app developers. We talked about social media and how to play the algorithms to become an influencer. I think I'd rather return my mother's phone call than continue *this* conversation."

He let her walk out. He told himself to let her go, to hold himself at a necessary distance. His feelings were too strong as it was. But the farther away she got, the more he knew he was totally blowing this.

"Amy," he called from the bottom of the main staircase.

She paused at the top to give him a haughty look from the rail.

"I don't *want* to care—" he bit out what felt like an enormous confession "—but I do."

"Good for you. I don't." She sailed along the gallery.

The hell she didn't! He took the stairs two at a time and opened the door to the guest bedroom that she had just slammed in his face.

She swung around to glare at him.

"I don't like having emotions I can't control," he said through his gritted teeth. "Perhaps I should ask your friend Bea to help me work through them?"

Such outraged hostility flashed in her bright green eyes, he nearly threw his head back and laughed. "See? You don't like it, either."

She folded her arms, chin up. "You chased me all the way up here to see if you could make me as pointlessly jealous as you are?"

"I'm not proud of it." He closed in on her. "But I needed to know whether you were capable of it."

"Jealousy comes from insecurity. I'm not an insecure person." She narrowed her eyes and held her ground. Temper crackled around her. She resisted his attempt to unfold her arms.

"Neither am I." He managed to draw her stiff arms open and kissed the inside of each of her blue-veined wrists. "But we haven't had time to become confident in each other, have we? So we're failing the test."

"You specifically told me not to believe in this!" She freed a hand to fling it out with exasperation. "You're the one who said it was a meaningless affair."

"I never said meaningless."

She tried to pull her arm away, but he held on to her wrist. Her struggle drew her closer. Her nose was even with his chin, her gaze wide and surprisingly defenseless beneath the sparks of anger.

That vulnerability dug into him the way her temper and his own conflicting emotions hadn't. He drew her in with great care, twining her one arm behind his lower back, then massaged her stiff shoulders.

"I've always known exactly what was expected of me," he said. "And I've always met and exceeded those expectations." His lips were tickled by flyaway strands of her hair. "But from the moment I met you, I have been off-center. I know what I should be thinking and saying and doing, but I can't make myself do it. Every instinct in me wants to *have* you." His arms tightened around her. "But I can't let that animal win. Not when I know how dangerous it is. The war inside me is killing me so you'll have to forgive the snarls." He ran his hand into her lower back.

It took a few circles of his palm before she released a noise that landed somewhere between defeat and petulance.

"This is new for me, too. From the job you hired me for to how I react to you…" She picked one of her red-gold hairs off his sleeve, then rested her hand where it had been. "I'm not being coy. This is hard to navigate."

"I know. I've made it hard. You have a right to be angry with me, which makes me less sure of you." He let one hand settle above her tailbone.

"I'm not angry or blaming you." Her brow pulled with consternation. "I took the job and slept with you. I caused us to be seen. I know how much of this is on me and that's hard, too. I'm worried about how our efforts to turn this around will pan out."

"It's going to be harder if we're fighting, no?"

"Whose fault is that?" she admonished, but grew pliant, leaning her thighs against his.

"Guilty." He let his fingers fan out to graze the upper curve of her backside. "Maybe we should kiss and make up. For the sake of our image."

"Humph." Her lips twitched. "Here in the privacy of this bedroom? Where no one can see us? A strong brand has to be reinforced consistently."

"Ooh. More shop talk, *amata mia*." He nuzzled his mouth into her throat, groaning with mock lust. "It makes me so hot."

She laughed and tried to shrug away from his tickling kiss. "Does it? Because I was going to say that I'm currently with the only man who interests me, but okay. Let me tell you about shareable infographics."

He lifted his head, accosted by the most intense flush of pleasure. The kind that should have had an orgasm as its source. And yes, he hoped to experience one of those very soon, but this was even more deeply affecting because it wasn't a biological reaction. It was an expansive, chaotic and thrilling reaction to a throwaway remark she had buried in nonsensical teasing. It was terrifying how much it meant to him.

"What?" she asked, smile faltering.

"Nothing." He cupped her cheek and set his mouth across hers, the avaricious beast in him howling to consume her, but something soft and equally ravenous urged him to be tender. To savor as he plundered. To pour himself into her even as he felt her start of surprise and tasted her broken sigh of capitulation.

Amy had been confused after their rooftop discussion, coming away wondering if she was allowing herself to be used again. She had wanted desperately to reach out to her friends to start putting all of this into perspective.

Neither had been available and for a few minutes, when she'd come back to the lounge, things between her and Luca had seemed to devolve into chaos. She had stalked up here insulted and filled with misgivings and now...

Now she was more confused than ever.

If he was using her, it was in the most tender way possible. His kiss was fierce and insatiable and shatteringly gentle. He was treating her like she was precious and irresistible. He unraveled her ability to think clear thoughts.

She knew nothing but her body and the feel of him where he touched her. The fingerprints he traced on her cheeks near her ear, the playful scrape of his teeth on her bottom lip, the brush of his thighs against hers and the wonderous way he cradled her breast.

The onslaught wasn't only physical. There was tremendous emotion welling in her as she heard his muted groan ring in his chest. She thrilled to the press of his erection into her middle and sighed with adoration when he touched his lips to her brow.

And she trembled. It was nearly too much, the way he made her feel so beautiful and treasured at once. The way he had shared his struggle. She felt it in the brief bite of his fingertips into her hips before he slowly eased her clothing away. Tasted it like whiskey on his tongue when he made love to her mouth before he kissed the nipples he'd exposed and slowly, erotically, made her writhe with need by sucking on them.

"Luca," she gasped.

His eyes were incandescent as he backed her toward the bed. Then he was over her, both of them with their clothing askew, but neither was willing to break apart to undress completely.

"I need you to take me inside you. I need that like I need air to breathe," he said, making her shiver.

With damp eyes, she nodded, needing it too. Needing the physical closeness to seal the schism that had been wrought by the betraying photo and everything that had come after.

Moments later, he had sheathed himself and, both still half-dressed, disheveled and frantic, they came together with a shudder of grand surrender to the passion they couldn't resist.

He held himself inside her as he brushed her hair from where it was caught on her eyelashes. She turned her mouth into the flexing curve of his biceps, tasting his skin and feeling drunk.

"I don't know if I'll ever be able to live without this." As the words left her, she realized she had spoken them aloud.

She saw the beast then. Caught the flash of feral possessiveness before his mouth was at the corner of hers, soft and tender and sweet again.

"Be with me now," he commanded.

He began to move. She had no choice but to lose herself to the exaltation that was the result of their lovemaking. The pleasure lifted her even as it seemed to strip her of any outer, protective layers, until she was nothing but pure being. Pure reaction.

Undone and completely vulnerable.

But he took care of her. Such care. Drawing her to the peak with those kisses of reverence and blatant hunger. Watching her with such pride and pleasure in her joyous ascent to climax.

"I want you with me," she gasped.

"I'm right here." His voice seemed to speak inside her head, they were so attuned.

And then they were splintering together, writhing and groaning and throbbing in perfectly synchronized culmination.

It was so powerful and magnificent, she couldn't open her eyes after. She stayed in that state of mutual bliss for ages, convinced they were actually one being.

"That was incredible," he whispered when they finally disengaged. He discarded the condom and they shifted to a more comfortable position. His fingers sifted through her hair then settled against her scalp, tangled in the strands. "Green-eyed monster slayed. I was a fool to think any man from your past could have any bearing on what we have."

His words should have been reassuring, but her eyes snapped open as one particular man from her past jumped into her head.

It wouldn't come out, she assured herself, while clammy fingers of apprehension squeezed her lungs. Was she being naive? Forewarned was forearmed. She ought to tell him.

It was so shameful, though. She hated to even recollect it. Trying to explain it, to dredge through the guilt and remorse and betrayal by her parents... His view of her would completely change. She didn't want to ruin this newfound closeness between them. Not right now.

His chest rose and fell beneath her ear as he exhaled into sleep. She snuggled closer and let unpleasant memories drift away.

"How does it feel to no longer be the most noteworthy person in the room?" Luca's twin asked as she appeared beside him.

Queen Sofia of Vallia was the height of elegance in one of their mother's vintage gowns and a tiara from the crown jewel collection. Her attendance at the foundation's gala was her first public event and their first appearance together since La Inversione, as the press had dubbed her bloodless coup.

Luca noted his sister's gaze was on Amy where she swiveled for the relentlessly flashing bulbs around her. Was Sofia criticizing the attention Amy was garnering? A twist of hostility wrenched through him aimed at the one person he'd always vowed to lay down his life to protect.

He sipped his drink, dampening his desire to remind her that she had been elevated to her current position at Amy's expense. "I never wanted to be. You know that."

"I was teasing." Her gaze narrowed at his tone. "You like her."

Which made him realize he was overreacting, damn it.

"I don't sleep with people I don't like," he muttered.

"Obviously. But you *really* like her. I was under the impression this was all for my benefit," she mused, looking back at Amy with consideration.

He took another gulp of his drink, guilty because this wasn't supposed to benefit him at all. Nothing was. Ever. He hadn't saddled Sofia with running their country so he could enjoy a sexual romp.

"I'll invite her to lunch," Sofia said. "Get to know her better."

"She's due back in London as soon as we return from Tokyo."

Her steady gaze asked, *And then what?*

He rubbed his thumb against the side of his glass, not ready to admit he was thinking of going there with her. There were so many variables and pitfalls. Sofia wasn't married or even looking for a consort. The public might be *for* Queen Sofia, but many were still taking sides *against* Amy Miller for costing them King Luca.

"She handles it well, doesn't she? Being in the sun," Sofia mused.

Amy was winning people over one bright smile at a time, but the attention would never stop. Nor would the judging. It was a sad and relentless fact of his life that he had to remain above reproach. He couldn't sentence her to those same strictures. Not forever.

Not when her smile was already showing signs of strain.

"Yes, but she's not wearing sunscreen." He set his glass on a drinks tray carried by passing waitstaff. "Excuse me while I rescue her."

Amy gratefully went into Luca's arms when he invited her to dance.

"How are you holding up?" he asked as he led her into a smooth waltz. Was there *nothing* this man didn't do perfectly?

"I underestimated what I was asking of my clients in the past, when I've said, 'Just smile while they take your photo.' My fault, I guess, for choosing this dress."

His expression flickered through amusement and ended up as something more contemplative. "There's a commentary there on how much attention we give to what women wear, but I'd rather not think too hard when I've finally got you to myself."

"I'll wear a tuxedo next year," she said, then faltered as she realized it sounded like she assumed she would be with him next year.

"Or pajamas," he suggested.

She relaxed. "I'm glad they've been well received, but I can't take the credit."

"Why not? Sofia and I wouldn't have ordered any if the option hadn't been presented."

Even so, the queen and former king had each pre-ordered a hundred pair, asking that they be donated to long-term care facilities throughout Vallia. With that example set, guests were ordering in factors of ten, rather than the one or two pair Amy had anticipated.

"Do you want to visit the pajama factory while we're in Asia?" Luca asked.

"Oh. Um…" She nearly turned her ankle again.

"While you're doing that award thing in Tokyo? I mean, yes. I'd love to connect with the manufacturer and be sure it's a fair wage factory, like they claim. Double-check the quality."

"Get a photo op? We'll go together."

"Look at you, doing my job for me."

"I'm in the midst of a career change. Willing to try new things."

She chuckled, more from happiness than humor, but he made her *so* happy. Glowingly, deliriously lighthearted and hopeful and filled with a sense that she was the luckiest person alive. Especially when his gaze swung down to connect with hers, conveying pride and sexy heat.

This optimism was strange because she had learned the hard way not to look to a man to make her happy. She knew it had to come from within, but even though she would have said she was very content prior to meeting Luca, she felt far more alive and excited now that she was with him. Colors were brighter, music more tear-inducing, her confidence unshakable.

She wondered if this was what being in love felt like—*Oh.*

He steadied her, pausing to give her a small frown. "How much have you had to drink?"

"One glass. I was just…distracted for a moment," she lied.

They resumed dancing, but her whole body was fizzing with the realization that her heart had gift wrapped itself and stolen under his tree.

She was in love with him. How it had happened so quickly didn't matter. It had. Because this wasn't a hero-worship crush gone wrong. Or sexual infatuation—although that was definitely a big part of it.

It was deep concern for his well-being. Admiration for his principles and intelligence and laconic wit. It was a compulsion to trust him with all of her secrets and a depthless yearning for him to return her regard.

The words clogged her throat, but it was too soon. Too public. Too new.

But as they continued dancing, she thought it with each step.

I love you. I love you.

The next days were busy.

Luca was in meetings to redefine his new role and Amy worked remotely, attempting to mitigate the damage her scandal had done to London Connection and her career.

She rarely had Luca to herself, and when she did, it was in bed. There they communicated in ways that were as profound as any conversation she might have wished to have, so she didn't worry that they weren't dissecting their relationship. It was growing stronger by the day.

The unrelenting media pressure only pushed them to rely on one another, rather than rending them apart. If an awkward question was directed at her, his hand would come out of nowhere to interlace with hers. When his bearing grew rife with tension over a late-night pundit's joke at his expense, she would slide her arms around his waist, asking nothing except that he allow her to soothe him. He would sigh and gather her in.

This morning he had commented to someone, "I'm likely to be in London for the next while—"

It had been part of a broader discussion, and she hadn't had an opportunity to ask if that meant he wanted to continue their relationship. They had agreed on two weeks, but she didn't need to do any soul-searching. Of course, she wanted to keep seeing him!

They were both in love. She was sure of it. If that put a dreamy, smitten look on her face, she couldn't help it.

Perhaps that's why she was garnering so many stares right now.

Or maybe it was because this morning, she and Luca had been granted an exclusive visit to Shinjuku Gyoen National Garden to view their cherry blossoms with some Japanese dignitaries. A handful of photographers had followed them, and those shots were likely being published right now.

Either way, her phone, which was facedown on the table and set to silent, was vibrating incessantly.

She ignored it and kept her attention on Luca. He spoke at the podium, switching back and forth between Italian and Japanese so she missed much of what he was saying. She could tell there was praise for collaboration and innovation on some tech solution commissioned for Vallia. He showed a photo of a port in Vallia, then one here in Japan, highlighting some advancement that had made a difference in both countries.

One of Luca's handlers stood behind him. The young man sent her an urgent glare.

Seriously? He could hear the buzz of her phone all the way over there?

She slid the phone off the table without looking at it and dropped it into her bag.

She had the sense of more glances turning her way, but reminded herself that a few rude stares were a small price to pay for the absolute wonder of being Luca's... They didn't need a label, she assured herself. None of the usual ones fit them anyway. "Girlfriend" was too high school. "Lover" was too edgy for a prince, "mistress" too eye-rollingly outdated.

Luca *had* been footing her bills since she'd met him. Even her charge from the hotel boutique in London had been reversed. Apparently, he'd had the clothes she'd bought that day put onto his own account.

That made her uncomfortable, but she pulled her weight in other ways. She was still managing the pajama campaign and offered constructive ideas to his team on how she and Luca were presenting themselves. They were equals.

Luca came to the good part, announcing a pair of names and the company they represented. Everyone clapped as a husband-wife team rose to collect the statuette Luca held.

The audience took advantage of the applause break to set their heads together and murmur, flicking speculative glances toward her. Luca joined his assistant behind the winners and glanced at the screen his assistant showed him.

He stiffened and his gaze lifted in a flash to hit hers like a punch.

Amy's stomach clenched. *What?*

As the couple at the podium finished speaking and left, they seemed disconcerted by the growing undercurrents in the room.

The cameraman who'd been filming the event turned his lens on her. A reporter shoved a microphone in Amy's face.

"Is it true? Did you cause a teacher to lose his position with Upper Swell School for Girls? Do you have a history of destroying men's lives?"

CHAPTER TEN

LUCA DISAPPEARED OFF the stage behind the curtain, abandoning her to the reckoning of harsh stares and harsher questions.

As Amy was absorbing the profound pain of his desertion, another reporter joined the first. People stared while she desperately tried to gather her handbag and light jacket, which was being pinned by a reporter. On purpose.

Panic began to compress her lungs. She struggled to maintain her composure. She was hot and cold and *scared*. As scared as she'd been the day she was told to leave the school and had no idea where she would go.

Do not cry. Do not, she willed herself while her throat closed over a distressed scream.

And these damned buzzards kept asking their cruel questions.

"Did you lure the prince into that nude photograph? Did someone hire you to do it? His sister?"

One of Luca's bodyguards shoved into the fray and shielded her with his wide body and merciless bulk. He grabbed her things and escorted her out of the nearest exit, but it was still a gauntlet of shouted questions and conjecture.

When he shoved her into an SUV, Luca was already in it. His PA sat facing him; his other bodyguard was in the front. The bodyguard who had rescued her took the seat facing her and pulled the door shut behind them.

"Is it true?" Luca asked stiffly. She hadn't seen this particular shade of subdued rage under his skin since he'd spoken of his father's death.

"I'm not talking about it here." Her voice was hollow. All of her was. It was the only way she could cope, by stepping outside her body and letting the shell be transported wherever he was taking her. If she let herself see and think and feel, she would buckle into hysterical tears.

"That's not a denial," he growled.

How had this happened? Why?

"Who—" She had to clear the thickness from her throat so her voice was loud enough to catch the PA's attention. "Who released this story?"

He told her the name of an infamous gossip site. "Their source is the wife of Avery Mason. She claims he confided in her early in their marriage."

Amy set her hand across her aching stomach and looked out the window.

"The flight plan has been changed, sir," Luca's PA informed him after tapping his tablet. "The team will meet us when we refuel in Athens."

No photo op at a factory in Jiangsu then. Big surprise. "The team" would be the same group of lawyers, spin doctors and palace advisers who had handled his first damning scandal and were continuing to massage it.

Obviously, *she* was off the job. Amy couldn't be trusted. Luca would control the messaging, and his lawyers would likely press her to sign something. Maybe Luca would sue her for defamation. The contract she'd signed with him hadn't stated explicitly that she was supposed to ruin him. They'd left that part as a handshake deal. Could that come back to bite her? She needed Bea!

The private airfield came into view. They drove up to his private jet, and even that short walk of shame was photographed from some hidden location that turned up on her phone when she checked it as the plane readied for takeoff.

"You're shaking," Luca said crisply. "Do you need something?"

A time machine? Her friends? She dug up one of the sleeping tablets she'd taken on the flight here, requested a glass of water and swallowed the pill.

Luca answered a call and began speaking Italian. His sister perhaps. He was cutting his words off like he was chopping wood. Or beheading chickens.

"Sì. No lo so. Presto. Addio."

She handed back her glass and texted Bea and Clare, already knowing it was futile. They were tied up with other things, and she didn't know how to ask for forgiveness when she was piling yet more scandal onto London Connection.

In a fit of desperation, she sent out a text to a few of her closest contacts, fearful she would be locked down in Vallia again. A commercial flight was out of the question. She'd be torn apart, but a handful of her clients flew privately throughout Europe. There was a small chance one of them might be going through the airfield Luca used in Athens.

As she was texting, her mother's image appeared on her screen as an incoming call.

Don't cry. Do not cry.

Amy hit ignore, then tapped out a text that she was about to take off and had to set her phone to airplane mode. It wasn't true, but she couldn't face the barrage that was liable to hit her. She turned off her phone and set it aside.

Luca tucked away his own phone and studied her.

The plane began to taxi. The flight attendant had seated herself near the galley. The rest of his staff were sequestered in their own area, leaving them alone in this lounge, facing one another like duelists across twelve paces of tainted honor.

"Yes. It's true," she said flatly, appreciating the co-cooning effect of her sleeping tablet as it began to release into her system, reducing her agitation and making her limbs feel heavy. It numbed her to the profound humiliation of reliving the most agonizing, isolating experience of her life. "I had an affair with my teacher in my last year of school. That's why I was expelled and why my parents disinherited me."

"How old was he?"

"Twenty-nine. I was eighteen."

He swore. "That's not an affair, Amy. He should have been arrested."

"Oh, he's a disgusting pig. I won't argue that, but I came on to him, even after he said we shouldn't. I told you I was spoiled. I wasn't used to taking no for an answer. I loved how enamored with me he seemed. How helpless he was to resist me."

She saw how deeply that hit Luca, pushing him back

into his seat. Making him reconsider his own infatuation with her.

Was she *trying* to hurt him with this chunk of heavy, sharp-edged history? Maybe. Kicking it at him felt like the only way she could handle touching it at all.

"I'd never had to face any consequences before that. If I was caught bringing alcohol into the dorm, my parents would make a donation to the school and smooth things over." That had been her father's solution, to avoid a fight with his ex over which one of them had to bring Amy back into their home. "I was friends with everyone. It was a point of pride that even if someone thought I was full of myself, I would win them over by flattering them and doing them favors." That had been her mother's legacy. If you didn't have a clear pressure point like money or maternal guilt to bring to bear, fawning and subtle bribery were good substitutes. "I refused to let up when he tried to turn me down."

"Grown men are not victims of teenage girls," he said with disgust.

"Not until his mother, the headmistress, discovers them. Then he's apparently a defenseless baby and the harlot who seduced him is served with an overdue notice of expulsion. *That's* when her parents finally decide she should be taught a lesson about the real world."

His flinty gaze tracked across her expression.

It was all she could do to hide how devastated she'd been. Still was. She looked away, out the window to where Tokyo was fading behind wisps of cloud.

A tremendous melancholy settled on her. The sleeping pill, but history, as well.

"It was covered up by his mother and mine. The gossip hadn't really got around anyway. Bea and Clare were the only two people who stood by me. They wanted to quit school in solidarity, but I didn't want them to throw away their futures just because I had. They helped with rent here and there, but I eventually found my feet with the online promotions and I was so…touched. So *proud* when Clare asked me to start London Connection with her. I felt like I was bringing value when I'd been such a mess in those early years. And now… Now I've stuffed it up anyway."

"Why did you take my assignment when you had something like this in your past?"

"I didn't expect to *relive* it. You're the one who decided to use me for your own ends because the opportunity was too good to pass up," she reminded him.

His head jerked back. "I would have made other decisions if I had known."

"Would you?" she scoffed.

"You didn't give me a chance to prove otherwise, did you? I came to you to manufacture a scandal so I wouldn't cause anyone else to be hurt. *I told you that.* But you didn't warn me that something like this was possible. You said this is a circle of trust, but you didn't trust me, did you?"

"Don't lecture me on *honesty*. Not when you—" She leaned forward in accusation, then abruptly had to catch her armrest as she realized the tablet was destroying her sense of balance. "When you were so convinced of your own perfection you had to *hire* someone to make you look bad. You want to talk about respecting a relationship? You hired me so that when you made your *one* mistake—" she showed him her single finger for emphasis "—it wouldn't really be yours. You wanted to be able to tell yourself that whatever happened wouldn't really be your fault. You want to believe this image—" she gestured to encompass his aura "—of being completely flawless, is *real*. Here's news, Luca. We all make mistakes. That's why my job exists! I'm *your* mistake. And now you'll have to live with that. So suck it."

She dropped back into her seat, feeling like a sack of bruised apples. The entire world was upon her, crushing her. She propped her cement-filled head on the weak joint of her wrist, growing too tired to cry, even though sobs were thickening her throat and sinuses.

"My mistake was believing the scarlet harlot of Upper Swell was going to live happily ever after with the Golden Prince."

"I never promised you that." He didn't shout it, but it struck like a sonic boom she felt with her heart.

"No," she agreed with growing drowsiness. "No, you said it was only going to be an affair and I believed you. But you made me fall in love with you." She blinked heavy lids over wet eyes. "That's on you, Luca."

Amy woke in Luca's stateroom several hours later. She wondered if he had carried her here or had one of his bodyguards do it. Whoever it was had removed her shoes and draped a light blanket over her.

She finger-combed her hair and used the toothbrush that had been designated hers when they'd embarked from Vallia, back when she and Luca had been in perfect sync and she'd believed…

She clenched her eyes. Had she really believed they had a chance at a future? *Come on, Amy. You're smarter than that.*

Wrinkled and fuzzy-headed, she crept back to her seat.

Luca was reclined in his seat and fast asleep. Her heart wrenched to see him there when he could have slept beside her in his own bed. If he had wanted to send the message that she would no longer wake to the sight of him sleeping beside her, this was it.

A flight attendant started to approach, and Amy waved her off. She should eat something so she didn't get air sick, but she was too anguished.

She turned on her phone and was tempted to turn it right back off again, but made herself go through some of the messages, looking for...

Her heart lurched as she picked up a reply to her SOS. One of her clients, Baz Rivets, was sober a year now, but had had addiction problems from the time she'd met him at one of his early pub gigs through to the international fame he and his rock band enjoyed today. She'd been beside him every time he'd gone in or come out of a program and regarded him as a friend, but she would never have expected him to go out of his way for her.

I thought I'd have to go back to rehab to see you again. We're detouring to Athens from Berlin. Will wait for you there, ducky.

It was enormously heartening, but also like hearing she could have lifesaving surgery on condition half her heart be removed.

With her throat aching, she replied with a heartfelt, "Thank you," and set aside her phone. Then she stared at the flight tracker, taking way too long to comprehend that they were above Turkey. Only a few hours to go before she would have to say goodbye to Luca.

He woke as they began their descent into Athens.

For one millisecond, as he glanced at her with disorientation, she saw a flash of the complex *hello* he usually wore when he woke next to her. It was discovery and pleasure and something magnetic and welcoming that always warmed her deep in her center.

This time, it was gone before it fully formed. She saw memory strike him so hard, he flinched. His expression blanked into steely, unreadable lines.

Whatever spark of hope still flickered within her died, leaving her more bereft than she'd ever felt. She looked to the window, teeth clenched against making apologies. Was this her fault? Not really. Everyone had a past, and she hadn't aired hers on purpose.

Did that matter when it was impacting him anyway? Her parents hadn't cared who was at fault ten years ago. *This can't get out, Amy. How did you let it happen?*

Her ears popped and, moments later, they were on the ground, taxiing to a stop outside a private terminal for personal and charter jets.

"I have to speak with my sister," Luca said, glancing up from his ringing phone. He unbuckled and rose, bringing the phone to his ear as he moved into the stateroom for privacy.

Amy searched wildly out the window as she began gathering her things. A team of trench coats and briefcases came out of the terminal and headed toward the plane. Fresh air came in as the steps were lowered.

Where was Baz? There! She saw the plane with the psychedelic logo on its tail and rudely shuffled her way past the confused faces of people trying to board.

It was raining and she hadn't bothered to pull on her light jacket, so she felt each stinging drop as she ran the short distance across the tarmac. Stairs appeared as the hatch was lowered on Baz Rivets's plane.

"Welcome to the naughty side, ducky!" Baz wore jeans, a torn T-shirt, a man bun and a scruffy beard. He opened his arms in welcome.

She ran up the steps, starting to cry, she was so overwhelmed. "I didn't know how to get home without being swarmed, but I didn't expect you to make a special trip for me!"

"You flew to Thailand and kept me out of *jail*. Giving you a lift home is the least I can do." He wrapped his arms around her. "You messy, messy girl."

"I never claimed to be otherwise, Baz. I really didn't."

"Oh. He doesn't look happy."

Amy turned to see Luca had come onto the steps of his own plane. He stared across at her, his dumbfounded rage so tangible she felt a jolt of adrenaline sear her arteries.

Baz kept one arm around her and drew her closer to his wiry frame. He wore the most neighborly of smiles as he waved and spoke with quiet cheerfulness through his clenched teeth, "That'll teach you, ya royal bastard. Amy should be treated like the queen she is."

I'm not. I was never going to be.

For a long moment, she and Luca stared at one another. He didn't call her back or come get her, though. And he turned away first.

It was a knife straight to her heart, one that would have kept her standing there waiting for the rest of her life in hopes he'd reappear to pull it out, but Baz nudged her inside.

"Come tell Uncle Bazzie all about it. Lads, put the kettle on for our sweet Ames."

* * *

Luca was clinging to his patience by his fingernails. His brain kept going back to asking *Why didn't she tell me this could happen?*

It didn't matter why. She hadn't. Intellectually, he understood that Amy was the victim of exploitation. That wasn't something she needed to tell anyone unless she wanted to.

But now his sister was in his ear saying, "I appreciate this isn't something she could control, but it's time to distance yourself from her."

"I know." His goal had been accomplished, and Amy's connection to him was making things worse for her.

The woman who had leaked the story wouldn't have been so well rewarded if she'd only been taking down a PR agent who worked with celebrities. No, Amy's romantic link to royalty had been the gold the story was really mining. It was a vein that would continue to be exploited as long as he and Amy were together.

Even so, when Luca saw Amy darting across the tarmac to the waiting plane, he nearly lost his mind.

He'd hung up on his sister and shoved his way outside in time to see her with— Who the hell was that? Some demigod celebrity, Luca realized as he took in the flamboyant logo that spoke of a live fast, die young rock culture. The jackass wore professionally distressed clothing and a smug grin as he claimed Amy.

Luca hated him on sight.

You made me fall in love with you.

If she loved him, she should have trusted him enough to tell him about her past. Enough to *stay*.

That's all he could think as he stared across at her

standing in that other man's embrace, the image like radiation that destroyed his insides the longer he stared.

"Sir, there are people in the terminal getting all this on their phones," someone said from inside his plane.

Brilliant. His final humiliation was being recorded for uploading to the buffet of public ignominy that was already so well stocked. Outstanding.

He went inside to take his seat, sick with guilt that he'd wanted to right a wrong and it had resulted in yet more wrong.

Everyone stared at him while he settled into his chair.

"Our first step is to make clear to her the legal and financial consequences she will face if she divulges any of this to the press," one of his lawyers piped up.

"We should make an immediate statement that she was *asked* to leave. Get in front of whatever photos come out from this." Another one tapped the window.

Luca had had the team meet him here in Athens in hopes they could find a way forward that wouldn't destroy both him and Amy. He had expected her to weigh in.

Now he could only stare in disbelief while another backstabbing idiot said, "Given her history, we could reframe the photos and make a case for you to take *back* the throne."

Luca swore and waved his hand. "Get off my plane. All of you."

Neither Bea nor Clare were in London when Amy arrived.

Bea, bless her, said Amy could use her flat. She was deeply grateful and sank into the familiar oasis of Bea's personal space.

But with both of her friends still away, it fell to Amy to keep London Connection running. She popped an email to her assistant to say she would do it remotely to minimize the disruption she was already causing at the office. She didn't mention her plan to resign. She would wait until Clare and Bea were back to tell them personally. For now, she focused on drafting a statement about her past and most recent disgrace.

It started out very remorseful, but the more she looked up statistics on sexual harassment and noted the delight trolls took in being sadistic toward women, and the punishment gap when a woman made a mistake versus a man, the more incensed she became.

She wound up writing:

How is it that a twenty-nine-year-old man was deemed to have more to lose than an eighteen-year-old woman?

Everyone had something to lose when this affair happened, but I—the person with the least life experience and fewest resources—became the scapegoat. I was expelled before I could take my A levels, destroying my university aspirations.

No one cared that my future was derailed. It was far more important to Avery's mother, the headmistress, that she keep her job and avoid a disciplinary hearing over her son's behavior. She convinced my parents to sweep it under the rug. They agreed because they had financial, social, and career pressures to protect.

Instead of urging me to call the police, which I was too humiliated to contemplate on my own,

my parents cut me off financially. I was literally
left homeless while Avery was immediately trans-
ferred to a position at another school.

What began as a PR spin became an essay on femi-
nism and the distance that still needed to be traveled.
When she was done, there was morning light outside.

Amy hit send to a senior editor of an old-school but
well-respected newspaper in America, then hired bodyguards to escort her to her own flat.

"'The king of Vallia hired me to assist with the Queen's
Foundation,'" Sofia read aloud from the same open letter that Luca was reading on his own tablet. "'At the
time of my professional engagement, we discussed extending my purview to other assignments, but those
discussions were discontinued after we became personally involved.'"

*Mio Dio, she knew how to gracefully pirouette with
prose*, Luca thought.

Perhaps Sofia was thinking it, too. He could feel her
staring at him from her position at the opposite end of
the table, prodding him for details on those halted discussions.

Luca and his twin had always breakfasted together
if they were both in the palace, even after Luca took
the throne. It allowed them to connect personally, but
also discuss any political developments or other rising
concerns. Luca had wanted Sofia to be in the know so
she could seamlessly take over when the time came.
She was keeping him equally well-informed as a cour-
tesy. She certainly didn't need him weighing in with
advice or opinions. Vallia's populace was adapting well

to the changeover, seeming energized and eager for the new order.

Luca wished he could say the same. He was miserable.

> *While I regret the anguish King Luca must have suffered from the photos of us that emerged, I feel no remorse over the fact he was pressured into giving up the crown as a result of our affair. Men should be held to account when they cross a line.*

"I like her," Sofia mused.

Me too, Luca thought, heart so heavy in his chest it was compressed and thumping in rough, painful beats that echoed in the pit of his gut.

He reached the end where an editorial note stated that Avery Mason's wife had recently retained an extremely pricey and ruthless divorce lawyer.

"Do you suppose that's why she sold the story?" Sofia asked as she clicked off her tablet. "To pay for her divorce?"

"And bolster her petition for one," Luca surmised. Perhaps she'd seen this as her only avenue for escaping her marriage. He couldn't spare much thought or empathy for her, though. Not when she'd ruthlessly used Amy to achieve her own ends.

The way you did? his conscience derided.

"A rebuttal is being drafted," Guillermo said, ever the helicopter guardian, hovering and batting away threats to his charges.

"Why?" Luca asked. "Do you not think men should suffer the consequences of their actions?"

"Signor." It was one of Guillermo's scolds that back-

pedaled even as his haughty demeanor reinforced his position. Luca Albizzi was never allowed to be seen as anything but faultless.

You were so convinced of your own perfection you had to hire someone to make you look bad.

"Guillermo, will you leave us please?" Sofia said.

Luca brought his focus back to his sister as Guillermo slipped away.

"I regret nothing," he said, which felt like a lie, but he still waved a dismissing hand at his tablet. "This will pass."

"Luca, I know," Sofia said in a voice that sent a chill of foreboding through him. "About the night Papa died. I made Vincenzo tell me everything." Vincenzo was the head of the palace's legal department.

Luca looked away, instantly thrown back to that grim night. "I was trying to spare you, not hide it from you."

"I know." She rose and came down the length of the table to stand behind him.

He tensed, not wanting comfort. He resisted her touch when her narrow hands settled on his shoulders and she squeezed his set muscles.

"I'm sorry you felt you couldn't tell me. That you've had to carry it alone."

"What was the point in forcing one more ugly memory onto you?"

"I know, but I needed to understand. Something changed in you after that night. At first, I thought it was the pressure of having to ascend. That you were angry the crown hadn't come to me, but it was more than that. I saw it more clearly when you were with Amy. She makes you happy, Luca, but you're fighting that every step of the way. Why?"

"Because look what happens when men in positions of power follow their base instincts!" He waved at the tablet where Amy's words were imprinted for the world to see. "Do you think that would have happened to her if she hadn't been tied to *me*?"

He would have risen to pace, but she didn't let him shrug her off. Her hands pressed him to stay in the chair as if she could impress her views into him with the action.

"You saw how upset she was the day our affair was revealed." He was still haunted by Amy's bleak expression. "She threatened to burn down the palace because she was terrified of exactly *this*."

"You didn't know about it, Luca."

"But I still wouldn't have done anything differently if I had. That's what makes me sick with myself. From the minute I saw her, I wanted her. I was attracted to her and yet I hired her anyway. I brought her here and gave in to what I felt. Pursuing what *I* wanted has destroyed her. So yes, she makes me happy. What the hell can I do about it when I'm a cancer that will only harm her?"

You made me fall in love with you.

He had to breathe through the pain every time he thought about her saying that. In the moment, he'd refused to let it in. His reflex had been to control the damage they faced, but while she'd been sleeping, her words had begun to penetrate and they'd replayed in his head continuously ever since, torturing him. Making him ache with what might have been.

"Do you know why I was away when Papa died?" Sofia asked.

"You were at a UN conference," he recalled dimly.

"The conference was over. I was hiding in a hotel room, worried I was pregnant."

Luca abruptly twisted in his chair to stare up at her.

"It was a false alarm," she hurried to say.

"Who?" he demanded in astonishment.

"Someone who was not anticipating being a father, let alone a queen's consort," she said tartly. "What I'm saying is, you are not the only person who has moments of weakness and fallibility." She cupped his cheek. "You're not the only one who wants to find a life partner and feel loved."

"I will stand behind you no matter what, Sofia. You know that." He took her hand to impress the words into her with a squeeze of her fingers. "You could have told me. If anything like that ever happens again, you can tell me."

"I know. And *I* stand behind *you* no matter what. Despite recent appearances," she said with a quirk of her mouth. Then she waved at his tablet. "Look how strong she is, Luca. Do you really think she's going to let *any* man destroy her? No. She has publicly declared she's keeping the life she has made for herself, and good for her. She is exactly the sort of woman you should be pursuing. She'll keep you honest."

You said it was only going to be an affair and I believed you.

He had tried to believe it himself, but he'd known that every minute with her was more than some flickering memory. It had been a stone in the foundation of something bigger. Something he wanted to make permanent. He'd already been contemplating going to London so they could continue to see one another.

"Do you have any idea how annoying it is that the women in my life are smarter than I am?" He rose.

"At least you're smart enough to realize that."

"Be warned, Sofia. If I'm going after *everything* I want, for me and you and Amy and Vallia, blood may get spilled. I won't always be nice about it."

She smiled. "I've always known you would slay dragons if you were allowed to carry a sword and weren't weighed down by a crown. You've made it possible for me to be who I need to be. I want you to be who *you* were meant to be." She offered her cheek for a kiss. "I love you and trust you."

"*Ti amo, sorella.* Don't wait up. I'll be gone as long as it takes to win her back."

I was going to resign, but you'll have to fire me.

Amy wrote that to Bea and Clare as she prepared to go into work two days later.

Clare was uncharacteristically silent, not answering texts or emails for the last few days, which was worrying, but Bea called her immediately. "I vote you be promoted to Executive Director of Executing Bastards. You're my hero. I love you."

"Where *are* you? When are you coming back?" Amy asked her.

"It's a lot to explain," Bea began.

"Oh, God. Wait," Amy said as her phone pinged with a text. "My mother is threatening to come see me. I haven't spoken to her since before Tokyo."

"You don't have to see her," Bea reminded her.

"That's what I'm going to tell her." Sort of. "I'll call

you back soon." Amy signed off and tapped her mother for a video call.

Her mother looked surprisingly frail, not wearing her usual makeup and designer day dress. Instead, she was in her dressing gown. Her skin looked sallow and aged and, if Amy wasn't mistaken, she was putting out a cigarette off-screen.

"There's a lot of paps outside, Mom. And I'm heading into work so don't come over here. I won't drag them to you, either."

"That's fine, but I *wish* you would have seen all of that old business from my point of view, instead of airing it publicly. In *New York*. Do you have any idea how traumatizing it would have been to put you through a court case over that prat? It was the best thing for you that we made it go away like that. You should be thankful."

"You have a right to your opinion. Is that all?" Amy propped up her phone so she could use two hands to load her bag.

"I've spoken to your father. He's arranging to release your trust fund as soon as possible."

"I don't need it, Mom." She kind of did, but... "I never wanted *money* from you and Dad," she added with a sharp break in her tone that she couldn't help.

"For God's sake, Amy. Have you never realized there was none? It was a recession! Your father borrowed from the trust to keep his company afloat. He stopped paying me support. That's why I married Melvin, so I could sell the house and make your tuition payments. You were adamant that you finished school with your friends. Then you got yourself expelled. I honestly didn't know what to do. We both thought you needed a dose of reality."

"And the reality was, I couldn't count on my parents to be honest with me."

"Do not play the victim here, Amy. You were an absolute pill."

"This is not a productive conversation, Mom. Let's take a break. A long one. I'll call when I'm ready to chat. If you don't hear from me by my birthday, you can call me then."

"In *five months*? No. That stupid Mason fool will not cost me my only child again. I swear, I want to track him down and stab him in the eye."

"Let me know what they set your bail at. I'll see if I can raise it online."

"You think I'm joking."

"You think I am."

"I'll see you at Wednesday's lunch," her mother declared.

Amy rolled her eyes, not caring that it made her mother sigh the way it always had, ever since she'd been a young, rebellious pill.

"I'll text you once I've checked my schedule at work," Amy conceded. "Bea and Clare are away and this is my first day back. It will be hectic."

A short time later, her bodyguards cut through the paparazzi and she entered London Connection. Despite Bea's supportive phone call, however, she wasn't sure of her reception.

"Amy!" someone shouted, and everyone stood up to applaud her.

Which made tears come into her eyes. She was deeply touched and had a queue of hugs to get through before she arrived at her desk and began putting things in order there.

It was a busy day. Some clients had dropped her and the agency, claiming they were "no longer a good fit," but the phones were even busier with potential new ones. Even more heartening were the emails from colleagues in her industry who not only expressed support for her personally, but told her how much they admired her professionally.

"I would rather work for you than the agency I'm at," more than one said. "Please let me know when you have an opening."

As Amy absorbed what an opportunity for growth they faced, she held a quick meeting with the department heads. She tasked them with helping her make a case for expanding London Connection that she could present to Bea and Clare the minute they were back.

It was exciting and consuming and kept her mind occupied so she wouldn't think about how thoroughly her letter had dropped the ax on any chance she might have had of a relationship with Luca. She kept waiting for his rebuttal to hit the airwaves, maybe something that would deride her for daring to be so comfortable with costing a king his crown. The arrogance! The cheek! Did she not know she had destabilized a nation?

There was only a short statement from the palace that they would not comment on the prince's personal life. When she arrived home, however, a pair of stoic-faced men in dark suits were waiting in the lobby of her building.

"Will you come with us, Miss Miller?"

"She will not," one of her own bodyguards said firmly, placing himself in front of her.

"It's fine, I know who he is," she said, nudging her man aside. Her heart began to race and she searched the face of Luca's bodyguard. He gave away nothing.

He probably didn't know what she faced any more than she did.

Would Luca rail at her? Force her to write a retraction? Have her thrown off a bridge?

There was only one way to find out. Despite her trepidation, she dismissed her own guards and went with the men.

They took her to a beautiful Victorian town house in Knightsbridge. The facade was white and ornate. Vines grew up the columns on either side of the black front door. She was shown across a foyer with a lovingly restored parquet floor and into a lounge of predominantly white decor. Three arched windows, tall and narrow and symmetrical, looked onto a garden where a topless maiden poured water from a jug into a fountain.

She looked at the figure and all she could think of was her walk with Luca the first day at his palace, when he'd confided in her about his father's death. He'd been so hurt by the things his father had done, and she'd set him up for more of it.

She rubbed her sternum, hating herself for that.

"It felt like home the minute I saw her," Luca said behind her.

Amy spun to find him leaning in a doorway, regarding her. Her heart leaped a mile high. She had missed him. So much. Then her heart took another bounce because he was so fiercely beautiful. And a third time because there was no anger in his expression. No vilification.

But no smile, either. The one that tugged at her cheeks

fell apart before it was fully formed, but she couldn't help staring at him. Drinking him in.

His neat, stubbled beard was perfectly trimmed across his long cheeks. His mouth was not quite smiling, but wasn't tense, either. Solemn. His blue eyes searched more than they offered any insight to his reason for bringing her here.

He had the ability to wear a blue button-down shirt and gray trousers as though it was a bespoke tuxedo. A suit of gleaming armor. Whether he called himself a king, a prince, or a man, he could lean in a doorway and command a room. He projected authority and strength, and despite his intimidating and unreadable expression and the very unsettled way they'd left things, her instinct was to hurry toward him.

She touched the back of a chair to ground herself. To hold herself back.

They'd been apart only four days. Their relationship from "ruin me" to being ruined had been a short ten. How was it possible that her feelings toward him were paralyzing her? She was on a knife's edge between hope and despair. There *was* no hope, she reminded herself.

But still he'd brought her here. Why?

"I—" she began, but had no clue what she wanted to say. Then his words struck her. "Wait. Did you just buy this?" She pointed at the floor to indicate the house.

"I did. Would you like a tour? It's not a faithful restoration. It was gutted and modernized. I think you'll agree that's a good thing."

He offered his hand.

She hesitated, then moved as though in a trance, desperate for this small contact. This was how miracles worked, wasn't it? Without explanation? She took his hand, and the feel of his warm palm against hers as he interlaced their fingers nearly unhinged her knees.

"I thought you'd be angry with me," she said shakily. "About the letter." Each cell in her body was coming back to life.

"I am. But not with you. I'm angry that you had to write it. The kitchen." He identified the room with a wave as they walked into an airy space of cutting blocks and stainless steel, pots and pans suspended from the ceiling, and French doors that led to a patio herb garden. "The chef has yet to be hired, but you remember Fabiana? I poached her from the palace."

"Yes, of course. Hello," Amy greeted the maid. "It's nice to see you again."

"Ciao." Fabiana gave a small curtsy before she went back to putting away groceries.

"You can access the stairs to the terrace out there. You've seen the garden through the windows. Staff quarters are downstairs. Dining room, office, powder room, you've seen the main lounge," he said as he walked her through the various rooms, all bright and fresh and sumptuously decorated in a soft palette of rose and gray, ice blue and bone white. Shots of yellow and burnt orange, indigo and fern gave it life.

"It's a charming touch to keep this," she said as she paused on the landing to admire the window seat that looked over the road. "I can imagine callers waiting here to see if they would be allowed upstairs by the duke or—" *Prince.*

"There might have been a receiving room up here once, but it's all master suite now."

It was. There was a sumptuous yet intimate lounge with a television and a wet bar, a dining nook for breakfast and other casual meals, a beautiful office with floor-to-ceiling bookshelves and a fitness room that would catch the morning light. The actual bedroom was enormous, and the master bath had a walk-in shower, two sinks, a makeup vanity and…

"That tub!" Amy exclaimed as she imagined stepping into what was more of a sunken pool. It was surrounded by tropical plants and candles, begging for an intimate night in.

"I thought you would like it. Look at the closet." It had an access from the bathroom and was the size of a car garage. There was a bench in the middle and a full-length, three-way mirror at the back. Alongside his suits hung gowns and dresses and a pair of green pants with a mended fly.

It struck her then, why he'd bought this magnificent house. She'd seen the headlines since their breakup.

King's Mistress Dethrones and Departs

Whatever magic had begun to surround her flashed into nothing. She was left with singed nostrils, and a bitter taste in the back of her throat.

She twisted her hand free of his and stalked through to the more neutral living area. Her adrenaline output had increased to such a degree that her limbs were twitching and her stomach ached. She couldn't decide if she wanted to spit at him or run to Baz Rivets again.

"I'm not making any assumptions," he began as he followed her.

"No?" she cried. "I won't live here. I won't be your— your *piece* in London, keeping your bed warm for when you happen to be in town."

"Stop it," he commanded sharply. "Think better of yourself."

His tone snapped her head back. He'd never spoken to her like that.

She folded her arms defensively. "I *am*."

"No, you're jumping to conclusions."

"What other conclusion is there?" She waved toward the closet.

In the most regal, pithy, arrogant way possible, he walked to a painting and gave it a light nudge to release a catch. It swung open, and he touched a sensor on a wall safe. It must have read his thumbprint because it released with a quiet snick.

He retrieved something before closing both the painting and the safe. Then he showed her a red velvet ring box and started to open it. "This was my grandmother's."

Amy was so shocked, so completely overwhelmed, she retreated in a stumble and nearly landed in an ignominious heap against the sofa.

She caught herself and managed to stay on her feet, then could only stare at him.

He gently closed the box. His expression became watchful, but there was tension around his mouth and a pull in his brows that was…hurt?

"As I said, I'm not making assumptions." He set aside the box—which made her feel as though he was setting her heart over there on a side table and abandoning it as he took a few restless steps, then pushed his hands into his pockets.

He snorted in quiet realization.

"Am I making another mistake? I don't like it," he said ironically. "I hurt you, Amy," he admitted gravely.

"I know I did. I hate myself for it. Especially because I don't know that I could have prevented it. As long as you were interested in me, I was going to pursue you and we would have wound up where we did. That's been hard for me to accept. I don't like thinking of myself as having such a deep streak of self-interest."

He glanced at Amy for her reaction, but she had no words. He *had* hurt her. "I didn't exactly run away."

Until she had.

She bit her lip.

He nodded. "You hurt me when you left the way you did. That's not a guilt trip. I only want you to know that you can. I stood there telling myself I was doing us both a favor by letting you go, but I was so damned hurt I could hardly stand it."

"Nothing happened with Baz," she muttered.

"I know. He's a client and you don't have relationships with clients." He sounded only a little facetious. More of a chide at himself, she suspected. "It was genuinely shocking to me that anyone could hurt me so deeply just by standing next to another man, though."

She was reminded of their spat about jealousy when they were at his villa on the lake. When he had pointed out they were too new to have confidence in their relationship.

"I want you to come to *me* when you're hurt and scared and don't know what to do." He pointed to the middle of his chest, voice sharpening, then dying to sardonic. "And I want you by my side when *I* don't know what to do. I've hardly slept, I was trying so hard to work out how to spin things so you wouldn't be destroyed by all of this. I wanted to talk it out with you." He laughed at the paradox.

"And then I threw you under the bus," she said contritely, mentioning what was looming like a bright red double-decker between them.

"Don't apologize for what you wrote."

"I wasn't going to." But she clung to her elbows, deeply aware that she couldn't do that to a man and not have him hate her a little.

Which made her gaze go to the velvet box. Maybe it wasn't a ring. Maybe she *was* jumping to conclusions. How mortifying.

She jerked her gaze back to his, but he had seen where her attention had strayed.

"I want to marry you, Amy."

She ducked her face into her hands, all of her so exposed she couldn't bear it, but there was nowhere to hide.

"We don't even know each other, Luca!"

Gentle hands grazed her upper arms, raising goose bumps all over her body before he moved his hands to lightly encircle her wrists.

"I'm telling you what I want, that's all. What I know to be true. You don't have to answer me right now. I'll propose properly when you're more sure."

"What would our marriage even look like?" she asked, letting him draw her hands from her face. "We're not a match that people want to accept. We don't even live in the same country!"

"We can work all that out," he said, as if it was as simple as buying groceries. "My future is up in the air right now. The only thing I know for certain is that I want to be with you. So I bought a house here. We can date or you can move in. You can work or not. I'll get started with my own ventures. Maybe we'll move to

Vallia at some point if it feels right. We can have a long engagement, so you have time to be sure. All of that is up for discussion, but I'd love for you to wear this ring when you're ready. I want people to know how likely I am to kill them if they malign the woman I love."

"You love me?" She began to shake.

"Of course, I love you."

"But you said…" She tried to remember what he'd told her about marriage. "You said you'd only marry someone vetted by… I'm not exactly the best choice of bride, Luca."

"If we make each other happy, that's all that matters. No. Wait," he corrected himself, cupping her face. "You are a bright, successful, badass of a woman who makes me a better man. How could anyone say that's a bad choice?"

"I make *you* better?" she choked out. "Hardly. You're perfect." It was annoying as hell.

"Exactly," he said with a shrug of casual arrogance. "I don't make mistakes. How could the woman I choose to spend my life with be anything but a flawless decision?"

"Oh, my God," she scoffed, giving him a little shove, before letting him catch her close. "You are a bit of a god, you know. It's intimidating." She petted his stubbled cheek before letting her hand rest on his shoulder.

"This is you acting intimidated? I can't wait until you're comfortable. You'll be hell on wheels once you trust me, won't you? Pushing back on me at every turn."

A pang of remorse hit her. "I should have trusted you and told you about Avery."

"It's a difficult subject. I understand."

"It wasn't just that," she admitted. "I was afraid of

how you'd react. Afraid you would push me away and I would never have a chance to get to know you better. Then I was afraid you'd judge me. That I'd lose you." Her eyes dampened. "And then I did lose you."

"No, you didn't. I'm right here." A smile ghosted across his lips. "We had a fight, and we'll have others because we're both headstrong and used to thinking independently. But we'll always come back to each other. Wear my ring and I'll prove that to you."

"You really think we could make this work?"

"There's only one way to know."

"Okay." Nerves had her hand shooting out between them as though they were finalizing a deal. "I'll live with you here and—"

He yanked her close and swooped a deep kiss onto her lips, one that sent her arms twining around his neck in joy. One of her feet came off the floor.

He used the leverage of taking her weight to pivot her toward the bedroom door, then broke their kiss to walk her backward.

"Wait. I need more of that first." He paused and drew her properly against him, squeezing out all the shadows and filling her with a golden light while his mouth sweetly and lazily got reacquainted with hers.

They both groaned and she whispered, "I missed you."

She might have cringed then because it had only been a few days. They'd been dark ones, though. The beginning of eternity without him.

But here he was murmuring, "Me too," before sweeping his mouth across hers with more heat and passion and craving.

"Luca," she gasped as need sank its talons into her.

"*Sì*. I need you, too," he said in a rough voice and picked her up to carry her through to the bedroom in long strides. When he set her on the bed, he came down with her and framed her face. "I need you, Amy. You. Never leave me again."

"Stay and fight?" she suggested on a shaken laugh.

"*Sì.*" He pressed his smile to hers and they didn't talk again for a long time.

"Amy," Bea murmured. She and Clare widened their eyes with awe as they entered Luca's home several weeks later. Hers too, he kept insisting, but she was taking things slowish.

Not so slow that she didn't introduce Luca by his new title as she drew her friends into the lounge.

"This is Luca. My fiancé." She gave an exaggerated wave of her wrist to show off the ring. It was an oval ruby with a halo of diamonds on a simple gold band, not extravagant, but invaluable for its sentimental and historical significance. He had proposed properly the day she officially moved in with him. She'd been staying with him since he'd come to London so, even though it all happened very quickly, it felt right to make it official. She was beyond honored to be his future wife.

"Oh, my God! Congratulations." Bea and Clare hugged her nearly to death and grew flustered when Luca accepted their congratulations by brushing away an offer to shake hands and embraced each of them.

"I'm delighted to meet you both. And I look forward to getting to know you better, but Amy's been missing you. I'll let you catch up." He touched Amy's arm. "I'll tell my sister she can release the statement on our engagement."

"Thank you." Amy wrinkled her nose. She had asked him to wait on announcing it until she'd had the chance to tell her two best friends in person. "You spoil me."

"Nothing less than you deserve, *mi amore*." He set a kiss on her lips, nodded at the other two women and disappeared up the stairs.

Clare and Bea stood there with their mouths open.

"You've been busy," Clare accused.

"Oh, please. You both have plenty of explaining to do about your own whereabouts these last weeks. Come." Amy led them to where the wine and glasses were waiting. "Dish."

EPILOGUE

"AND THE WINNER for Most Innovative Integrated Media Messaging goes to London Connection, for their Consent to Solar Power campaign on behalf of AR Green Solutions."

Bea and Clare shot to their feet in excitement while Luca said a smug, "I knew it," beside Amy. He rose to help her out of her chair.

Amy needed help. She was eight months pregnant going on eleven. She had been on the fence about attending this ceremony, but it was her last chance for a night out and a rare opportunity to catch up with her best friends.

Of course, when they had planned it, Amy hadn't known she was pregnant again. It had been thrilling news to learn she was expecting their second child, but a surprise, considering it happened a mere twelve weeks after their daughter Zabrina had been born.

Despite how busy she was as a mother, Amy was keeping her hand in with London Connection. She had personally supervised the team who had come up with this promotion for the solar tiles Luca was producing with his partner Emiliano.

They were heading straight to Vallia in the morning,

though. Sofia was not even engaged, let alone showing signs of producing the next ruler. This baby would be third in line for the throne after Luca and Zabrina. Everyone wanted this babyto be born there.

For the most part, Amy had been feeling good. Tired, but Luca was a hands-on father, and they had a nanny along with other staff who were always willing to cuddle a princess.

Even so, Amy leaned on Bea and Clare as they all went onto the dais. "Can you believe this is our life?" she asked them.

They were both beaming, all of them at the top of their individual worlds.

But as had always been their dynamic, both women gave Amy a little shove toward the microphone, letting her take the heat of the spotlight for all of them.

"I wouldn't be where I am without these two wonderful women beside me and the brilliant men who conceived these panels, most especially my husband who didn't dismiss me when I said 'What if we show your workers asking Mother Nature for consent?'"

A ripple of laughter went through the room at the unusual campaign.

"I'm the one who said she was out of her mind," Clare interjected, making Amy laugh because that was exactly what her friend had said, before assuring her she trusted her and encouraging her to go for it.

Something happened when Amy laughed, though. A release. She felt the flood of dampness and cringed with an agony of embarrassment.

"Ames?" Bea squeezed her arm. "What happened? Are you okay?"

"This is not a stunt for more publicity, I swear." Amy

shaded her eyes and looked for her husband who was already moving quickly toward her, an anxious expression on his face. "But I'm about to make a scene."

"*Amore*, what's wrong?"

"I'm so sorry, Luca. My water broke."

As the whole room erupted, Luca gathered her into his side. "Of course, it did," he said ruefully. "Never a dull moment. Do you know how much I love you for that?"

Her love for him was touch and go for the next few hours while she labored to bring their son into the world, but at dawn, when she woke to see him cradling their newborn, her feelings toward him defied words.

He barely looked any worse for wear despite the fact he'd been up all night. His love for her and their son glowed from his expression when he noticed she was awake.

"Do you know how much I love *you*?" she asked.

"I think I do," he said, caressing her jaw and kissing her temple. "But tell me anyway."

* * * * *

MILLS & BOON

Coming next month

CINDERELLA'S NIGHT IN VENICE
Clare Connelly

As the car slowed to go over a speed hump, his fingers briefly fell to her shoulder. An accident of transit, nothing intentional about it. The reason didn't matter though; the spark of electricity was the same regardless. She gasped and quickly turned her face away, looking beyond the window.

It was then that she realized they had driven through the gates of City Airport.

Bea turned back to face Ares, a question in her eyes.

'There's a ball at the airport?'

'No.'

'Then why…?' Comprehension was a blinding light. 'We're flying somewhere.'

'To the ball.'

'But…you didn't say…'

'I thought you were good at reading between the lines?'

She pouted her lips. 'Yes, you're right.' She clicked her fingers in the air. 'I should have miraculously intuited that when you invited me to a ball you meant for us to fly there. Where, exactly?'

'Venice.'

'Venice?' She stared at him, aghast. 'I don't have a passport.'

'I had your assistant arrange it.'

'You—what? When?'

'When I left this morning.'

'My assistant just handed over my passport?'

'You have a problem with that?'

'Well, gee, let me think about that a moment,' she said, tapping a finger to the side of her lip. 'You're a man I'd never clapped eyes on until yesterday and now you have in your possession a document that's of reasonably significant personal importance. You could say I find that a little invasive, yes.'

He dropped his hand from the back of the seat, inadvertently brushing her arm as he moved, lifting a familiar burgundy document from his pocket. 'Now you have it in your possession. It was no conspiracy to kidnap you, Beatrice, simply a means to an end.'

Clutching the passport in her hand, she stared down at it. No longer bothered by the fact he'd managed to convince her assistant to commandeer a document of such personal importance from her top drawer, she was knocked off-kilter by his use of her full name. Nobody called her Beatrice any more. She'd been Bea for as long as she could remember. But her full name on his lips momentarily shoved the air from her lungs.

'Why didn't you just tell me?'

He lifted his shoulders. 'I thought you might say no.'

It was an important clue as to how he operated. This was a man who would do what he needed to achieve whatever he wanted. He'd chosen to invite her to this event, and so he'd done what he deemed necessary to have her there.

'Your business is too important to our company, remember?' She was grateful for the opportunity to remind them both of the reason she'd agreed to this. It had nothing to do with the fact she found him attractive, and everything to do with how much she loved her friends and wanted the company to continue to succeed.

'And that's the only reason you agreed to this,' he said in a deep voice, perfectly calling her bluff. Was she that obvious? Undoubtedly.

Continue reading
CINDERELLA'S NIGHT IN VENICE
Clare Connelly

Available next month
www.millsandboon.co.uk

Copyright ©2021 by Harlequin Books S.A.

Special thanks and acknowledgement are given to Clare Connelly for her contribution to the *Signed, Sealed...Seduced* miniseries.

COMING SOON!

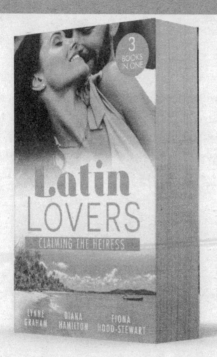

might just be true love...

MILLS & BOON

HEROES

At Your Service

Experience all the excitement of a
gripping thriller, with an intense romance
at its heart. Resourceful, true-to-life
women and strong, fearless men face
danger and desire - a killer combination!